Vision of the Disinherited

THE MAKING OF AMERICAN PENTECOSTALISM

ROBERT MAPES ANDERSON

HENDRICKSON
PUBLISHERS
PEABODY, MASSACHUSETTS 01961-3473

26590324

VISION OF THE DISINHERITED
The Making of American Pentecostalism

Copyright © 1979 by Hendrickson Publishers, Inc.
P. O. Box 3473
Peabody, Massachusetts, 01961–3473

ISBN 1–56563–000–9

First printing, September 1992

Reprinted from the edition originally published by Oxford University Press, Inc.

Copyright © 1979 by Oxford University Press, Inc.
Assigned 1991 to Robert Mapes Anderson
Assigned 1992 to Hendrickson Publishers, Inc.

Printed in the United States of America

Library of Congress Cataloging-in-Publication Data

Anderson, Robert Mapes, 1929–
    Vision of the disinherited: the making of American Pentecostalism   /
Robert Mapes Anderson.
        p.   cm.
    Originally published: New York: Oxford University Press, 1979.
    Includes bibliographical references and index.
    ISBN 1–56563–000–9 (pbk.)
    1. Pentecostalism—United States.   2. Pentecostal churches—United
States.   3. United States—Church history—20th century.   I. Title.
    BR1644.5.U6A5   1992
    289.9′4′0973—dc20   92–30434
                                                                   CIP

The photo on the cover depicts the baptism of Hanna Wiley, in Joplin, Missouri, and is used courtesy of the Assemblies of God Archives.

For Ann

Acknowledgments

I would like to express my thanks to those who have assisted me in various ways during the course of this work. Professor Robert D. Cross of the University of Virginia and Professor Robert T. Handy of Union Theological Seminary gave me invaluable advice as they guided this study through its dissertation stage at Columbia University. Professor Martin E. Marty of the University of Chicago and Professor Robert J. Kaczorowski of Wagner College read the entire manuscript. The librarians at Oral Roberts University and the headquarters staffs of the Assemblies of God, the Church of God (Cleveland, Tenn.), the Pentecostal Holiness Church, and the Church of God of Prophecy were uniformly gracious in making research materials available to me. Wagner College and its Faculty Affairs Committee granted me financial aid and sabbatical leave to complete the manuscript.

Contents

List of Tables

Abbreviations

FGBMF   Full Gospel Business Men's Fellowship.

PEF   Files of the *Pentecostal Evangel,* Springfield, Missouri.

RB   United States, Bureau of the Census. *Census of Religious Bodies*. Washington, D.C.: U.S. Government Printing Office (cited with date of census).

Preface

Since this study first went into print the world of Pentecostalism has come to be much better known. To the list of already familiar Pentecostal personalities—Aimee Semple McPherson, Oral Roberts, and Elvis Presley—others have been added: Jimmy Swaggart, Jim and Tammy Faye Bakker, Pat Robertson, Amy Grant, Ronald Reagan's Secretary of the Interior James Watt, Jimmy Carter's sister Ruth Carter Stapleton (more accurately a charismatic), and the on-again, off-again Pentecostals, Little Richard and Jerry Lee Lewis.

Despised and ridiculed by the few people who even knew of it during its first fifty years of existence, Pentecostalism has come to be recognized as a major religious force and an important segment of the political Right in America. Moreover, it is now the fastest growing segment of Christendom with an estimated 100 million adherents worldwide.

The Pentecostal drive for acceptance and respectability that began after World War II seemed to be succeeding. But since the mid-1980s the reputation of Pentecostalism has been seriously tarnished by revelations of the sordid sexual escapades of Jimmy Swaggart and Jim Bakker, by Bakker's imprisonment for financial fraud, and by the exposure of the fraudulent practices of several millionaire Pentecostal televangelists. But scandal has plagued the Pentecostal movement from its earliest years, and yet it has survived and grown dramatically. Recent declines in membership growth and contributions may well prove to be temporary.

The American public seems to thrive on sensationalism. This is not a sensationalist study. Rather, it aspires to be a detached, scholarly analysis of a movement that has had more than its fair share of "sensational" personalities, episodes, and practices. One need not sensationalize a movement that has been so sensational in and of itself.

It is most gratifying that this study has been widely acclaimed by leading scholars in the field of religious history. Even believing Pentecostal scholars have on the whole received it favorably, though not without reservations. One would not expect them, of course, to take kindly to my view that Pentecostalism—and all religion—is an entirely naturalistic and wholly human phenomenon. Yet, even those historians whose religious convictions are incompatible with this view must operate in accordance with it; supernatural and superhuman explanations are inadmissible in professional historical writing.

It has been noted that I have given less weight to the specifically religious dimensions of Pentecostalism than to non-religious dimensions like class, race, ethnicity, and power. This was by design.

Religious thought and behavior have a degree of relative autonomy within society that makes it possible to write histories of their internal development with little regard to external developments. For the social historian, such histories are useful but seriously inadequate. Surely, religious developments cannot be explained by religion itself; this would be tautological. Nor can religious movements be explained primarily (or as they are by some, entirely) in terms of their theology; this would be a kind of cognitive reductionism. There is no such thing as a religious occurrence that is not also a historical, social, economic, political, and cultural occurrence. Every religious movement, then, is produced and shaped by a convergence of all these and other forces. Religious change must be seen in relationship to the multiple changes in the larger society. This is a reciprocal relationship, but one in which the impact of religion on the rest of society is modest and has been diminishing for more than a century, while the impact of the larger forces in society on religion has been powerful and increasing.

There are deficiencies in this book that need correction—in particular, the influence of Africanized Christianity on the origin and shaping of American Pentecostalism as a whole, and the treatment of African American Pentecostals themselves. These subjects are of much greater importance than would appear from the book in its present state. The major difficulty in assessing that importance was, and to a large extent still is, the paucity and unavailability of source materials. Another shortcoming herein is the neglect of Pentecostal attitudes on gender issues, which were relatively progressive in the early years and mostly conservative thereafter. Happily, as the supplementary bibliography indicates, some work has been done to correct these deficiencies, and the door is open for further scholarly progress.

Whatever its deficiencies, I have decided to reissue the book essentially unchanged. It has stood the test of time well, and, although subsequent scholarship has contributed much toward a more complete understanding of Pentecostalism, I have not felt it necessary to alter my original interpretations or conclusions.

Chapter one explores the psychological and linguistic character of speaking in tongues, and the biblical basis for its practice. Here, Pentecostalism is placed in the context of the history of ecstatic religion, and of Christianity.

Chapter two explains the various cross currents within the latter nineteenth century Holiness movement from which Pentecostalism emerged.

In Chapter three the earliest stage of the Pentecostal movement in the lower Midwest under Charles Fox Parham is traced.

Chapter four describes the remarkable Azusa Street revival of 1906 in Los Angeles, sparked by William Joseph Seymour, and the movement's sudden expansion across the nation and around the world.

The thesis of chapter five is that the Pentecostal message was initially structured around the central theme of the imminent, apocalyptic, Second Coming of Christ; and that speaking in tongues, miraculous healings, exorcisms, and other ecstatic practices are best understood in relationship to that central theme. This was perhaps my most original finding when I first wrote this book. Since then it has become a virtual truism.

Chapters five and six develop group profiles of Pentecostal leaders and followers in terms of region, class, race, ethnicity, and religious orientation.

Chapter eight assesses the opposition met by the new movement and the fading of the initial revival phase.

In chapters nine and ten the internal conflicts and fragmentation of the movement are examined. Here, it is argued that the theological disputes at issue were largely shaped by social differences and involved personal struggles for political power. It is also suggested that this fratricide, paradoxically, contributed to the growth and stabilization of the movement.

Chapter eleven deals with the social ideology of the Pentecostals. Here, it is maintained that the movement initially constituted a radical critique of the status quo, but that it was soon transformed, in effect, into a conservative bulwark of the social system.

The last chapter is interpretive and speculative. Here conclusions are drawn as to why the movement emerged, why people joined it, what they got out of it, and what impact it has had on the larger society.

At a recent convention, a group of South African Pentecostals (one Afrikaans, one African, one of mixed ancestry) told me that my book had opened their eyes to parts of their religious heritage they had never known about, and that this had helped them to develop a more relevant Pentecostal stance on the racial and other social issues that have for so long troubled their homeland. This most gratifying outcome went well beyond my limited aims. I have tried to recount the story of early American Pentecostalism and offer some insights and explanations without regard to how it might please or infuriate, or what use might be made of it. If this book contributes to the reader's understanding of Pentecostalism, it will have achieved its purpose.

Supplementary Bibliography

The literature on Pentecostalism has mushroomed in the past dozen years or so. New or improved depositories provide extensive materials for researchers. The excellent bibliographical aids noted below make it superfluous to list any but a few of the more significant works published since 1977 that bear on the history of American Pentecostalism prior to the 1930s. The *Newsletter* of the Society for Pentecostal Studies (Gaithersburg, Maryland) attempts to keep up with the steady flow of literature. The same society's journal, *Pneuma*, is also useful.

I *Depositories*

David du Plessis Center for Christian Spirituality, Fuller Theological Seminary, Pasadena, Calif.

Assemblies of God Archives, Springfield, Mo.

Hal Bernard Dixon, Jr., Pentecostal Research Center, Cleveland, Tenn.

The Arch, Pentecostal Holiness Church Archives, Bethany, Okla.

Pentecostal Historical Center, United Pentecostal Church, Hazelwood, Mo.

Asbury Theological Seminary, B.L. Fisher Library, Wilmore, Ky.

Institute for the Study of American Evangelicals, Billy Graham Center, Wheaton College, Wheaton, Ill.

Pentecostal Collection, Schomberg Center for Research in Black Culture, New York Public Library, New York, N.Y.

II *Bibliographical Guides*

DuPree, Sherry. *Bibliographical Dictionary of African-American, Holiness-Pentecostals, 1880–1990.* Wash., D.C.: Middle Atlantic Regional Press, 1989.

Jones, Charles Edwin. *A Guide to the Study of the Pentecostal Movement.* 2 vols., Metuchen, N.J.: Scarecrow Press, 1983.

Jones, Charles Edwin. *Black Holiness: A Guide to the Study of Black Participation in Wesleyan Perfectionist and Glossolalic Pentecostal Movements.* Metuchen: Scarecrow Press, 1987.

Mills, Watson E. *Glossolalia: A Bibliography.* Lewiston, N.Y.: Edwin Mellen Press, 1985.

Mills, Watson E. (ed.). *Speaking in Tongues: A Guide to Research on Glossolalia.* Grand Rapids: Eerdmans, 1986.

Mills, Watson E. *Charismatic Religion in Modern Research: A Bibliography.* Macon, Ga.: Mercer Univ., 1985.

Payne, Wardell J. *Directory of African American Religious Bodies.* Wash., D.C.: Middle Atlantic Regional Press, 1991.

III *Published Original Sources*

Blumhofer, Edith L. *"Pentecost in My Soul": Explorations in the Meaning of Pentecostal Experience in the Early Assemblies of God.* Springfield, Mo.: Gospel Pub. House, 1989.

Corum, Fred T. and Rachel A. Harper Sizelove (comp.). *Like As of Fire: Newspapers from the Azusa Street World Wide Revival.* Wash., D.C.: Middle Atlantic Regional Press, 1991.

Dayton, Donald W. et al. *The Higher Christian Life: Sources for the Study of the Holiness, Pentecostal, and Keswick Movements.* 48 vols. New York: Garland, 1984.

Golder, Morris E. *The Life and Works of Bishop Garfield Thomas Haywood (1880–1931).* Indianapolis: privately published, 1977.

Haywood, G. T. *The Life and Writings of Elder G. T. Haywood.* Portland, Ore.: Apostolic Book Pub., 1984.

Mason, Mary. *The History and Life Work of Elder C. H. Mason, Chief Apostle and His Co-Laborers.* Memphis: Church of God in Christ, 1987.

Urshan, Andrew David. *The Life Story of Andrew D. Urshan.* Portland, Ore.: Apostolic Book Pub., 1982.

Warner, Wayne E. (ed.). *Touched by the Fire: Eyewitness Accounts of the Early 20th Century Pentecostal Revival.* Plainfield: Logos International, 1978.

IV *Books, Articles, and Theses*

Abell, Troy. *Better Felt Than Said: The Holiness Pentecostal Experience in Southern Appalachia.* Waco, Texas: Baylor Univ., 1982.

Beaman, Jay. *Pentecostal Pacifism: The Origins, Development & Rejection of Pacific Belief Among the Pentecostals.* Hillsboro, Kansas: Center for Mennonite Brethren Studies, 1989.

Blumhofer, Edith L. *The Assemblies of God.* 2 vols. Springfield, Mo.: Gospel Publishing House, 1989.

Blumhofer, Edith. "Women in Evangelicalism and Pentecostalism." In Melanie May (ed.), *Women and Church: The Challenge of Solidarity in Times of Turmoil.* Grand Rapids: Eerdmans, 1990.

Burgess, Stanley M. and Gary B. McGee (eds.). *Dictionary of Pentecostal and Charismatic Movements.* Grand Rapids: Zondervan, 1988.

Cohen, Norman J. (ed.). *The Fundamentalist Phenomenon.* Grand Rapids: Eerdmans, 1990.

Colletti, Joseph. "Ethnic Pentecostalism in Chicago, 1890–1950." Ph.D. diss., University of Birmingham, England, 1990.

Crews, Mickey. *The Church of God: A Social History.* Knoxville: University of Tennessee, 1990.

Darrand, Tom C. and Anson D. Shupe. *Metaphors of Social Control in a Pentecostal Sect.* N.Y.: Edwin Mellen, 1983.

Dayton, Donald W. *Theological Roots of Pentecostalism.* Reprint. Peabody, Mass.: Hendrickson, 1987.

Dayton, Donald W. and Robert K. Johnston (eds.). *The Variety of American Evangelicalism.* Downers Grove, Ill: InterVarsity Press, 1991.

De Caro, Louis. *Our Heritage: The Christian Church of North America.* Sharon, Pa.: Gen. Council, Christian Church of North America, 1977.

Dieter, Melvin E. *The Holiness Revival of the 19th Century.* Metuchen: Scarecrow Press, 1980.

Ervin, Howard M. *Conversion-Initiation and the Baptism of the Holy Spirit.* Peabody, Mass.: Hendrickson, 1984.

Faupel, D. William. "The Everlasting Gospel: The Significance of Eschatology in the Development of Pentecostal Thought." Ph.D. diss., University of Birmingham, England, 1989.

Garrett, Clarke. *Spirit Possession and Popular Religion: From the Camisards to the Shakers.* Baltimore: Johns Hopkins, 1987.

Goff, James R., Jr. *Fields White Unto Harvest: Charles F. Parham and the Missionary Origins of Pentecostalism.* Fayetteville: Univ. of Arkansas Press, 1988.

Golder, Morris E. *History of the Pentecostal Assemblies of the World.* Indianapolis: privately published, 1973.

Gregory, Chester W. *The History of the United Holy Church of America, Inc., 1886–1986.* Baltimore: Gateway Press, Inc., 1986.

Harrell, David Edwin, Jr. *Oral Roberts: An American Life.* Bloomington: Indiana Univ., 1985.

Harrell, David Edwin, Jr. (ed.). *Varieties of Southern Evangelicalism.* Macon: Mercer Univ., 1981.

Howell, J. H. "The People of the Name: Oneness Pentecostalism in the U.S." Ph.D. diss., Florida State Univ., 1985.

Hunter, Harold D. *Spirit-Baptism: A Pentecostal Alternative.* N.Y.: Univ. Press of America, 1983.

Hunter, James Davison. *American Evangelicalism.* New Brunswick: Rutgers Univ., 1983.

Kenyon, Howard N. "An Analysis of Ethical Issues in the History of the Assemblies of God." Ph.D. diss., Baylor Univ., 1988.

Lawless, Elaine J. *God's Peculiar People: Women's Voices and Folk Tradition in a Pentecostal Church.* Lexington, Ky.: Univ. Press of Ky., 1988.

Lawless, Elaine J. *Handmaidens of the Lord: Pentecostal Women Preachers and Traditional Religion.* Philadelphia: Univ. of Pa., 1988.

Lovett, Leonard. "Black-Holiness Pentecostalism: Implications for Ethics and Social Transformation." Ph.D. diss., Emory Univ., 1979.

McGee, Gary B. (ed.). *Initial Evidence: Historical and Biblical Perspectives on the Pentecostal Doctrine of Spirit Baptism.* Peabody, Mass.: Hendrickson, 1991.

MacRobert, Iain. *The Black Roots and White Racism of Early Pentecostalism in the USA.* N.Y.: St. Martin's, 1988.

Maloney, H. Newton and Lovekin, A. Adams. *Glossolalia: Behavioral Science Perspectives on Speaking in Tongues.* N.Y.: Oxford Univ., 1985.

Marsden, George M. *Fundamentalism and American Culture: The Shaping of Twentieth-Century Evangelicalism, 1870–1925.* N.Y.: Oxford Univ., 1980.

Mills, Watson E. *A Theological-Exegetical Approach to Glossolalia.* N.Y.: Univ. Press of America, 1985.

Nelson, Douglas J. "For Such A Time As This: The Story of Bishop William J. Seymour and the Azusa Street Revival: A Search for Pentecostal-Charismatic Roots." Ph.D. diss., Univ. of Birmingham, England, 1981.

Paris, Arthur Ernest. *Black Pentecostalism: Southern Religion in an Urban World.* Amherst: Univ. of Mass., 1982.

Reed, David A. "Origins and Development of the Theology of Oneness Pentecostalism in the US." Ph.D. diss., Boston Univ., 1978.

Richardson, James Collins. *With Water and Spirit.* Wash., D.C.: Spirit Press, 1980.

Robeck, Cecil M., Jr. (ed.). *Charismatic Experiences in History.* Peabody, Mass.: Hendrickson, 1985.

Spencer, Jon Michael. *Protest and Praise: Sacred Music of Black Religion.* Minneapolis: Fortress Press, 1990.

Tenney, T. F. *The Flame Still Burns: A History of the Pentecostals of Louisiana.* Tioga, La.: Focused Light, 1989.

Turner, W. Clair, Jr. "The United Holy Church of America: A Study in Black Holiness Pentecostalism." Ph.D. diss., Duke Univ., 1984.

Wacker, Grant. " 'Playing for Keeps': The Primitivist Impulse in Early Pentecostalism," in Richard T. Hughes, ed., *The American Quest for the Primitive Church.* Urbana, Ill.: Univ. of Ill. Press, 1988.

Waldvogel (Blumhofer), Edith L. "The Overcoming Life: A Study in the Reformed Evangelical Origins of Pentecostalism." Ph.D. diss., Harvard Univ. 1977.

Warner, Wayne E. *The Woman Evangelist: The Life and Times of Charismatic Evangelist Maria B. Woodworth-Etter.* Metuchen: Scarecrow Press, 1986.

Weber, Timothy P. *Living in the Shadow of the Second Coming: American Premillennialism, 1875–1925.* N.Y.: Oxford Univ., 1979.

Wheelock, Donald Roy. "Spirit Baptism in American Pentecostal Thought." Ph.D. diss., Emory Univ., 1983.

Williams, Cyril G. *Tongues of the Spirit: A Study of Pentecostal Glossolalia and Related Phenomena.* Cardiff, Wales: Univ. of Wales Press, 1981.

Wood, Dillard L. and William H. Preskitt, Jr. *Baptized With Fire: A History of the Fire Baptized Holiness Church.* Franklin Springs, Ga.: Advocate Press, 1983.

Vision of the Disinherited

Introduction

On Sunday, April 3, 1960, Father Dennis J. Bennett informed his rather staid, affluent parishioners at St. Mark's Episcopal Church in Van Nuys, California, that he had recently "found" a new religious experience. The Holy Spirit, he said, had granted him the "gift of tongues," the miraculous ability to speak a language he had never learned. The incident aroused a controversy that led to Bennett's resignation and his reassignment to St. Luke's Church in Seattle, a tiny inner-city mission.[1]

But that was not the end of the matter. An interest in speaking in tongues and other "gifts of the Spirit" soon gave rise to a new "charismatic" movement, at first in the Episcopal Church, and then elsewhere. Bennett's story was picked up by local newspapers and by national periodicals, including *Time*. By the spring of 1963 the existence of a "charismatic revival" was widely acknowledged. Within all the major Protestant denominations, in the Roman Catholic Church, and in several colleges and seminaries, including Yale, small groups of believers met to speak in tongues and to lay hands on one another for healing and "casting out devils." Special denominational committees were formed to study the development, reports and resolutions were issued concerning it, and leading churchmen pronounced publicly upon it, usually in varying degrees of condemnation or condescension. In the years since, the Charismatic movement in the churches has continued to grow, especially in the Roman Catholic Church.[2]

The roots of this Charismatic revival, as many discovered to their surprise, lay in a religious movement that had been in existence for more

3

than half a century. The recent Charismatic or "neo-Pentecostal" movement is but a small by-product of an older Pentecostal movement that is the subject of this study.

The problem of defining one's subject matter is particularly acute for the student of Pentecostalism. The usual definition proposed by Pentecostal writers, and accepted by many others, has been purely doctrinal. The movement, they say, is characterized by its unique teaching that "speaking in tongues is *the* initial, physical evidence of Baptism in the Holy Spirit."[3] As will become clear in the following pages, however, this doctrine was not developed in that form until a dozen years after the 1906 Los Angeles revival that marked the rise of the movement to national and international significance. And, at that time, this doctrine was the occasion for a division in the movement because not all Pentecostals accepted it, nor do all accept it today.[4]

Martin Marty is closer to the truth when he maintains that Pentecostalism's distinctive feature is the *practice* of speaking in tongues, that is, behavior, not doctrine, is decisive.[5] Some difficulties are presented by this definition because other non-Pentecostal groups like the Irvingites and the Mormons have practiced speaking in tongues. However, tongue-speaking has not held the same central position in the structure and function of these other groups that it has in Pentecostalism.

Pentecostalism should be viewed as a specific form of a general class of ecstatic religions, and also, initially, of a general class of millenarian movements—each of which classes includes a very wide spectrum of Christian and non-Christian religions over the course of human history. I have tried to suggest both the similarities and dissimilarities between Pentecostalism and these other movements.

My working definition has been that Pentecostalism is a movement that emerged on the world scene in 1906 during a Los Angeles revival in which speaking in tongues was regarded as a sign of Baptism in the Spirit for the individual, a sign of a Second Pentecost for the Church, and a sign of the imminent Second Coming of Christ. I have designated as "Pentecostal" all groups, by whatever name they may use, whose origins can be traced to that revival.

This study is limited to the formative phase of the Pentecostal movement from the late nineteenth century to the early 1930's. The Depression years were years of phenomenal growth for the Pentecostals, but by then the movement had entered a different stage of development; much of the spontaneous element had become ritualized and what had been a fluid movement had largely crystallized into a number of denominations. While my primary focus has been on Pentecostalism as a social movement, I have been ever mindful of the interaction between theological and sociological influences, between ideas and action.

There are several reasons for giving the Pentecostals a more prominent place in the historic record than they have so far been granted. First, the sheer dimensions of the movement clamor for scholarly investigation and explanation. There are today literally scores of Pentecostal denominations and millions of Pentecostal believers scattered all around the world. In the United States alone there are about 150 known Pentecostal organizations with a total membership of well over two million. In addition, there are unknown numbers of completely autonomous Pentecostal congregations meeting in private homes, rented halls, and store-fronts across the nation. Moreover, the vitality of the movement is attested to by its continued growth in the United States, its impressive success in the underdeveloped regions abroad, and its recent inroads into the established churches.[6]

Second, a thorough study of the Pentecostal movement would have clear implications for our understanding of Fundamentalism in American religion. The Pentecostals have always prided themselves on their commitment to what they believe to be the "fundamentals" of historic Christian orthodoxy. Since the late 1920's when it declined to relative unimportance within the major denominations, Fundamentalism has been perpetuated as strongly by the Pentecostal churches as by any others. Any analysis of Fundamentalism must necessarily take the Pentecostal movement into consideration, but this has hardly been the case. When this is done, however, the inadequacies of existing historical interpretations of Fundamentalism will be readily apparent.[7]

The almost totally apolitical character of the Pentecostal movement, for example, raises serious questions about the interpretation of Fundamentalism as an essentially political movement. Pentecostals did indeed take delight in the political battles of other Fundamentalists who tried to impose Fundamentalist theological views on the major denominations, and Fundamentalist "moral standards" (prohibition and anti-evolution legislation) on the larger society. But the Pentecostals themselves showed little inclination to leave the sidelines and join the fray directly. The Pentecostals regarded both state and church as incurably corrupt, abstained from political activity aimed at altering them, and placed their hopes for change in an imminent Second Coming.

Interpretations of Fundamentalism which identify it as primarily theological in nature must take into account a Pentecostal doctrinal spectrum of such variety and complexity that even unitarianism may be found within it. Even if it could be agreed that there is some common theological thread uniting all Fundamentalists, our understanding of the movement on that basis alone would be deficient, for the Pentecostals are not the only Fundamentalists who regard experience, not theology, as of primary importance in the religious life. Most Fundamentalists and all Pentecostals believe that the "new birth" experience,[8] not doctrinal belief, makes one a Christian. While many Pentecostals consider acceptance of certain doctrines, like the "five points,"[9] a necessary condition for salvation, none would think this sufficient—the same may be said of many other Fundamentalists.

Our understanding of the Fundamentalist movement has been greatly advanced by the work of Ernest Sandeen, who has laid bare its connections with millenarianism and the Princeton theology. Sandeen characterizes the Fundamentalist movement as a "self-conscious, structured, long-lived, dynamic entity with recognized leadership, periodicals and meetings."[10] Yet, if the Pentecostals were not fully a part of the "entity," they had nevertheless very clear connections with it. They fully subscribed to all the basic tenets of Fundamentalism, they recognized the authority of the same leaders (in all matters except their pronouncements on the Pentecostal movement), they read their periodicals, and they attended their meetings. Therefore, despite the initial hostility of the main body of Fundamentalists to the Pentecostals, it seems to me that the Pentecostal movement should be regarded as a part of the Fundamentalist movement. Indeed, Sandeen's assertion that the closest institutional parallel to Fundamentalism is Puritanism, rightly opens the door for this interpretation. Initially, Pentecostals stood in somewhat the same relationship to other Fundamentalists as the Quakers did to other Puritans. After all, the Fundamentalists had no real grounds for condemning the Pentecostals, since they merely carried Biblical literalism—the bedrock of Fundamentalism—to its logical conclusion. Appropriately, when the main body of Fundamentalists ultimately organized as the National Association of Evangelicals in 1948, they included the Pentecostals. Only a hard core of Fundamentalists, organized as the American Council of Churches, has persisted in refusing to acknowledge the Fundamentalist character of Pentecostalism.

A third reason for examining the Pentecostal movement lies in the light it throws upon a vast subculture in America that is no less real simply because its outlines are obscure. What I have in mind is a subculture, or perhaps more accurately a constellation of subcultures, that is described only in part by words like "hill-billy," "rural," "small town," "country and western," "Southern," and "Midwestern." Such labels over-emphasize the differences between the life-styles referred to, and create an illusion of geographical isolation that does little justice to the facts. It seems to me that these terms refer to the remnants of an older, rural-agrarian culture whose dominance began to wane more than a century ago. Yet, while consistently and increasingly overshadowed by the newer, urban-industrial culture, this older life-style has survived in varying degrees and in modified forms in all parts of the nation, and has interacted in complex ways with the dominant style.

One aspect of this older subculture is its consistent commitment to "the old-time religion." The Pentecostal movement was one attempt among many to preserve or restate what was believed to be the old-time religion, and as such it was an authentic expression of that older, folkish culture. However differently it has been defined, the old-time religion stands in unmistakable contrast to the liberal, intellectual, and socially oriented religion that has come to typify mainstream Protestantism—or at least, its leadership. Dogmatic, emotional, often intolerant, anti-intellectual, and tribal, the thrust of the old-time religion is almost diametrically opposed to that of the major denominations.

Moreover, despite innumerable variations, there is a style of worship common to believers in the old-time religion that differs from that of the mainline denominations and reflects the ethos of its folkish tradition. Stereotyped preaching, praying, and "testifying," in a simple, straight-forward, sentimental, often "folksy" manner, are characteristic. So, too, is its musicology that combines hymns of the mournful "Old Rugged Cross" type with those of the hand-clapping "Give Me That Old-Time Religion" variety, and leans more toward "honky-tonk" piano, guitar, banjo, and tambourine than to the organ.

Indeed, it is in the realm of music that the cross-currents within this folk culture and its interaction with the larger culture are most clearly discerned. The precise connections between the hymnology of the old-time religion and jazz, "country and western," folk, rock, and folk-rock are clearly suggested by Louis "Satchmo" Armstrong's assertion that rock came straight out of A.M.E. Zion by way of jazz, by Elvis Presley's Pentecostal upbringing, and by the testimony of the ear.

Fourth, through a study of the Pentecostal movement, we may gain an insight into the roots of religion as emotional experience and expression. In the ecstatic flow of Pentecostal "tongues" there echoes the cry of endless generations of worshippers from countless religions since the emergence of the human race. In the soul-shattering elemental peak-experience that Pentecostals call "Baptism in the Holy Spirit," there is mirrored an age-old struggle of men and women to possess and be possessed by supernatural power.

To have endured so long, to be continually revived in new forms like Pentecostalism, to thrive even in the centers of modern urban culture, ecstatic religion must satisfy human needs that are widespread indeed. It may be that behind the Pentecostal determination to seize and be seized by the Holy Spirit in "the Baptism," behind the forms and content of all ecstatic religious experience, there lies a common human urge to seize and be filled with life itself. Yet, while the capacity to achieve ecstasy is probably universal, or nearly so, it would be a mistake to leap from this to the conclusion that ecstatic religion is rooted in a human nature common to all men. I doubt that such a fixed and constant human nature exists, and in any event, an appeal to such has no explanatory value. I think it better to view ecstatic religion as one way substantial numbers of people in varying circumstances have interacted with their material and social environment.

Finally, and very important from my perspective, we can learn from the study of the Pentecostal movement something about the way in which movements of the "disinherited" that arise out of protest against the social order are transformed into religious forces that serve to perpetuate that order.

In this study I have attempted to determine what kinds of people in what kinds of circumstances became Pentecostals, and how Pentecostalism helped them and hindered them in dealing with those circumstances. I have tried to understand, *from the inside,* the motivations of the Pentecostals as individuals and as a group. But I have been equally concerned with understanding Pentecostalism *from the outside.* I have tried to determine the historic intellectual and social sources of the movement, of which the Pentecostals themselves were unaware but which were more determinative of the movement than the ideologies and intentions that filled their consciousness. In short, I have been as much interested in the historic background and social context in which the Pentecostal consciousness took shape as in that consciousness itself. I have tried to assess the social functions of the movement for its adherents and for the larger society.

Whatever else it may be, religion is a cultural tool by which man adapts to his material, social, and psychic environment. Because of this, the specific form of any religion is largely determined by the particular cultural tradition, particular social milieu, and particular psychic structure of its adherents. As an adaptive mechanism, each religion must adjust to change in each of these aspects of the lives of its adherents. Therefore, only a broadly conceived social history can adequately deal with any particular religion. This is the perspective that guided me in my study of the Pentecostal movement.

I

The Charismatic Tradition

In his classic work on religion, the German theologian Rudolf Otto maintained that the "real innermost core of all religion" is a "unique original feeling response," a sense of the "aweful," incomprehensible, and overpowering qualities of existence; a response that is wholly emotional and devoid of all moral and rational elements. In its raw, elemental state the religious consciousness conceives of its object as a blind and overpowering force, or a spirit. The goal of the religious impulse is possession of and by this spirit, and the means to that end are often crudely mystical, enthusiastic, magical, and orgiastic.[1]

Christianity, no less than other religions, has been engaged in a perennial struggle to contain this primitive impulse without destroying its creative potential. The struggle began in the earliest years of the Christian era, for the Apostolic Church was, among other things, a community of the Spirit,[2] and the atmosphere of its worship is perhaps most nearly approximated today in storefront Pentecostal missions. From its origins, the Church has lived in a state of enduring tension between the charismatic and the institutional, freedom and order, emotion and intellect.

The Church has usually been able to moderate and contain the effects of enthusiastic movements within its ranks. But from time to time the charismatic has triumphed over the institutional, and small groups have broken away to heed the wooing of the Spirit.[3] In these charismatic, Spirit-centered movements the expression of religious experience has taken forms well known to students of primitive religion and revivalism. Ascetic and orgiastic techniques are cultivated to achieve ecstasy in the belief that unusual psychological and physical states are synonymous with possession of or by the Spirit. Worship is characterized by overt emotional expression and a wide range of unusual phenomena like the loss of feelings in certain parts of the body, falling into catalepsy and trance, visual and auditory hallucinations, clapping, stamping, leaping, running, climbing, falling, rolling, and jerking.[4] Strange and unusual vocalizations, mysterious, ambiguous, and unintelligible speech have often been regarded as evidence of the "Numen," or divine presence. Such speech disorders are but one type of a general class of motor dysfunctions that includes crying, sighing and groaning, stuttering, barking and crowing, complete muteness, and sustained automatic discourse.

The common feature of these varied phenomena is that they are carried out in an automatic, involuntary way that convinces those who exhibit them and often onlookers as well that they are being controlled by some force beyond themselves. For this reason such behavior has long been considered an indication of possession by some spirit, good or evil.[5] Belief in spirit possession often leads to altered states of consciousness that produce unusual psychological and physical effects. Since these effects are dissociated from full consciousness, they are perceived as coming from some external, supernatural force. Thus, the consequences of the belief in spirit possession confirm that belief and the circle of faith is closed.

Since at least the time of Plato, speaking in tongues has been recognized as ecstatic speech; speech that is dissociated from thought and flows forth involuntarily and automatically. The conclusion that the tongue-speaker is in an altered state of consciousness is supported by the consensus of those historians, sociologists, anthropologists, theologians, psychologists, psychiatrists, and neurophysiologists who have studied the phenomenon.[6]

Possession and trance are not necessarily connected, although they often are.[7] In the early Pentecostal movement there is little doubt that they almost always were. Speaking in tongues was believed to be speaking in a state of consciousness that was altered because of possession by the Holy Spirit. The expectation of the early Pentecostals was that the state of the speaker as well as his "words" would make it obvious to all that he was indeed possessed by or "filled" with the Holy Spirit. It is clear that speaking in tongues was an ecstatic phenomenon in the early years of the movement because it was accompanied by the emotional excesses and gross physical behaviorisms that are typical of crisis cults of the deprived. It is less clear today because these secondary features have been greatly minimized (where they have not disappeared altogether) as the natural consequence of the Pentecostals' gradual conformity to middle-class standards of "respectability." The neo-Pentecostals, because they were predominantly middle-class adherents of mainline denominations from the outset and have largely remained there, have rarely displayed obvious ecstatic behaviorisms. For all the attenuation of the grosser secondary ecstatic phenomena, however, possession belief and ecstatic trance have been mutually reinforcing and all but inextricable in the minds of Pentecostals, old and new alike.

The words "possession" and "trance" and the psychological states they represent have had a distinctly negative connotation in Western culture until their recent positive evaluation by "counterculture radicals." Because of this, Pentecostals and neo-Pentecostals insist that they are not possessed and not in trance, ecstasy, or any other altered state of consciousness. But the internal evidence of their own descriptions of the experience belies their protestations. "It is not ye that speak," proclaimed an early Pentecostal periodical, "but the Holy Ghost, and he will speak when He chooses. . . . When singing or speaking in tongues, your mind does not take any part in it."[8] In a work widely recognized by Pentecostals as one of the most authoritative statements of Pentecostal doctrine and experience, we are told that the Baptism in the Spirit with speaking in tongues "is God's method whereby the Holy Spirit may possess men completely and be able to control them."[9] A prominent neo-Pentecostal says, "At a given point in this experience the seeker finds his tongue being taken over and a new language being formed by a power other than his own. . . . These expressions are given apart from the processes of thought."[10]

Every Pentecostal and neo-Pentecostal tongue-speaker insists that he is speaking under the control, power, or influence of the Holy Spirit. It is not he himself who speaks, or at least not he alone, but the Holy Spirit who speaks through him or with him. He believes this because he feels himself to be under the control of some power other than his own. What the Pentecostals themselves describe is precisely Spirit possession, though they express it in different terms.

Some observers accept the Pentecostals' view of the matter, some attribute the speech to diabolical spirits, and some to madness. Yet nearly all agree with the tongue-speaker that he is under the control of something other than himself because he appears so. Practitioners and observers of tongue-speaking arrive at these beliefs because the tongue-speaker is in an altered state of consciousness[11] which gives the *illusion* of the presence of some force external to himself. The state may be called "Baptism in the Spirit," ecstasy, trance, hypnosis, or dissociation, but these are merely different terms for similar forms of the same basic psychological mechanism: the alteration of consciousness from its normal, ordinary, day-to-day state. Pentecostals, old and new, clearly regard speaking in tongues as "possession trance"; their objection is to the words, not to the reality they represent.

Those few students of the subject who insist that a person speaking in tongues is usually in a perfectly normal state of consciousness[12] fail to recognize that altered states of consciousness run the full gamut from near full consciousness to complete unconsciousness. Thus, many experienced tongue-speakers are able to enter a state of dissociation with such little effort that neither they nor others are aware of the change. Yet the underlying alteration of consciousness is normally there, as it is in the case of all automatic behavior. As the anthropologist Felicitas Goodman rightly states, "the glossolalia utterance [is] superimposed . . . upon the substratum of the hyperarousal dissociation,"[13] but any other form of automatic behavior could as well be superimposed upon that state.

Goodman has demonstrated that there is a cross-cultural regularity in the intonation curve of tongue-speech. This striking uniformity strongly supports Goodman's contention that there is also a uniformity in the neurophysiological state of those who speak in tongues—a theory proposed by George Barton Cutten nearly fifty years ago and given added weight by the work of William Sargant twenty years ago.[14] Yet, so far, this theory has not been scientifically demonstrated. Studies designed to measure altered states by electro-encephalographic readings have been inconclusive. "There are," concludes one authority on altered states, "really no verifiable objective or subjective criteria that may be used to determine when hypnosis [or, as the context shows, any other altered state] is or is not present." We must therefore rely solely upon the testimony of those who have experienced altered states and those who have observed them.[15] In the case of Pentecostal and neo-Pentecostal tongue-speakers, the internal evidence of such testimony is overwhelmingly in favor of concluding that they are normally in an altered state of consciousness.

It must be conceded, of course, that speaking in tongues may be imitated successfully by people who are not in an altered state. From the beginning of the Pentecostal movement to the present, seekers of the

"Baptism" have been encouraged to imitate tongue-speech because of the intuitive realization that the simulation of ecstatic movements facilitates the induction of ecstasy itself. The critical point to be recognized here is that in order to be considered a tongue-speaker a person must convince others, and usually himself, that he is not speaking by his own power. He must *feel* himself to be in an altered state or, at least, *appear* to be so to others. No speech, whatever its form or content, will be identified as speaking in tongues by Pentecostals or neo-Pentecostals if it is believed to be delivered in a state of ordinary day-to-day consciousness. The tongue-speaker must, in Pentecostal terminology, be speaking "in the Spirit," and not "in the Flesh."

In short, speaking in tongues is speaking in an actual state of altered consciousness or in an imputed one. The speaker may or may not be in a psychologically defined state of altered consciousness (which as we have seen cannot be unambiguously and objectively determined anyway), but he must be in a culturally defined state of altered consciousness.

In his superb study of ecstatic religion, the anthropologist I. M. Lewis suggests a formula that makes perfect sense: "If someone is, in his own cultural milieu, generally considered to be in a state of spirit possession, then he (or she) is possessed."[16] What is true of possession is equally true for all of its expressions, including speaking in tongues. If a person says he speaks in tongues and others agree with him, then he is speaking in tongues, regardless of his actual psychological state and regardless of what he may say. Short of this, the student of tongue-speaking will be led into a futile and fruitless attempt to distinguish between "authentic" and "inauthentic" speaking in tongues on the basis of criteria other than cultural and historical. Such distinction is inappropriate for the scholar who seeks to approximate scientific objectivity. Pentecostals themselves distinguish between the "true" speaking in tongues and speaking in tongues that is mere imitation, "of the flesh," or "of the devil," but the classification of any particular incidence of tongues is determined by the shifting norms and prejudices of particular Pentecostals, who often disagree with one another because it is a purely subjective distinction.

Most of us who have been raised in the highly rationalized atmosphere of modern urban culture are prone to believe that those who cultivate non-rational and ecstatic experiences must be mentally ill or, in some sense, abnormal." Because of this, a brief word on the mental and emotional health of tongue-speakers seems in order. While the data on the psychological health of tongue-speakers are somewhat ambiguous, it appears that for the most part they fall within the "normal" range.[17] They tend, however, to be persons who have experienced a greater amount of stress in life than most and are, therefore, more dependent, more suggestible, more neurotic, and more inadequate in interpersonal relations than the general population.[18] Speaking in tongues may, of course, be experienced by any normal person since dissociation in varying degrees is common to all people, but that does not mean that an otherwise "normal" person is in a normal state at the time he dissociates and engages in speaking in tongues or any other form of automatic behavior. Whatever the state of their mental and psychological health in ordinary day-to-day life, tongue-speakers are, while engaged in speaking in tongues, in an altered state, with few exceptions.

The belief in and practice of ecstatic possession may or may not be healthy, depending upon the cultural norms of the society in which they occur.[19] Where possession and ecstasy are culturally normal, as in many Asian, African, and Latin American cultures, Pentecostalism is fully normal and healthy—a fact that goes far toward explaining why the Pentecostal movement has had so much more success in these areas than in the United States and Europe. In America, however, this belief and this practice have been neither culturally nor statistically normal. Therefore, while Pentecostals *as individuals* may be categorized as "normal" on the basis of certain accepted psychological criteria, Pentecostal*ism*, with some justification, has been regarded as unhealthy by the wider society, or at best only marginally healthy. It seems to me, however, that Pentecostalism might better be regarded, like a fever in the human body, as a symptom of some unhealthiness in the American social body. From this perspective, Pentecostalism, far from being a disease, is an attempt to regain health, a struggle against some illness in the larger society.

With few exceptions, American Pentecostal spokesmen have consistently claimed that all speaking in tongues is speaking in a language previously unknown to the speaker. It might be an extant language, a dead language, the language of angels, or a divine language, but always a language and not unintelligible jargon.[20] Initially the Pentecostals believed that all speaking in tongues was speaking in a known foreign language. As W. T. Gaston, later Chairman of the Assemblies of God, said, "all supernatural tongues are UNKNOWN TONGUES to the SPEAKER of them, but may be understood by the hearer—will be, if a foreigner is in the house whose native tongue is spoken."[21] By the mid-20's the notion of "angelic" and "heavenly" or "divine" languages was added.[22]

European Pentecostals, however, have not been dogmatic on this point. T. B. Barratt, chief founder of the Pentecostal movement in Scandinavia, hinted as early as 1908 at the possibility that some speaking in tongues might be unintelligible when he distinguished between "the rhapsodic speaking in tongues" and the "gift of tongues."[23] Dutch Pentecostal G. R. Polman stated that most Pentecostal speaking in tongues was unintelligible and that speaking in foreign languages was rare in the movement. English Pentecostal leader Donald Gee concurred in this view.[24] Some American neo-Pentecostals lean to the European view. Samarin found that of sixty-nine contemporary tongue-speakers, fifty believed thay were speaking a human language, three believed they were speaking a "heavenly language," and sixteen doubted that they were speaking any language.[25]

Here we must introduce an important distinction between two notions of speaking in tongues: glossolalia and xenoglossy. The term "glossolalia" is used today to refer both to unintelligible vocalization and to the miraculous use of language the speaker has never learned. To avoid this ambiguity some scholars have limited the use of the term glossolalia to unintelligible vocalization only, and have adopted the term xenoglossy for speaking in a language unknown to the speaker.

When American Pentecostals use the term glossolalia, they almost always mean xenoglossy, but their claims to xenoglossy are unsupported. In the earliest years of the Pentecostal movement, the German scholar Mosiman carefully investigated many cases of Pentecostal tongue-speech in Chicago and in several cities in Germany. Not once did he hear any foreign language, nor was he able to authenticate a single claim that any tongue-speaker had spoken in a language previously unknown to him. This same conclusion had been reached in the 1830's by several linguists who studied the tongue-speech of Mary Campbell, the Scotswoman who inspired the Irvingite movement. For seventy years now nearly every non-Pentecostal observer of tongue-speakers has recognized its non-linguistic, "gibberish" character.[26]

Until the recent neo-Pentecostal movement no objective studies of the actual content of tongue-speech existed. So far, studies now completed or in progress have concluded that speaking in tongues is incoherent, repetitive syllabification having neither the form nor the structure of human speech. A study analyzing the tape-recorded tongue-speech of some sixty persons in Southern California showed that none spoke a word of any known language and that when the same tape was "interpreted" by several persons claiming the "gift of interpretation," no two interpretations were at all similar. William E. Welmers, Professor of African languages at UCLA, arrived at the same conclusion on the basis of his investigations. A group of government linguists listened to the tape-recorded tongue-speech of Harold Bredesen, a neo-Pentecostal leader who claimed to speak Polish and Coptic Egyptian, and found no resemblance to any language. Bredesen's tongue-speech was also analyzed by a conference of linguists in Toronto who together had done field work in over 150 aboriginal languages in more than 25 countries. They found it had a "very high repetition of individual sounds and syllables," and concluded it was "highly improbable that this is a human language." John Sherrill, journalist and convert to neo-Pentecostalism, played some forty different samples of tongue-speech for a group of six linguists from Columbia University, Union Theological Seminary, and General Theological Seminary, who agreed unanimously that none spoke any words of any language. All of this corroborates what early observers of the Pentecostal movement concluded on the basis of their subjective impressions.[27]

The most thorough linguistic analysis of speaking in tongues has been made by William J. Samarin. Samarin found that none of the numerous cases of tape-recorded tongue-speech that he meticulously analyzed involved anything more than an occasional word or phrase of a foreign language, which anyone could have picked up. Moreover, without exception, the tongue-speech of Samarin's respondents lacked all of the elements essential to any language, even a hypothetical or newly created one: vocabulary, grammar, syntax, and a systematically related phonological-semantic structure. He concluded that speaking in tongues bears "no systematic resemblance to any natural language, living or dead," although it has some superficial similarities to language.[28]

Samarin chose to include in his study only those instances of tongue-speech that were phonologically structured and that superficially resembled language. But while his is a good enough description of the form of tongues cultivated among Pentecostals today, it is inadequate as a universal definition. Historically, nearly every form of vocalization known to man has been considered speaking in tongues, because it is not the form or content of the speech itself but the attribution of it to some outside power that is the criterion for identification. The linguistic character of tongue-speech is not necessarily different from that of vocalization in general. It is not even limited to speech, but includes any sound that can proceed from a human mouth.[29]

Speaking in tongues is a cultural phenomenon that cannot be reduced to a psychological or linguistic phenomenon merely. It need not and probably will not lend itself, without exception, to any uniform psychological or linguistic definition. The only acceptable historical definition is that speaking in tongues is any vocalization uttered in an actual or imputed state of altered consciousness that is attributed by some group to a spirit or power other than the speaker.

Yet, while there is no reliable evidence to support them, the testimonies of hundreds of Pentecostals who say that they heard people speak languages they had never learned and did not know they were speaking cannot all be simply dismissed as self-conscious fabrications. Neither, however, should they be uncritically accepted as true, since all the testimonies derive from Pentecostal believers. Where it is asserted that non-Pentecostals confirmed the real linguisticality of tongue-speech, these witnesses are either unnamed, cannot be found, or are incompetent to judge.[30] The only reliable evidence is the growing volume of recorded tongue-speech which in every single instance flatly and unambiguously contradicts Pentecostal claims to xenoglossy.

How then can the Pentecostal testimonies be explained? Thomas Sporri, professor of psychiatry at the University of Berne, believes that tongue-speech is similar to that of people who can imitate the melodic accent and rhythm of a language without having learned it, in a way that is convincing to all but linguists.[31] A more plausible explanation may be found, as Mosiman suggested, if we shift our focus from the tongue-speaker to those who hear him. The Pentecostal hears what he has been led to expect and what he wants to hear. The numerous "appearances of Mary" and UFO sightings are widely acknowledged to be mass visual hallucinations and are not uncommon. Why should we not also acknowledge mass auditory hallucinations? Short of discounting Pentecostal eyewitness reports as simple deceptions, this seems to be the only satisfactory explanation for them.

One final point should be made. We must recognize the *possibility* of someone's speaking a foreign language which he has never consciously learned but to which he has been exposed. George Barton Cutten cited several reasonably well-attested instances of this phenomenon,[32] but the most spectacular and best authenticated of all such cases is that of Helene

Smith, who spoke Sanskrit and manufactured a whole new language while in trance. Through painstaking analysis, Thomas Flournoy showed that Helene Smith had been exposed to Sanskrit, and also was able to trace her private language to the previously known sources from which it was created.[33] Ian Stevenson, director of the division of parapsychology at the University of Virginia, has made a comprehensive review of all published cases of alleged xenoglossy and has also made a detailed study of an American woman who spoke Swedish.[34] Despite Stevenson's insistence that the woman had never been exposed to the Swedish language before, it is likely that this, and all other cases noted, were instances of cryptomnesia.

Cryptomnesia, in the context of this discussion, is the ability to recall in trance a language that one has heard or seen but never consciously committed to memory. Pentecostals may seize upon this as a scientific basis for their claims, even though none of these cases involved a Pentecostal and none involved the claim of speaking in tongues. Nevertheless, given the fact of cryptomnesic xenoglossy, we must acknowledge the *theoretical* possibility that some Pentecostals have spoken languages they never learned. Cryptomnesia requires a deep state of dissociation, which was quite common among the early Pentecostals. Today Pentecostals rarely achieve this state, and so cryptomnesic xenoglossy is very unlikely. We will never know, however, whether cryptomnesic xenoglossy occurred among the early Pentecostals because their speech was not recorded.

Simple xenoglossy—the ability to speak a language with which one has had absolutely no prior acquaintance—is, of course, utterly incredible. That scholars should have to deal seriously with this claim is a tribute to the abiding strength and contemporary resurgence of pre-scientific modes of thought. On the basis of the evidence, we must conclude that Pentecostal speaking in tongues is simply glossolalia, that is, unintelligible, non-linguistic utterance.

Except where it is essential to differentiate between "xenoglossy" and "glossolalia," I have chosen to use "speaking in tongues" throughout this study. In recent years some Pentecostals have been using glossolalia (though they almost always mean xenoglossy), but the early Pentecostals and most contemporary ones as well have used "speaking in tongues" almost without exception. The reader will understand that for me "speaking in tongues" always means glossolalia, but for the Pentecostals it means xenoglossy.

Speaking in tongues as a sign of Spirit possession has a history whose origins very likely lie deep in mankind's past. Reports of the practice extend from ancient to modern times in virtually every region of the world. What astonishes the novice student of tongue-speaking is how extraordinarily common this seemingly exotic practice has been and still is. The phenomenon has certainly been far more extensive and frequent among non-Christians, but our concern is with the Christian tradition.[35]

Christianity was born out of Judaism and, indeed, the Palestinian Christians apparently remained for some time a sect within Judaism.[36] Thus, Christianity was heir to much in the Judaic tradition. The ancient Hebrews had recognized ecstatic speech as a sign of authentic prophecy, though with them it was usually an exalted form of discourse in which the message was sometimes obscure or ambiguous rather than a meaningless jargon. By the dawn of the Christian era, however, the older view that true prophecy was delivered in a state of spirit possession had been replaced by the teaching that "the spirits of the prophets are subject to the prophets."[37]

Concomitant with the political unification of the Mediterranean world by Rome, there occurred the interpenetration of various ideas and practices of Greek, Roman, Jewish, and Oriental religions and the rise of a baffling array of new sects and cults, "mysteries" and "gnoses." In this religious milieu, ecstasy was common property. Various enthusiastic elements, including speaking in tongues, were evident in the inspired prophecies of the Oracle of Apollo at Delphi, the popularity of mysterious, magical and meaningless phrases, the Thracian cult of Dionysius, the Egyptian cult of Osiris and Isis, the Syrian cult of Adonis, the Phrygian cult of Attis and Cybele, and the Persian cult of Mithras. In the "mysteries," rebirth to immortality through ritual participation in the death and resurrection of the cultic deity was often, perhaps usually, an ecstatic experience. In the "gnoses," each person's knowledge (gnosis) of his own divine origin and eternal essence in and of itself brought salvation, but in its most exalted form gnosis was also a transfiguring ecstatic experience.[38]

The common explanation of these ecstatic practices was provided by Hellenistic pneumatology. "Pneuma" or Spirit was thought to be a divine substance, which, through possession, gave men all sorts of miraculous powers.[39] The pneumatic state was one of ecstasy in which the "pneuma banishes the human 'nous' [or] 'mind' "[40] and acts or speaks through man. The deity spoke out of the pneumatic's mouth in words that neither he nor anyone else could understand unless they were translated by the Pneuma itself. To prove that he was indeed a pneumatic, a person had to demonstrate the presence of the Pneuma within him by engaging in ecstatic behavior, especially ecstatic speech. Indeed, according to Ernst Käsemann, "in the Hellenistic epoch every Jew *and* Gentile knew of the existence of the self-manifestation of the divine Spirit, because inspiration and ecstasy were universally accepted phenomena."[41]

It is hardly surprising then that early Christianity shared many of the concepts and practices of its religious environment. To compete successfully against its rivals, it had to meet them on their own terms, yet at the same time to distinguish itself from them. It did this by embracing pneumaticism but it redefined and restructured the practice and asserted the superiority of Christian pneumaticism over pagan by claiming more and greater miracles. The prevalence and near universality throughout early Christendom of supernaturalism, pneumaticism, enthusiasm, ecstasy, glossolalia, revelations, visions, and miracles have been affirmed by virtually every scholar of the subject. Eduard Schweizer, specifying ecstasy, glossolalia, healing, and miracles, says, "The fact that Paul presupposes such phenomena in Thessalonica as well as Galatia, in the church of Rome . . . as well as that of Corinth, seems to show that this is not just the accompanying remnant of a primitive concept." Johannes Behm asserts that in the study of glossolalia "we are concerned with an ecstatic phenomenon which is shared by both Jewish and Gentile Christianity." Indeed, Ernst Käsemann maintains that "enthusiasm was the *characteristic* expression of the young Christian religion" (my italics).[42]

Nevertheless, we should be careful to avoid the conclusion either that speaking in tongues and ecstatic practices generally were spread throughout early Christendom or that they constituted the dominant content of Christianity. While the Corinthian church was by no means unique in the prominence it gave to pneumaticism, neither was it typical.[43]

The New Testament literature is filled with revelations, visions, dreams, prophecies, ecstatic transports, miracles of healing, exorcisms, raising the dead, and other supernaturalism, all of which are attributed to the workings of the Spirit (Pneuma). Speaking in tongues, however, is explicitly mentioned only in the Gospel of Mark, the book of Acts and the first letter to the Corinthians, although it very probably is alluded to elsewhere.[44] All authorities agree that the reference to tongues in Mark

16:17 is a later interpolation since it is not found in any manuscript dating before the 5th century.[45] This passage, therefore, throws no light on speaking in tongues in the New Testament church.

In Paul's first letter to the Corinthian church (A.D. 54 or 55), one of the earliest documents of Christian literature,[46] the practice of speaking in tongues and the pneumatology undergirding it are described more fully than anywhere else in the New Testament. Speaking in tongues, Paul says, is a charism, a gift of the Spirit, which no man can understand, not even the speaker himself, because his " 'nous' [mind or understanding] is swallowed up." The speech itself is meaningless and inarticulate. The tongue-speaker, says Paul, will appear to be a madman unless he or someone else can interpret—a power which constitutes another gift of the Spirit. This is a straightforward description of glossolalia that fully agrees with those of Plato, Philo, Irenaeus, and Celsus.[47] It has been suggested that there is some ambiguity in Paul's use of the phrase "tongues of men and angels" (I Cor. 13:1), and of "phonon" (I Cor. 14:10f.), which may be translated "languages." These allusions simply reflect the generally held view that it is the Pneuma who speaks His language through the pneumatic, but any human language is almost certainly excluded.

The second chapter of the book of Acts describes the day of Pentecost following the crucifixion of Jesus as the time when the Holy Spirit descended on the disciples at Jerusalem and thereby inaugurated the Church age. The event is described in miraculous terms: a wind shakes the house where the believers are gathered, tongues of fire appear on their heads, and they all speak in languages which they do not know, but which are understood by foreigners who gather to hear them. Thus, speaking in tongues here is surely described as xenoglossy. However, some of the onlookers are astonished (Acts 2:7,12) and accuse the tongue-speakers of drunkenness (Acts 2:13,15). These attitudes are clearly inexplicable as a response to xenoglossy, but are quite understandable as a response to glossolalia. Because of this, nearly all scholars acknowledge that while xenoglossy is meant, there is unmistakable internal evidence of glossolalia in the same account. Moreover, nearly all agree that the Acts 2 account is the only place where speaking in tongues is described as xenoglossy and that all other references and allusions to it in the New Testament must be understood as glossolalia, including those by the very same author of Acts throughout the remainder of his volume.[48]

How is the contradiction in the Acts 2 account of tongues at Pentecost to be resolved? At least one scholar believes that there is not enough evidence here or elsewhere to determine what was meant by speaking in tongues.[49] Some insist that there is no contradiction and hold the untenable position that since xenoglossy is meant in Acts 2, all other references to it in the New Testament are to be understood as xenoglossy.[50] In his monumental commentary on the book of Acts, Haenchen recognizes the glossolalic element in the Pentecost account and acknowledges that everywhere else in Acts speaking in tongues means ecstatic, incomprehensible speech, yet he draws no conclusion from this concerning the authenticity of the xenoglossic element.[51] Haenchen, in short, simply fails to recognize that the contradiction requires a resolution.

But the best scholars, excluding Haenchen, conclude that the speaking in tongues of Acts 2 is quite simply and only glossolalia and that the xenoglossy is a later interpretation imposed on the event by the author of Acts. Johannes Behm says that the Acts 2 account, like all other New Testament references to speaking in tongues, "bears essentially the same characteristics as the glossolalia depicted by Paul" and "may be understood only in the light of . . . I Cor. 14:2ff." He maintains that the internal evidence of Acts 2 "makes quite impossible the idea of foreign languages." He concludes that the author may have used two different sources of which "The historical kernel is a mass ecstasy on the part of the disciples which includes outbreaks of glossolalia," and that "The Lucan account of Pentecost . . . is a legendary development of the story of the first significant occurrence of glossolalia in Christianity." Krister Stendahl says that the xenoglossy of Acts 2 is the author's "theological interpretation of the phenomenon of speaking in tongues," which is nowhere else in the New Testament understood as speaking a foreign language.[52]

In analyzing speaking in tongues in the New Testament we must be careful to distinguish between what really happened, what the sources say happened, and what the author's interpretation was. The weight of the New Testament evidence and of scholarly opinion surely points to the conclusion that glossolalia is what actually occurred in the early Church wherever and whenever speaking in tongues is said to have taken place, but Paul, in keeping with Hellenistic pneumatology generally, *interprets* it as a heavenly or angelic language, while the author of Acts, writing between A.D. 80 and 100[53] when the practice was being driven out of the main body of the Church, *interprets* it as a miraculous speaking in foreign languages.

In his treatment of speaking in tongues in I Corinthians, Paul placed his chief emphasis on limiting the practice by imposing stringent regulations on its use (one at a time, no more than three in any meeting, and only when it is interpreted), and by downgrading its value relative to all other gifts of the Spirit.[54] The reason for this is undoubtedly that the Corinthians considered tongues the highest[55] or, more likely, quite simply *the* gift of the Spirit.[56] At Corinth, Christ and the Spirit were considered one and the same; hence, unless one could prove by speaking in tongues that he had the Pneuma-Christ indwelling him, he was merely "psychical" and not "pneumatic," that is, either a second-class believer or none at all.[57] This and other enthusiasms lay at the root of the divisiveness in Corinth.[58] While Paul himself claimed to be a pneumatic who spoke in tongues more than anyone at Corinth, throughout his life he waged a ceaseless battle to prevent enthusiasm from overwhelming Christianity and making it just another "mystery" or "gnosis."

Paul's argument against the Corinthian extremists was that every believer has the Spirit (Pneuma) and every believer also has some gift of the Spirit (charism).[59] This surely implied that every believer was both a pneumatic and a charismatic despite the absence of any extraordinary visible manifestations. Further, in criticizing the zealots who were dividing the church by claiming some superiority based on their ostentatious display of demonstrative gifts like tongues, Paul was raising doubts as to whether they were pneumatics after all. What we see here is an attempt by Paul to head off the dangers of uncontrolled enthusiasm by redefining pneumaticism and charismata in such a way as to make ecstasy and physical manifestations subordinate or independent phenomena.[60] This was crucial because the church was initially pneumatic in spirit and charismatic in organization,[61] and if possession of the Pneuma and its charismata meant *only* uncontrolled ecstaticism then the survival of Christianity itself would have been in doubt. "The theological and practical conquest of enthusiasm," says Käsemann, "was the first test to which the young church was exposed, and nothing less than its whole existence and future depended on its mastery of this problem."[62]

This struggle became all the more imperative as enthusiasm became closely linked if not equated with the "incipient gnosticism" within the Church. Gnosticizing Christians claimed direct revelations that were equal or superior in authority to the Old Testament Scriptures and the pronouncements of the Apostles. Such revelations were presumed valid because they came through those in a state of ecstatic possession by the Pneuma and were confirmed by signs and miracles.[63]

The need to combat gnosticism and enthusiasm led to the creation of a new church order based on ecclesiastical authority to replace that based on pneumaticism and charismata.[64] That struggle began toward the last quarter of the 1st century and continued for about a century before the victory was complete in the main body of the Church. Aside from a few scattered references to the practice of speaking in tongues like those of Irenaeus and Celsus in the 2nd century, the last clear record of it in Christendom until modern times concerns the Montanist movement originating in Phrygia in the mid-2nd century. Montanus and his associates Prisca and Maximilla prophesied and spoke in tongues but they taught that these gifts were reserved for themselves alone, so that the survival of Montanism into the 5th century cannot be viewed as the survival of pneumaticism in general or tongues in particular. By the end of the 2nd century gnosticism and enthusiasm had been thoroughly routed. "From the saying, 'The Church is where the spirit is,' the struggle with gnosticism led to the new thesis: 'the Church is where the bishop is.' . . . The spirit revealed himself now . . . not as formerly in prophets and those who spoke in tongues, but in the bishop and the clergy whom the bishop led."[65]

By the 4th century, not only had the practice of speaking in tongues disappeared from the main body of the Church, but apparently all knowledge of its true character as well. Unaware of the ecstatic nature of tongues, later Christian writers like Chrysostom, Augustine, and Aquinas interpreted the New Testament references to speaking in tongues as xenoglossy and thereby set the pattern of explanation for most commentators until fairly recent times. This erroneous conception, for example, undergirds the medieval stories imputing xenoglossy to various saints; all such stories are, to say the least, highly suspect. Except for an occasional reference here and there, speaking in tongues dropped out of the historical record of Christendom for some fifteen centuries after the early years of Montanism.[66] Indeed, the Church came to regard speaking in tongues as an infallible sign of diabolic possession.[67]

Yet, with few exceptions, the Pentecostals have maintained that speaking in tongues has had a continuous history from the Apostolic age to the present. Although, they say, the practice fell into eclipse at an early point, a succession of small groups kept it alive until its full restoration to the Church in the 20th-century Pentecostal revival. By assuming that tongue-speaking was present wherever there is evidence of religious enthusiasm, the Pentecostals have constructed a history of the "true," or at least "spiritual," Church from the day of Pentecost to the present. They have compiled long lists of "authorities" to show that tongue-speaking was practiced by the sub-Apostolic church, the Waldensians, Albigensians, mendicant friars of the 13th century, Anabaptists, Camisards, Quakers, Shakers, Methodists, Mormons, Swedish Readers, and many others; and that Luther, Finney, and Moody spoke in tongues while Wesley endorsed it.[68] These claims are, with the exception of the Camisards, Shakers, and Mormons, without factual foundation, as some Pentecostal writers like Kendrick and Nichol have recognized.[69] Some of them depend upon forced interpretations of primary sources, others are based upon secondary works presumed to be authoritative. After the outbreak of the Pentecostal revival in Los Angeles in 1906, numbers of individual Pentecostals reported having spoken in tongues prior to it, and others reported that speaking in tongues had been a common practice among certain Holiness fellowships in Tennessee and North Carolina and the Holiness Baptists of Georgia and South Carolina in the 1890's, as well as the "Gift People" of New England since 1854, and one or more sects in Armenia and southern Russia since the mid-19th century. Until these claims are closely investigated, however, the proper attitude is skepticism since all are ex post facto and documented poorly or not at all.[70]

A close scholarly study of the sources necessary for writing the history of tongues in Christendom is yet to be done. Such a history would have to make a distinction between incidental cases of tongue-speaking, which may have occurred intermittently throughout the history of the Church, and the belief and practice of speaking in tongues by identifiable Christian groups. On this basis the only groups after the Montanists for whom speaking in tongues is well attested were the French Protestant Camisards in the late 17th century, Ann Lee's Shaking Quakers, who adopted the practice from émigré Camisards and carried it to America in 1774, and the Irvingite, Mormon, and Spiritualist movements, which grew out of the Anglo-American revivalism of the 1830's and 1840's.[71] In short, as a recognized and approved practice, speaking in tongues has apparently been non-existent in the great, historic Christian churches since the Apostolic era, and has been limited to a few sects on the fringes of Christianity only since the late 17th century. Moreover, speaking in tongues did not dominate the theology and worship even of these few sects to the degree it eventually did those of the Pentecostal movement.

If we turn to individual instances of speaking in tongues, however, it is quite possible that such have occurred sporadically throughout Christian history, since wherever the conditions exist for producing one kind of automatic behavior they exist for all others. Automatisms other than speaking in tongues certainly were present among the members of many of the groups claimed by Pentecostals as part of the tongue-speaking tradition. Edwards, Wesley, and Finney observed various automatisms in their revivals, including shouting and barking. Speaking in tongues, therefore, may well have occurred in their meetings, and in other enthusiastic movements at various times in Christian history.

Aside from the specific practice of speaking in tongues, the Pentecostals are indeed the spiritual heirs of a formidable flock of enthusiasts down through the ages. But we should be careful to recognize that while modern Pentecostalism is phenomenologically related to these other movements, no evidence as yet exists to show any direct, historical connection with them, not even with the contemporaneous groups—the Shakers, Mormons, Irvingites, and Spiritualists—who had previously practiced tongue-speaking. For the Pentecostals, as for the great many enthusiastic groups in the Christian past, the ultimate religious experience is to possess or be possessed by divine power evidenced by extraordinary sensations and physical manifestations. In this sense, the Pentecostals stand within a tradition that reaches back to the Corinthian zealots.

II

The Holiness Background

The immediate origins of the Pentecostal movement are to be found in the nineteenth-century Holiness movement. The outstanding characteristics of the Holiness movement—literal-minded Biblicism, emotional fervor, puritanical mores, enmity toward ecclesiasticism, and, above all, belief in a "Second Blessing"[1] in Christian experience—were inherited and perpetuated by the Pentecostals. Initially a faction within the Holiness camp, the Pentecostal movement drew much of its membership and nearly all of its leadership from Holiness ranks. Except for the issue of speaking in tongues, in the early days there was little to distinguish the Pentecostal believer from his Holiness brethren.

John Wesley reinvigorated the ancient Judeo-Christian tradition of holiness with his doctrine of sanctification. While that doctrine was sufficiently flexible, or perhaps ambiguous, to allow for various emphases, Wesley's central concern was with the limitation or removal of sin in the believer.[2] Methodism entered the American religious environment during the Great Awakening of the eighteenth century, and from then until the close of the following century, revivalism and holiness were to march side by side. Revivalism had the dual purpose of converting sinners and rousing the faithful to a life of piety and service, in short, of holiness.[3]

Charles G. Finney—lawyer, revivalist, theologian of a sort, and president of Oberlin College—gave the doctrine of sanctification a new formulation in the 1830's. The Oberlin definition of "entire sanctification" had little to do with sinlessness. Rather, it meant perfect trust and consecration that expressed itself in social activism. Finney counseled his converts to join the fight for good government, Christian education, temperance, abolitionism, and relief of the poor, asserting that the spirit of the Christian "is necessarily that of the reformer." In Finney's theology, revivalism, holiness, and reform merged to form a single entity.[4]

During the revival of 1857–58, holiness of either the Wesleyan or Oberlin variety swept through most of the major Protestant denominations.[5] By midcentury, the bulk of American Protestants had come to share a common ideology. Mined from various veins of the common lode of Christian tradition, forged in the Second Awakening, and hammered out in the intermittent revivals down to 1858, evangelical Protestantism was Arminian in doctrine, revivalistic in method, and perfectionist in purpose; and perfectionism meant the regeneration both of the individual and of society.[6]

The cataclysm of civil war was followed by a period of industrial expansion accompanied by widespread materialism, corruption, and social dislocation. The Church's response was a renewal of the call to holiness.

The resurgence of the Holiness movement was both international and interdenominational, but in America it was a predominantly Methodist undertaking. The centennial year of Methodism, 1866, was commemorated across the nation by weekday prayer gatherings, conventions, and camp meetings centering on the holiness theme. The following year, at Vineland, New Jersey, the National Camp Meeting Association for the Promotion of Holiness was organized, and over the next decade some three dozen national camp meetings and scores of regional and local ones were held under its auspices. Numerous other interdenominational Holiness institutions were established, and Holiness periodicals proliferated. By 1886, weekday holiness meetings were being held in every major city; at least 238 in the nation as a whole.[7]

But the heroic efforts of Methodist leaders and others to tap anew the springs of piety were being undermined by other developments that would eventually drive many holiness believers out of the established denominations.

The Protestant churches of the North and West had won an honored position in the nation by their support of the anti-slavery movement, the Republican Party, and the war against the South, and they prospered within the new order created by urban industrialization.[8] In the years from 1870 to 1890, the number of congregations in the nation rose by nearly 130 per cent and the value of church buildings by nearly 100 per cent. From 1880 to 1900 church membership increased at a faster rate than the population as a whole. The Methodists increased their membership by about 57 per cent in those two decades, and added an average of 800,000 new recruits to their rolls in each decade from 1870 to 1910.[9]

Success was accompanied by a shift in the class composition of the Protestant denominations. Their memberships had probably always been drawn chiefly from the middle classes, but a century of revivalism had brought hosts of lower-class people into the fold. By the close of the Civil War, however, many lower-class church members had attained middle-class status, in part by practicing the virtue of self-discipline inculcated by the Protestant ethic and in part as the result of the upward push given them by the new waves of immigrants entering the social structure at the bottom.[10]

Through the medium of its predominantly middle-class constituency, the materialism and secularism that characterized the larger culture invaded the Church. Organization, education, and growth in power and prestige overshadowed personal piety and social service. Church boards, dominated by solid businessmen, adapted the methods of the marketplace to the work of the Church. Requirements for admission were lowered to increase membership and income, and church discipline was largely abandoned. Horace Bushnell's doctrine of Christian nurture was used, perhaps misused, to provide a theoretical basis for a shift from personal conversion to education as the normal door of entrance into the Church— a door far more congenial to middle-class inclinations.[11]

The focus of evangelizing efforts shifted from the frontier regions. and the urban working classes to the upper and middle classes. Moving out of downtown working-class neighborhoods, the churches constructed smaller, more ornate edifices in more fashionable residential areas, hired professional singers and organists, and developed greater formality in worship. Even in the poorer parishes there was "the same extra attention paid to the rich . . . and the same thrusting of the poor into nooks and corners."[12]

In the last quarter of the nineteenth century, the identification of Protestantism with middle-class culture was almost complete. Indeed, Christianity at that time had become, in the eyes of a later generation of historians, a "culture religion." Leading churchmen, viewing society from their upper-middle-class perspective and inclined to believe that a system in which the Church prospered must be good, even Christian, bent their efforts to celebrating and sacralizing the status quo. Nowhere was this more evident than in the preaching of the "Princes of the Pulpit." The

Gospel of Wealth, a conglomeration of the doctrines of individualism, classical economics, and Social Darwinism, if not advocated by all clergymen, was proclaimed by a sufficient number to give it the apparent endorsement of Protestantism as a whole.[13]

But many devout holiness people, who were predominantly of lower-class status, found little cause to praise the new urban-industrial order, and to them the accommodation of the Church to middle-class culture was "friendship with the world" and thus "enmity with God." Yet while holiness believers deplored the secularism of Church and society they shared the social conservatism of the "Princes of the Pulpit." By concentrating upon individual moral character as the source and solution of all problems, personal and social, they reinforced the social system.

Beginning in the 1880's, however, a new movement within the Protestant churches arose to challenge the status quo and recall the Church to its prophetic tradition of social criticism. The Social Gospel movement reached out to ameliorate the conditions of the disadvantaged and joined the vanguard of social reform that would culminate in the Progressive movement at the turn of the century.[14]

An alliance between the Social Gospel and Holiness movements on the basis of common dissatisfaction with Church and society was, perhaps, a possibility. There was precedent for such an alliance in the interlocking of reform and revivalistic holiness during the days of Finney. But Social Gospelers tended to regard the Holiness movement as an irrelevancy, and Holiness people were prone to view socialized religion as antithetical to personal, heart-felt religion.[15] Indeed, the Social Gospel was considered another evidence of the overemphasis given "worldly" matters by the Church as a whole. In any event, by the time the Social Gospel was an important force, a portion of the most ardent Holiness believers was already breaking away from the denominations.

Holiness people were repelled, too, by the currents of theological liberalism in the denominations. The "Higher Criticism" of Scripture undermined the authority of the Bible; the comparative study of religion, by placing Christianity in a relativistic framework, deprived it of its unique and absolute character; and evolutionary theory in both its biological and social applications detracted from the supernatural and personal attributes of the Deity—so it seemed, at least, to many Holiness believers.[16]

That theological liberalism and socialized religion had independent lines of development (though they tended to merge later), and that both were resisted by the conservative ecclesiastics who presided over the secularization of the Church, were not recognized by many Holiness people. Unaware of the complex cross-currents at work, they concluded that these trends were inextricably linked and that together they constituted proof of the apostasy of the Church.[17]

The Holiness movement began as an attempt to reassert and extend pietistic values within the Church and the larger culture. But the increasingly middle-class orientation of the major denominations and their accommodation to new social and intellectual forces were bringing in a new set of values that were incompatible with pietistic ones. The result was a growing separation of the Holiness faction and the larger body of church members; the former in aversion to the presumed "worldliness," if not sinfulness, of the middle-class majority, the latter in embarrassment over the "puritanical" and "fanatical" attitudes of Holiness believers. To a large extent the alienation mirrored the divergent class composition of the opposing camps.

Gradually abandoning hopes of purifying the churches from within, many Holiness advocates looked for the creation of a separate fellowship of the sanctified.[18] A more radical phase of Holiness first appeared in rural areas of the Midwest and South in the late seventies. Holiness evangelists in these regions began to concentrate upon the externals of holiness—dress and behavior—and to exhort the faithful to come out from among the "worldly" churches. Soon, numerous Holiness "bands," camp meetings and state and local associations, independent of denominational controls and including non-church members as well as church members, sprang up across the country.[19]

"Come-outism" provoked "crush-outism." Denominational authorities felt compelled to reconsider their attitudes toward interdenominational Holiness institutions. In 1881 the bishops of the Methodist Church, North, rejected a lay appeal for a national Holiness convention under church sponsorship, asserting that, "It is our solemn conviction that the whole subject of personal holiness . . . can be best maintained and enforced in connection with the established usages of the church." From then on the Northern bishops tried to limit or withdraw support from Holiness institutions not subject to official Methodist supervision.[20]

Despite Holiness schisms in the ranks of the Methodist Church, South, in California, Texas, and Missouri during the 1880's, the bishops of that church refrained from official condemnation until 1894. But in their annual address of that year, they denounced independent Holiness organizations, and deplored their alleged claim to "a monopoly of the experience, practice and advocacy of holiness'' and their tendency to ''separate themselves from the body of ministers and disciples.''[21]

The independent Holiness movement was fundamentally a movement of protest against the overall social crisis of the 1890's. The frustrations and anxieties of those church members most adversely affected by the general crisis found oblique expression in the Holiness movement, which was specifically directed against those changes in the major denominations that were themselves attempts to deal with that crisis.

The major criticism leveled at the Holiness movement by denominational leaders centered on its disregard for the authority, organization, and ''established usages'' of the church. Resistance to the Holiness movement was necessary in order to make the accommodations that would keep the overwhelming majority of church members in the fold, retain the financial support of the wealthy and middle-class, and maintain the prestige of the churches in the social order. As long as the Holiness movement remained in the churches to challenge the policies that were designed to achieve these goals, it constituted a threat to those who held positions of power in the denominational hierarchies. Thus, on one level the Holiness issue involved, however uneven, a struggle for power.

It was not only Holiness institutions that were coming under fire within the major denominations, but the doctrine of sanctification as a second act of grace, as well. The attack was launched in the South with the publication of J. M. Boland's *The Problem of Methodism,* and in the North with the publication of James Mudge's *Growth in Holiness Toward Perfection, or Progressive Sanctification.* By the mid-nineties the anti-Second Blessing forces had carried the day in both Southern and Northern Methodism.[22]

The rejection of ''orthodox'' Holiness doctrine—sanctification as a second act of grace—by the major denominations accelerated and completed the trend toward division already well under way. Most of the national, state, and local Holiness associations lost their interdenominational character, and many members of those organizations severed their connections with the older churches.[23]

Thus, once outside the churches, the Holiness movement constituted a highly vulnerable, amorphous mass that invited strenuous competition for the rewards of prestige, power, and material gain that would accrue to those who succeeded in organizing it and securing leadership over it. Pentecostalism became, for some, a weapon in that struggle for power. As the Holiness movement crystallized into a constellation of organizations, those contestants for leadership who had lost out or were insecure in their positions found in Pentecostalism a means by which they could assert or legitimize their authority. They could appeal to the ecstatic experience of tongues as proof of their greater "spirituality" and therefore of their right to precedence. The countercharge was that the Pentecostals were demon-possessed and therefore unworthy of any hearing at all. Everywhere, Holiness associations and denominations would be split over the Pentecostal issue.

Even before the separation of the main body of Holiness believers from the denominations, there had been differences among Holiness believers over the permissible limits of emotional expression in worship, codes of dress and behavior, and over the doctrine of the Second Blessing. The removal of denominational restraints and the loose associationist or completely autonomous character of independent Holiness congregations exacerbated those differences. The rise of the Pentecostal movement must be seen against the background of a Holiness movement riven with controversy over the bounds of "liberty in the Spirit," divided into three factions over the doctrine of Baptism in the Holy Spirit, and coalescing into several dozen separate denominations.

The scenes of turbid emotionalism in the meetings of the Holiness evangelist Mrs. Mary B. Woodworth-Etter were typical of the Holiness movement, and increasingly so in the 1890's. The pages of Mrs. Woodworth-Etter's memoirs teem with references to the most extraordinary "manifestations of the Spirit." In a Methodist church in Willshire, Ohio, in 1880 people "came to the altar screaming for mercy"; at another in Monroeville, Indiana, in 1883, "the aged sisters fell prostrate and became cold and rigid as if dead." During a five weeks' campaign in Hartford City, Indiana, the following year, "Men, women and children were struck down in their homes, in their places of business, on the highways, and lay as dead. They had wonderful visions, and arose converted, giving glory to God." In the spring of 1885, during a campaign in a Universalist church in Columbia City, Indiana, "The Lord showed me . . . that I had the gift of healing." [24] At a camp meeting attended by "25,000 souls," near Alexandria, Indiana, the following summer,

> The power of God fell on the multitude. . . . Many fell to the ground. Others stood with their faces and hands raised to heaven. The Holy Ghost sat upon them. Others shouted, some talked, others wept aloud. Sinners were

converted, and began to testify and praise God. I was overpowered and carried to my tent.[25]

The camp meeting at Muncie, Indiana, in the summer of 1886 was "a real Pentecost revival." In 1890, during a seven months' campaign in St. Louis, Missouri, Mrs. Woodworth-Etter later said, she first heard speaking in tongues at her meetings. "Several," she wrote, "spake very intelligently in other languages as the Spirit gave them utterance."[26]

By the time she returned to St. Louis fourteen years later, she said, speaking in tongues had assumed greater proportions. A Swedish woman spoke in "many different languages," one "sister" sang in Greek and Latin, another spoke in eight different languages, and a "brother" spoke in three languages, "sang in the Spirit, and laughed in a manner resembling the laughter of several other nations." In the spring of 1905 at an Indianapolis tent meeting, "one sister spoke in unknown tongues all night. This was before the Holy Ghost fell at Los Angeles, California." Soon after that, Mrs. Woodworth-Etter became a leading light in the Pentecostal movement.[27]

Benjamin Hardin Irwin, a preacher in the Iowa Holiness Association, began to teach a crisis experience beyond conversion and sanctification—a "baptism of fire"—in the mid-90's. Despite attacks on this "Third Blessing Heresy" by most Holiness leaders, the fire-baptized movement spread all through the Midwest and South, culminating in the organization at Anderson, South Carolina, in 1898, of the Fire-Baptized Holiness Association, a loose fellowship of nine state associations. Fire-baptized meetings were characterized by such utter abandon and extreme physical displays that J. H. King, a close associate of Irwin's, was repelled at times. But Irwin encouraged the saints to press on, adding three more "baptisms" for which to strive. The explosive, emotional nature of these experiences is suggested by their names—dynamite, lyddite, and oxydite—but their meaning may have been no clearer to those who sought them than to later students of the movement.[28]

In the southern Appalachians, a small group of former Baptists, calling themselves the Christian Union, experienced a revival in 1896. "Spiritually starved souls" crowded into the one-room schoolhouse at Camp Creek, North Carolina, to join in weeping, shouting, trance, and ecstasy. Later, in prayer meetings at the home of the layman William F. Bryant, speaking in tongues and miracles of healing were reported to have taken place.[29]

Southern California was a center of Holiness extremism. Bishop Alma White's "Pillar of Fire" movement, which had its center in Denver, Colorado, and was best known for its practice of "marching in the Spirit," had considerable appeal in Los Angeles and the surrounding towns. The "Burning Bush" movement, which began in the independent Metropolitan Church in Chicago, was active in the same locale. The free-lance Holiness evangelist Frank Bartleman, who had first-hand experience with both movements, believed they "had spoiled the spirit of the saints greatly" in Los Angeles, making them "hard, censorious, critical and bigoted." At a Holiness camp meeting in the Arroyo mountains in 1905, Bartleman complained of the "evanescent froth and foam . . . religious ranting and bombast." Summing up the sentiments of many within and without the Holiness movement, Bartleman said, "We had a tremendous lot of fanaticism in the Holiness movement."[30]

Extreme forms of emotional expression were accompanied by extremist teachings. Among these were prohibitions against eating meat, sweets, and "medicinal foods," against wearing neckties and other "worldly ornamentations," and against using hair curlers and cosmetics. There were demands for public confession of the most personal "sins," and for fasting to the point of complete physical exhaustion. And, too, there were widespread denunciations of doctors as "imposters," medicine as "poison," and denominational ministers as "servants of corruption," "blind leaders of the blind," and "false teachers"; and criticisms of secret societies, labor unions, and divorce and remarriage.[31]

Such developments exposed the Holiness movement to ridicule and opposition; even staunch Holiness believers turned away. Mrs. Woodworth-Etter, who had at one time been welcomed into Methodist, Baptist, Lutheran, United Brethren, Bible Christian, Quaker, Universalist, and "General Eldership" churches in the early years, found "all" the ministers in Springfield, Illinois, united against her during her campaign there in 1899. From then on, her meetings were held almost exclusively in rented halls and tents. J. P. Widney, co-founder with Phineas Bresee of the Los Angeles Church of the Nazarene, returned to the Methodist fold out of distaste for the "noise and confusion" in Nazarene services. By 1900, defections from the Fire-Baptized Holiness Association to the denominations resulted in the dissolution of seven of the nine Fire-Baptized state organizations. By 1902 the Christian Union group of Appalachia, "riven and besmirched by fanaticism," had been reduced to about twenty members. The Church of God (Centralia, Missouri), an extremely decentralized organization founded in 1896 by "come-outers" from the South-west Holiness Association in the rural areas of Missouri and eastern Kansas, was "racked in its early decades by controversy over sacraments, church order, and by some who believed in 'the fire' as a third work of grace." [32]

"Wild-fire" threatened to consume the Holiness movement and leave nothing but ashes. It was clear that discipline was needed to prevent this. The loose organizational structure of most Holiness groups was an encouragement to anarchy. The reins would have to be tightened. Thus began a trend toward increased organization and regulation. Joseph H. King, successor to Irwin (who had been repudiated for alleged "romantic involvement") as General Overseer of the Fire-Baptized Holiness Association, introduced organizational reforms designed to preserve that work from extinction in 1900. A small remnant of the Christian Union reorganized itself as the Holiness Church at Camp Creek in 1902 "to correct the deficiency in the Church structure" which it held responsible for "fanaticisim" and loss of membership. The Church of the Nazarene and those groups that were later to merge with it bolstered their organizations and moved toward the creation of a new national denomination. Analogous developments were occurring among Holiness groups everywhere, and by 1907 no less than twenty-five Holiness denominations had sprung into existence. [33]

A major restraining influence on emotional expression in Holiness circles was exerted by the professional revivalists of the day. The leading revivalists were first and foremost evangelists, but all were recognized advocates of holiness as well, and many of their converts swelled the ranks of the Holiness hosts. Most prominent among these were Dwight L. Moody, sometime salesman and YMCA worker who dominated revivalism for the last quarter of the nineteenth century; Reuben A. Torrey, sometime president of both the Moody Bible Institute of Chicago and the Los Angeles Bible Institute; Adoniram J. Gordon, founder of the Gordon Bible Institute; Albert B. Simpson, father of the Christian and Missionary Alliance; and J. Wilbur Chapman, evangelist of international renown. All of these men professed to have been Baptized in the Holy Spirit, and all preached and wrote extensively on the subject, though, as we shall see, they gave it a different meaning from the one generally held by Holiness people. [34]

Revivals from the time of the Great Awakening to the Finney campaigns had been characterized by the active participation of the audience.

When "the power fell," impelling people to cry out and pray aloud, and at times give vent to their emotions in physical displays, preaching often became secondary, sometimes non-existent. But after the Civil War, professional revivalists frowned more and more on such demonstrations. Moody discouraged emotional expression and taught his co-workers that meetings "getting out of hand" should be broken into with a hymn. In England he was commended for the good order of his meetings. "Mr. Moody," reported a British journal, "suffered no fools, and every symptom of hysteria which often breaks out in such movements was promptly suppressed."[35]

Others followed Moody's lead and, in time, only managed audience participation was permitted by the revivalists. "No emotional outcry was needed or wanted to interrupt a smooth-running performance." Later, Billy Sunday would act out the physical gyrations of an earlier revivalism, but his congregations were allowed to experience these only vicariously. Those who attempted to share the limelight by interjecting "Amens" or "Hallelujahs" in his meetings were given clear warning and then thrown out by the ushers. The revival was stripped of its spontaneity and became at once more conventional and more theatrical.[36]

Conversion, too, was denuded of its drama. In the days of Edwards, of Cartwright, and of Finney, conversion had been a climactic spiritual experience preceded by soul agonies and followed by euphoria. Beginning with Moody, conversion became little more than a simple business transaction. All that was required was the assent of the will signified by a walk to the altar, a handshake, signing a card, or simply raising a hand while the rest of the audience remained with heads bowed in prayer, lest they embarrass the "convert." The professional revivalists "left a little room for the supernatural, but not much for earthly visions, raptures, transports or soul searching . . . the convert was not to expect 'ecstasies'."[37]

Revivalistic campaigns became highly organized business ventures that seemed to rule out the older conception of revival as something sent by God in his own way and in his own time. This was the logical end result of Finney's emphasis upon the techniques for inducing revival. It also reflected the increasing commercialization of American life and the demands imposed upon revivalism by the conditions of urban society. But for many Holiness people, business methods smacked too much of the world.[38]

Some revivalists, like Sam P. Jones, "the Moody of the South," began to emphasize what Holiness people considered the social aspects of religion at the expense of its personal aspects. Although Jones most often expressed his social concern in assaults upon such "social sins" as drinking, dancing, card-playing, theater-going, swearing, and novel-reading, devout Holiness zealots actually considered him and others of his ilk "part of the social gospel movement."[39]

Even more disturbing were the fading of "hell-fire and damnation preaching," and the launching of attacks upon the Holiness movement itself. Jones, for example, "ridiculed those old Methodists who claimed that religion was a change of heart," said that he "heartily disliked" Holiness people, and classified "extreme holiness cranks" along with Second Adventists and Christian Scientists as "non-conformists."[40]

These changes in revivalism were not looked upon with favor by many people in the Holiness camp. The restraints imposed upon emotional expression by the new revivalism were often regarded as "quenching the Spirit." The increasing tendency of officials in Holiness denominations to establish order and regulation drew a similar response, and with the organization of each new denomination and the adoption of each new precept, a group of "come-outers" broke away.[41]

The First General Holiness Assembly held in Chicago in May of 1885 adopted a doctrinal statement, which read:

> Entire Sanctification more commonly designated as "sanctification," "holiness," "Christian perfection," or "perfect love," represents that second definite stage in Christian experience wherein, by the baptism with the Holy Spirit, administered by Jesus Christ, and received instantaneously by faith, the justified believer is delivered from inbred sin, and consequently is saved from all unholy tempers, cleansed from all moral defilement, made perfect in love and introduced into full and abiding fellowship with God.[42]

This was the "orthodox" position on sanctification held by the bulk of those Holiness people who left the major denominations. But a rival view, most closely associated with the English Keswick movement, was to split the American Holiness movement down the middle.

The origins of this development lie in the early part of the nineteenth century. During revivals in the British Isles in the 1820's, a "back-to-the-Bible" movement within the Anglican Church resulted in the founding of a small splinter group called "the Brethren." In 1827 their first congregation was established in Dublin by Edward Cronin. Among its earlier members was the shoemaker John Nelson Darby, who soon emerged as the dominant leader of the Brethren movement. At a conference held in Powerscourt Castle, Dublin, in 1830, Darby formulated the dispensational teachings that became the backbone of Brethren doctrine. Significantly, some Irvingites were present at that conference.[43]

Darby maintained that the Bible could be "rightly divided" only by first recognizing that God had established different ground rules governing his relations with man for different epochs or dispensations. An understanding of this enabled one to distinguish between those Biblical injunctions intended for people of earlier dispensations and those intended for today. The dispensation of grace had begun with the Christian era, and would soon be ended by the Second Coming of Christ, which would usher in the next dispensation, the Millennium.[44]

Darby propagated his teachings in America during a series of visits between 1862 and 1877. Dwight L. Moody was acquainted with Brethren teachings before his rise to fame, and first visited England in 1867 in part to learn more about the Brethren and their doctrines. Among those Brethren whom he met on that occasion was Harry Moorehouse, the "Boy Preacher," who soon afterwards came to preach in Moody's Chicago church. Association with Moorehouse marked a turning point in Moody's thinking and preaching. Thereafter, he leaned more and more to Brethren notions.[45]

The Moody-Sankey campaign in Britain from 1873 to 1875 was supported by a group of ministers, banded together for that purpose, that included primarily Brethren, Anglicans, and Calvinist Baptists and Presbyterians. In 1875 this group met for what proved to be the first of a continuing series of annual conferences at the resort town of Keswick in the mountainous Lake District of Cumberland County in northwest England. The Keswick group pledged themselves to the furtherance of revivals, missionary work, and the "higher life."[46]

Keswick leaders accepted the general outlines of Darby's dispensational framework and concentrated upon the study of Biblical prophecy to determine "the signs of His coming." They concluded that one such sign would be a great world-wide revival that would give every living person a last chance to accept the gospel. They expected that the Holiness movement would culminate in a Second Pentecost in which the Holy Spirit would endow believers with extraordinary powers to carry out the rapid evangelization of the world. This belief, and the resistance to Wesleyan perfectionism arising from their Anglican and Calvinist backgrounds, led the Keswick group to give the doctrine of Baptism in the Holy Spirit a different meaning from that held by most Holiness people in America.[47]

They rejected the "orthodox" Holiness contention that sanctification and Baptism in the Holy Spirit were one and the same experience. Rather, they believed sanctification to be a life-long process of increasing growth in grace that began at conversion but was never completed, and held that the Baptism in the Spirit was a separate "enduement of power." At first, there was some uncertainty over whether the Baptism in the Spirit was a second act of grace or a gradual process marked by successive "fillings" of the Spirit, but the latter view finally prevailed.[48]

Soon after his return from England, Moody gave increasing emphasis to Keswick teachings and became closely associated with Keswick proponents more avid than himself, including the Holiness-revivalists Torrey, Gordon, Simpson, and Chapman, and the Bible teacher-convention speakers C. I. Scofield, James M. Gray, and Arthur T. Pierson.[49]

The ready acceptance of Keswick doctrines by these men may be explained in part by their acquaintance with the works of Asa Mahan and Charles G. Finney, who gave heavier emphasis to the empowering aspects of Baptism in the Spirit than to its purifying facets, and in part by their predominantly Calvinist backgrounds.[50] Moreover, the Keswick teaching on the Baptism of the Spirit, fortuitously or otherwise, was more suitable from the standpoint of the professional revivalists. They relied heavily upon the major denominations for cooperation, support, the use of church buildings, and a source of "converts" for their campaigns; the "orthodox" Holiness view of "the Baptism" was becoming increasingly unpopular with both clergy and laity in the denominations.

Keswick views were widely disseminated by means of annual Bible conferences like those at Northfield, Massachusetts, from 1880 to 1902 and at Niagara Falls from 1883 to 1897; at the series of International Prophetic Conferences here and abroad beginning in 1876, and in the global preaching tours and publications of Keswick champions on either side of the Atlantic.[51] The writings of Keswick proponents, often printed in inexpensive paperback editions, were read in Holiness circles throughout the English-speaking world; some were translated into foreign languages and reached a still wider public.[52]

On the eve of the new century, C. I. Scofield observed, no doubt with some exaggeration, that:

We are in the midst of a marked revival of interest in the Person and work of the Holy Spirit. More books, booklets and tracts upon that subject have issued from the press during the last 80 years than in all previous time since the invention of printing. Indeed, within the last 20 years more has been written and said upon the doctrine of the Holy Spirit than in the preceding 1800 years.[53]

Many of these works, added Scofield, "speak of new Pentecosts."

The twin themes of a coming Pentecostal revival, sometimes called "the latter rain," and of a Spirit baptism of power, run through this literature. References to the gift of healing as a characteristic of both the revival and "the Baptism" are abundant; and to speaking in tongues, occasional.[54]

The outlines of future Pentecostal doctrine were most clearly sketched out by Reuben A. Torrey in *The Baptism with the Holy Spirit,* which was first published in 1895 and then reissued in several editions that ran into many tens of thousands of copies by the early twentieth century. Torrey rejected both the extreme Holiness view that the Baptism in the Spirit was an act of grace which "eradicates man's sinful nature," and the more moderate view that it was "primarily for the purpose of cleansing from sin." Rather, it was "for the purpose of empowering for service." Torrey insisted that "the Baptism in the Holy Spirit is a definite experience of which one may know whether he has it or not." The problem was to find how one could know for certain. Telling of his search through Scripture for a solution,[55] Torrey said:

> In my early study of the Baptism with the Holy Spirit, I noticed that in many instances those who were so baptized "spoke with tongues," and the question came often into my mind: if one is baptized with the Holy Spirit will he not speak with tongues? But I saw no one so speaking, and I often wondered, is there anyone today who actually is baptized with the Holy Spirit. This 12th chapter of 1st Corinthians cleared me up on that, especially when I found Paul asking of those who had been baptized with the Holy Spirit: "Do all speak with tongues?"[56]

Having speculated on, but rejected, what was later to become the doctrine of Baptism in the Holy Spirit held by mainstream Pentecostalism, Torrey went on to conclude that the believer knows he has received the Baptism when he has fulfilled God's requirements for obtaining it. If one repents, renounces sin, is baptized in water, obeys God, asks for the Baptism, and believes he has received it, then he knows he has it "because the Bible says if you do these things you will receive it." Manifestations may occur, but none are necessary except the reality of new power in

Christian service. Summing up, Torrey said, "simply ask, claim, act."[57]

Differences over the doctrine of Baptism in the Holy Spirit split the Holiness camp into two major factions and one minor faction. The Wesleyan wing held Baptism and sanctification to be one and the same second act of grace, primarily designed to resolve the problem of sin in the believer, though there were differences within that wing over whether sanctification was instantaneous and complete or progressive and incomplete. The Keswick wing distinguished between sanctification, which was regarded as a gradual and incomplete process commencing at conversion, and the Baptism in the Spirit, which was an enduement of power; though here, too, there were differences over whether the Baptism was a second act of grace or a process. Finally, some Holiness people, most notably the Fire-Baptized adherents, held to the "orthodox" Holiness view of sanctification as a second act of grace and the Baptism as a third; a very few followed Irwin's lead in believing there were still other such acts as well. Yet by the turn of the century most Holiness people were agreed on the imminent, premillennial, apocalyptic Second Coming of Christ, preceded by a great world-wide revival of Pentecostal dimensions.[58]

The Keswick movement, as we shall see,[59] was absolutely crucial to the development of Pentecostalism. Thus, I find it necessary to reject the central thesis of Synan that "the historical and doctrinal lineage of American Pentecostalism is to be found in the Wesleyan Tradition."[60] To the contrary, that wing of the Pentecostal movement which had earlier connections with Wesleyanism became Pentecostal by accepting Keswick (i.e. Calvinist) teachings on dispensationalism, premillennialism and the Baptism of the Holy Spirit. This acceptance led logically to their ostracism by the "orthodox" Wesleyan Holiness movement, which held them guilty of the "Third Blessing heresy." The majority of Pentecostals were entirely consistent when they later rejected the Wesleyan view of sanctification as a second act of grace.[61] Those Pentecostals who did not follow suit in this rejection, however, cannot accurately be called Wesleyan since their doctrine is an amalgam of Wesleyanism and Keswick-Calvinism. In short, the Pentecostal movement was as much a departure from the Wesleyan tradition as a development from it. Synan's own denomination, formerly the Fire-Baptized Holiness Church and now the Pentecostal Holiness Church, had departed from Wesleyanism when it embraced Irwin's teaching of the Baptism of Fire as a third act of grace, before the Pentecostal movement emerged.

The expectation of a global Pentecostal revival was not restricted to Holiness circles. The approach of the twentieth century aroused the hopes of many other Christians for such a revival. Discrepencies in the Western calendar led Biblical scholars to date the opening of the new century anywhere from January 1, 1896, to January 1, 1901. Thus, in September 1896, the *Homiletic Review* sent out a call to some 100,000 churches to prepare for the new epoch by renewed prayer for world revival, a call that evoked enthusiastic response. In the January 1897 issue of the same journal, C. H. Payne, Corresponding Secretary of the Methodist Church, North, published the first of a series of articles entitled "The Coming Revival." Payne, stating what he believed would be the revival's outstanding characteristic, said, "It will be a revival of original Christianity."[62]

As the new century dawned with little sign of the expected revival, hopes began to wane. But they were reawakened by the news of a revival in Australia during Torrey's campaign there in 1901. The revival was attributed to the prolonged efforts of prayer circles organized in Australia to prepare for Torrey's arrival. The Keswick convention of 1902 set for itself the task of organizing similar circles to bring revival elsewhere, and by the end of the next year innumerable groups were praying for revival in England, Wales, India, Canada, and the United States.[63]

In the summer of 1903 a Welsh "Keswick" convention was established at Llandrinrod Wells, deep in the Cambrian Mountains near the English border.[64] Before the end of the year, local revivals were breaking out here and there, and the year following brought a revival that swept through Wales and then London, Liverpool, and all the British Isles. The recognized leader of the Welsh revival was Evan Roberts, a twenty-six-year-old miner-blacksmith and ministerial student. Spontaneity and complete "freedom in the Spirit" (some said, "hysteria") were the outstanding characteristics of the revival.[65] "In the Welsh revival," said an American observer, "there is no preaching, no order, no hymn-books, no organs, no collections and no advertising."[66] F. B. Meyer, a Presbyterian clergyman associated with both the English and the Welsh Keswick conventions, wrote:

> We have seen and heard things which have unveiled the spirit-world, and are so totally dissimilar from the stereotyped religious forms that we are wont to pursue, as to usher us into a new world—should we not say into that old world which Pentecost introduced, and of which I Corinthians 12 is a specimen! . . . The personality and work of the Holy Spirit are in every prayer and on every tongue. The pent-up power of godly people which has too long

been restrained, has broken loose, and before it the ministers are silenced. One told me that he felt that things would never again be as they had been in this direction, but that liberty of utterance would have to be conceded (during a part at least of the ordinary services) to the speech of the Holy Ghost through consecrated lips.[67]

Yet, though silenced, the ministers as a whole welcomed and supported the revival enthusiastically, as well they might, since estimates of new church members in Wales alone ran from 20,000 to 70,000. Unlike the later Pentecostal revival, the Welsh revival began in the churches and remained there.[68]

Some observers of the Welsh revival, hearing unfamiliar speech in prayer and preaching, reported that worshippers were speaking in tongues, though this was not claimed by leaders of the revival.[69] What the observers were witnessing was the ancient and sacred Welsh "hywl," described by a knowing participant as,

> Speaking in a strange, weird, curious, mesmeric manner: it is a unique kind of incantation, thoroughly musical, and at times, it resembles an ancient chant . . . it is the Welsh "hywl" in its rare beauty and grandeur.[70]

The world-wide attention given by the religious and secular press brought religious leaders and workers from afar to meet Roberts and study the revival at first hand. The evangelists Torrey, Alexander, and "Gypsy" Smith were only the most prominent of hundreds of Americans who visited Wales and returned home to preach and write on the subject, and to lead their followers in prayer for the extension of revival to their own nation and others.[71]

By the close of 1905, "great revivals" had broken out in the Khassia and Lushai hills to the south and west of the Ganges River of India, where the Welsh mission stations in that country were concentrated, and in southern Norway under the preaching of an obscure seaman named Lunde. Moreover, "sparks" of revival were being reported from Sweden, Germany, Uganda, Madagascar, Egypt, Persia, China, Australia, the Gilbert Islands, Chile, Brazil, and some fifteen places in the United States and Canada.[72]

The post-Civil War Holiness movement had begun within the old-line denominations. But secularization, formality in worship, theological liberalism, and, later, socialized religion—developments related to the increasingly middle-class orientation of those denominations—led substantial numbers of lower-class Holiness people to leave their churches and strike out on independent courses. By the turn of the century, emotional extremism and doctrinal controversy fragmented the movement. To prevent chaotic collapse numerous Holiness denominations were organized. But institutionalization was necessarily attended by some compromise on, among other things, doctrine and the acceptable limits of emotional expression in worship. Similar trends toward regularization divested revivalism and conversion of their spontaneity, mystery and awe.

To the absolutist mentality of many Holiness people, all compromise was "sin," organization was "ecclesiasticism" or "churchianity," and any restraint in worship was "quenching the Spirit." None of this could be countenanced by the true believer. Thus, within the Holiness movement was lodged a growing body of discontented true believers, some in the Holiness denominations, most in tiny associations or independent churches and missions, all determined to press on for still newer horizons of spiritual experience. For them, only a dramatic Christianity of intense emotion could be satisfying.

The doctrinal basis for such a form of Christianity was laid by the Keswick wing of the Holiness movement, while an atmosphere heavy with hopes of a new Pentecost and inspired by the Welsh revival provided a favorable milieu. In the United States, even before the Welsh revival, the seeds of the Pentecostal movement were being planted by Charles Fox Parham in the lower Midwest.

III

The Apostolic Faith Movement

The earliest adherents of the Pentecostal movement identified themselves as believers in "the Apostolic Faith." Charles Fox Parham formulated, or, as Pentecostals would prefer, restated, that faith at least as early as 1901.[1] Parham's Negro disciple, William Joseph Seymour, introduced a simplified version of it during the Los Angeles revival of 1906.

Parham was born at Muscatine, Iowa, on June 4, 1873. His father, whose English ancestors had settled in Philadelphia in the eighteenth century, had gone west, first to Iowa where he married a girl of German descent, and, five years after the birth of Charles, to a farm near Cheney, Kansas. In infancy, Parham was "taken with a fever" and "dreadful spasms," the first of a series of debilitating illnesses that kept him in "constant pain" until his eighteenth year. At the age of nine he was striken with "inflammatory rheumatism" and developed a tapeworm. During this bout, he received a "call" to the ministry and began reading the Bible avidly, though he had not yet been "saved." At an age when other boys were doing men's chores, young Parham was confined to bed except when he was well enough to do some housekeeping or herd the cattle to and from pasture.[2]

When he was thirteen years old, his mother died, and in the aftermath Parham was converted under the preaching of "Brother Lippard of the Congregational Church House." It was a Damascus road experience.

> There flashed from the heavens a light above the brightness of the sun; like a stroke of lightning it penetrated, thrilling every fibre of my being; making me know by experimental knowledge what Peter knew of old, that He was the Christ, the Son of the Living God.[3]

Filled with zeal, Parham became a regular church-goer and a Sunday-school teacher.

It was hardly surprising that the ailing, motherless, introverted youth had turned to religion. Not that he was raised in the church, for he had hardly attended a religious service before adolescence. But for one seeking integration and purpose in life in late 19th-century Kansas, there were few alternatives to religion.

The state of Kansas was born in the midst of a fratricidal conflict that served as prologue for the Civil War. Characteristics of individualism, fierce partisan loyalty, and intolerance that often turned to violence were perpetuated there in politics and religion for several generations. "Holy" was a fitting epithet for Kansas, where folk-dancing in kindergarten was outlawed, and the only songs heard in school were hymns and temperance ditties. Not only was the sale of liquor and tobacco prohibited by law, but students who came from high schools that allowed their faculties to smoke were refused admittance to state colleges. In such a place the career of prophet was avidly pursued by many. Parham was to stand as a minor figure in a school of prophets that reached from John Brown to Carrie Nation and beyond.[4]

In preparation for the ministry, Parham entered Southwestern College, a Methodist school at Winfield, Kansas, in 1889. Soon after embarking upon his studies, the frail sixteen-year-old youth veered aside from his original intention in favor of a career in medicine. "The devil," he later said, "tried to make me believe I could be a physician and a Christian too." In retrospect, he concluded that in entertaining the notion he had been guilty of "backsliding," for which God "chastised" him with a new attack of rheumatic fever. Lying in a daze from an overdose of morphine, he overheard the prediction of his imminent death by a doctor called in to examine him. Parham confessed in prayer that he had sinned in contemplating a medical career, and promised to obey the "call" to preach if he should live. There then "came" to him "all those wonderful lessons of how Jesus healed," and Parham felt assured that He would also heal him.[5]

Parham's recovery was not total. He was "healed" of "all ailments," but his ankles "remained helpless." After learning to "walk upon the sides of my feet, or rather upon my ankles with my feet thrown out to the side," he returned to college. Shortly, it was "revealed" to him that education was a hinderance in the service of God, and he decided to quit college. At that moment, "God instantly sent the virtue of healing like a mighty electric current through my body and my ankles were made whole."[6]

Leaving Southwestern on his own two feet, he went directly to preaching. He was licensed by the Methodist Church, North, in 1892, and given a dual pastorate over the churches at Eudora and Linwood, not far from Lawrence, Kansas, at the age of eighteen. The experience was a disappointment. For all his zeal and sense of mission, two years of labor yielded him but one solitary convert.[7]

During his first year in the ministry, however, while conducting revival services in a schoolhouse near Tonganoxie, Kansas, he was befriended by the Thistlethwaites, a Quaker family. Mrs. Thistlethwaite's father, David Baker, persuaded Parham to abandon the doctrine of eternal punishment in favor of the teaching of the total annihilation of the wicked. It was probably while under this holiness Quaker's influence that Parham also came to reject water baptism, to accept sanctification as a second act of grace, and to regard church membership as a matter of indifference.[8]

Trouble with his Methodist superiors arose because Parham began to preach against the traditional doctrine of hell as a place of eternal punishment, and because he advised his audiences to join any church or none at all, since salvation had nothing to do with church membership. Under fire, he left the Methodist Church in 1894, asserting that he could no longer accept a salary raised by "suppers and worldly entertainment," and deploring, in typical "come-outer" Holiness fashion, the "sectarian churchism" of the denominations.[9]

After living for a time with a Captain and Mrs. M. J. Tuttle in Lawrence, he obeyed the "call" to enter the evangelistic field "on faith" (that is, with no visible means of financial support) and preached among Holiness people wherever he found an opening. He kept up his friendship with the Thistlethwaites and was married to one of the daughters, Sarah, by a Friends minister on New Year's Eve, 1896, after which they embarked on an evangelistic tour through Kansas and Missouri. About the time their first child was born in September 1897, Parham developed "heart disease in the worst form." While praying for a sick man soon after this, the Scripture text "Physician, heal thyself" came to Parham. He prayed for his own healing, recovered, and immediately threw away all his medicines, gave up doctors "forever," and cancelled his insurance policy.[10]

The experience led him to center his work on divine healing. After beginning this new ministry in Ottawa, Kansas, he moved to Topeka and was operating Bethel Healing Home there by the fall of 1898. It was a combination of rest home and Bible school, where people were admitted on a "faith basis," i.e., on condition that they trust God for all their needs with no visible means of support. According to his wife, Parham's teachings at that time were: "Salvation, Healing, Sanctification, the Second Coming of Christ, and the Baptism of the Holy Spirit, although we had not then received the evidence of speaking in other tongues." In short, he was a typical Holiness preacher with Keswick leanings. In connection with the home and school, a mission was opened and a bimonthly periodical, *The Apostolic Faith,* was published. For the first time, Parham tasted success, but contentment eluded him.[11]

From itinerant evangelists who stopped to preach in his mission, Parham heard about the workings of the Spirit in Holiness centers of the North and East. A gnawing dissatisfaction with his inner experience led him to seek out Frank W. Sandford, who presided over one of the more prominent of these centers. Sandford was a former Free Baptist minister who had left that church to strike out "in faith" as an independent in 1893. By 1898 the "Holy Ghost and Us" society that he had founded was operating a Bible and missionary training school large enough to accommodate 500 students in a complex of buildings named "Shiloh" that stood high on a hill overlooking the Androscoggin River in the town of Durham, Maine. Parham and about eight others from his Topeka mission enrolled in Sandford's school in the summer of 1900.[12]

Parham spent about six weeks at Shiloh and was greatly impressed. On the journey to and from Maine ne stopped to visit the communitarian settlement of the healer-evangelist and self-styled "Prophet" John Alexander Dowie in Zion City, just north of Chicago; the "Eye-Opener" mission work in Chicago itself; "Malone's" work in Cleveland, Ohio; Simpson's Nyack, New York, institute; and other sites of Holiness experimentation. In each place Parham sought in vain for a teaching and experience of Baptism in the Holy Spirit that "tallied with the Word of God." He went back to Topeka convinced that no one had yet found the "true Baptism."[13]

On his return, Parham was denied access to his Healing Home and mission by the preacher he had left in charge during his absence. Choosing to "resist not evil," and, perhaps more interested just then in his search for the "true" Baptism in the Spirit, he decided to open a new Bible school patterned after Sandford's.[14]

Through the agents of the American Bible Society of Philadelphia,

Parham secured the use of an unfinished mansion on the outskirts of Topeka. Surely one of the more grotesque examples of Victorian architecture ever constructed, "Stone's Folly," as it was known locally, was a jumble of red brick, white stone, balustrades, ornate cornices, stained glass windows and doors, with cupolas, tall chimneys and a soaring observatory. Each of the completed rooms was finished in paneling of different exotic woods.[15]

The "College of Bethel" was opened on October 15, 1900, with about three dozen persons, including "students" and their children in attendance. Most of them had been ministers or religious workers for some years in Methodist, Baptist, Quaker, and independent Holiness churches and missions. All of them were of the Holiness persuasion and shared Parham's desire for a new experience of the Spirit, and for new power in evangelistic work.[16]

Perhaps typical of the group was Agnes N. Ozman. Born of German descent in Albany, Wisconsin, Miss Ozman had grown up under the watchful eyes of her devout Methodist parents on the Nebraska prairies. In adolescence she found the experience of sanctification and embarked on a lifelong spiritual odyssey. She attended T. C. Horton's Bible school at St. Paul, Minnesota, and Simpson's Nyack institute, visited Dowie's utopia, and worked intermittently for twelve years as a home missionary with various groups before ending up in Kansas City mission work in the fall of 1900. There she attended a meeting where Parham announced the opening of his school in Topeka and asked for volunteers. "My heart," she said, "felt a stir within for a greater fulness of the Spirit," and she was off on still another search for the ultimate experience. At the time, she was twenty-nine years old, temperamentally high-strung and nervous, and suffering from consumption of long standing.[17]

In imitation of Sandford's Shiloh techniques, the Bethel school was operated "on faith," the Bible was the only textbook, a "prayer-chain" in three-hour shifts was maintained in one of the tower rooms, several rooms were set aside for a healing home, and much time was given to prayer and fasting. Parham was the only regular teacher, but numerous evangelists visited to preach and teach. Parham taught by extemporaneous exposition of the Bible, verse by verse; the students learned by rote. House-to-house canvassing was carried out during part of the day, and, in the evening, services were held in a downtown mission. The group had all things in common, shared their material possessions and money, ate at the same table, performed household chores, worked in the mission, and prayed and studied in concert, their "only object utter abandonment in obedience to the commandments of Jesus, however unconventional."[18]

Over it all, Parham presided. Now twenty-seven years old, he presented a singularly curious spectacle. Whether by birth, or as a result of his childhood ailments, or, as Parham believed, because of the "poisons," that is, medicines, administered to him, at full maturity he was a dwarflike figure. Slight, spare, and "extremely delicate looking," he had a pale face, bushy eyebrows, a full mustache, and an "abnormally large" brow crowned with masses of brown hair.[19] But a reporter sent to get a story on the "strange religion" at Bethel said, "Mr. Parham does not impress one as being a peculiar man. Indeed he is a right good fellow and is earnest in his life's work."[20] A convert of later years described him as the students at Bethel no doubt saw him:

> A personable, gifted, accomplished, original and forceful thinker and a vivid, magnetic personality with superb, versatile platform ability, he always held his audience in the curve of his hand. People sat spellbound, one moment weeping, the next rocking with laughter. . . . His humility, his meekness and consecration impressed everyone most favorably.[21]

Perhaps his unusual physical appearance was more an asset than a liability for one propagating so unusual a gospel.

The story of the "outpouring of the Spirit" at Bethel College has come down to us weighted with miracle and wonder.[22] Parham first convinced his students that what most of them called the Baptism in the Spirit was, in fact, either sanctification or "the anointing that abideth," and that their task was to discover the "true" Baptism. Agnes Ozman described her reaction to this:

> I like some others was decided for a time that I had my Baptism and had received as I thought the Holy Ghost at a time of consecration or in sanctification in being separated unto the Lord. But after hearing Mr. Parham proclaim with much assurance and with power that the Holy Spirit was yet to be poured out, and to be given to believers, my own heart became so hungry for the promised gift and Comforter I began to cry out for this mighty fulfillment of promise. At times I longed for the Holy Spirit to come in more than for my necessary food and at night a desire was felt more than for sleep and I knew it was the Lord.[23]

Before leaving for a three-days' campaign in Kansas City near the end of December 1900, Parham told the Bethel group to study the subject of the Baptism separately and in solitude. Directing them to read carefully the second chapter of the book of Acts, Parham said,

> The gifts are in the Holy Spirit and with the baptism of the Holy Spirit the gifts, as well as the graces, should be manifested. Now, students, while I am gone, see if there is not some evidence given of the baptism so there may be no doubt on the subject.[24]

Returning to the school on the morning of December 30, Parham called the students together and asked for their findings.

> To my astonishment they all had the same story, that while there were different things occurred [sic] when the Pentecostal blessing fell, that the indisputable proof on each occasion was, that they spake with other tongues.[25]

Now miraculously enlightened on the "true" Baptism, and buttressed by some seventy-five kindred souls who came for the New Year holidays, the group prayed, fasted, and held services night and day, awaiting the coming of the Spirit in a Second Pentecost. Then, in the words of Agnes Ozman,

> Near eleven o'clock on this first day of January it came to me to have hands laid upon me to fulfil Scriptures. I remembered somewhere in the Bible the believers had hands laid upon them during prayer when they received the Holy Spirit. I asked Bro. Parham to pray and to lay hands on me that I might receive the Baptism in the Holy Ghost and as he prayed and laid hands opon [sic] my head I began to speak in tongues glorifying God. Bless HIM! I talked several languages for it was manifested when a dilect [sic] was spoken. Glory to God![26]

Miss Ozman claimed that for the next three days she spoke only in Chinese and wrote only in Chinese characters. "Some of the writing has been interpreted," she said, "and it is wonderful messages."[27] The others, prodded on by Miss Ozman's example, "tarried" together in an upper room cleared for the purpose, "scarcely eating or sleeping." On the evening of January 3rd, while Parham was holding a meeting in a Free Methodist church in Topeka, the fire fell on the company at Bethel. Lillian Thistlethwaite, Mrs. Parham's sister, described the event.

> We prayed for ourselves, we prayed for one another. I never felt so little and utterly nothing before. A scrap of paper charred by fire is the best description I can give of my feelings. Then through the Spirit this message came to my soul, "Praise Him for laying on of hands." Then a great joy came into my soul and I began to say, "I praise Thee," and my tongue began to get thick and great floods of laughter came into my heart. I could no longer think

words of praise, for my mind was sealed, but my mouth was filled with a
rush of words I didn't understand. I tried not to laugh for I feared to grieve
the Spirit. I tried to praise Him in English but could not, so I just let the
praise come as it would in the new language given, with floodgates of glory
wide open. He had come to me, even to me to speak not of Himself but to
magnify the Christ,—and oh, what a wonderful, wonderful Christ was revealed. Then I realized I was not alone for all around me I heard great rejoic-
ing while others spoke in tongues and magnified God.[28]

Howard D. Stanley, another of those present that night, related his
story with crude grammar and spelling.

I saw the clovend tonges as of fire came down into the room and my vocal
cords and tongue changed and I was speaking another language and so was
most of the others.[29]

When Parham entered the dimly-lit room later that evening, he saw
twelve ministers sitting, kneeling, and standing with up-raised hands,
engulfed in a miraculous "sheen of white light above the brightness of
many lamps." Falling on his knees behind a table while the company
sang with angelic voices "Jesus, Lover of My Soul" in "at least six different languages," Parham sought the same experience.

He distinctly made it clear to me that He raised me up and trained me to
declare this mighty truth to the world, and if I was willing to stand for it,
with all the persecutions, hardships, trials, slander, scandal that it would en-
tail, He would give me the blessing. And I said, "Lord I will, if You will
just give me this blessing." Right then there came a slight twist in my
throat, a glory fell over me and I began to worship God in the Sweedish [sic]
tongue, which later changed to other languages and continued so until the
morning.[30]

As related, the whole episode at Bethel is too pat to be true. In some
respects the accounts used by Pentecostals undermine their own miraculous interpretation, and in other respects additional eyewitness accounts,
ignored by Pentecostal historians, flatly contradict the accepted version.

In the first place, although it cannot be said for certain that Parham
taught his students that speaking in tongues was proof of Spirit baptism
from the outset, it is very likely that he had reached that conclusion for
himself beforehand. Parham had long been concerned about the conflicting views on the Baptism, and had read much, traveled far, and con-
versed extensively with Holiness leaders on the subject. It is difficult to
believe that he was not familiar with the ideas of Torrey and others. Fur-

thermore, his school was primarily for training home and foreign missionaries, and Parham had long believed that God could give people the miraculous ability to preach in foreign languages without any study on their part.

> I had felt for many years that any missionary going to the foreign field should preach in the language of the natives. That if God had ever equipped his ministers in that way He could do it today. That if Balaam's mule could stop in the middle of the road and give the first preacher that went out for money a "bawling out" in Arabic that anybody today ought to be able to preach in any language of the world if they had horse sense enough to let God use their tongue and throat.[31]

Parham had himself spoken automatically in English on several occasions before opening the school at Topeka. Using the royal "we," Parham told of those experiences.

> We ourselves had known the power of the Holy Ghost in our lives to a wonderful degree for many years, and had such wonderful anointings that we were carried far beyond ourselves, many times for ten, fifteen and twenty minutes words of living truth (Our minds took no part, but in which we became an interested listener) flowed from our lips; yet this was but the anointing that abideth, not the Baptism of the Holy Ghost as many believed it to be.[32]

According to Pentecostal mythology, the doctrine that speaking in tongues is the evidence of Baptism in the Holy Spirit was miraculously revealed when the students at Bethel unanimously reached that conclusion after independent study of the Scriptures. But Parham had specifically instructed them to search the second chapter of Acts for the indisputable evidence of Spirit baptism, and it is just this section of the New Testament where speaking in tongues is tied most directly to the descent of the Holy Spirit. It seems clear that Parham had previously formulated the doctrine in his own mind but, in order to make it appear to be a miraculous divine revelation, set the stage for his students to "discover" the doctrine he intended them to. But this story of the students' discovery is based on only three accounts: those of Parham, his wife, and his wife's sister. The only other eyewitness accounts I could find—those of Agnes Ozman and Howard Stanley—tell a different, contradictory tale.

Miss Ozman claimed that she knew nothing about the doctrine of Baptism in the Spirit with speaking in tongues until *after* her experience of January 1, 1901, when it was revealed to her only. Then, she said, she had to convince the others that "it was Bible" by pointing them to Acts 2:4 and Acts 19:1–6.

> Before receiving the Comforter I did not know that I would spea[k] in tongue[s] when I received the Holy Ghost for I did not know it was Bible. But after I received the Holy Spirit speaking in tongues it was revealed to me that I had the promise of th[e] Father as it is written and as Jesus said. . . . And now I will put in print and say I did not know then that anyone else would speak in tongues.[33]

Stanley seemed to confirm this story when he said, "Agnes Ozman was the one that made clear to me that when we were filled with Holy Spirit that we would speak in other tongues."[34]

Furthermore, the position that Miss Ozman first spoke in tongues on January 1, 1901 is insupportable. In her earliest account of the events of that day, Agnes Ozman said, "About three weeks before this, while three of us girls were in prayer, I spoke three words in another tongue." This was corroborated by Lillian Thistlethwaite, who said Miss Ozman "had received a few words while in the Prayer Tower." And the earliest newspaper account I could find, dated January 9, 1901, and based on an interview in which Parham was quoted, says that Miss Ozman first spoke in tongues "about two weeks ago."[35]

In view of the scanty and conflicting evidence, we are compelled to speculate. It seems most probable that Parham arrived at his doctrine of the Baptism in the Spirit with speaking in tongues sometime during the year 1900. At the Bethel school he led the group in their studies in such a way as to make them believe the doctrine was not his own "man-made" idea, but came by revelation. Miss Ozman made the intended connection between speaking in tongues and the Baptism in the Spirit, and, being temperamentally predisposed, experienced slight disturbances of speech soon after she entered Bethel in early December. With expectations heightened by the dawning of a new century, Miss Ozman achieved fully automatic speech, and a few days later others were carried into the experience. In retrospect, the episode took on such cosmic significance to the Parhams that they remembered it as totally divine and supernatural.

The miraculous story of Bethel College gives us insight into the Pentecostals' self-image. Their movement, according to the accepted story, was founded in nearly the exact manner in which the Church was founded on the day of Pentecost. The 40 students plus about 75 visitors at the time of Miss Ozman's Spirit baptism made roughly 120 persons, the same as on the day of Pentecost. The outpouring of January 3rd in an "upper room," the speaking in tongues, the visible tongues of fire, and the multitude of newspapermen and linguists alleged to have flocked there, are almost exactly as Pentecost is described in the second chapter of Acts. In addition, there is much symbolism in the story, some of it based on sacred numerology, a popular topic with Pentecostals to this day. It was about three days from the time the students began to search the Bible for the "true" doctrine of the Baptism until they reached their verdict, another three days till Agnes Ozman spoke in tongues on January 1, and still another three days till the general outpouring of January 3rd. The number three symbolizes the Trinity, and three times three is the numerical equivalent of perfection. Parham and the twelve ministers who were in the "upper room" on the night of January 3 correspond to Jesus and the disciples.

All was not love and harmony at Bethel. Less than a week after the Spirit fell, one of the saints, S. J. Riggins, defected and told the local newspapers that the school was "a fake." As it turned out, he rendered a service to Parham, for not until then did the story receive coverage. In a short time, reporters from Kansas City, St. Louis, Cincinnati, and elsewhere came to Bethel and wrote about the "strange sect" whose adherents claimed to speak languages that they did not understand. One article included a sample of Lillian Thistlethwaite's tongue-speech and its "interpretation."

> "Euossa, Euossa use, relia sema cala mala kanah leullia sage nalan. Ligle logle lazle logle. Ene mine mo, sah rah el me sah rah me." These sentences were translated as meaning, "Jesus is mighty to save." "Jesus is ready to hear," and "God is love." [36]

The newspaper reports, on the whole, were only mildly bantering in tone, though they were considered "almost blasphemous" by the Apostolic Faith believers. Bethel was referred to as the "Parham School of Tongues," the prayer tower as "the tower of Babel," and their "new religion" as "queer and strange." Yet press coverage, favorable or otherwise, attracted attention to the new movement. Parham was inspired to launch out with his message. Planning a campaign across the country to the Northeast, Parham moved first on Kansas City with an "Apostolic Band" of seven workers. [37]

His arrival was heralded by front-page news coverage, but after two weeks the group returned to the Topeka school in failure. Another, larger band then went out with Parham to try its luck in Lawrence, with the same dismal results. Nor was Topeka any more hospitable to Parham's gospel. By mid-summer, "Stone's Folly" had been sold out from under the Bethel group, and only a hard core of disciples followed Parham to Kansas City where he opened another unsuccessful Bible school.[38]

There the faithful few began to leave, one by one. Howard Stanley went to open a mission in Lawrence which, he said, "had nothing to do with the bible school" (i.e., Parham's).[39] Agnes Ozman returned to mission work somewhere in the Midwest, and repudiated her experience at Bethel (though she was reclaimed to Pentecostalism soon after the Los Angeles revival of 1906).[40] When the Kansas City school closed after four months, the saints had all scattered, "some preaching, others to other things." Parham, deserted by all but his wife and her sister, and mourning the death of his year-old son the previous spring, was utterly despondent. Looking back on these days years later, Mrs. Parham said they were "hated, despised, counted as naught, for weeks and weeks never knowing where our next meal would come from, yet feeling that we must maintain the faith once for all delivered to the saints."[41]

The winter of 1901–02 found the Parhams in Lawrence, Kansas, where they remained for a year and a half, preaching here and there, but still to no avail. "The people," said Mrs. Parham, "seemed slow to accept the truth, some declaring it was not the power of God which enabled us to speak in tongues."[42] During these months Parham, the rejected prophet, formulated his ideas and put them into print under the title *A Voice Crying in the Wilderness.*[43]

Success came in the fall of 1903, after Parham shifted his emphasis back to healing, and carried his gospel into the mining region at the juncture of Kansas, Missouri, and Oklahoma known as the Tri-State District. Parham was invited to hold meetings in Galena, Kansas, by Mrs. Mary A. Arthur, a devout Methodist who professed to have been healed through Parham's ministry at the health resort of Eldorado Springs, Missouri, the previous summer.[44]

Galena lay at the center of the Tri-State District, which for half a century would be the richest lead and zinc producing area in the world. Mining operations had begun there as early as the 1870's, but large-scale production did not start until 1899. Galena was a typical, wide-open, frontier boom-town "where everything went," and the sight of dead bodies lying between the saloons, brothels and tent shacks on the morning after was commonplace. In a region where memories of old-time camp meeting revivals were still very much alive, but where the established denominations had already abandoned that tradition, Parham met with an enthusiastic response.[45]

Meetings were held first in a tent pitched alongside the Arthur home, and then in a rented warehouse with seats for 2,000. The revival continued night and day all winter long, attracting "thousands" from a hundred mile radius. One newspaper account reported that more than 500 were converted, some 250 were baptized in the icy waters of the Spring River, and many received "what they term 'the Pentecost' and are enabled to speak in foreign tongues. . . . but of all the wonderful things which have transpired in connection with these meetings, nothing has attracted the attention of the public as has the 'healings'."[46]

Parham left the work at Galena in the charge of Mrs. Arthur and Mrs. Fannie Dobson, who opened a mission there, while he launched out to hold revivals of lesser dimensions in Baxter Springs and Melrose, Kansas, and in Joplin, Missouri. His converts and workers carried the movement to Columbus, Kansas, Carthage, Missouri, and Miami, Oklahoma. As a result of these campaigns, several Apostolic Faith missions and house meetings were established in the Tri-State District.[47]

In the spring of 1905 another fruitful field was opened to Parham: the boom-towns of the Houston-Galveston area, which sprang up overnight following the Spindletop oil strike near Beaumont four years earlier. Mr. and Mrs. Walter Oyler, who had attended Parham's meetings in Galena and Joplin, invited him to hold house meetings in their home in the prairie village of Orchard, Texas. Finding a favorable reception, Parham returned to the missions of the Tri-State District where he raised funds and recruited workers for a major campaign in Houston, the largest city in Texas.[48]

In July 1905 some two dozen Apostolics (adherents of the Apostolic Faith Movement) descended on Houston, working in teams from house to house and visiting the jails during the days. In the evenings Parham, "clad in the robes of a bishop," marched through the streets at the head of his Oriental-costumed entourage, stopping here and there to preach on corners, and leading the inspired and the curious to meetings in a rented hall.[49]

A spectacular healing brought Parham the free advertising of newspaper coverage. The wife of a prominent lawyer in Houston, whose suit for injuries suffered in a street-car accident had been widely publicized, was carried up the stairs to the "upper room" in Bryan Hall and prayed for by Parham. Rising from her chair, she "walked about the hall in a state of ecstatic joy, shouting, clapping her hands, and praising the Lord." Parham, however, had his greatest success, not in Houston, but in the town of Brunner just outside Houston. There he won over the independent Holiness mission of W. Fay Carothers, and for some years that church was the headquarters of the Apostolic Faith Movement in Texas.[50]

By the fall of 1905, their ranks swelled by some two dozen more workers, the Apostolics fanned out in bands to evangelize the towns and cities southward to Galveston. In December, Parham rented a large, two-story frame house in Houston, and announced the opening of a Bible school for training still more workers needed to "firmly establish this great growing work in Texas." The school was operated along the same lines as Bethel had been, but with the additional innovation of teaching by the Holy Spirit directly through "prophecy," and through "messages" in tongues and interpretation.[51]

Among the students at the Houston school was William Joseph Seymour, the man who later carried the Apostolic Faith Movement to Los Angeles. Seymour was a Baptist preacher of Holiness persuasion who had been born a slave in Louisiana and been "saved and sanctified" under the "Evening Light Saints". He had worked as a waiter in Indianapolis before stopping at Houston en route to the West Coast. Stocky and somewhat disheveled in appearance, customarily quiet and unassuming, but fervent in prayer and preaching, Seymour had a vaguely unsettling effect on others—an effect enhanced by the blindness of one eye. To admirers and critics alike his demeanor suggested untapped depths of awesome power, divine or diabolic.[52]

In Houston, Seymour visited a Negro mission and heard someone speak in tongues, probably Parham's black "governess" Lucy Farrow, who frequented the Holiness missions of her race in that city, sometimes accompanied by Parham. At any rate, Seymour showed up at Parham's school and asked to be admitted. Parham hesitated for fear of provoking racist opposition to his work, but Seymour finally prevailed. Accepting the doctrine of Baptism in the Spirit with speaking in tongues, Seymour became a "seeker," but failed to attain the experience until he reached Los Angeles.[53]

While working among the black Holiness missions in Houston, Seymour met Neeley Terry. Back in her home city of Los Angeles Miss Terry had been a member of a black Baptist church whose ranks had been split when an itinerant evangelist, "Sister Hutchinson," began preaching sanctification as a second act of grace during a revival campaign there. The church officials closed the doors against Sister Hutchinson, who promptly led a group of the disaffected, including Neeley Terry, in opening a store-front mission on Santa Fe Avenue, in a black neighborhood alongside the railroad tracks on the east side of town. On her return to Los Angeles, Miss Terry told the Santa Fe congregation about Seymour, and persuaded them to engage him as an associate pastor.[54]

When he received the invitation Seymour discussed it with Parham, who tried to convince him to remain in Houston to "tarry" for the Baptism and continue to work among his race there. But once again Seymour won out, and Parham gave him railroad fare out of the common treasury. With prayer and the laying on of hands, Seymour was dispatched from Houston to Los Angeles sometime in January 1906.[55]

It was a turning point. As he laid his hands on the kneeling Seymour, Parham was unknowingly passing on the leadership of the movement to others. He would continue to have a following in the Midwest, but would never achieve prominence among Pentecostals nationally. What had been under Parham a relatively small, localized movement, was to assume international proportions through the Los Angeles ministry of the obscure, chunky black man who sat gazing out the sooted train window, lost in prayer and meditation as the Texas plains slid behind him.

IV

The Pentecostal Revival

The Los Angeles which Seymour entered was a bustling city, then in a boom that would taper off in the years following the Panic of 1907 only to be resumed by 1910. The fastest growing city in the nation from 1880 to 1910, Los Angeles had doubled its population in the 1890's and more than tripled it in the next decade. The sprawling, residential character of the city reflected the rural, anti-urban sentiments of its inhabitants. And, while industrial growth was even then eroding the rustic aspects of the city, the frontier ethos was still strong, and would linger on well into the future.[1]

Most of the native white majority were recent migrants from the Midwest, having sold their farms and businesses to enjoy their middle and declining years in the salubrious climate for which Los Angeles had been a byword since the "health craze" of the 1880's. The high rate of mobility, both into and within the city, exacerbated the psychological effects of urban life: loneliness, ennui, alienation and despair. The consequent "quest for community" often found expression in attempts to recreate the familiar rural relationships of the past. But the community they sought was not broadly enough conceived to include all the residents of Los Angeles.[2]

The native white Anglo-Saxon Protestant majority carefully shunned the multiplying minority groups of the city. Between 1900 and 1910, some 31,000 Europeans, 5,500 blacks, 5,000 Mexicans, and 4,000 Japanese filtered into the downtown ghettoes of the central city or gravitated to the segregated pockets on its fringes. Blacks, Orientals and Mexicans—all considered "non-white" by standards then prevailing—accounted for 5.6% of the population in Los Angeles in 1910; southern and eastern Europeans for about 4.2%. Together, the "non-whites" and all immigrants made up about 22% of the population.[3]

If the old-stock, middle-class, rather elderly majority could not recapture the homogeneous quality of their Midwest youth, they could at least turn to the comforts of religion. According to the census of 1916, one in three people was a church member, but the actual proportion was no doubt considerably larger since Los Angeles was already becoming a breeding ground for new sects, many of which were not listed in census reports.

If the atmosphere of worship and the sense of fellowship in many mainline denominational churches failed to satisfy the longing for community, it was not so in the churches of the newer, revivalistic sects. And some 11.5% of those church members appearing in the census were affiliated with churches other than the major denominations. By 1906 there were over a hundred churches preaching the "full gospel" in Los Angeles. The Church of the Nazarene had 1,695 members in four churches in Los Angeles, and an uncertain number in six other churches in the surrounding region. Churches of the Pentecostal Union ("Pillar of Fire"), the Metropolitan Church Association ("Burning Bush"), Peniel Missions, the Christian and Missionary Alliance, and numerous independent churches and missions were active in promoting holiness and revival. Moreover, many denominational churches like the Methodist Episcopal, North, had been carried into the Holiness camp in the 1890's, and some at least were still preaching the "higher life" and praying for revival. Similar conditions prevailed in the churches of nearby Pasadena, San Diego, Hermon, Santa Barbara, and San Pedro.[4]

Even those Angelenos who were not affiliated with any church clung fiercely to the pietistic values and mores of 19th-century Evangelical Protestantism. Answering a criticism of the "rural beliefs, pieties, superstitions and habits" of Los Angeles, one spokesman declared, "She deliberately chooses to be dubbed 'Puritan,' 'Middle-West Farmer,' 'Provincial', etc., and glories in the fact that she has been able to sweep away many flaunting indecencies that still disgrace older and more vice-complacent communities."[5]

Not only was the general moral and religious climate of Los Angeles such as to predispose at least some of its inhabitants to the Pentecostal movement, but when Seymour arrived a revival was already in progress, a revival in which the expectation of Pentecostal gifts and signs figured prominently.

Inspired by the news of the Welsh revival, the Holiness believers of the city had been praying for a similar outpouring of the Spirit. In the spring of 1905 F. B. Meyer, the English Keswick champion and a participant in the Welsh revival, spoke to large audiences in Los Angeles. Joseph Smale, pastor of the First Baptist Church, returned in July from a visit to Wales and began prayer meetings in his church that led to a sixteen-week revival. A member of the First Methodist Church said of the "prayer band" there, "We prayed that Pentecost might come to the city of Los Angeles." During the summer, the spirit of revival was evident in the "Burning Bush" and Peniel missions, and in several independent churches and missions. Special revival campaigns were held in tents in the city and at camp meetings in the nearby Arroyo mountains.[6]

A prominent figure in developing and spreading the revival in the Los Angeles region was Frank Bartleman, a Holiness preacher who arrived in the city in December 1904, after a decade of itinerant evangelism all over the nation. After hearing Meyer speak, Bartleman read the accounts of the Welsh revival by S. B. Shaw and G. Campbell Morgan, began corresponding with Evan Roberts, and threw himself wholeheartedly into the work of promoting revival in southern California. Night and day he visited and preached in various churches, wrote tracts and articles for Holiness periodicals, and distributed the booklets by Shaw and Morgan and thousands of other tracts in the missions, saloons and brothels, and on street corners. "The spirit of revival," he said, "consumed me."[7]

Bartleman was most closely associated with Smale's First Baptist Church, where nightly meetings ran into the small hours of the morning, and where Smale prophesied "the speedy return of the apostolic 'gifts' to the church." In September 1905, an attempt by the officials of the First Baptist Church to curb the revival precipitated the defection of Smale, Bartleman, and the "most spiritual" church members, who rented Burbank Hall and organized the New Testament Church. Revival continued with all-night prayer meetings in which the saints were "led to pray for a Pentecost. It seemed almost beginning." Then, in February of 1906, as Bartleman remembered it,

> One afternoon after a service in the New Testament Church, seven of us seemed providentially led to join hands and agree in prayer to ask the Lord

to pour out His Spirit speedily, with "signs following." Where we got the idea from at that time I do not know. He must Himself have suggested it to us. We did not have "tongues" in mind. I think none of us ever heard of such a thing.[8]

It was into this charged atmosphere that Seymour came, early in 1906. In his first sermon at the Santa Fe Holiness mission, on a Sunday morning, he preached on Acts 2:4, declaring that no one had the real Baptism in the Holy Spirit unless he spoke in tongues. Sister Hutchinson and the saints at the mission believed that the Baptism and sanctification were one and the same experience, an experience most of them claimed to have had. Seymour's teaching required that they repudiate their own belief and experience concerning the Baptism. Although they had heard about the speaking in tongues in Houston from Neeley Terry, they believed that it was only one of the gifts of the Spirit that were to be poured out upon sanctified believers, those who had already been Baptized in the Spirit. When Seymour returned for the afternoon service he found the doors padlocked against him.[9]

Feeling compelled to continue his work at all costs, Seymour resorted to cottage prayer meetings, first in the home of "Irish" Lee and his wife, black adherents of one of the Peniel missions, and later in the home of another black couple, the Baptist "Brother and Sister" Asbury, who lived at 214 North Bonnie Brae Street in the depressed section north of Temple Street. In the beginning, Seymour's flock consisted primarily of Negro washwomen. Seymour was handicapped in that he himself had not yet spoken in tongues and was not successful in inducing it in others.[10]

But news of Seymour and his teaching spread by word of mouth from the first. The Lees discussed the new development with members of Peniel Hall; a Mr. and Mrs. C. M. McGowan, who heard Seymour's sermon at the Santa Fe mission, reported it to members of their church, William Pendleton's Holiness Church on Hawthorne Street; and Frank Bartleman, ever attuned to "the movement of the Spirit" in Holiness circles, began visiting Seymour's house meetings sometime in March, as did Arthur Osterberg and some of the members of his independent Full Gospel Church.[11]

Lack of real success, however, led Seymour to write Parham for assistance, and sometime in late March or early April Lucy Farrow and "Brother" J. A. Warren arrived from Houston. Lucy Farrow had already spoken in tongues and soon became famous for her ability to induce it in others at the touch of her hands. Shortly after their arrival "the power fell" in the Bonnie Brae meeting on April 9th; within a few days, several, including Seymour, found the Pentecostal experience.[12]

The following Sunday morning, one of the black "sisters" from the Bonnie Brae meetings visited the New Testament Church and spoke in tongues. This "created quite a stir," and led a number of those present to go to Seymour's meeting that same afternoon. Encouraged by the "break" in the work, Seymour opened meetings in a rented hall a few days later.[13]

Renowned among Pentecostals ever since as the center from which their movement radiated around the world, 312 Azusa Street was a run-down former African Methodist Episcopal church on a side street in the central urban ghetto amid wholesale houses, stockyards, stables, a lumberyard, and a tombstone shop. It had been converted into a stable and storage warehouse on the ground floor with a rooming house above. A relatively small, flat-roofed rectangular building finished with white-washed clapboards, the only indication of its origins was a single gothic-style window above the entrance. Seymour and his tiny flock cleared an area on the ground floor of discarded building materials and other debris, and arranged seating for two or three dozen persons by placing planks across empty nail kegs. Two empty packing boxes served as a pulpit.[14]

Like the story of the Bethel College "outpouring of the Spirit," that of the Los Angeles revival has been greatly embroidered and distorted. The initial visitation of the Spirit on the saints at Bonnie Brae is said to have "stirred the whole city," and attracted such crowds that even the Azusa Street building, rented out of necessity to accommodate the crush, was inadequate. A great revival is said to have continued night and day at Azusa for three years from the day of its opening. One account has it that the house on Bonnie Brae collapsed from the jumping, stamping and dancing "in the Spirit," though, miraculously, no one was injured.[15]

Actually, the saints at Azusa had little real success until July at the earliest. Soon after the meetings began at Azusa, the *Los Angeles Daily Times* reported the "weird babel of tongues" heard amongst a "new sect of fanatics." But, as the report indicated, the meetings' newsworthiness lay in their bizarre character. It did not have revival dimensions and thus no further articles appeared in the *Times* until September. When Bartleman attended one of the first meetings at Azusa he found only "about a dozen saints there, some white, some colored."[16]

The work, it seems, received its first major impetus from the San Francisco earthquake of April 18th. The quake aroused widespread religious concern throughout the nation, and Azusa mission in Los Angeles profited from it. The Dallas *Baptist Herald,* commenting on the disaster, voiced the sentiments of many people at the time when it said the event was designed to "shock us into attention to his words that life is but a span and that eternity is all in all."[17]

Earth tremors were felt in Los Angeles and other parts of southern California for several days after the San Francisco upheaval. Bartleman believed the incident had "opened many hearts," and attempted to capitalize on the situation by mass distribution of his tracts, "The Last Call" and "The Earthquake Tract." Within three weeks' time, seventy-five thousand of the latter had been sown broadside in the missions, churches, and saloons, and on the streets of Los Angeles and other communities in southern California, and fifty thousand in the San Francisco area. "The San Francisco earthquake," said Bartleman, "was surely the voice of God to the people on the Pacific Coast. It was used mightily in conviction, for the gracious after revival."[18]

Still, the work seems to have moved by fits and starts until late summer. Glenn A. Cook, a former Baptist and then a free-lance Holiness preacher who became active in the Azusa mission early in its history, said, "The meetings had been running about a month when the power fell." But when Rachel Sizelove first visited the mission in June, the situation was exactly as Bartleman had found it in mid-April. "There were," she wrote, "about twelve of God's children, white and colored, there tarrying before the Lord. . . ." As Bartleman said, "The 'Ark of God' moved off slowly, but surely, at 'Azusa.' Gradually the tide arose in victory. But from a small beginning, a very little flame."[19] Then, sometime in July, Bartleman reported to the *Way of Faith:* "Pentecost has come to Los Angeles."

Sporadic success in those early months was, to a large extent, due to the utter dependence of those at Azusa upon what they believed to be the direct operation of the Spirit. Asserting that all human efforts at promotion of the work were antithetical to reliance on the Spirit, they refused to advertise the meetings other than by word of mouth. "No bills," wrote Ewart, "were printed to advertise the meetings at the commencement. Neither were there any worldly newspapers patronized." Even people passing the building could not have known about the meetings going on there unless they happened by at those times when "the power" impelled the saints to raise their voices in shouts and songs, since no announcements of services were posted outside, nor was a name affixed to it for fear of "grieving the Spirit."[20]

But in September, after Bartleman had been writing about the Azusa work in holiness periodicals for about two months, the *Los Angeles Daily Times* returned to cover the meetings, and other local papers came as well. The newspaper accounts were heavy with "ridicule and abuse," but, as Bartleman acknowledged, they gave the work "much free advertising," and "this brought the crowds." The concerned, the curious, and the mockers flocked to Azusa Street, and the revival for which the small band around Seymour had prayed finally came.[21]

Bartleman depicted, with perhaps some overstatement, the effects of the revival on the city:

> In the early "Azusa" days both heaven and hell seemed to have come to town. Men were at the breaking point. Conviction was mightily on the people. They would fly to pieces even on the street, almost without provocation. A very "dead line" seemed to be drawn around "Azusa Mission" by the Spirit. When men came within two or three blocks of the place they were seized with conviction.[22]

As attendance increased, the entire ground floor of the mission was cleared to provide more seats, and an "upper room" was opened on the second floor for those "tarrying for their Pentecost." The mission was open twenty-four hours a day, and people in prayer could be found there around the clock. Meetings ran continuously from ten in the forenoon until midnight and sometimes two or three the following morning: Sermons were few and short, and almost always emphasized Acts 2:4 or Mark 16:17–18. For the most part the meetings were given over to singing, testifying, and praying. Under "the power of the Spirit," people spoke in tongues, interpreted, prophesied, cast out demons, healed innumerable diseases, wrote in tongues, saw visions, played musical instruments without any previous training, and harmoniously sang new songs composed spontaneously by the Spirit in what was known as "the heavenly chorus."[23]

Bartleman's description vividly captures the atmosphere at Azusa mission.

> No subjects or sermons were announced ahead of time, and no special speakers for such an hour. No one knew what might be coming, what God would do. All was spontaneous, ordered of the Spirit. We wanted to hear

from God, through whoever he might speak. . . . The meetings started themselves, spontaneously, in testimony, praise and worship. . . . We had no prearranged programme to be jammed through on time. Our time was the Lord's. We had real testimonies, from fresh heart-experience. . . . A dozen might be on their feet at one time, trembling under the power of God. . . . All obeyed God, in meekness and humility. In honor we "preferred one another." The Lord was liable to burst through any one. We prayed for this continually. Some one would finally get up annointed for the message. All seemed to recognize this and give way. It might be a child, a woman, or a man. It might be from the back seat, or from the front. It made no difference. We rejoiced that God was working. . . . The meetings were controlled by the Spirit, from the throne.[24]

There was no need at Azusa mission for the standard revival technique of "the invitation" to sinners at the close of the service.

Some one might be speaking. Suddenly the Spirit would fall upon the congregation. God himself would give the altar call. Men would fall all over the house like the slain in battle, or rush for the altar enmasse, to seek God. The scene often resembled a forest of fallen trees.[25]

Then, in a burst of "glory," they would "come through" to salvation, or sanctification, or baptism in the Spirit, with shouts and songs of praise, speaking in tongues, leaping, running, jumping, kissing, and embracing one another.[26]

Initially, the Azusa mission had a multi-racial, multi-ethnic character. "God makes no difference in nationality," said the first issue of the mission's periodical, "Ethiopians, Chinese, Indians, Mexicans and other nationalities worship together." Other ethnic groups represented at one time or another in those early days were Portuguese, Spanish, Russians, Norwegians, Frenchmen, Germans, and Jews. One of the Azusa leaders estimated that more than twenty different nationalities were represented at the meetings. "It is," said an eyewitness of the work, "noticeably free from all nationalistic feeling. . . . No instrument that God can use is rejected on account of color or dress or lack of education." The ethnic minority groups of Los Angeles found themselves welcome at Azusa, and some would discover there the sense of dignity and community denied them in the larger urban culture.[27]

A great many of the earliest attendants were ministers, evangelists, missionaries, and religious workers. A number of Holiness preachers, like Glenn A. Cook who supervised the correspondence of the mission, went there intially to "straighten Seymour out" on his doctrine, only to be converted to it. Azusa became a magnet, attracting clergy and laity of various denominations, not only from Los Angeles and southern California, but from all across the country. "One reason for the depth of the work at Azusa," said Bartleman, "was the fact that the workers were not novices. They were largely called and prepared for years, from the Holiness ranks, and from the mission field, etc. They had been burnt out, tried and proven. They were largely seasoned veterans."[28]

As the work grew, the Azusa mission was organized as the "Apostolic Faith Gospel Mission," a name that was painted in crude letters across the side of the building. A committee of twelve elders was appointed for handling the finances and correspondence, publishing a free monthly periodical, and issuing ministerial credentials. Of the twelve, three were blacks: Seymour, Jennie Moore, who later married Seymour, and a "Sister Prince"; the others were Hiram W. Smith (a former Methodist pastor), "Brother and Sister" G. W. Evans, Clara Lunn, Glenn A. Cook, Florence Crawford and her daughter (about ten years of age), and two others.[29]

The move toward "organization" was deplored by Bartleman, who said of it: "The truth must be told. 'Azusa' began to fail the Lord also, early in her history. God showed me one day that they were going to organize. . . . Sure enough the very next day . . . I found a sign outside 'Azusa'. . . ." While continuing to maintain friendly contact with the Azusa Street mission, Bartleman opened a new work in a building at the corner of 8th and Maple Streets on the edge of the largest black district in the city. True to his convictions, he refused ever to create "an organization," or even to give the place a name. It was known simply as "8th and Maple."[30]

Shortly afterwards, Bartleman was joined in his work by William Pendleton and some forty members of his congregation who had been evicted from the Hawthorne Street Holiness Church over the issue of speaking in tongues. And Elmer Fisher, a former Baptist pastor from Glendale who had joined Smale's New Testament Church, led a group out of it to establish the Upper Room Mission on South Spring Street, not far from Azusa mission. By late summer then, there were three Pentecostal missions in Los Angeles.[31]

Emissaries from these missions introduced the Pentecostal message into other churches in the city. Anna Hall, from Azusa, preached in an Armenian church on Boston Street, reportedly "in their own language as the Spirit gave utterance," and found that they claimed to have practiced speaking in tongues in their homeland for several decades. Adolph Rosa, a Methodist minister who had been raised a Roman Catholic, accepted the Pentecostal gospel and preached it in the People's Church. Bartleman itinerated among the Peniel and other Holiness missions and churches in Los Angeles and the surrounding towns and cities.[32]

Some of the Holiness churches in the city found themselves losing members to the Pentecostal missions. Arthur Osterberg closed his Full Gospel Church and went with his congregation to Azusa. A. G. Garr, pastor of a mission of the Metropolitan Church Association, led the bulk of the "Burning Bush" workers into the Azusa mission. Joseph Smale had to go to Azusa to "look his people up."[33]

Recent migrants to Los Angeles who were converted to the new movement returned to their hometowns, impelled by a belief common among the early Pentecostals that they had an obligation to bear witness of their experience to their friends and relatives. Thus, Iva Campbell went back to East Liverpool, Ohio, introduced the Pentecostal gospel, and from there the work spread to Akron and Cleveland, and from Cleveland to Homestead, Newcastle, and Pittsburgh, Pennsylvania. Rachel Sizelove carried the message to Springfield, Missouri; Glenn A. Cook to Indianapolis; others to Fort Worth, Seattle, and Benton Harbor, Michigan.[34]

Visitors from afar, attracted to Azusa mission by press reports and by the voluminous correspondence carried on by Cook, Clara Lunn, Bartleman, and others, found "their Pentecost," and went back to evangelize. G. B. Cashwell, a preacher active in the Fire-Baptized Holiness movement in the Southeast, carried the Pentecostal movement first to his home town, Dunn, North Carolina, and then propagated it among the adherants of the Fire-Baptized Holiness Church, the Holiness Church of North Carolina, the Church of God (Cleveland, Tennessee) and other Holiness people in Tennessee, the Carolinas, Georgia, Alabama, and Mississippi. Charles H. Mason, black co-leader of the Church of God in Christ, visited Azusa and carried the Pentecostal message back to his own church and other Negro churches in the Southeast.[35]

In the spring of 1907, the indefatigable Bartleman embarked "by faith" on a nationwide tour from California to Maine to South Carolina and back to California again, bearing the Pentecostal tidings to the Pillar of Fire people in Denver; to Christian and Missionary Alliance churches, missions, camps, and schools at Conneaut, Cleveland, Youngstown, Akron, and Alliance in Ohio, at New Castle, Pittsburgh, and Beaver Falls in Pennsylvania, at Nyack and New York City in New York, and at Old

Orchard in Maine; and to independent Holiness missions, faith homes, and schools in Chicago, Cincinnati, St. Louis, Topeka, Columbia (South Carolina), Washington, D.C., and Denver, Colorado Springs, and Trinity, Colorado. He returned to Los Angeles in December, having "preached Pentecost" scores of times to dozens of audiences.[36]

Aside from these visitors and "free lancers," the Azusa Street mission commissioned numbers of foreign and home missionaries, thirty-eight in all as early as October 1906, with many more later. Candidates for "the field" were chosen by messages in tongues and interpretation, told where to go through visions and prophecies, equipped by the Holy Spirit with the languages of those to whom they were sent, and dispatched with the laying-on of hands by the twelve elders "as the apostles of old."[37]

Sometimes as individuals, more often in bands, these emissaries fanned out from Azusa. One band, including Mrs. Crawford, her daughter, and Mr. and Mrs. Evans, went north to Oakland, Portland and Seattle. Using as a base of operations a Holiness mission in Portland that was "turned over" to her after accepting the Pentecostal evangel, Florence Crawford then carried the movement eastward to Minneapolis and St. Paul.[38]

Missionaries en route to their ports of embarkation proclaimed the Pentecostal tidings along the way, in their hometowns and elsewhere. Mr. and Mrs. A. G. Garr, "called" to the Far East, stopped in Chicago, and won many from the "Burning Bush" in Danville, Virginia. Lucy Farrow, en route to Africa, established a work in Norfolk, Virginia; Mr. and Mrs. Hutchins and their teen-age niece Leila McKinney, bound for the same destination, preached in Chattanooga. Andrew Johnson, one of the earliest Norwegian-American converts at Azusa, stopped in Chicago en route to Jerusalem by way of Scandinavia. A number of these missionaries converged on New York City in the late fall of 1906, and while awaiting passage introduced the Pentecostal movement in at least two Holiness missions.[39]

In the Midwest, Parham's Apostolic Faith workers, encouraged by the events in Los Angeles, stepped up their efforts. Pentecostal bands worked the territory from Texas to Iowa, and some moved east through Louisiana, Mississippi, and Alabama. Parham himself, following up on an opening made by some of his group in Zion City, Illinois, took advantage of the divisions there that led to Dowie's ejection on charges of misappropriation of funds and polygamy (either actual or contemplated). Within a week several hundred Zionites joined Parham's movement. Two of the converts, Marie Burgess (later Brown) and Jessie Brown, were dispatched by Parham to New York City, where they opened a Pentecostal mission on 42nd Street near 7th Avenue after the Holiness missions rejected them.[40]

Most important for the rapid dissemination of the Pentecostal message was its propagation at convocations of Holiness people gathered from all across the nation and around the world. Champions of the new movement hastened from one Holiness camp meeting to another: the Christian and Missionary Alliance meetings, attended by people of various affiliations, at Beulah Park in Cleveland, Ohio, Rocky Springs Park near Lancaster, Pennsylvania, Beaver Falls and Pittsburgh, Pennsylvania, and Old Orchard, Maine; and Holiness association meetings also at Old Orchard and at South Framingham (near Boston); Wilmore, Kentucky; Falcon, North Carolina; and Durant (near Miami). Pentecostal zealots attended conventions in various Holiness schools and homes: "Mother Moise's" Home in St. Louis; Beulah Rescue Home in Chicago; the Alliance Rest Home in Alliance, Ohio; Beulah Holiness Bible School in Beulah, Oklahoma; God's Bible School in Cincinnati; Elim Faith Home and Bible Institute near Rochester, New York; the Alliance Bible and Missionary Training Institute at Nyack, New York; Bethel Holiness School at Magnolia, North Carolina; and the Altamont Bible Institute at Greenville, South Carolina. From these places the Pentecostal evangel was carried by new converts back to the innumerable religious groups and locales from which they came.[41]

Widespread publicity of the Los Angeles revival, especially in the Holiness periodical press, which reached those most likely to accept it, paved the way for the spread of the movement. In the South, J. M. Pike's *Way of Faith* (Columbia, S.C.) carried articles and reports in nearly every issue beginning in mid-summer, 1906. Through the reading of these, the independent Holiness principal of Altamont Bible Institute, J. Nickels Holmes, and many Fire-Baptized and other Holiness people were prepared for the Pentecostal message that G. B. Cashwell brought to them from Azusa, where he had gone after reading the same articles. Alliance people read about the movement in their periodical, *The Christian and Missionary Alliance;* the *Apostolic Light* (Salem, Ore.) broke the ground for Mrs. Crawford's success in the Pacific Northwest; the *Gospel Witness* (Louisville, Ky.) in the Ohio Valley; and the *Herald of Light* (Indianapolis, Ind.) and others, elsewhere. In the first year or two of the revival Frank Bartleman alone wrote more than 550 articles for the religious press.[42]

The Azusa mission's own publication exerted more influence, perhaps, than all of the above together. Having abandoned its original prejudice against advertising, the mission had a large committee of workers compiling lists of the names of friends, relatives, acquaintances, churches, preachers, and others, to whom they sent free of charge a four-page monthly entitled *The Apostolic Faith*.[43] The first issue, September 1906, numbered five thousand, the second ten thousand; by the end of 1907, forty thousand per month were being printed, and a year later, when the place of publication was transferred to Mrs. Crawford's headquarters in Portland, Oregon, eighty thousand were distributed each month. Among Holiness people who received the paper, became seekers as a result, and emerged as Pentecostal leaders were Thomas Ball Barratt, a Norwegian Methodist awaiting passage home at the Alliance Home in New York City; A. H. Argue, then pastor of a Holiness church in Winnipeg; C. A. McKinney, pastor of an Alliance church in Akron, Ohio; and J. H. King, overseer of the Fire-Baptized Holiness Church.[44]

Moreover, once introduced in a new locale, the movement was almost certain to receive sensationalist coverage in the secular newspapers. Though often critical and derisive, these accounts attracted numbers of curiosity seekers from a variety of social backgrounds, most of whom went away amused or appalled, but at least a few of whom remained to pray. Bartleman, referring to press coverage of the Pentecostal-dominated Alliance camp meeting in Alliance, Ohio, in the summer of 1908, said, "The newspapers were more abusive and untrue than ever. But they did our advertising for us, free."[45]

By such means the movement was diffused and planted in widely scattered places here and abroad. By the end of 1908 reports of the falling of Pentecostal power and the establishment of Pentecostal centers were pouring in from New York City, Baltimore, Philadelphia, Washington, D.C., Chicago, Zion City, St. Paul, Minneapolis, Atlanta, Birmingham, Cleveland (Ohio and Tennessee), Indianapolis, Portland, Seattle, San Francisco, and Oakland; and from the British Isles, Scandinavia, Germany, Holland, Egypt, Syria, and Jerusalem; from Johannesburg and Pretoria, South Africa; and from Shanghai, Hong Kong, Ceylon, and Calcutta.[46]

Initially, the use of Holiness resources and institutions was of enor-

mous, perhaps crucial, significance for spreading the Pentecostal movement. But the Pentecostals began early to develop their own independent
resources, partly, as we shall see, in response to the closing-off of their
openings in the Holiness camp.

In a very short time a veritable deluge of new Pentecostal periodicals,
almost all mailed free of charge, inundated Holiness people everywhere,
at home and abroad. A. H. Argue, who found the Pentecostal experience
at William Durham's North Avenue Mission, a center of the new movement in Chicago, had thirty thousand copies of his *Apostolic Messenger*
(Winnipeg, Canada) distributed in 1907, and seventy thousand in 1908.
J. H. King changed the name of the official organ of the Fire-Baptized
Holiness Church from *Live Coals of Fire* to *The Apostolic Evangel* to
reflect its new Pentecostal character in 1907, and ran it into bankruptcy
the following year as a result of his policy of free distribution in vast
numbers. William Piper, pastor of the Stone Church, another Pentecostal
center in Chicago, was publishing fifty thousand copies of his *Latter Rain
Evangel* in 1908. Among the more than fifty other Pentecostal periodicals
published in the first half dozen years of the movement were *The Pen-
tecost* (Indianapolis), *The Pentecostal Record* (Spokane, Washington),
Pentecostal Wonders (Akron, Ohio), *Trust* (Rochester, N.Y.), *The Upper
Room* (Los Angeles), *Apostolic Rivers of Living Waters* (New Haven,
Conn.), *The New Acts* (Alliance, Ohio), and *Grace and Truth* (Memphis,
Tenn.), as well as several foreign language periodicals like *Sanhedans
Tolk* (Paulsbo, Washington), a Norwegian paper, and *Wort und Zeugnis*
(Milwaukee), a German monthly. A complete list of Pentecostal periodicals published in the early years of the movement is unlikely ever to be
compiled, but the number of those known is impressive. Hollenweger
lists twenty-four; Clyde Bailey said he was receiving over thirty papers as
early as 1908; and I have gathered a list of more than twice that number
published in the United States alone. These were circulated around the
world, just as those published abroad were circulated here.[47]

A number of the Holiness camps, faith homes and schools mentioned
previously, like the Falcon, North Carolina, and Durant, Florida, camp
grounds, and the Beulah, Oklahoma, Elim, New York, and Greenville,
South Carolina, schools, were captured by the Pentecostals and became
centers of the movement. Several conventions were held every year in
each of these places, and in the new camps established by the Pentecostals at Alliance, Ohio, Fort Worth and Dallas, Texas, Eureka Springs,
Arkansas, Davis City (near Des Moines), Iowa, Meridian, Mississippi,

Mercer, Missouri, Portland, Oregon, South Framingham, Massachusetts, Paterson, New Jersey, and literally dozens of other places, especially in the South and Midwest.[48]

Several Pentecostal churches became the sites for frequent all-Pentecostal regional and national conventions, like Piper's Stone Church in Chicago, the Brunner Tabernacle in Houston, and Glad Tidings Tabernacle in New York City.[49]

Short-term Bible schools were held to indoctrinate the new converts and train workers for "the field," many of them initiated by D. C. O. Opperman, formerly of Dowie's Zion City, where he had been an elder and the superintendent of schools (in which it was taught that the earth is flat). From 1908 to 1914, Opperman conducted month-long "Schools of the Prophets," often teaching by tongues and interpretation, in Houston; Hattiesburg, Mississippi; Joplin, Missouri; Anniston, Alabama; Hot Springs and Eureka Springs, Arkansas; and Des Moines and Ottumwa, Iowa. J. H. King taught Bible classes at various Pentecostal Holiness camps across the country annually, and A. J. Tomlinson at the Church of God encampments at Durant, Florida.[50]

Within a few years, more permanent, longer term schools were established: Opperman's Ozark Bible and Literary School at Eureka Springs, Arkansas, D. W. Myland's Gibeah Bible School in Plainfield, Indiana, the Pentecostal Missionary Training and Bible School in North Bergen, New Jersey, T. K. Leonard's Gospel School at Findlay, Ohio, R. B. Chisolm's at Union, Mississippi, Andrew L. Fraser's in Chicago, the Pacific Bible and Missionary Training School in San Francisco, and others.[51]

The more prominent leaders soon established themselves in comfortable though modest circumstances as editors of periodicals, Bible school principals, and administrators of small Pentecostal denominations. Often, they continued to itinerate around a national—and, indeed, an international—circuit of Pentecostal centers for a few months of the year as well. But for the average Pentecostal preacher who had to break new ground, life was hard going for many years.

The Pentecostals were willing to pool their meager resources for publishing ventures, the training and support of missionaries, and the holding of camp meetings and conventions; all these contributed directly to spreading the gospel widely and rapidly. But they were unwilling to spend time or money on building churches or even helping local congregations to rent places of worship, for they were convinced that such efforts were futile in the face of the imminent Second Coming.

Thus, rank-and-file Pentecostal preachers stumped the country, preaching wherever they could get a group together. Increasingly refused the use of denominational and Holiness church buildings, they held meetings in school houses, warehouses and rented store-fronts; in private homes and under brush arbors, in tents or in open fields and forest clearings, in funeral parlors, gas stations, and cafes. They preached to millhands in their factories, to road gangs by the wayside, to workmen in railroad yards and iron works, and to farmhands in the cotton fields. They exhorted sinners from courthouse steps and city parks, and in dance halls, gambling houses, and "red light" districts. They journeyed by wagon and horseback, and finally by foot, into remote and rugged mountain regions.[52]

While the Pentecostal movement had perhaps more than its due share of venal and sordid preachers, it had, too, men and women of solid character. These lived often in extreme poverty, going out with little or no money, seldom knowing where they would spend the night, or how they would get their next meal, sleeping in barns, tents and parks, or on the wooden benches of mission halls, and sometimes in jail. Bands of workers would pool their funds, buy a tent or rent a hall, and live communally in the meeting place, subsisting at times on flour and water, or rice, or sardines and sausages.[53]

Having proclaimed their gospel, they would pack up and move on after a few days or weeks, leaving small cells of converts to shift for themselves. Often people of small income, and imbued with the belief in the approaching end of the world, these groups would meet in one another's homes or rent a store-front. For years, few congregations owned their meeting place, and even those who could afford it, like Florence Crawford's church in Portland, Oregon, preferred to rent. Wherever possible, the meeting place had to be above the ground floor, an "upper room" in which to re-enact the Pentecostal scene of Acts 2.[54]

Few congregations could support a pastor, if they could get one, and regular salaries were neither offered nor expected. Nor were collections taken. All contributions were given voluntarily and at the initiative of the giver, perhaps stuffed into the hand or pocket of the preacher, or placed in a box at the back of the meeting place.[55]

Typical of the great privations endured by some Pentecostal pioneers is the story of Walter J. Higgins who, together with his wife, accepted the pastorate of a Pentecostal assembly in Morehouse, Missouri. They were provided with living quarters in a crawl-up attic furnished with one iron bed, one table, and several wooden crates for chairs. They lived on sorghum molasses and potatoes three times a day, and Higgins went about his duties with the soles of his shoes literally worn through to his feet. Small wonder that many Pentecostal preachers worked at manual labor to support themselves.[56] What Frank Bartleman said of himself could well have been said by many another Pentecostal pioneer:

> I made my choice between a popular, paying pulpit, and a humble walk of poverty and suffering. . . . I chose the streets and slums for my pulpit. . . .[57]

The Pentecostal movement came upon the religious world in 1906 like a meteor. The novelty of speaking in tongues aroused interest and curiosity in diverse circles, and seemed initially to fulfill the expectations of many in the Holiness camp who were praying for the restoration of the gifts and powers of the early Church. Inspired by the Welsh revival of 1904, localized revivals had already begun in many places where the Pentecostal movement was introduced. The new movement spread rapidly and widely, but was rather quickly ostracized, not only by the denominational churches, which were little affected, but more especially by the main body of Holiness believers. The Pentecostal movement was largely limited in its initial appeal to the smaller, newer Holiness bodies, and to the "independents" and "come-outers" on the fringes of the Holiness movement. Soon deprived of their openings in the Holiness camp, disorganized and severely limited in material resources, the Pentecostals found their chief asset in the spirit of sacrifice and the enormous drive of their leaders, who went throughout the land warning sinners of the impending wrath of God and exhorting the faithful to prepare themselves for the Coming Christ.

V

The Pentecostal Message

In the spring of 1914, a convention of Pentecostal saints met in the garish Grand Opera House of Hot Springs, Arkansas, to seek greater "cooperation, fellowship and unity according to the Scriptures." Looking back on the years since the Los Angeles revival, they rejoiced that:

> Almost every city and community in civilization has heard of the Latter Rain outpouring of the Holy Ghost, with many signs following, and . . . hundreds of missionaries have consecrated themselves and gone forth until almost every country on the globe has heard the message, and also the prophecy which has been predominant in all this great outpouring, which is "Jesus is coming soon" to this old world in the same manner as He left it to set up His Millennial kingdom. . . .[1]

If they overstated the universal sweep of the movement, they nevertheless clearly and accurately pinpointed the central theme of the early Pentecostal movement: "Jesus is coming soon."[2]

The very first issue of Azusa mission's paper noted that "Many are the prophecies spoken in unknown tongues and many the visions that God is giving concerning His soon coming." So frequent and universal were such prophecies at Azusa and elsewhere that, by January 1908, the same periodical could say, " 'Jesus is coming soon' is the message that the Holy Ghost is speaking today through nearly everyone that receives the baptism with the Holy Ghost." George B. Studd said of his fellow worshippers at the Azusa mission,

They were earnestly looking for the coming of the Lord, and continually witnessing thereto. It seemed a watchword with them, especially when God blessed any one, they would so often say, "Oh, Jesus is coming so soon."[3]

At the Pentecostal-dominated Christian and Missionary Alliance camp meeting in Alliance, Ohio, in 1908, "The supreme thought was that of Jesus' soon coming, and the evangelization of the world in preparation for this." In a Cleveland, Tennessee, revival of the same year, A. J. Tomlinson preached on "the near and soon coming of our Lord," after which "several conversations were held in unknown tongues prophesying the soon coming of our Lord. Three years was definitely given for some sign."[4]

In April of 1909, William H. Piper, the highly-regarded pastor of the Stone Church in Chicago and editor of the *Latter Rain Evangel,* wrote:

> There are at least sixty thousand people today in all parts of the world who, within the last five years have been baptized in the Holy Spirit, and have spoken in the unknown tongue. Nearly every one of these has uttered the prophesy—Jesus is coming soon. Scandinavian, Japanese, Chinese, German, Italian, English and well-nigh every nationality . . . tells us in other tongues the same prophecy, JESUS IS COMING SOON.[5]

As late as 1916, A. G. Jeffries, a prominent preacher in Assemblies of God circles, wrote,

> What does all this mean? Does it not presage the end of time? Is not this whole movement a prophecy of the coming of Him "whose right it is to reign"? I believe it is. . . . The ineradicable conviction is on the saints of God that Jesus is coming soon. . . . "Even so, Come Lord Jesus."[6]

Speaking in tongues and healing, because of their frequency in Pentecostal meetings and because of their spectacular character, appeared to be the central message of the Pentecostal movement, especially to non-Pentecostals. But, in the early years at least, speaking in tongues and healing were subordinate elements in what was first and foremost a millenarian movement.

The Pentecostal belief in an imminent, apocalyptic return of Christ was itself part of a larger myth[7] that provided a unified view of past, present and future—a myth that derived its validity from its correspondence to the real life experiences of those who accepted it. From the Pentecostal perspective, history seemed to be running downhill—at least, for the Pentecostals—and the world seemed to be at the point of collapse—their world, at any rate. The myth served to bring order out of the chaotic social experiences that gave rise to it.

The myth began with the traditional Christian teachings of the fall of man in Adam and his redemption in the substitutionary atonement of Christ. It went on to assert that the Church fell into apostasy and sin at an early date—no later than the reign of Constantine in the early fourth century—and that its history, as well as that of mankind as a whole, has been a devolutionary one. But a "saving remnant" stood fast against the general decline, and God progressively "restored" to them the true Apostolic faith, which had been "lost." Now, after six thousand years of human history (corresponding to the six days of creation), a final consummation was in the offing. A great "Latter Rain" outpouring of the Spirit (corresponding to the "Former Rain" on the day of Pentecost) would immediately precede the apocalyptic Second Coming. Finally, in the Millennium (which corresponds to God's day of rest following creation), a new social order of peace and harmony would be established under Christ, in which position and prestige would be dispensed in accordance with one's faith and service to God during life.[8]

The myth, of course, was not at all unique. Similar myths had persisted since the Apostolic age, and it was substantially the same myth believed in by Keswick-oriented people and premillennialists generally in the Holiness movement. Holiness people found the Pentecostal movement attractive in part because its message fit so well into the general outlook already held by them.

The only aberrant feature of the Pentecostal myth was speaking in tongues. Yet, while all Pentecostals agreed on the basic myth and on speaking in tongues as a significant element in it, they differed over details. Numerous versions of the myth existed in the Pentecostal camp. One such version was outlined by Charles Parham in *A Voice Crying in the Wilderness,* written in 1902, and in *The Everlasting Gospel,* first published in 1911. Although not all of Parham's notions were accepted by other Pentecostals, it is, perhaps, more useful to examine one version of the Pentecostal myth than to generalize about many.

Parham's interest was focused almost exclusively on eschatology—doctrines of the end of the world and the future state of the soul.[9] All other matters were peripheral, or integrated into his eschatological scheme. Even conversion was looked upon as something so elementary that it required but scant mention. Parham sketched out what he considered the "steps of grace in a Christian life" as "Enlightenment and Conviction, Repentance, Conversion, Healing, Consecration, Sanctification, Anointing of the Holy Ghost, Baptism of the Holy Ghost, and Redemption and Glorification.'' Of these eight steps, only the last two, which were inextricably linked to the ''Last Days,'' came in for extended treatment. Parham was a seeker after the life of the Spirit, and that life was conceived of, not as an evolutionary growth in grace, but as a progression of crisis experiences hedged about with internal and external signs and wonders. Having long since passed through all the earlier steps, which seemed somehow prosaic, it was only the one most recently achieved— the Baptism of the Holy Ghost—and the one he earnestly sought— Redemption and Glorification—that captured his imagination. And, it should be added, these last ''steps of grace,'' though attained by a select few over the dispensational eras of God's dealings with man, were especially reserved for the last days. They were themselves eschatological signs.[10]

In God's reckoning, according to a widely held view that Parham accepted, one day equals a thousand years. The world was created in six thousand years, at the end of which God created a race of men in his own image—''the Sons of God.'' After resting for a thousand years, God ''formed'' a second race of men on the eighth day ''from the earth (earthy)''—the Adamic race. When Cain, a member of the Adamic race, killed his brother Abel, he ran away and took for his wife a member of the sixth day creation—the Sons of God.

> Thus began the woeful inter-marriage of races for which the flood was sent in punishment, and has ever been followed by plagues and incurable diseases upon the third and fourth generation, the off-spring of such marriages.[11]

Only Noah, who was ''perfect in his generation, a pedigree without mixed blood in it, a lineal descendent of Adam,''[12] was spared in the flood which destroyed all the rest of the eighth-day race, and the entire sixth day race. The purity of the Adamic race was preserved by a line running from Noah through Shem, Abraham, and Isaac to Jacob, who was the father of the twelve tribes of Israel (Jacob received the name ''Israel'' as a result of his wrestling match with God). In 975 B.C. (according to Parham) the Israelites were carried captive into Assyria and only one tribe, Judah, remained. The others were separated and scattered, one going to India (''from whom descended modern Hindus'') and Japan, the others wandering through northern Greece and into Germany where they were known as Anglo-Saxons—''The word Saxon being a derivative of ISAAC'S SONS.'' It was these tribes which conquered the British Isles, and later migrated to the United States and around the world.[13]

> Today the descendants of Abraham are the Hindus, the Japanese, the high Germans, the Danes (tribe of Dan), the Scandinavians, the Anglo-Saxon and their descendants in all parts of the world. These are the nations who have acquired and retained experimental salvation and deep spiritual truths; while the Gentiles—the Russians, the Greeks, the Italians, the low German, the French, the Spanish and their descendants in all parts are formalists, scarce ever obtaining the knowledge and truth discovered by Luther,—that of justification by faith or the truth taught by Wesley, sanctification by faith; while the heathen,—the Black race, the Brown race, the Red race, the Yellow race, in spite of missionary zeal and effort are nearly all heathen still; but will in the dawning of the coming age be given to Jesus for an inheritance.[14]

Over the millenniums God dealt with man in various ways,[15] but with little success until, with the coming of Christ, He instituted a period of grace in which man was offered salvation with no condition other than faith in the substitutionary atonement of Christ.[16] The Church was established by Christ and charged with the propagation of the true faith. But soon after the Apostolic age the Church gave way to the paganism and heresy of Roman Catholicism, though a saving remnant maintained some semblance of ''the faith once delivered to the saints.''

Beginning with the Reformation, God progressively restored the lost truths of the Apostolic faith. Luther was used to restore the doctrine of justification by faith alone; Wesley recovered the doctrine of sanctification; the Holiness movement revived healing as a part of the gospel; and now the Baptism in the Holy Spirit with speaking in tongues was being restored. Yet, despite the restoration of the Apostolic faith, Christendom and ''the world'' were rejecting it, and falling into still greater apostasy and sin.

According to the widely accepted Biblical chronology of Archbishop James Ussher (1585–1656), the six thousand years alloted to human history would end somewhere between 1896 and 1901 and the Millennium would shortly follow. The signs of the Second Coming were everywhere in evidence: wars, earthquakes, plagues and pestilence, immorality, crime, vice, divorce and remarriage, disrespectful children, increasing education, more rapid modes of transportation and communication, the growth of huge organizations in business, labor and religion, and the spread of radical ideologies; the Church becoming ever more apostate, the faithful given over to worldliness and falling prey to "seducing spirits and doctrines of devils," like Christian Science, Mormonism, Spiritualism, Higher Criticism, Darwinism, the Social Gospel, and Ecumenicism; and the Jews already returning to their homeland as the Zionist movement gathered momentum. And, standing out above all these signs, the outpouring of the Spirit upon the true believers in the Apostolic faith with all the signs and gifts "following after."

In the "Latter Rain" outpouring the Apostolic church and faith would be restored in all their pristine purity. Ecumenicism would be achieved, not by man-made organization, but by the direct leading of the Spirit in the creation of a fellowship of all true believers. Apostles and prophets would once more be set in authority, not by the whim of man, but by the Spirit himself whose will would be clearly recognized by all those truly filled with the Spirit.

Only one sign of the end remained to be fulfilled: the global propagation of the gospel—"not the gospel of the churches, but the Gospel of Christ and the Apostles." For this task God was restoring to the Church in these last days the true baptism in the Holy Spirit. Those who would take part in the last great mission of evangelism must receive this baptism to avoid "wasting thousands of dollars, and often their lives in vain attempts to become conversant in almost impossible tongues which the Holy Ghost could so freely speak,"[17] and to receive "the power for witnessing in your own or any language of the world."[18]

Moreover, the Baptism in the Holy Spirit was necessary to "seal" the believer against the torments to be visited upon the world by the coming Antichrist during the Great Tribulation. Already, the spirit of Antichrist was "abroad in the world," and the time of anguish and disaster was "shaping up."

> It is needless to minimize the fact, the world faces the greatest crisis in history. An age-old civilization is threatened with dissolution. A scarlet colored beast appears upon the horizon, and threatens the overthrow of all governments. . . . The wave of Bolshevism, now sweeping Europe, is as sure to reach this country in its devastating influence, as the plagues of Europe have always found their way to this country. You could no more quarantine against this power than you could against a pestilence originating in Europe.[19]

An international class conflict is to bring about a new political order. In Europe, the old Roman Empire is restored as a Social Democratic confederation of nations under the rule of "the King of the South" and with the blessing of the Pope, while all other lands are absorbed by Russia whose Czar will become "the King of the North." The United States is punished for "mingling the blood of thousands of human sacrifices upon the altar of her commercial and imperialistic expansion" [20] and emerges as a Social Democratic empire encompassing the entire Western Hemisphere and ruled by a king.

The King of the South establishes a reign of peace and justice, but suddenly dies. While lying in state, he is apparently resurrected, but in fact it is the Antichrist who is Judas Iscariot reincarnated in the body of the King of the South. With the endorsement and advice of the Pope, who now becomes "the False Prophet," the Antichrist declares himself Christ and has his statue set up to be worshipped in the Holy of Holies in the restored Temple at Jerusalem. Using the absolute power made possible by the previous consolidation of all churches into one, all unions into one, and so on, the Antichrist forces all, on pain of death, to worship him and to be branded on the hand and forehead with his insignia, "the Mark of the Beast." Then he embarks on a crusade to "Christianize" the world by war. The United States is invaded and undergoes another siege of death and devastation, but is not completely destroyed or subdued because the Antichrist is forced to withdraw in order to meet the threat posed by the King of the North who has amassed a great army and is moving on Jerusalem.

In the meantime, a select group of 144,000 believers has been taken out of the true Church, which is the "Body of Christ," to become the "Bride of Christ," as a rib was taken out of Adam to become his bride. The Bride, in turn, "gives birth" to another select group of 144,000, the "Man-Child"—"those who reach the highest perfection attainable for human beings." [21] The Great Tribulation period of seven years begins with the removal of the Man-Child in the Rapture, and the flight of the Bride into "the wilderness." In "Redemption," the last "step of grace," the members of the Body, already baptized in the Spirit and sealed against whatever wrath may be unleashed against them, are clothed with resurrection bodies and, "like Jesus, have power to appear and disappear at will . . . [and] to traverse the earth at will." [22] Those Christians who are saved and sanctified, but who, because they were not "looking for His coming," never received the Baptism in the Holy Spirit or "Redemption," are the Saints to whom the Body preaches during the Tribulation, telling them that their last chance to share in the final resurrection and the

Millennium is to refuse the "Mark of the Beast" and to accept martyr-dom at the hands of the Antichrist. The Antichrist, unable to touch either the Raptured Man-Child, the Bride or the Body (whose "Redemption" has rendered it immune), turns in great fury on the Saints, many of whom refuse the Mark of the Beast, choosing rather to die "for the testimony of Jesus."

When the armies of the Kings of the North and of the South meet in the valley of Armageddon just northwest of Jerusalem, Christ returns, splitting the Mount of Olives at the touch of his feet, and with the hosts of heaven slays the opposing armies in rivers of blood that reach to the horses' bridles. At the conclusion of the slaughter the Antichrist and the False Prophet are thrown into the lake of fire and the Devil is bound for a thousand years. Sitting in power and majesty at Jerusalem, Christ presides over a new era of peace, plenty and happiness. The Body, the Bride, the Man-Child and the resurrected martyrs are rewarded with positions of authority over the "unsanctified, and all the masses of sinners and heathens who know not God." At the close of the Millennium the Devil is let loose on the earth "for a season" to test those converted under the reign of Christ, after which he is cast into the lake of fire where the Antichrist and the False Prophet are, and they are tormented forever.

Now the "White Throne Judgment" begins. All the unsaved dead from the beginning of the world are resurrected and judged by Christ according to their works. The righteous but "unsanctified" are given "everlasting human life" on the "new earth," while the unrighteous—"only those who are utterly reprobate"—are thrown into the lake of fire, and totally and eternally annihilated. Finally, the sanctified are given "everlasting spiritual life" in the "new heavens," and "Christ having finished His work; yields all into the hands of the Father, takes His place among the brethren and 'God is all and in all' through the countless cycles of eternity."[23]

It is clear from this synopsis of Parham's thought that he was peculiarly attuned to the fatuities of his age. He was a catch basin for many of the ideas germinating on the fringes of the revivalist-holiness tradition since the days of Finney and before. Those beliefs that were later to be called Fundamentalism, though seldom mentioned explicitly, are evident throughout, especially the bedrock of literal Biblicism. Many of the notions woven into the fabric of Parham's scheme may be traced back to very ancient times, but it is likely that Parham derived them from the religious milieu of his own day, corroborating and modifying them in the light of his own experience and his study of the Bible. His lack of religious training in childhood, the influence of his father-in-law's eccentric Quakerism, and his shifts from Congregationalism to Methodism to Holiness had left him singularly free from inhibitions about innovating and appropriating ideas from various Christian and pseudo-Christian traditions.

Apocalypticism and millenarianism have had such a continuous life in Christian history and are so prominent in the New Testament that no search for origins would seem necessary. But there was a strong resurgence of millenarianism during the last quarter of the nineteenth century, in Britain as well as in America. The roots of this movement lay in the Irvingite, Darbyite, and Millerite movements of the 1830's and 1840's. In America, millenarianism gained wide currency in evangelical circles through numerous Bible and prophetic conferences, and through such periodicals as *Truth* and *Watchword*.[24]

Premillennialism, dispensationalism, and the concept of the Baptism in the Holy Spirit as an enduement of power for evangelization were staples within the Keswick wing of the Holiness movement. Moreover, apocalyptic eschatology formed a prominent part of the teachings of the Seventh Day Adventists and the Jehovah's Witnesses who were emerging into prominence at the time Parham wrote. Healing was widely taught and practiced among Holiness people as well as among the Quimby–Christian Science–New Thought constellation of sects and the Spiritualists. Parham was most strongly influenced on this subject by John Alexander Dowie and A. B. Simpson. Variant Anglo-Israel theories, all of which claimed a racial and moral superiority for the "Anglo-Saxon race," based on its lineal descent from Jacob, were being propounded at the Prophetic Conferences of the day. Notions similar to those of speaking in tongues and "Redemption of the Body" were common among the Spiritualists.[25]

Parham indirectly acknowledged his debt to these contemporaneous religious movements, and even recognized the affinity between his own doctrines and theirs, especially those of Christian Science and Spiritualism.

> When we heard and studied the pretended claims of Medical, Mental, and Christian Sciences, hypnotism, etc., we said: God has the real of which these sorceries are the counterfeit. We found Him who bare our sicknesses (Matt. 8:17) and was lifted up for us even as Moses lifted up the serpent in the wilderness [for Healing] (John 3:14). When beholding the power of spir-

itualism, for though 99 per cent of it is slight of hand it does contain certain forces, as the possession of mediums, speaking under the control of evil spirits, etc. We said, God has the real of this; and, lo, when the power of Pentecost came we found the real, and everyone who has received the Baptism of the Holy Spirit has again spoken in tongues, having the same confounding evidence of Acts 2nd chapter, also 10:44–48 and 19:6.

Again, when like the Witch of Endor, they materialize spirits, we said, God has the real, that He may be glorified. . . .

. . . we refute the counterfeit materializing and dematerializing of spirits by a revelation of the glorious church, who have true Bible power to appear and disappear as the Father shall have need of them.[26]

What Parham, and the Pentecostals after him, shared in common with these other movements was an ultrasupernaturalistic world-view and a belief that the common-sense world of reality was on its last legs. For some, like the Spiritualists, the natural order was being broken into by the spiritual. For others, like the Jehovah's Witnesses, the social order was disintegrating and hurtling toward an apocalypse to be followed by a new spiritual order. The Pentecostals saw both processes at work.

Parham's ideas reflect not only the influence of his religious milieu, but also the broader social climate of his day. Anglo-Israelism was a subtle religious modification of the Anglo-Saxon racism that captured the imagination of people on both sides of the Atlantic at the turn of the century. And it, in turn, was but one facet of the white supremacist thinking underlying the wholesale degradation of the Negro in the southern United States, and non-white peoples around the world during the era of the "New Imperialism." Moreover, anticatholicism and antiunionism, the detestation of both "plutocracy" and "Bolshevism," and the ambivalent feelings of sympathy and fear toward the working classes—all were characteristic of the small-town, white Anglo-Saxon Protestant mentality, especially as given expression in the Progressive movement.[27] Prophecies of impending doom involving the loss of old values, social disintegration, class struggle, war and imperialism, and panaceas hingeing on the theme of restoration were recurrent motifs in the rhetoric of Populists, Progressives, socialists and in the works of various social commentators of the period both here and abroad.[28]

Parham's complicated plan of salvation with its eight "steps of grace," his obscure distinctions between the Saints, the Body, the Bride and the Man-Child, his fantastic notion of the "Redemption of the Body," and the bizarre details surrounding the emergence of the Antichrist were too esoteric to commend themselves to very many people. More importantly, perhaps, his belief in the annihilation of the wicked[29] undermined what many evangelical and holiness people still believed to be the primary impetus to conversion—the fear of eternal punishment. Finally, the thinly-veiled Anglo-Saxon racist strain in Parham's scheme made its acceptance by minority racial and ethnic groups difficult and unlikely.

Seymour had spent at most a few weeks in Parham's Houston school before leaving for the West Coast—not long enough to learn and absorb Parham's entire version of the Second Coming myth. Thus, the message that radiated from Azusa mission was stripped of those abstruse and objectionable features which no doubt accounted in part for Parham's failure, after some five years of effort, to ignite the kind of response Seymour did in Los Angeles. Yet the myth propagated from the Azusa Street mission did include a devolutionary view of history and eschatological fantasies substantially similar to those in Parham's scheme.[30]

It is within the context of this Pentecostal myth of the Second Coming that the disparate features of the movement are best understood. The early Pentecostals believed they were living in the Last Days, that "moment" toward which all of history had inexorably moved. Theirs was the age of the Spirit, without counterpart save for the first century of the Christian era. And, as "the first Pentecost *started* the church, . . . the second Pentecost, *unites* and *perfects* the church unto the coming of the Lord."[31] Thus, the Pentecostals expected to experience all the extraordinary activities of the Spirit recorded in the Acts of the Apostles. As A. J. Tomlinson expressed it:

> We can expect nothing less in glory and power in the evening light than that which broke out over the eastern hills in the early morning of the gospel age. . . . The Holy Spirit was given to the disciples in the morning to give them the power to accomplish just what they did accomplish. He is given us today for the same purpose.[32]

Such expectations led the Pentecostals to cultivate the same unusual psychic phenomena that characterized the early Church, and to consider them, as did the first century Christians, the works of the Spirit. Given such circumstances, it is not entirely surprising that extraordinary phenomena should in fact appear among them; and this in turn confirmed and intensified their eschatological convictions and expectations.

Speaking in tongues was but one of the spiritual powers claimed by the Pentecostals, as it had been but one of those possessed by the Apostolic

Church. The gift of tongues, as we have seen, was considered a sign of Baptism in the Spirit, but that Baptism was only one aspect of the "Latter Rain" outpouring of the Spirit which was itself a sign of the Second Coming.[33] The early Pentecostals did not consider speaking in tongues the message of their movement, but rather a means by which the message was confirmed, legitimized and propagated. The message was "Jesus is coming soon."

Parham's belief that the primary purpose of speaking in tongues was to make possible the fulfillment of the last sign of the end—the miraculous propagation of the gospel in the languages of all the peoples of the world—was not, like some of his ideas, an idiosyncrasy merely. Nor was it, as Pentecostal apologists would have us believe, an aberration entertained only by a few extremists. It was, rather, a fundamental and nearly universal notion during the first few years of the movement.

The Azusa Street mission maintained from the first that

> The divine plan for missionaries was that they might receive the gift of tongues either before going to the foreign field or on the way. It should be a sign to the heathen that the message is of God.

And that they believed this was in fact happening is clearly asserted.

> The gift of languages is given with the commission, "Go ye into all the world and preach the Gospel to every creature." The Lord has given languages to the unlearned, Greek, Latin, Hebrew, French, German, Italian, Chinese, Japanese, Zulu and languages of Africa, Hindu and Bengali and dialects of India, Chippewa and other languages of the Indians, Esquimaux, the deaf mute language, and, in fact, the Holy Ghost speaks all the languages of the world through his children.[34]

Parham was reported to have "preached in different languages over the U. S., and men and women of that nationality have come to the altar and sought God." Alfred G. Garr and his wife went to the Far East with the conviction that they could preach the gospel in "the Indian and Chinese languages." Lucy Farrow went to Africa and returned after seven months during which she was alleged to have preached to the natives in their own "Kru language." The German pastor and analyst Oskar Pfister reported the case of a Pentecostal patient, "Simon," who had planned to go to China using tongues for preaching. Numerous other Pentecostal missionaries went abroad believing they had the miraculous ability to speak in the languages of those to whom they were sent.[35]

These Pentecostal claims were well known at the time. S. C. Todd of

the Bible Missionary Society investigated eighteen Pentecostals who went
to Japan, China, and India "expecting to preach to the natives in those
countries in their own tongue," and found that by their own admission
"in no single instance have [they] been able to do so."[36] As these and
other missionaries returned in disappointment and failure, Pentecostals
were compelled to rethink their original view of speaking in tongues. A
very few, like Charles F. Parham, stood steadfast against the evidence.
While conceding that "to my knowledge not a single missionary in the
foreign field speaks in the tongue of the natives as a gift from God,"
Parham nevertheless insisted that

> All the early missionaries for five hundred years spake in the languages of
> the natives . . . [and] if God ever gave this gift he can today and that it
> should be proof of the calling of every one going to the foreign fields that
> they should be thus equipped by God with the gift of tongues.

Offering himself as living proof of this, Parham added,

> For twenty-five years I have spoken and prayed in other languages to the
> conversion of foreigners in my meeting.[37]

Most Pentecostals, however, rather quickly shifted their position to
square with the realities of the situation.

> It is clearly not the purpose of God to bestow a language that will work auto-
> matically upon heathen and sinners of other lands and tribes. When the Spirit
> was first poured out in California a few years ago a sad mistake was made by
> some who acted upon the belief that all they had to do was to reach some
> heathen land and the language would be always the very dialect needed.[38]

This became the standard refrain of Pentecostal apologists when discussing the movement's initial belief in tongues as a means for world evangelization. They dismissed as unusual exceptions, sincere but misguided individuals, those who in fact had been typical.[39]

One would think that the experiences of these first-generation Pentecostals would have led them to abandon the notion that speaking in
tongues was speaking in a foreign language, but such was not the case.
Only the *permanent* gift of *preaching* in a foreign language *at will* was
repudiated. Pentecostals continued to believe that in the exercise of his
sovereign will God often spoke through a speaker-in-tongues to foreigners in their language. As we have seen in Chapter One, recent research is in unanimity on the non-linguistic character of speaking in
tongues. But had the early Pentecostals been aware of these findings they

would likely have been little affected by them. Speaking in tongues was for them a divine encounter, a subjective experience of the Spirit, which no amount of objective evidence could annul. There were some Pentecostals in America who conceded that speaking in tongues was sometimes unintelligible, and many Europeans who acknowledged it was usually so, yet they continued to speak in tongues and to believe it was the work of the Spirit. For what was important to the tongue-speaker was not the actual sounds themselves—that became a problem only for the dogmatic apologists of the movement—but rather the sense of possessing and being possessed by the Holy Spirit. Rapt in what he believed to be mystical union with the divine, the tongue-speaker released a flow of speech expressing emotional needs and aspirations so deeply buried in the lower depths of his consciousness that it seemed to come from the Spirit. And from this sense of nearness to the deity came the strong conviction that "Jesus is coming soon."

Speaking in tongues was not the only phenomenon of the first Pentecost repeated in the second. All of the unusual events reported to have occurred on the first day of Pentecost were claimed by the early Pentecostals: the tongues of fire, the wind and the shaking of the meeting place. The signs which according to the spurious Mark 16:15–20 were to "follow them that believe," were also reported to have been wrought in their midst: casting out demons, snake handling, drinking deadly poisons, and healing the sick. Indeed, all the signs, wonders, and miracles recorded in Acts and elsewhere in the New Testament were allegedly repeated in the early Pentecostal movement—and more. Whatever the validity of their claims, the Pentecostals believed their movement to be a duplication in detail of the early Church.[40]

> The Pentecostal Movement . . . leaps the intervening years crying "Back to Pentecost." In the minds of these honest-hearted, thinking men and women, this work of God is immediately connected with the work of God in the New Testament days. Built by the same hand, upon the same pattern, according to the same covenant, they too are the habitation of God through the Spirit. They do not recognize a doctrine or custom authoritative unless it can be traced to that primal source of church instruction, the Lord and His apostles.[41]

The more extreme phenomena, such as snake and fire handling, were largely restricted in practice to Pentecostals in the most backward and culturally isolated regions of the Ozarks and the lower Appalachians, where such customs were sanctioned by time-honored folkways. Only a few Pentecostal denominations like the Church of God groups, however, gave official approval of snake and fire handling, and even these usually qualified their endorsement of such practices.[42]

But visions, trances, dreams and transports, dancing and various physical gyrations, loud singing and shouting, prolonged prayer, and fasting were universally and enthusiastically approved by all Pentecostals, with the sole reservation that they be "in the Spirit" and not "in the flesh." The distinction was construed differently from one denomination to another, and from one congregation to another.[43]

The "manifestations of the Spirit" other than speaking in tongues that were most widely reported and endorsed by Pentecostals were miracles of healing. It was believed that as salvation was purchased by the crucifixion of Jesus, physical healing was secured by his scourging, the proof-text being I Peter 2:24: "Who his own self bare our sins in his own body on the tree . . . by whose stripes ye were healed." Healing might come through laying on of hands by one having the "gift of healing," anointing with oil by the elders, application of "prayer handkerchiefs," "aprons," and even Pentecostal periodicals, or simply by "the prayer of faith" of the individual believer.[44]

Every manner of disease and disability was alleged to have been cured, and the most spectacular miracles were claimed, including the growth of new fingers on the hand of a woman who had lost the originals in an accident.[45] Numerous persons testified to having seen the dead restored to life.[46] Healing, like speaking in tongues, became a valuable "drawing card" for the Pentecostal movement, attracting newspapermen and the curious, as well as the crippled and infirm.[47] In the intense emotional atmosphere of Pentecostal meetings, people suffering from functional disorders caused by psychic and nervous disturbance could no doubt experience "cures" that are to be explained by the same causes. Others found symptomatic relief, at least temporarily.

The report of a committee appointed by the Vancouver, British Columbia, Ministerial Association suggests the probable results of divine healing in Pentecostal circles generally. In 1925, following a campaign by the healer-evangelist Charles S. Price in Vancouver, a committee consisting of eleven ministers, eight doctors, three college professors and one lawyer investigated 350 alleged healings resulting from Price's Pentecostal meetings. Of these, the committee found that 5 had become insane, 39 had died, 17 were worse, 212 showed "no change," 38 showed some improvement, and 5 were considered cured. The committee concluded that "no case had benefitted that could not have received the same benefit by methods known to medical science."[48]

So grossly exaggerated and often fabricated were the reports of divine healing that Pentecostal editors eventually refused to print them without substantiation, which usually meant the testimony of some Pentecostal whose word was accepted at face value by the editor in question.[49] Some, like Stanley H. Frodsham, editor of the *Pentecostal Evangel,* explained that healing, like salvation and other acts of grace, could be lost, and acknowledged the very small number of those who "kept" their healing. Frodsham accepted as valid the report of a newspaperman who followed up fifty cases of alleged healings and concluded that only two were in fact authentic. Again, Frodsham reported that a mail survey of one thousand persons "healed" in Pentecostal meetings produced only one respondent.[50] Looking back on nearly forty years of acquaintance with the movement's healing activities, Donald Gee noted with sadness "the small number of definite miracles of healing compared to the great numbers who were prayed for."[51]

Yet there were many Pentecostals who saw people rise from their sick beds and wheelchairs, or throw away their crutches at the laying on of hands and prayer. That they often returned to their former state or became worse soon after was not known to most who had witnessed the "miracles." And even when it was known it seems to have made no difference in their belief that healing had in fact occurred. Thus, for example, Mrs. Woodworth-Etter continued to say her husband had been healed of tuberculosis at the 1913 World Wide Pentecostal Camp Meeting in Los Angeles, even after he died of that ailment a year later; and Mrs. Marie Burgess Brown, sixty years after the episode, could say her brother was healed of the same disease by John Alexander Dowie, although he died shortly after Dowie prayed for him.[52]

What seems to have mattered was not the real or imagined cause or cure, nor the relative merits of divine and mundane healing, but the "moment" or experience itself. Those who experienced or witnessed the act of healing were strongly impressed that they stood in the presence of supernatural power, and what passed before or after had no effect on that impression. As with speaking in tongues, so with healing, the unusual and, to them, inexplicable was felt to indicate the operation of the supernatural. Moreover, these feelings intensified their eschatological expectations and convictions. For healing, like tongues, was believed to be another sign of the Second Coming.

> The great agitation on the subject of divine healing the world over is an evidence that God is getting the bride in readiness for the translation, and as the Church of God comes to its full development and gifts, we shall have more healings, and that which is greater.[53]

Healing and "casting out demons" were almost synonymous terms in Pentecostal vocabulary. Robert A. Brown, addressing a meeting of the General Council of the Assemblies of God in 1923, spoke for most Pentecostals when he said, "I believe all sickness is the work of the devil."[54] Sickness was usually believed to be the result of sin or unbelief. At times, however, God might allow sickness to come upon believers not guilty of any infractions of the divine will in order to test their faith, but even then the ailment itself was viewed as a "demonic assault" on the body. Healing prayers almost always included a commandment to the "deaf spirit," the "cancer demon," and so on to "come out in the name of Jesus." Pentecostals exulted that "all kinds of diseases were driven out of the bodies of men, women and children."[55]

The testimony of an anonymous Pentecostal is illustrative of the identification of illness with demon-possession, and of the typical Pentecostal technique for dealing with the infirm.

> For five years I was devil-possessed. . . . I was taken to Sister Etter's meeting in Chicago. . . . They tried to take me to the chair to be prayed for. Immediately I got angry and began to curse and swear, the devils taking full possession. It took five men to hold me.
>
> Sister Etter began to rebuke the insane and all other devils to come out. The power of Satan got broken. The devils came out screaming.[56]

The Pentecostal attitude toward sickness and healing grew out of an underlying animistic outlook so thoroughgoing that it came close at times to being a total explanation for human behavior, as when the *Church of God Evangel* warned its readers to resist "Discouraging Demons," "Sensitive Demons," the "demon of Sleep," "Contrary Demons," "Criticizing and Fault-Finding Demons" and "Exaggerating Demons."[57] Indeed the common denominator of the two most prominent features of the Pentecostal movement—tongues and healing—was this animistic philosophy. Both involved the invasion and control of the individual by a foreign spirit. In tongue-speaking the Holy Spirit was the agent; in sickness, evil spirits. Healing was a process of driving out the evil spirits through the greater power of the Holy Spirit. For this reason, numerous articles and pamphlets were written to instruct the faithful in the arts of exorcism.[58]

The extraordinary activity of evil spirits, Pentecostals believed, was evidence of a wholesale counter-movement of the demonic world against its impending destruction. If the Holy Spirit was in these Last Days preparing the way for the Coming Christ, so too were Satan and his demonic hosts preparing the way for the Antichrist, and rallying for the final cataclysm between the forces of Light and the forces of Darkness. Thus, demon activity was also a sign of the Second Coming.

As Pentecostal expectations for an imminent Second Coming began to wane, a significant change occurred in Pentecostal ideology. The dominant theme of the Second Coming and the subordinate practice of speaking in tongues underwent an exchange of roles in the structure of Pentecostal thought. Initially, the intense belief in the immediate end of the world elicited the ecstatic response that found its expression in speaking in tongues. The speaking in tongues, in turn, legitimized the belief in the imminence of the Second Coming. The key factor was the immediacy of a resolution of the problems of the Pentecostals.

Once the belief in a Second Coming ceased to be an immediate individual expectation, it could no longer hold the central place in Pentecostal thought. Thus, speaking in tongues, which retained its immediacy, moved to the center of Pentecostal ideology. The former hope of immediate physical escape from their unhappy world through the Second Coming was replaced by the reality of immediate psychic escape through ecstasy.

Belief in the imminent Second Coming could from time to time arouse expectations, but it could not sustain them on a continuing basis. Therefore, it became a subordinate, largely formal doctrine, rather than a lively hope. Speaking in tongues then ceased to be primarily an eschatological sign and a means for hastening the Second Coming (through miraculously preaching the gospel to all the peoples of the world in their own languages). Rather, speaking in tongues became an end in itself, and the central teaching of the Pentecostal movement.[59]

The consistently dominant theme of the early Pentecostal movement was "Jesus is coming soon." That premillennialist notion rested on a myth that explained the origins, development and goal of human history

in a single, unified bloc. The myth was composed of traditionally orthodox Christian beliefs, and of heterodox teachings dating back to the Apostolic age and resurgent in quasi-Christian movements of the 19th century. In its broad outlines, the Pentecostal myth was substantially the
same as that of the Keswick wing of the Holiness movement.

The myth provided the Pentecostals with a pessimistic explanation of
past and present that coincided with their own social experience, while at
the same time it held out hope of triumph and reward in the immediate
future. It was both pessimistic and optimistic.

The temper of the Pentecostal movement, the atmosphere of its worship, and the meaning of its most striking outward features—speaking in
tongues and healing—are best understood within the context of the myth
of the Second Coming. In time, however, the failure of eschatological
hope would undermine the structure of the original myth and speaking in
tongues would replace the Second Coming as the central feature of the
Pentecostal message.

VI

Apostles and Prophets

Who were these men and women who went forth, often with "neither purse, nor scrip," to "turn the world upside down" in emulation of the first-century Christians? Many of them will never be known, others are only names. Even some of the most notable, like Seymour, must remain in obscurity because Pentecostals remembered little of the "founding fathers" aside from their "spiritual" qualities: humility, saintliness, ability to quote scripture and work "miracles," fervency in prayer, preaching, and "soul-winning."

Yet, from their diaries, memoirs, and autobiographies, and from bits and pieces in periodical literature, I have compiled biographical material on forty-five leaders who joined the Pentecostal movement during its earliest years, all of them before 1914, most of them before 1909. Many of them advanced to prominent positions in one or another Pentecostal denomination, several to the highest. All have been recognized as leaders of the movement by Pentecostal writers.[1]

Since the selection of the sample was largely dictated by the limitations of the sources, it is in no sense scientific. The leaders of some important, though minor, factions of the movement could not be included for lack of information. There are only five women and two blacks among the forty-five. As a group, foreign-born leaders are represented in about the right proportion, but their ethnic distribution is not. Ten of the fourteen foreign-born leaders came from English-speaking countries, and only one each from Norway,[2] Italy, Mexico, and Persia. More Italian and Scandinavian, and some German and Slavic leaders should have been included.

In other respects, the sample is fairly representative. The most prominent early leaders of the four largest Pentecostal denominations—the Assemblies of God, the Church of God in Christ, the Church of God (Cleveland, Tennessee), and the Pentecostal Holiness Church—are all included, as are two outstanding leaders of the Oneness faction of the movement. Doctrinal divisions among those in the sample are roughly proportionate to those in the movement as a whole. Of the forty-five, seventeen remained true to the original Second Work Trinitarian faith, twenty-four became Finished Work Trinitarians, and four moved on to the Oneness position.[3] At least ten different Pentecostal groups are represented, and several independents who moved freely from one group to another are included.

The Pentecostal leaders were young. More than a third of the sample joined the movement before reaching the age of thirty, more than two thirds before forty. During the movement's initial thrust in the years between 1906 and 1912, most of them ranged in age from the mid-twenties to the early forties. Aimee Semple McPherson was an eighteen-year-old bride when she went to China as a Pentecostal missionary, and was making national headlines while still in her twenties. Howard Goss joined in the work with Parham (who was then twenty-nine) at the age of nineteen, was a recognized leader of the Apostolic Faith movement in the lower Midwest in his early twenties, and the prime mover in creating the Assemblies of God at the age of twenty-eight. J. Roswell Flower, another founder of the Assemblies of God, was only twenty-six at the organizing convention of 1914. Most rank and file Pentecostal preachers were even younger than those in the leadership sample. Goss said of the workers in those early days, "90% of us were so very young."[4]

They grew up almost exclusively in rural surroundings. Of the thirty-seven whose early environment is known, not one was reared in a city; only four are known to have spent their childhood in small towns. Nearly all had been born during the years from 1870 to 1885 at a time when the urban proportion of the national population rose from 26% to 34%.[5] Yet, wherever it could be determined, the childhood residence of every Pentecostal leader was rural. Few had ever seen a large city before reaching maturity.

Of the thirty-one native-born Pentecostal leaders, eighteen came from the South, eight from the states of the upper Mississippi valley, and only

four from the most populous and urbanized area of the nation, the Northeast. Of the fourteen immigrant leaders, four came from the agrarian
regions of the Canadian Midwest, and two from frontier areas in Australia.

The picture of a predominantly rural-agrarian background is reinforced
by an analysis of the occupations of their fathers. Of the thirty-two about
whom we have information, the principal occupation of twenty-six was
farming; four were blue-collar workers; one, Thomas B. Barratt's father,
was the manager of a small mine. Only one could be called a professional: the father of Nickels John Holmes was a Presbyterian minister and
teacher at Laurensville Female College, in South Carolina. But Holmes'
father was also the owner of a sizeable plantation, and it is difficult to say
whether his principal vocation was that of farmer or minister-professor.[6]

Indeed, several of these fathers had dual occupations or left farming for
other employment. Ambrose J. Tomlinson's father was a partner in a
building contracting business in addition to operating a farm. Frank Bartleman's father became the owner-manager of a feed store; and Watson
Sorrow's left the farm to work as a millhand. Four, the fathers of A. H.
Argue, George N. Eldridge, Richard B. Hayes, and J. Roswell Flower,
were ministers or preachers on the side.[7]

Although a few Pentecostal notables, like Holmes, Barratt, and possibly Tomlinson, grew up in economic security, most were raised in humble circumstances, though probably not much more humble than those of
many Americans in the latter part of the nineteenth century. Other than
these three, none could even be classified as solidly middle-class.

Several were victims of abject poverty. Smith Wigglesworth and Frank
Bartleman both described their families as "very poor." J. H. King
remembered his childhood as one of constant struggle and deprivation.
His father, a tenant farmer with "no education, no money, no home and
no horse," migrated frequently round about the South Carolina back
country, dragging his wife and eleven children from one single-room log
cabin to another. "The struggle," said King, "to secure the bare necessi-
ties of life was, in itself, a warfare. . . . Poverty reigned in our home."
Mary Woodworth's drunkard father died when she was ten years old,
leaving his widow and eight children penniless. To survive, Mary and
others of the brood were hired out to live and work with nearby farm
families. Howard Goss and his eight brothers and sisters ran barefoot
through the mud and dust of Galena, Kansas.[8] If such destitution was not
the common lot of the Pentecostal founders, few indeed were those

among them who had not known the rigors of manual labor at an early age, and many were they whose hands had been calloused to the plow handle. As a group, they were almost exclusively farmer-labor working class in origin.

Given the economic status of their families, one would hardly expect anything more than an average or below-average education as the norm for Pentecostal leaders. We have information on the educational backgrounds of only twenty-seven in our sample of forty-five. Recent Pentecostal writers, determined to minimize the widespread belief that theirs was a movement of the ignorant and uneducated only, are often quick to point out the educational attainments of the founding fathers, and have sometimes embellished them.[9] Silence concerning the education of the other eighteen, therefore, almost certainly indicates no more than a secondary school education, and very probably less than that.

One of the twenty-seven, Smith Wigglesworth, had no schooling at all and was virtually illiterate. Another, Mary Woodworth-Etter, did not complete elementary school. Five ended their formal education in adolescence. Six attended Bible school, and one, Robert A. Brown, took the two-year reading course by correspondence for licensing as a Wesleyan Methodist minister. Two went through seminary, and one, William Piper, graduated from a normal school (teachers' "college") in Pennsylvania. J. Roswell Flower "studied law" briefly. Surprisingly, nine had some "college."[10]

What in these cases passed for advanced education, however, must be carefully scrutinized. Those who went to Bible school should not be thought to have had a secondary-school eduction. The Bible schools concerned—Moody's, Horton's, Simpson's, and Godbey's—did not require graduation from high school or even grade school, before admission. The academic subjects in these schools were limited to the elementary or, sometimes, the secondary level. Indeed, a Bible-school education was little more than a program of indoctrination in the Holiness ideology by rote memorization of scriptural proof-texts. Agnes Ozman, a student at Horton's, Simpson's, and Parham's schools, was, as her correspondence shows, at most semi-literate.[11]

Nor should a seminary education presume a high school diploma. J. H. King was admitted to the School of Theology at U. S. Grant University in Chattanooga with only eighteen months of grade school behind him. George N. Eldridge entered the Oak Hill Seminary at Ft. Knox, Maine, despite having left school at age fifteen.[12]

As for the nine "college-educated," seven attended obscure denominational institutions for ministerial training, which rarely offered academic subjects above the secondary level. And seven of the nine dropped out before graduation, at least two, Parham and Mason, in obedience to what they believed to be the will of God. Parham, it will be remembered, had the equivalent of less than a year at Southwestern Methodist, while Mason had little more at Arkansas State Baptist. Bartleman studied nights for only one year at Temple College, at that time an infant institution for training Baptist ministers. Daniel Awrey attended an unnamed college in Delaware for six months.[13] George F. Taylor spent a year at the University of North Carolina and Nickels J. Holmes about two years at the University of Edinburgh. Arch P. Collins, the first regular chairman of the Assemblies of God, attended Baylor University, a Baptist school in Texas, but did not graduate. Barratt entered the Wesleyan "college" at Taunton, Somersetshire (later Queen's College), at the age of eleven and graduated when only sixteen.[14]

The last of the nine "college" men, Eudorus N. Bell, another Chairman of the Assemblies of God, graduated from John B. Stetson College, a Baptist school in DeLand, Florida, went on to three years at the Baptist Seminary in Louisville, Kentucky, and studied for several years at the University of Chicago, though there is no evidence that he took a degree at the last institution. In short, none of the Pentecostal leaders can be said to have had much higher education except Bell.[15]

Yet, leaving aside the question of quality, that twenty-one out of forty-five, or 46% of the leadership sample, could lay claim to any post-adolescent education indicates somewhat more schooling than one would have found in an average cross-section of the American population at the turn of the century. As compared with the education of other Protestant clergymen, however, their education was considerably less than average. While nine of the forty-five, or 20%, had some college, by 1926 nearly 60% of the ministers of the seventeen largest white Protestant denominations had some college, and 33% had both college and seminary. Moreover, it must be remembered that we have been concerned here, not with the education of the Pentecostal clergy as a whole, but rather with their most prominent leaders. The education of the Pentecostal elite, as compared with that of the leaders of other religious groups of the day, was exceedingly meager.[16]

Although the fathers of only five of the forty-five in our sample were ministers or preachers, and the mothers of only two are known to have been religious workers, nearly all of the Pentecostal leaders grew up in homes in which religion figured prominently. Their parents are often described as "godly," "devout," and "religious." Most were raised in the evangelical-pietistic tradition that dominated 19th-century Protestantism. Of the forty-one whose original religious affiliations are known, sixteen were Methodists, ten Baptists, four Congregationalists, two Presbyterians, two Roman Catholics, and one each United Brethren, Quaker, Disciples of Christ, and Lutheran. Two, Florence Crawford and Howard Goss, said they were raised as "infidels," but they were hardly less obsessed with religion than the others. Both were nourished on religious argumentation, though from an opposing standpoint.[17]

A pattern of shifting religious allegiances was nurtured in the childhood of some Pentecostal leaders. The parents of six changed their religious affiliations one or more times before their children grew to manhood, two of them several times. Together, the parents of J. Roswell Flower had connections with the Church of England, the Presbyterian and Methodist churches, the Dowie movement, and the Christian and Missionary Alliance before they became Pentcostals. Fred Vogler's parents, originally Lutherans, moved on through the Baptists to the Salvation Army while still in Australia, and finally emigrated to America primarily to enjoy the benefits of residence in Dowie's puritanical utopia.[18]

Whatever sustenance their religious heritage afforded them was little enough to offset the deprivations imposed on the Pentecostals in their formative years, deprivations that were not social and cultural merely, but often physical and psychological as well. Frank Bartleman, like Parham, was afflicted with ailments from infancy: gastric fever, double vision, varicose veins, frequent toothaches, and "almost daily . . . sick headaches and dyspepsia." "I hungered," he wrote, "for sympathy and love, but was misunderstood largely, except for precious mother." His father, who "had little sympathy or understanding for weakness," berated, ridiculed, and beat him frequently. "I had been told so often," said Bartleman, "that I would never amount to anything that I had about come to believe it." Looking back to the culmination of his systematic degradation at the hands of a brutal father, Bartleman wrote, "I remember as a little child my father asking me in a sarcastic, disparaging manner, what I was living for." Small wonder that the youth felt "death . . . always on my track" and "saw no future." And smaller wonder still that he should write with a bitterness only faintly muted by sorrow, "I learned to fear, and I am afraid almost to hate, my father."[19]

While one should not rush to a generalization from this particular story, Frank Bartleman's childhood experience need not be considered unique among a group that came from families of similar social circumstances. It is not unreasonable to suppose that others may well have been subjected to the bitterness, censure, and physical violence common to working class families. Here and there among the writings of Pentecostals less forthright than Bartleman, one catches a glimpse of authoritarian figures moving in the background.[20]

Personal loss and physical suffering marked both the childhood and the adult experience of many Pentecostal notables. Like Mary Woodworth (later, Woodworth-Etter), Bell, Collins, Eldridge and S. Clyde Bailey each lost a parent in childhood. Marie Burgess came from "a T. B. family," saw her three sisters and mother die of the disease, and was herself afflicted with "a touch of it." Spinal meningitis left Florence Crawford "a physical wreck" who "could not take two steps" without "a body harness." The physical ailments and handicaps of Parham, Seymour and Agnes Ozman have already been mentioned. George F. Taylor was crippled from infancy. M. M. Pinson, a Tennesseean who pioneered in Pentecostalism in the South, but could not be included in our sample because of insufficient data, was obliged to wear a built-up shoe to compensate for his dwarfed leg.[21]

Personal tragedy, frustration, and despair, common to the human condition as they are, seem peculiarly pronounced in the life story of more than one Pentecostal leader. Indeed, personal tragedy so closely preceded the conversions of some that one is all but compelled to recognize a causal relationship between these experiences.

The death of Mary Woodworth's father set her on a course that led to marriage in adolescence to a poor farmer, and a life of drudgery relieved only by the stark grief of burying five of her six children in infancy or early childhood. Plagued by frequent visions of children in Heaven and sinners in Hell, she lived out her youth in quiet but desperate anxiety and frustration, finding release only in middle age as a Holiness evangelist, and fulfillment not until her declining years as the Pentecostal movement's most renowned practicioner of divine healing before the rise of "Sister Aimee."[22]

Aimee Semple (later McPherson), widowed at age nineteen while stranded in Hong Kong and eight months pregnant, returned home in despair with her fatherless child, only to marry unhappily, fall ill, undergo two operations, and slip off to escape her husband in the dead of night with a babe-in-arms and a toddler at her side. "I was," she said, "obeying God." It was on the emotional wreckage of such experiences that "Sister Aimee" launched her career as Pentecostal evangelist.[23]

J. H. King, his hopes for a career in the Methodist Episcopal Church, South, dashed when his application for an exhorter's license was rejected, enlisted in the army in his late teens, found he "could not endure the awful immoralities," and secured a discharge after only four months's service. Shortly after, he married hastily, a move he described as "the saddest thing I ever did in my life." Feeling he was on the verge of insanity, King separated within months and, true to his Holiness convictions, remained single until the death of his estranged wife some thirty years later. Following his marital failure, he served an unsatisfying and unsuccessful stint in the ministry of the Methodist Episcopal Church, North, joined the Fire-Baptized Holiness movement, and, as overseer of the Fire Baptized Holiness Church, came to rest at last in the Pentecostal fold.[24]

Thomas Barratt's twelve-year-old daughter died in May 1904, and his brother-in-law shortly afterwards. The day after his arrival in New York City on a fund-raising tour in the fall of 1905, he received word of his mother's death. Added to this, his mission proved futile. Writing of his frustrations after a year in this country, he said, "Almost all the English churches here have closed against me. I fought on, attempting many plans, but everything failed. At last the Lord denied me the privilege of preaching entirely." It was precisely at this point in his life that Barratt found the Pentecostal experience and became one of its chief apostles.[25]

Richard Baxter Hayes became a Pentecostal only a few short months after his eleven-year-old son died for lack of the medical attention refused by Hayes and his wife, who were "out on divine healing." Shortly before renouncing his atheism and turning to the Apostolic Faith, Howard Goss stood by as his twenty-one-year-old brother ("John was my ideal") died an atheist's death. Dan T. Muse, later general overseer of the Pentecostal Holiness Church, was "dying of printer's consumption" when he found the Pentecostal experience.[26]

Encumbered with an arduous past, subjected to an undue share of sorrow and adversity, for many of the sons life was, as it had been for the fathers, an unremitting struggle. An analysis of the occupational histories of those in our sample for whom we have such information, reveals a haphazard scramble to secure a livelihood by whatever means lay closest to hand, but almost always, behind the striving, a kind of instinctual groping or drifting toward the pulpit. And, by the time they cast their lots with the Pentecostal movement, every one of the forty-five save Goss and Muse had become ministers, preachers, missionaries, or dedicated religious workers of some sort.

Yet very few of those who preached the gospel were able to live off the gospel. Most found it necessary to look to secular employment for their income, and some continued to do so after taking up the Pentecostal torch. Marie Burgess, who was a demonstrator of Zion City's products in a Chicago department store, is the only one of the five women in our sample known to have had regular employment for any period of time. Only a few of the men, like Bell and Barratt, who held positions in the established denominations, or others, like Mason, Tomlinson, and King, who were already the top leaders in Holiness denominations, are known to have derived their income mainly or solely from their ministry at the time they became Pentecostals. And most of these had been employed in some occupation—farming usually—at an earlier time in their lives.[27]

I have gathered information on the occupations of twenty-four who had been regularly employed in secular positions before or at the time of their conversion to the Pentecostal gospel. Together, they had held at least sixty different jobs, aside from their religious vocations. At least thirteen had worked at two or more different secular occupations. Because of the incompleteness of the employment records of most, the sketchiness of some job descriptions, and the diversity of positions held by a number, it is not possible to classify accurately each of the twenty-four. But an analysis of the sixty jobs held by them may suggest the occupational status of the group as a whole.

Eight of the twenty-four men followed their fathers into farming, but only one, S. Clyde Bailey, is not known to have passed on to some other vocation; three others turned their hands to agriculture temporarily, somewhere along the line: this amounts to a total of eleven farming jobs out of the sixty. Seventeen positions were unskilled jobs like laborer, factory-hand, mill-hand, section-hand, miner, house painter, and lumberjack. Thirteen other jobs were semi-skilled: butcher, miller, barber, printer, carpenter, and plumber. Eleven were white-collar positions like salesperson, hotel clerk, office clerk, and postmaster. Three were managerial or entrepreneurial: fruit rancher, owner-manager of a variety store, and manager of a co-op dairy. Finally, four of them were school teachers, one of whom, Holmes, later became a lawyer.

The work histories of Bartleman and Bosworth are the most complete of any in the sample, and though they are somewhat atypical in the number and diversity of positions held, they exemplify the group's job-hopping tendency. The types of occupations they engaged in are thoroughly typical.

Frank Bartleman began as a farmer and by the time he was thirty-five years old had been, successively, butcher, potter, section-hand, shoe clerk, hotel clerk, ditch digger, fruit-picker, house painter, gardener, and carpenter's helper. Concurrent with these secular occupations, or sandwiched in between, Bartleman had also worked as a colporteur (Bible salesman) from time to time, and served as pastor, preacher, or evangelist with the Baptists, Salvation Army, Wesleyan Methodists, Pentecostal Union, several independent holiness missions, and finally with the Peniel Missions in southern California.[28]

Fred Francis Bosworth had held jobs as cornetist, traveling salesman, factory-hand, grocery clerk, butcher, shop-hand, sawyer, house painter, barber, postmaster, City Clerk, bookkeeper, and, at the time of his conversion to Pentecostalism in his twenty-ninth year, leader of Dowie's Zion City music band. Other than the ordination that accompanied his appointment to his last job, Bosworth is not known to have held any religious position until after joining the Pentecostal movement.[29]

Taken as a whole, the status of the sons was, given the declining prestige of farming in late 19th-century America, perhaps somewhat above that of their fathers. In their secular employment the Pentecostal leaders ran the gamut from the bottom of the working class on up to the lower middle class. True, many of them before becoming Pentecostals and all of them, eventually, were ministers of a sort, a vocation that would ordinarily place them in the middle class. But status is a somewhat indefinite term connoting not only place in a social system, but also prestige. Thus, while as ministers they could hardly be called working-class, as *Holiness,* and later *Pentecostal,* ministers they were relegated to a place very near the bottom of the prestige structure.

The prestige even of the established denominational ministry was declining by the late 19th century, and the Holiness and Pentecostal clergy stood on the fringes or outside the religious establishment. Even in the small towns of the agrarian sections of the nation, where men of the cloth continued to be highly regarded well into the 20th century, Holiness and Pentecostal preachers would not be considered among the respectable clergy for many years (if they are as yet). The class character of their congregations, the emotionalism of their services, their meager education, and their employment in secular occupations, often of menial character—all denied them the status accorded other ministers.[30]

Indeed, the regard which their secular occupations alone would normally have entitled them to was depreciated by their religious affiliations, whether they were ministers or not. Always a factor in determining status, religious affiliation must be given considerable weight in evaluating that of our leadership sample, who projected an image in which their most important identification was that of Holiness, and later, Pentecostal, believer. Because both Holiness and Pentecostal sects were held generally in exceedingly low regard, the overall status of the Pentecostal was bound to suffer.

Without developing precise definitions and systematic indices for weighting family background, education, occupation, income, residence, life style, and other factors included in the concept of status, we cannot arrive at a definitive classification of these Pentecostal leaders. My own conclusion, based on the information presented and substantiated by impressionistic evidence is that, both before and after joining the Pentecostal movement, the group as a whole lay in a sort of limbo between working and middle class. Neither quite one nor the other, they were marginal men and women.

The ambiguity of their social position helps explain the anxiety, the restless energy, the impetuous striving so evident in the lives of the Pentecostal leaders. The shift from the farmer and working-class status of their fathers to that of working-middle-class contributed to that anxiety. The farm life so many of them had known, with all its rigors, its deprivations, and its own kind of insecurities, had after all a certain stability, a certain rhythm and regularity. A farmer might be hard pressed to meet the next payment to a bank or a land-owner, or even to spread the next meal on the table,[31] but he knew who he was. His close-knit relationship with the soil and the seasons gave him a certain stolid dignity and self-assurance. He might, like King's father, migrate frequently, but he always knew what lay ahead: the ploughing and grubbing, the sowing and tending, the harvest.

Cut off from their roots in the soil, the Pentecostals found themselves lacking not economic security merely—that they had hardly known—but inner security as well. The fervent quest of the Pentecostals for absolute religious certainty was a measure of the intensity of their anxiety and insecurity, a quest strikingly apparent in the propensity of the Pentecostals to move from one religious group to another, from one set of beliefs to another, from one religious experience to the next. Spiritual odysseys like those of Parham, Miss Ozman, Mrs. Woodworth-Etter, and Frank Bartleman were by no means unusual among our sample of forty-five. To a man, they were seekers.

By the time they joined the Pentecostal movement, all of our 45 leaders had some religious affiliation except Goss, who went straight from atheism to Pentecostalism. Florence Crawford had rejected her "infidel" upbringing and become a Methodist of holiness persuasion some years before her association with the Azusa Street mission. Together, the 44 Pentecostal leaders had held no fewer than 102 different religious affiliations.[32] The incompleteness of the data almost certainly implies an even greater number. Of the 44, 11 are known to have been associated with only one religious group before becoming Pentecostals, but that one was often a Holiness denomination or association, or an independent Holiness church or mission of recent origin. The only affiliation I could find for Alfred G. Garr, for example, was with the Metropolitan Church Association, originally an interdenominational organization established sometime after Garr had reached manhood. It is certain that Garr, and others like him, had been adherents of some denomination prior to their Holiness connections, but where evidence is lacking I have refrained from speculation.[33]

Of the others, 18 had been associated with at least 2 different groups, 11 with 3, and 4 others with 4 or more. Some of these, too, undoubtedly held more affiliations than are indicated. In some cases, connections with more than one Holiness organization is clearly implied, but where I could not determine this for certain, I have counted only one.

Of the 102 affiliations, 24 were Methodist (including at least five Wesleyan Methodist), 14 Baptist, 4 Congregationalist, 3 Presbyterian, 2 each Roman Catholic and Quaker, 1 each Lutheran, Church of England, Disciples of Christ, United Brethren, Plymouth Brethren, and Church of God (General Eldership); 5 were Salvation Army members[34] (some of them simultaneously with membership in the Methodist Church). The other 42 affiliations were all with the newer Holiness denominations, associations, independent churches, and missions, among which the Christian and Missionary Alliance claimed 7, the Fire-Baptized Holiness Church 6, the Christian Catholic Apostolic Church in Zion 5, and the balance were scattered among a diversity of smaller or unspecified Holiness groups.

The steady shift away from the more formal, established denominations toward the newer Holiness institutions intimates the predisposition of those in the leadership sample to some such movement as the Pentecostal. At the time of their conversion to Pentecostalism only 6 of the 44 who had some religious affiliation were Methodists and only 8 were Baptists. Aside from these 14, all had severed their relations with the mainline denominations. The other 30 had moved over into some Holiness group, and, wherever there was sufficient evidence to make a judgment, those who were Methodists and Baptists were found to be Holiness believers as well.

The drift of the Pentecostal leaders, with few exceptions, was consistently toward religious groups that were more "enthusiastic." Both of those in our sample who had been raised as Roman Catholics passed through a transitional evangelical Protestant phase before joining the Pentecostal movement. Francisco Olazabal, a prominent figure among Mexican-American Pentecostals, was a convert to Methodism and a minister of that fellowship. Louis Franciscon, a trail-blazer of the new movement among Italians here and abroad, was first a Presbyterian and then co-pastor of an independent Holiness church in Chicago.[35]

All of those who had at some time been Congregationalists or Presbyterians, held interim affiliations with some more evangelistic group before moving on to Pentecost. Marie Burgess, raised a Congregationalist, was associated with independent Holiness churches and missions, and held ordination in Dowie's Christian Catholic Apostolic Church in Zion when she was drawn into the Pentecostal fold. Nickels John Holmes left the Presbyterian ministry to organize the independent Tabernacle Church in order to more freely preach holiness.[36]

Even those shifts from one mainline denomination to another were dictated by a desire for greater commitment to revivalistic holiness. J. H. King went from the Methodist Episcopal Church, South, to the Methodist Episcopal Church, North, primarily because in Georgia the latter was more sympathetic to Holiness doctrine and practice. A similar rationale lay behind Francis M. Britton's switch from Methodist to Baptist, and Richard B. Hayes's from Baptist to Wesleyan Methodist. More obvious and more typical was A. H. Argue's progression from Methodist to Salvation Army to Christian and Missionary Alliance, and then to the Pentecostal camp.[37]

The anxious quest for religious certainty and satisfaction that led the Pentecostals progressively from the staidly orthodox denominations on through increasingly revivalistic sects to the radical outer fringes of the

Holiness movement and then to Pentecost is epitomized in the experience
of Smith Wigglesworth, who said of himself:

> I was saved among the Methodists when I was about eight years of age. A
> little later I was confirmed by a Bishop of the Church of England. Later I
> was immersed as a Baptist. I had the grounding in Bible teaching among the
> Plymouth Brethren. I marched under the Blood and Fire banner of the Salva-
> tion Army. . . . I received the second blessing and a clean heart under the
> teaching of Reader Harris and the Pentecostal League . . . in Sunderland in
> 1907, I knelt before God and had an Acts 2:4 experience.[38]

The Pentecostal leadership was drawn from two principal sources: the
ministry of the miniscule, radical Holiness sects, and the ranks of those
Holiness preachers who hesitated to join any organization at all—those
whom Timothy Smith characterized as "restless individuals unable to accept much real discipline save their own." The new movement initially
attracted those who had been outlawed from the main body of Holiness
believers by the National Holiness Association's ban on "those who
made healing, premillennialism and Keswick views their 'hobby.' " This
was aimed at such groups as the Christian and Missionary Alliance and
the "Third Blessing" Fire-Baptized movements.[39]

Nearly all of the forty-five Pentecostal leaders under consideration
came out of the Christian and Missionary Alliance, or the Fire Baptized,
Dowie, Burning Bush, and other splinter Holiness factions that advocated
healing and other gifts of the Spirit and premillennialism. All these
groups rejected the mainstream Holiness view that sanctification and the
Baptism in the Holy Spirit were synonymous. All looked for a Second
Pentecost having both collective and individual aspects, which would restore the miraculous gifts and powers of the Apostolic Church—a notion
that lay at the heart of the Keswick movement.

Many of the Pentecostal leaders had direct, personal contact with Keswick-oriented champions and institutions. Barratt had read Moody's and
Torrey's sermons, and had met Torrey, Alexander, and Simpson on his
1905–06 tour of the United States. George N. Eldridge had known Simpson, and A. H. Argue had been healed through Simpson's ministry.
Stanley H. Frodsham's wife attributed her healing to the reading of Simpson's tract "Gospel of Healing," and as a result went to study at his
Nyack, New York, school. Agnes Ozman, it will be recalled, was also a
student at both Simpson's and Horton's schools.[40]

Francisco Olazabal and Marie Burgess attended the Moody Bible Institute in Chicago. Andrew Urshan, the Persian Pentecostal evangelist, was active in the Moody Church in Chicago when he first came into contact with the Pentecostal movement. Bartleman, who spent a few weeks at the Moody Institute in Chicago, also worked in Moody's Philadelphia campaigns of 1895 and 1896, and attended the Northfield Conference of 1896. Mrs. Woodworth-Etter worked in Moody's meetings in New York City, and A. J. Tomlinson visited his meetings in Chicago in 1894 and "elsewhere" at other times. Nickels J. Holmes read the works of Moody, Simpson, and Murray, and met Moody, A. T. Pierson, and A. J. Gordon at the Northfield conferences of 1891 and 1892.[41]

The connection between the Keswick and Pentecostal movements does not rest solely on a demonstration of personal contact between the leaders of both. There are many evidences of the influence of Keswick ideas upon the Pentecostals both before and after their conversion to the new movement.

The Bible school of the Fire-Baptized Holiness Church at Royston, Georgia, based its curriculum on James M. Gray's *Synthetic Bible Study* and used other works by Keswick writers like A. T. Pierson. When that church merged with the Holiness Church of North Carolina to form the Pentecostal Holiness Church, its official organ, the *Pentecostal Holiness Advocate,* advertised the fourteen volume *Moody Library* and other Keswick-oriented works regularly.[42]

The Assemblies of God was dominated by former Alliance people, some of whom, like G. N. Eldridge, J. W. Welch, and D. W. Kerr, had held prominent positions in that organization. The Assemblies' Reading Course for ministers included the works of Moody, Torrey, Simpson, Murray, and Pierson. C. I. Scofield's edition of the Bible, a major vehicle of Keswick doctrine, was used extensively in Assemblies Bible schools.[43]

Aimee Semple McPherson's Foursquare Gospel, allegedly revealed to her in a vision, was little more than Simpson's Four-Fold Gospel of Christ as Savior, Healer, Baptizer in the Holy Spirit, and Coming King, with Baptism in the Spirit redefined to specify speaking in tongues.[44]

Finally, Scofield's Bible and the works of nearly all the major Keswick proponents were widely advertised in various Pentecostal periodicals, and were avidly read by Pentecostals everywhere.[45] Thus, the Keswick notion of an enduement of Pentecostal power dominated the thinking of individuals and institutions that were to prove most receptive to the Pentecostal gospel. Indeed, acceptance of the new movement seemed both logical and natural.

The composite picture of the Pentecostal leader that emerges from our analysis is that of a comparatively young man of humble rural-agrarian origins. Often a victim of physical as well as cultural and economic deprivation, he nevertheless managed to secure a smattering of advanced education of relatively low quality. Peculiarly subject to the loss or estrangement of those closest to him, his primary relationships deeply tinged with melancholy, cut loose from his roots in the soil, highly mobile and unstable in residence, occupation, and religious affiliation, hovering uncertainly between working class and middle class, he sought a resolution of the anxieties stemming from his social experience, not by clinging to the faith of his fathers but by the intensification of the pietistic, emotional, and world-rejecting elements of that faith.

The salient characteristics common to all of our forty-five leaders are their mobility and their marginality: spatial, occupational, and religious. Wandering from place to place, from job to job, from church to church, they could hardly have avoided an acute awareness of the transiency and impermanence of their existence. It was but a short step from this to a conviction that the present world system was collapsing, and a new one struggling to be born. The Pentecostal message confirmed this conviction, and provided a framework for the articulation in religious terms of what was largely social discontent. The belief in a Second Pentecost by which the believer would receive blessings and powers denied him in this world, and of an imminent Second Coming that would reverse his present fortunes, paved the way for acceptance of the Pentecostal movement.

VII

The Faithful

The Pentecostal faithful everywhere were drawn from the humbler orders of society. "One of the most common reproaches that the world delighted in heaping upon us," recalled an early Pentecostal Holiness preacher, "was the fact that those who accepted the truths and experience taught in those meetings were illiterate and that only the common classes were favorably impressed." Not only were the economically and culturally deprived—the "honest poor"—attracted, but also, as one Pentecostal put it, "the 'scum' of society . . . habitual drunkards, veteran gamblers and even immoral women and infidels."[1]

The movement's initial appeal was to old-stock whites either in the rural environs of their origin or in urban areas to which they migrated. But at a very early point the movement also attracted ethnic minorities of both native and foreign birth, especially in the larger cities. Shortly afterward, a substantial proportion of the movement consisted of recent European immigrants, among whom Scandinavians, Germans, Italians, and Slavs were most numerous, and of older-stock minorities like Afro-Americans and Mexican-Americans.

Regionally, the Pentecostal movement found its readiest response in the South. The very partial returns of the 1916 census showed 81% of all Pentecostals residing in the South; the 1926 census reported 55% in that region; and one of every two Pentecostals reported in the 1936 census[2] was still to be found in the states south of the Mason-Dixon line. Yet during these years the proportion of the national population living in the South remained at approximately 30%.[3] Another one in four resided in the urban-industrial region from New England to the Mississippi River. The upper Midwest claimed about one in nine Pentecostals, the Pacific Coast about one in ten, and the rest were sparsely scattered in the Mountain states.

In the movement as a whole, the 1936 census showed more than three Pentecostals residing in urban areas for every two living in rural environs. In the South the movement was more rural than urban while in the greater Northeast and on the West Coast it was overwhelmingly urban in character.

Within the South the Pentecostal movement achieved its greatest success in the upland regions centering on lower Appalachia and the Ozark Plateau. In Appalachia, the Church of God (Cleveland, Tennessee) was a struggling Holiness group with fewer than a dozen congregations clustered at the juncture of Tennessee, North Carolina, and Georgia when it embraced the Pentecostal movement. We have already noted that ecstatic religious experience, including speaking in tongues, was reported to have accompanied a revival in that area a decade earlier. But there is no hint of speaking in tongues in that church's records until 1908 when G. B. Cashwell, fresh from Azusa Street mission, preached at the Church of God's Annual Assembly in Cleveland, Tennessee, and led many into the Pentecostal experience, including the overseer, Ambrose J. Tomlinson.[4]

The membership of the Church of God at this time consisted almost entirely of impoverished farmers who barely eked out a living from the barren hillsides. So primitive was life in those regions that Tomlinson wrote in his diary, "The rude huts, the rough home-made bedsteads, the stone fireplaces and stick and clay chimneys remind one of colonial days."[5] Tucked away in inaccessible mountain hollows, the homes of the faithful could often be reached only by leaving wagon or horse to clamber over precipitous footpaths, dodging rattlers and copperheads along the way. In winter, people stayed home from meeting for lack of clothing, and children ran barefoot through snow and ice.[6] Some reacted like frightened animals at the mere sight of a stranger. "I have gone to places," said Tomlinson, "where the people were so wild that as I entered the front door the whole family ran out at the back door."[7] Poverty, hunger, and illiteracy were endemic.[8]

Under the dynamic leadership of the newly Spirit-baptized Tomlinson, the Church of God grew rapidly, planting or absorbing congregations all through the southeastern states from Kentucky to West Virginia to Florida, though its center of strength remained in the Appalachians and

Table 1. Regional Distribution of 26 Pentecostal Denominations, 1936 (computed from United States Bureau of Census, *Religious Bodies, 1936,* 3 vols., Washington, D.C.: Government Printing Office, 1941)

Denomination	New England	Middle Atlantic	East North Central	West North Central
Apostolic Faith Mission				146
Apostolic Overcoming Holy Church of God				
Assemblies of God	1,818	12,752	20,628	24,063
Calvary Pentecostal Church				
Church of God (Cleveland, Tennessee)	171	1,218	4,495	1,787
Church of God (Original)	161	28	27	207
Church of God (Tomlinson)		1,806	922	963
Church of God in Christ	529	4,539	4,393	2,613
Church of God in Christ (Pentecostal)			(est) 90	
Church of the Living God, Christian Workers Fellowship		24	706	563
Church of the Living God, The Pillar and Ground of Truth				
Congregational Holiness Church				
Fire-Baptized Holiness Church of God of America	51	206	53	
Italian Pentecostal Assemblies of God	71	1,476		
House of the Lord			80	
International Church of the Foursquare Gospel		317	2,384	1,971
International Pentecostal Assemblies	82	1,003	2,659	475
National David Spiritual Temple, Christ Church Union				1,412
Pentecostal Assemblies of Jesus Christ	60	559	7,563	1,347
Pentecostal Assemblies of the World	133	735	3,160	787
Pentecostal Church, Inc.		26	1,690	1,347
Pentecostal Church of God of America		98	708	682
Pentecostal Fire Baptized Holiness Church				
Pentecostal Holiness Church		148	76	421
United Holy Church of America	85	1,184	224	
Unorganized Italian Christian Churches of North America	371	5,813	2,247	229
Membership Totals by Region	3,532	31,932	52,105	39,013
Per Cent of All Pentecostals	1.0	8.9	14.6	10.9

South Atlantic	East Central	West South Central	Mountain	Pacific	Totals
52		39	50	2,001	2,288
	863				863
10,488	6,593	42,272	6,530	22,899	148,043
			166	880	1,046
19,582	12,600	4,310	374	281	44,818
370	951	525			2,269
6,374	5,747	1,750	697	92	18,351
3,866	5,130	8,508	524	1,462	31,564
46	42	32			210
10	876	2,268	22	56	4,525
82	18	4,558	5	175	4,838
1,778	389				2,167
1,532	131				1,973
					1,547
222					302
27	452	618	1,173	9,205	16,147
1,324	59	188	26	517	6,333
		128		340	1,880
2,314	380	3,234	385	228	16,070
84	263	138		413	5,713
197	1,327	3,520	705	869	9,681
215	182	1,180	40	1,191	4,296
1,017	331				1,348
8,930	581	2,605	68	126	12,955
5,670	341			31	7,535
405	80	73		349	9,567
64,585	37,336	75,946	10,765	41,115	356,329
18.1	10.5	21.3	3.0	11.2	100.0

Table 2. Urban-Rural and Racial Distribution by Region of Combined Memberships of 26 Pentecostal Denominations, 1936

Region	Total Membership	Urban	Rural	Per Cent of Total		White Denoms.	Black Denoms.	Inter-Racial Denoms.	Per Cent of Total		
				Urban	Rural				White	Black	Inter-Racial
New England	3,532	2,937	595	83.2	16.8	2,774	698	60	78.5	19.8	1.7
Middle Atlantic	31,932	26,511	5,421	83.0	17.0	24,685	6,688	559	77.3	20.9	1.8
East North Central	52,105	44,519	7,586	85.4	14.6	35,836	8,706	7,563	68.7	16.9	14.4
West North Central	39,013	24,662	14,351	63.2	36.8	32,291	5,375	1,347	82.8	13.8	3.4
South Atlantic	64,585	32,484	32,101	50.3	49.7	50,759	11,512	2,314	78.6	17.8	3.6
East South Central	37,336	13,535	23,801	36.3	63.7	29,292	7,664	380	78.5	20.6	0.9
West South Central	75,946	38,690	37,256	50.9	49.1	57,080	15,632	3,234	75.2	20.6	4.2
Mountain	10,765	6,302	4,463	58.6	41.4	9,829	551	385	91.4	5.1	3.5
Pacific	41,115	32,881	8,234	79.9	20.1	38,310	2,577	228	93.4	6.0	0.6
Totals	356,329	222,521	133,808	62.4	37.6	280,856	59,403	16,070	78.8	16.6	4.6
Adjusted Race Totals*	—	—	—	—	—	279,423	60,836	16,070	78.4	17.7	3.9

*The total membership of the Church of God (Cleveland, Tenn.) included 1,405 blacks organized separately, and the International Church of the Foursquare Gospel, 28. Since these denominations were not really interracial, and since the census did not break down their statistics by race, I have included these blacks under "WHITE DENOMS." in the regional computations.

the surrounding Piedmont country. By the early 1930's the Church of God was the second largest Pentecostal communion.[9]

It was largely through Cashwell's ministry also that the Fire-Baptized Holiness Church, centered in the uplands of the Carolinas and Georgia, and the Holiness Church of North Carolina were swept into the Pentecostal fold. These two groups merged as the Pentecostal Holiness Church in 1911. By the end of the 1920's, the Church of God, the Pentecostal Holiness Church, their schismatic offspring, and several smaller organizations were well established in the rural agrarian communities and the mill towns of the southern Piedmont. In the same region, numbers of black assemblies were established or organized by the Church of God in Christ, the United Holy Church of America, and the Fire-Baptized Holiness Church of God of America.[10]

It will be recalled that it was in the frontier mining towns of the Western Ozarks that Parham's Apostolic Faith Movement scored its earliest victories. With the infusion of Pentecostal emissaries from Azusa mission and elsewhere following the Los Angeles revival, the movement gained a firm hold throughout the entire Ozark Plateau and peripheral areas. While autonomous congregationalism was at first strong in this region, most of the Pentecostals were eventually gathered into denominations. By far the most important of these was the Assemblies of God, the largest and most nearly national of all Pentecostal bodies. Yet, despite its growth elsewhere in the nation, the Assemblies' center of strength remained in its place of origin, the greater Ozark region.[11]

The peculiar responsiveness of the inhabitants of the Ozarks to the Pentecostal movement attracted workers from the Pentecostal Holiness Church and from the Church of God groups. By the end of the 1920's, the Assemblies faced competition on its home grounds from these denominations and from others growing directly or indirectly out of schisms in its own ranks. Although some blacks in this region found their way into these organizations, most gravitated toward the Church of God in Christ and the Church of Living God groups.[12]

The southern Pentecostal movement had a more distinctly rural character than the 1936 census suggests. The census defines urban churches as those located in cities or incorporated areas of more than 2,500 people. Some churches conforming to the definition were situated in small agrarian towns and drew their constituencies almost entirely from the surrounding rural areas. More importantly, many more "urban" churches in the South, and in the Midwest as well, drew their memberships from recent rural migrants to urban areas, which gave those churches a rural ethos.[13]

The inhabitants of the towns and smaller cities surrounding the southern Appalachians and the Ozarks were largely displaced agrarians from the outlying rural areas. The agrarian crises of the late nineteenth century and of the 1920's and 1930's sent waves of farmers from Appalachia flooding into the Piedmont mill towns, and from the Ozarks into the mining towns along the western and southern slopes of the Plateau or out onto the plains of central Oklahoma and north Texas. Operators of textile mills in the southern Piedmont sent recruiting agents into the hill country, scattering promotional handbills as they went. In Gaston County, North Carolina, Liston Pope found that by the mid-1920's the membership of every Pentecostal church was 100% millhands.[14]

Rural attitudes and patterns of behavior were more likely to survive in towns and small cities than in large urban centers, and the southern Pentecostal movement was more successful in the former than the latter. The Church of God (Cleveland, Tennessee), for example, is listed in the 1936 census as 41.4% urban, yet only 14% of its membership resided in cities with a population of more than 25,000, and probably most of these were to be found in the North, where the Church of God was most heavily urban.[15]

Reports of local revivals gathered from Pentecostal periodicals and the writings of early Pentecostals include the names of scores of mountain communities in the Appalachians like Bluefield and Richlands, Virginia; Bryson City and Murphy, North Carolina; Ducktown and Tellico, Tennessee; and Dahlonega, Georgia. But increasingly the work in this area centered in the mill towns of the Piedmont country: Danville, Virginia; Gastonia, North Carolina; Greenville and Anderson, South Carolina; Toccoa and Gainsville, Georgia; Cleveland and Athens, Tennessee.

In the Ozarks the movement had great success in such mountain towns as Hot Springs, Malvern, and Eureka Springs, Arkansas; Thayer, Branson, and Ozark, Missouri. Here, too, there was a shift outward to the mining towns on the rim of the Ozarks: Joplin and Webb City, Missouri; Galena and Baxter Springs, Kansas; Picher, Muskogee, and McAlester, Oklahoma; and the homestead communities from Tulsa westward. By the late 1920's the Assemblies of God was reporting more revivals in Oklahoma than in any other state.[16]

While Pentecostal campaigns were held in a number of the larger cities of the South, success there in the early years was modest. More often than not, churches were established in outlying towns or suburbs, and not in the central cities. Thus, in the Houston-Galveston area the movement was initially successful in the suburb of Brunner and the outlying towns of Katy, Richmond, Alvin, and Angleton, only modestly so in Houston, and not at all in Galveston. In the Birmingham area, Pentecostal assemblies were first established in Parrish, Dora, and Kimberley, some twenty miles north of industrial Birmingham. Pentecostal evangelists like Tomlinson and Mrs. McPherson had much success in Durant, Wimauma, Clearwater, and other towns surrounding Tampa Bay, but little in Tampa itself.[17]

All of the principal white Pentecostal denominations with heavily southern constituencies established their headquarters in small towns in either Appalachia or the Ozarks. The parent Church of God and its offspring, the (Tomlinson) Church of God, located their headquarters not in Memphis or Nashville, but Cleveland, Tennessee, at that time a town of fewer than 5,000. The Pentecostal Holiness Church established its offices first in Royston and later Franklin Springs, both small towns in the Piedmont region of northeastern Georgia. The headquarters of the Congregational Holiness Church was at Griffin, some thirty miles south of Atlanta. Even the Assemblies of God, which was more Midwestern than Southern, moved its offices from St. Louis, where its officials admitted they had made no progress in propagating the movement, to Springfield, Missouri, in the heart of the Ozarks. The Pentecostal Church of God of America moved from Chicago to Joplin, Missouri.[18]

On the other hand, black Pentecostal denominations of the region, whose memberships were predominantly urban, located their headquarters in larger cities: the Church of God in Christ in Memphis; the Fire-Baptized Holiness Church in Atlanta; the United Holy Church of America in Goldsboro, North Carolina; the Church of the Living God: Christian Workers for Fellowship in Oklahoma City; and the Church of the Living God: the Pillar and Ground of Truth in Winston-Salem.[19]

The flight from the farms of the nation that had sent so many into the mill, mine, and agrarian towns surrounding the lower Appalachians and the Ozarks, carried others still farther afield. Joined by displaced blacks from the rich soil of the Tidewater South and by whites from the arid Middle Border, the upland farmers of the South streamed into the burgeoning urban centers of the nation. The limited means of many propelled them into the deteriorating boarding, rooming, and tenement house neighborhoods where they mingled with masses of newcomers from abroad or lived near them in tight ethnocentric enclaves.

As farmers, many had learned the rudiments of carpentry, masonry, and other trades to maintain their farms and increase their incomes. These often found skilled employment in the cities and some were able to escape to more desirable neighborhoods. Others, more limited by their agrarian origins, found semi-skilled or menial employment. Still others drifted into the subculture of poverty, crime, vice, alcoholism, and drug addiction.

It was almost exclusively from among these ethnically heterogeneous, struggling working classes and impoverished unemployed that the Pentecostal movement drew its following in the urban areas of the nation. Vast differences in race, national origin, language, religion, and custom created psychic distance between these urban dwellers. Yet they shared at least some things in common. Most had come from rural-agrarian backgrounds, nearly all had experienced cultural transplantation; most lived in similar social circumstances and were to some degree excluded from full admittance into the mainstream of middle-class urban society. The early Pentecostal movement built upon this base of commonality by preaching the unity and solidarity of all true believers and providing a common spiritual experience that transcended mundane distinctions. In a remarkable display of amity that ran against the prevailing winds of Anglo-Saxon ethnocentrism, old-stock American, Scandinavian, German, Italian, and Russian, black and brown, red and yellow together achieved a new sense of dignity and community in fully integrated Pentecostal services.

Recalling his early ministry in San José, the English immigrant Stanley Frodsham said, "We did not observe the color line in Pentecostal assemblies in California."[20] In the multi-ethnic Azusa Street meetings in 1906, the Southern white, G. B. Cashwell, knelt beside a black youth who "prayed him through" to the Pentecostal experience, Cashwell's initial prejudice overcome when "the Lord whispered to him, 'This young man is deeply in earnest and I have sent him.' "[21] In the same city, German services were held every Monday night in the Upper Room Mission.[22] When Charles Parham visited E. Liddecoat's Midnight Mission in Los Angeles, he found the hall crowded with "the poor and unemployed . . . white men, Negroes and Mexicans."[23] One band of workers from Los Angeles preached to Chinese and Japanese dockworkers in Spokane, Washington; another opened a mission serving steelworkers in Pueblo, Colorado, who together spoke seventeen different languages.[24]

In Mrs. Crawford's Portland, Oregon, mission, "There was no color line. The red, the yellow, the black and the white all worshipped together." Monday night services were in German; Saturday night in Swedish or Norwegian. Those converted in that mission included "Fallen humanity of every type and description . . . drunkards . . . and drug addicts" as well as "many tradesmen: contractors, engineers, bricklayers, carpenters, iron and concrete workers, electricians, painters, plumbers, sheet metal and furnace workers."[25]

Even before the Los Angeles revival, Parham had tapped this new ethnically heterogeneous constituency in Houston, where he garnered black converts like Seymour, Miss Farrow, and "Brother" Johnson, and some Mexican-Americans. At the 1913 summer encampment of Parham's group in Baxter Springs, Kansas, "White people, colored people and Indians all took part in the meeting and as Brother Parham remarked, 'We had the Gospel in black and white and red all over.' " For years, Parham held integrated meetings throughout the lower Midwest.[26]

Dan T. Muse, Pentecostal pioneer in Oklahoma, worked among the "homeless men and women" both black and white in Oklahoma City, many of them "addicted to narcotics, alcohol and slovenly living . . . broken down lawyers, doctors, common prostitutes and perverts." Later, he worked a strip of territory east and south of the city where recent immigrants from Ohio, Missouri, Kansas, and Germany homesteaded the recently opened Indian Territory.[27]

Jonathan Perkins, a Methodist minister, attended Pentecostal services in Wichita in 1909 and went away in disgust over the failure of those in charge to "keep niggers in their place." Fourteen years later, Perkins was converted to the movement in a predominantly black meeting in the same city. "I had to wade through a whole camp meeting of them when I got the Baptism," wrote Perkins; "God surely broke me over the wheel of my prejudice."[28]

Not only in the Midwest and the western reaches of the South, but in the deep South as well, integrated meetings were common. Fred Bosworth, pastor of a Pentecostal church in Dallas in the years before and after 1912, was beaten by local whites for befriending blacks; and Watson Sorrow recalled integrated meetings in various parts of Georgia during the early years.[29]

In Atlanta, Mrs. Woodworth-Etter preached to black assemblies and had blacks seated at the rear of the rented hall in which she held her principal meetings during her 1914 campaign in that city. The following year, her services in Atlanta were crowded with "the poor who could not attend the Chapman-Alexander meetings" in progress elsewhere in the city. Among those in attendance were many Cubans, Italians, and French. At Colorado Springs her audience consisted primarily of miners representing a variety of nationalities.[30]

Aimee Semple McPherson had her first real success among impoverished, illiterate blacks and whites in Florida in the winter of 1917–18. Describing her audiences at the Pleasant Grove Camp grounds in Durant (near Tampa), she said, "Many of the people are very poor. Some cannot even read or write, but how hungry they are for God." In Miami, "The tabernacle was filled, night after night, with precious black pearls to be gathered for Jesus. . . . . The people are very poor and go to meetings in aprons and overalls." In Key West she went from door to door inviting both black and white to her tent meetings. "Glory!", she wrote, "All walls of prejudice are breaking down, white and colored folks to the altar together . . . white and colored joined hands and prayed . . . people so hungry after God that color is forgotten even here in the Southland." Similar audiences flocked to her meetings in West Palm Beach.[31]

The following winter "Sister Aimee" preached to standing room only in the 3,500 seat Temple Auditorium in Los Angeles. In appreciation of her ministry, her working-class converts constructed a home for her, digging the cellar, laying the foundation, erecting the framework, lathing, plastering, and making the furniture with their own hands. In 1920, Mrs. McPherson preached above the roar of locomotives in a warehouse hard against the tracks and switches of the rail center at Piedmont, West Virginia, her listeners drawn from the workers in the surrounding coal mines, paper mills, lumber yards, and rail terminals.[32]

The fame of "Sister Aimee" spread widely among various Gypsy tribes after one of their number professed to being healed during her Denver campaign in the summer of 1921. The next year, Gypsies thronged to her meetings in Wichita, Rochester and Denver. At the opening of Angelus Temple in Los Angeles on the first of January, 1923, some five hundred Gypsies weighted down with gifts of flowers and money were in attendance.[33]

Mrs. McPherson's appeal was by no means limited to the disinherited: she was also successful among middle-class church people in Baltimore, Philadelphia, Denver, and elsewhere, although this success accrued more to the mainline denominations than to Pentecostal churches and missions; and that success was made possible in part at least by her caution in restraining "fanaticism" and in limiting the distinctly Pentecostal aspects of her work to "tarrying places" set apart from the tents, halls, and sanctuaries in which she preached. Once established in Los Angeles, her following was drawn more from the lower middle classes of rural white migrants than from those humbler classes who frequented the smaller Pentecostal missions of the city.[34]

The proportion of blacks in the Pentecostal movement would have been raised substantially from the roughly 20% shown in the 1936 census had the independents—those who belonged to autonomous assemblies—been included. Black Pentecostals were urban rather than rural by a ratio of three to one while the ratio of urban to rural whites was only four to three, and "independency" was strongest in urban areas. Moreover, black Pentecostals generally were more firmly attached to independency than whites as a whole. On the Pacific Coast, for example, the 1936 census reported only some 2,500 black Pentecostals constituting but 6% of all Pentecostals. But independency was the norm in southern California, the center of the movement on the West Coast, until the mid-1920's when large numbers of whites were gathered into the Foursquare Gospel Church of "Sister Aimee" and the Assemblies of God. The blacks, however, largely clung to autonomous churches like Azusa mission, which never appeared in any census return.[35]

More than 50% of black Pentecostals were to be found in the South, but blacks constituted only 20% of all Pentecostals in that region, a lower proportion than in the larger population. Another 28% of all black Pentecostals were located in the Northeast where they made up about 22% of the movement. The highest black to white ratio shown by the census of 1936 was in the East North Central district, where there was nearly one black Pentecostal to every three whites. This reflects the success of the unitarian Pentecostal Assemblies of the World and the Pentecostal Assemblies of Jesus Christ in organizing many formerly independent black congregations in the years between the 1926 and 1936 censuses. The ratio in that region is probably more representative of the actual situation elsewhere in the greater Northeast than is shown in the census.[36]

Black Pentecostals everywhere were heavily urban—much more so than their white brethren. In the Northeast and on the West Coast, more than nine in ten blacks resided in cities, and even in the South, where white Pentecostals were rural by a ratio of ten to seven, blacks were urban by ten to six.[37]

Mexicans were present at Azusa mission at an early date, and they soon initiated missions of their own. Within a decade, Pentecostal preachers of Hispanic extraction like Francisco Olazabal, Frank Ortiz, and J. F. Lugo together with non-Hispanics like John Preston, Alice Luce, and "Brother" Murcutt had firmly planted Pentecost among the "floating population" of migrant Mexicans in many cities and towns from San José to Los Angeles to San Diego and throughout the outlying farm valleys. By 1925 a Bible school was opened at San Diego primarily for preparing Spanish-speaking Pentecostals to minister to their people here and abroad.[38]

Not only in California, but all along the Mexican-American border, and especially in Texas, Mexicans were swept into the Pentecostal movement. Oscar Nelson was not alone among the Pentecostal preachers who encountered a rebuff from non-Hispanics in the region and thereafter concentrated on reaching the Spanish-speaking populace. Recalling his shift in focus, Nelson wrote, "The Lord told us, 'The white people have rejected the gospel and I will turn to the Mexicans.' "[39]

Some of those prominent in the work among peoples of Hispanic extraction in California assisted also in establishing the work in Texas. A few early pioneers like Joseph Roselli and M. M. Pinson had some success among Mexicans in cities like Houston and the nearby town of Pasadena (where by 1916 it was reported that "nearly all the Mexicans here at Pasadena have the Holy Spirit now. . . .") and in San Antonio, Angleton and elsewhere.[40]

Perhaps the most outstanding leader of the movement among Mexicans in Texas, however, was H. C. Ball. Prepared by his work in Methodist missions with these people before his conversion to Pentecostalism, Ball held his first revival in the obscure town of Ricardo in southeast Texas in the summer of 1915. Within a year he had established his headquarters in Kingsville where he had a thriving congregation, opened a short-term Bible school and began publishing a periodical, La Luz Apostolica, and Spanish language hymnals, tracts, and pamphlets.[41]

By the fall of 1917 the Assemblies of God alone, of which Ball was a member, had established Mexican congregations in fifteen Texas towns and cities. At their 1919 General Council, the Assemblies set aside a special fund for the Mexican work. The Fourth Annual Mexican Convention of that denomination in Dallas in 1922 reported an estimated fifty assemblies with a total of some 1,500 members. Since the census of 1926 showed the Assemblies of God with 3,800 constituents in Texas, at least two of every five of its members there were Mexicans. By 1925, the Assemblies had established a more permanent, long-term Bible school at San Antonio for training Mexican preachers, many of whom had "come from the cotton fields" with little or no education.[42]

While numbers of Mexicans were found in the Houston-Galveston, Fort Worth-Dallas, and San Antonio areas, the Assemblies of God work in Texas was most heavily concentrated in the smaller cities and towns along the Mexican border; towns like Brownsville, San Benito, Odem, Mercedes, Mission, and Rio Grande City. In the counties in which these towns were located, Mexicans moved frequently back and forth across the border and consistently made up more than a third of the population.[43]

In 1929 the Assemblies of God organized a Latin American District Council, which included primarily Mexican-Americans in Texas and California. In the same regions Mexican Pentecostals of unitarian faith founded the Apostolic Assembly of the Faith in Jesus Christ at least as early as 1916. More orthodox Mexican believers established the Iglesia Santos Pentecostales; others were organized into the Church of God (Cleveland, Tennessee), and no doubt there were still other Mexican missions, churches, and fellowships.[44]

The American Indian chief who found the Pentecostal experience during Parham's Galena revival of 1903 was but one of the first of many Indians to embrace the new movement. Mrs. Woodworth-Etter drew many Indians to her meetings in Petoskey, Michigan, and Sioux City, Iowa, and had a revival on a reservation near Winnebago, Nebraska. Numbers of Osage Indians frequented Mrs. McPherson's meetings at Wichita in the spring of 1922. By the late 1920's the Assemblies of God had a thriving work among Indians drawn from at least twelve different tribes in northern California and in Oregon.[45]

Scandinavians were won to the movement during the early years, not only in Minnesota and the Dakotas, but also in Los Angeles, Portland, Oregon, Chicago, and New York City. Conventions of Scandinavian Pentecostals were held even in Boston and in Hartford, Connecticut, at least as early as 1914. Many, perhaps most, Scandinavians, however, steadfastly resisted "organization," making it difficult to estimate even remotely the real dimensions of the work among them. A similar attitude tended also to prevail among German-American Pentecostals, but some measure of their strength is suggested by the organization of a German District Council within the Assemblies of God as early as 1922, the first foreign-language branch established by this group.[46]

The Pentecostal movement had considerable success among recent immigrants from the rural-agrarian regions of southern Italy in cities like Chicago, New York, Buffalo, Philadelphia, St. Louis, and Providence, Rhode Island. By the end of the 1920's there were more than two hundred Italian Pentecostal assemblies in the nation.[47]

Reports of "the Spirit falling upon Serbs and Croats" in Granite City, Illinois, and on Hungarians in Ecorse, Michigan, and of the establishment of Russian missions in Los Angeles and New York City were but slight indications of the success of the Pentecostal movement among Americans of Slavic extraction. By the early 1930's the (Tomlinson) Church of God was publishing literature in Russian, Ukrainian, and Polish; and this group had only a fraction of the Northern urban constituency of either the Assemblies of God or the Church of God (Cleveland, Tennessee). The Scranton church of the Assemblies of God had some fourteen or fifteen different nationalities, including many Slavs, represented in its congregation of anthracite miners, and it became the mother church of many other assemblies in the Lackawana Valley. J. Roswell Flower and his wife, who pastored the Scranton church, were careful to teach their children to "show no partiality in their relationships with different nationalities," and to be "especially diligent to raise no racial barriers."[48]

In his study, *One Thousand City Churches,* during the mid-1920's, the sociologist H. Paul Douglass observed a preponderance of Scandinavian working-class people in a Pentecostal "Church of the Elect" in a "western city"; of "refugees from the Ozarks" in a Pentecostal mission located in the "blighted area" of a Midwestern city; and of rural migrants in a hall situated in the midst of a predominantly Negro and Jewish section of "a Massachusetts city."[49]

In no other city did the Pentecostal movement achieve greater success in the early years than Chicago. As early as July 1906 several Holiness missions in Chicago, on hearing of the Los Angeles revival, began to pray for a similar "outpouring of the gifts of the Spirit" in their own city. In the summer and fall of that year bands of workers from Azusa mission and from Parham's Apostolic Faith group introduced the Pentecostal message in Zion City, just north of Chicago, and in Chicago itself. In Zion City, Dowie had only recently come under fire for his handling of funds and his alleged bigamy, and was battling with his former assistant, Voliva, for leadership. Parham entered the fray and succeeded in making deep inroads among Dowie's followers. Out of the Dowie movement came a host of zealous Pentecostal converts who joined with those from Los Angeles and the lower Midwest in planting the movement among Holiness people in Chicago and beyond.[50]

The members of John C. Sinclair's Holiness mission in Chicago heard of the Los Angeles revival in the summer of 1906 and accepted the new gospel soon after a band of workers from Azusa mission visited them in August. Sinclair found the Pentecostal experience in November and propagated the new message in various missions of the city. William H. Durham, pastor of a Holiness mission on North Avenue, went to visit Azusa mission after talking with Sinclair, and found the Pentecostal experience there early in 1907. He returned to make the North Avenue Mission a leading center of the work in Chicago. In the spring of 1907, William H. Piper, pastor of the Stone Church, accepted the new movement and still another Pentecostal lighthouse was established in the city.[51]

A group of Persians from "the Moody church" were won to the movement sometime during the spring of 1907. Finding their home church unreceptive to the new gospel, they joined Durham's mission for a while and then left to open a mission of their own under the leadership of Andrew Urshan, a former student at the Moody Bible Institute.[52]

Italians of Holiness persuasion who had been holding meetings in one another's homes for several years began attending Durham's church at about the same time. They, too, with Durham's encouragement, opened a work of their own under the leadership of Louis Franciscon. The Congregazione Christiana of Chicago became the mother church of other Italian Pentecostal assemblies not only in Chicago and elsewhere in America, but in Italy and Latin America as well.[53]

F. A. Sandgren, a Norwegian elder in Durham's mission, used his Scandinavian religious periodical, *Folke Vennen* (People's Friend), to spread the Pentecostal tidings among its Holiness subscribers in Chicago and the upper Midwest. By the end of 1909 there were several Swedish, Norwegian, and Danish Pentecostal missions in Chicago. Soon after, several German missions were opened.[54]

In May of 1908, the Pentecostal evangelist A. H. Argue reported some thirteen or fourteen missions proclaiming the Pentecostal gospel in Chicago. A list of "principal" Pentecostal assemblies in that city published in the *Pentecostal Herald* in 1917 showed 18 missions, including 3 German, 3 Scandinavian, 1 Persian, and 1 "Mission to the Jews." But this list included only 1 black and no Italian assemblies, both of which were numerous in the city. By 1920, the same periodical claimed there were 25 to 30 Pentecostal congregations in Chicago, which made it "the greatest Pentecostal center in the world." This too was certainly an underestimate.[55]

The census of 1926 showed 28 Pentecostal assemblies with a total membership of 2,720 in Chicago, 90% of whom were black; the 1936 census reported 39 with 3,950 members, of whom only 33% were black. In neither census did the figures even approximate the real number of Pentecostal churches and believers. The 1936 census listed only 17 black Pentecostal assemblies in Chicago, but a 1928 study showed at least 45 in that city, and there were probably some black Pentecostal congregations among the 25 "other" Negro churches listed in that study. In any event, the 45 alone constituted no less than 1 in 6 of all Negro congregations of all faiths in Chicago.[56]

Several students of religion attended white Pentecostal meetings in Chicago in the early years. All observed a high proportion of immigrants—especially Italians. Scandinavians, and Germans—and all agreed on the generally low socio-economic status of those in attendance.[57]

In New York City, news of the Los Angeles revival was discussed in the Christian and Missionary Alliance rest home where Thomas Barratt was awaiting passage home to Norway. Barratt became a seeker and corresponded with the Azusa Street mission. In November, Barratt met Mrs. Lucy Leatherman, the wife of a doctor who had visited Parham's Topeka school some half dozen years earlier. She had recently come from Azusa mission and was on her way to Jerusalem as a Pentecostal missionary. Mrs. Leatherman invited Barratt to attend a Holiness mission where a woman who had recently found the Pentecostal experience in Canada was conducting services. In this "place of no reputation" at 250 West 14th Street, the "Spirit fell" on several, and Barratt first spoke in tongues as Mrs. Leatherman and "a Norwegian brother" laid hands on him. The mission leaders, however, apparently rejected the new movement, since from then on the Pentecostal believers began attending the Union Holiness Mission at 351 West 40th Street.[58]

Several teams of missionaries from Azusa mission en route to the foreign field converged on that small, black Holiness mission in late November and early December of 1906. A number of converts were won, not only from among the predominantly "poor and uneducated class" of blacks and whites who made up the bulk of the congregation, but also from the few "people of refinement and culture" in attendance. Following the departure on December 8 of Barratt and all the Pentecostal missionaries except Mrs. Leatherman, however, the mission returned to its former "dead condition."[59]

Mrs. Leatherman wrote Charles Parham in Zion City asking for someone to come and establish the work in New York City. Parham sent Marie Burgess, who had been won from "Dowie-ism" to Pentecostalism during house meetings conducted by Parham's advance workers in October of 1906. Armed with several weeks' experience in preaching the new gospel in Holiness missions and churches in Chicago, Detroit, and Toledo, Miss Burgess arrived in New York City with a co-worker, Miss Jessie Brown, early in January 1907.[60]

On their first visit to the 40th Street mission, the two women found more preachers on the platform than worshippers in the seats. One of those present was "Brother" Boyle, the owner of a lumber business and an active Alliance worker. Boyle prevailed upon the somewhat skeptical black pastor, Elder Sturdevant, to let the women hold a series of meetings, promising to fill the hall with his acquaintances in Alliance and other Holiness missions. After two or three weeks of packed meetings, Sturdevant decided against the new movement and asked Miss Burgess and her assistant to leave.[61]

For several months the work continued in house meetings among a small group of loyal converts. In March or April Parham came East and held a two weeks' campaign in the Volunteers of America mission on West 42nd Street, adding some of their number to the growing ranks of Miss Burgess's flock. In May the group opened a store-front mission at 416 West 42nd Street under the name "Glad Tidings Hall—Apostolic Faith Mission" with 96 folding chairs, and a portable organ provided by Robert A. Brown, the Wesleyan Methodist preacher who later married Miss Burgess. At the first service two derelict alcoholics were converted.[62]

Within a few months the assembly moved down the block to the Volunteers' hall at 454 West 42nd Street, whose officials remarked. "You might as well have our place. . . . You take all the people and we don't have anybody to come anymore." By 1913 remodeling expanded the seating capacity from 175 to 300. As in Chicago and elsewhere, numbers of immigrants were attracted to the new movement, and foreign language services were held weekly in German and in Norwegian occasionally. By

1922 Glad Tidings was the leading Pentecostal assembly in the East and had spawned at least nine other missions in the greater New York area, including three Russian, two Italian, and several Scandinavian and German assemblies. During the 1920's, Glad Tidings established a children's mission in Chinatown and a summer camp at Beacon, New York, purchased a Baptist church on West 33rd Street, and began broadcasting its services on radio.[63]

During the earliest years several Pentecostal missions were established independently of Glad Tidings. A mission on 38th Street near 7th Avenue under the leadership of Mrs. Maud Haycraft, the Free Gospel Church in Queens, and no doubt other Holiness assemblies accepted the Pentecostal gospel. In May of 1908 a handful of Pentecostals opened a mission in the notorious San Juan Hill district at 227 West 61st Street. In the fall of 1911 a Swedish Apostolic Faith mission was opened at 211 East 51st Street in the equally notorious prostitution center of the city known as the "Tenderloin."[64]

The origins of the movement among New York's black populace are obscure, but the work received impetus with the arrival of Bishop R. C. Lawson in the city in 1917. Preaching at first on street corners and in house meetings, Lawson soon opened the Refuge Church of Christ of the Apostolic Faith in the heart of Harlem at 52–56 West 133rd Street. Within a few years Lawson and his associates had planted a dozen or more branches throughout the city. By the early 1920's at least a half dozen black Pentecostal missions of various affiliations or none at all studded Harlem from 131st to 133rd Street.[65]

The Pentecostal movement made substantial headway among newcomers in Brooklyn's "Little Norway," an area centering on lower 7th Avenue. Several independent Holiness missions were swept into the new movement in the earliest years. By the mid-1920's, Scandinavian Pentecostal missions like Ebenezer Tabernacle, Salem Gospel Tabernacle, the Evangelical Mission, and the Carroll Street Mission had sprung up in south Brooklyn, and at least two on the north shore of Staten Island.[66]

An Italian Pentecostal assembly was founded in the city as early as 1908, and the work grew rapidly among this ethnic group in Manhattan's "Little Italy," in the Coney Island area, and on the north shore of Staten Island.[67]

The census of 1936 reported sixty-six Pentecostal congregations in New York City, eighteen of which are identifiable as black (Lawson's churches were not included), fourteen as Italian, the rest of undetermined ethnic composition. It is clear from the reports of the New York City work in Pentecostal periodicals and from discussions with Pentecostal leaders, however, that nearly all Pentecostal assemblies did have a distinct ethnic character (most still do). Often, reference was made to congregations in terms of their ethnic character, the most frequent being "colored," and then, in order of decreasing frequency, Italian, Norwegian, German, Russian, and Greek. Although Spanish-speaking Pentecostal churches mushroomed in the city during the 1930's, there were very few before that period.[68]

The rural-agrarian origins and the new conditions of life in urban areas shared by old-stock Americans, black and white, and by recent immigrants from abroad were important, perhaps essential, in predisposing some to the Pentecostal movement. Yet, since only a relatively small proportion of these new urban masses were won to the movement, other factors must have been equally important. Chief among these was the general religious background and orientation of those who became Pentecostals.

Native-born American converts to Pentecostalism were overwhelmingly Southern in either residence or background, and it was in the South that the revivalistic-pietistic tradition, of which Pentecostalism was but the most recent expression, continued most strongly into the early 20th century. While liberal theology, socialized religion and ecumenicism were emerging as major trends in American Protestantism in the nation as a whole, the South resisted these trends more strenuously and successfully than any other region except the rural Midwest.[69]

Liberal theology made but slight headway among Southern Baptists and Methodists, who together constituted 90% of all church members in the South. The extremely modest educational requirements for licensing and ordination precluded the liberalization which exposure to higher education was having on Northern churchmen. There was in the South a high degree of religious solidarity based on a common commitment to conservative 19th-century orthodoxy, and the few "modernist" seminarians who challenged that commitment found themselves an ostracized minority. Thus, the Fundamentalist controversy had but slight impact upon Southern Baptists, Methodists, and Presbyterians, unlike its divisive effects on Northern denominations.[70]

The Southern version of the social gospel tended to be expressed in legal battles to impose putatively religious standards upon society as a whole. Prohibition by local option throughout most of the region long before the ratification of the 18th Amendment was one evidence of this. The adoption of laws restricting the teaching of evolution in public schools by seven Southern states was another.[71]

General consensus on conservative theology and cooperation in crusades to Christianize society by statute, however, hardly implied organizational unity or even amity among Protestant communions of the South. Unlike the North, where ecumenicism and merger were characteristic, the normal pattern of inter-church relations in the South was competition and schism.[72]

Patterns of religious belief and behavior differing more in degree than kind from those of the South were to be found as well in the Midwest. There also "the old-time religion" of evangelistic-pietistic-fundamentalist Protestantism persisted well into the 20th century.[73]

Yet in one important respect the mainline denominations of the South and the Midwest were moving in the direction of their Northern counterparts. They were becoming increasingly disenchanted with overtly emotional revivalism. While revivalism continued to be common in the South relative to the rest of the nation, it was also becoming less common relative to the South's own religious traditions. More and more revivalism was being driven out of the cities, and even where it persisted, institutionalization was divesting it of emotional power and expression. Much more slowly and cautiously than in the North, but no less certainly, the major Baptist and Methodist communions of the South were moving away from fervent revivalism and toward formalism.[74]

The turn away from old-style revivalism gave the religion of the mainline denominations a coldly rationalistic, legalistic, and formalistic aura in the eyes of the lower social classes whose attachment to emotional religion remained unshaken. Added to this, the old-line denominations, again like their Northern counterparts, were becoming defenders of the status quo, the spokesmen for the burgeoning bourgeoisie of the New South. The effect of this, as elsewhere, was to drive the working classes out of the churches.[75]

The greater strength of the revivalistic-pietistic tradition among the masses of the South and Midwest, and the increasing departure from that tradition on the part of the major mainline denominations played an important role in the rise of the Pentecostal movement in those areas. It also helps explain the attraction of the movement for migrants from those regions in the urban centers of the North and Far West. Pentecostalism perpetuated the still-extant features of mainstream rural Protestantism in the South and Midwest—fundamentalism, puritanism and sectarianism— and revived and intensified overtly emotional revivalism, once prevalent but by the turn of the century undergoing eclipse.

As for the religious orientation of new immigrant Pentecostal converts, some, like the foreign-born leaders in our sample, had been affected by the Holiness movements in their homelands. Many of the Norwegian Pentecostals of south Brooklyn and Staten Island, for example, had come from the extreme southwest corner of Norway, a kind of "burnt-over" district whose frenetic religious history has been likened to that of southern California.[76] Some Italian Pentecostals had been Waldensians, Presbyterians, or Holiness believers before their conversion to Pentecostalism, yet most came directly from Roman Catholicism. There may be, however, more than a little substance to one Italian-American Pentecostal's statement that, "Having been accustomed to believing in miracles as former Roman Catholics, it was not difficult for the people to accept the truths of Pentecost and Divine Healing."[77] Similar beliefs in miraculous religion were prevalent among Harlem's blacks[78] where the Pentecostal movement met with much success. As for American Indian converts to the movement, the Ghost Dance religion that swept the Plains Indians in the late 19th century was characterized by ecstatic expressions and ultrasupernaturalistic beliefs having more than a little resemblance to Pentecostalism.[79]

It would be a mistake to claim too much from such fragmentary evidence. Yet most Pentecostal converts came from peasant roots, and it may well be that those whose religious heritage was other than that of evangelical-pietistic Protestantism were predisposed to Pentecostalism by the mystical, supernatural, even animistic and magical notions common to those who live close to the soil.[80]

Like the apostles and prophets whom he followed, the typical Pentecostal believer came from rural-agrarian beginnings. If he remained on the land it was likely to be in dying agrarian regions like Appalachia and the Ozarks, where he tumbled from subsistence farmer to tenant, cropper or migrant farmhand. Sometimes he moved on to nearby mill, mine, and oil towns. More often, he left the ploughed fields and dusty villages of his youth, whether here or abroad, to wander into the jumbled ghettos of the nation's inner cities, turning his hands to tasks he considered inferior to farming. Whether rural or urban in habitat, the typical Pentecostal found himself in straitened circumstances, and relegated to a social position lower than his forebears. If he was a member of a racial or ethnic minority group, as was often the case, he was held in still lower esteem.

Mobility and marginality, both spatial and social, were as characteristic of the Pentecostal faithful as of their shepherds. As ruralite the Pentecostal was a tiller of marginal soils in the last isolated pockets of the old frontier—a member of a depressed agrarian proletariat. As urbanite he lived in deteriorating neighborhoods along the new urban frontier—a member of a struggling industrial proletariat. In either case, he stood outside or on the fringes of mainstream middle-class white Anglo-Saxon Protestant society.

Economically, socially, culturally, and even physically displaced and deprived, the convert to Pentecostalism often found in this new-old version of Christianity an ideological and emotional affinity to his religious heritage, broadly conceived. The world-view of Pentecostalism was wholly congenial to the supernaturalistic cast of mind acquired in his youth, and brought clarity and meaning to his disoriented social circumstances. He found in Pentecostalism the marginal religion that expressed and dignified his marginality, but also contained some potential for assimilation into the core culture. In the ecstasy of "the Baptism" he gave symbolic expression to his social experience; the dissociation and disorganization of his psychic and physical mechanisms constituted a reflection of the chaotic, disorganized social world in which he lived, and also a cathartic mode of accommodation to that world. Moreover, in the unrestrained atmosphere of Pentecostal worship, the distinctions and prejudices encountered in the larger culture were often swept away, giving birth to a new sense of community and a new sense of status.

VIII

Proscription and Abatement of the Revival

The Pentecostal revival reached a crest in 1907, began to lose its force in the following two or three years, and passed into relative obscurity soon after. Except for a brief period following World War I when Aimee McPherson drew national attention to the movement, it remained a little-known oddity outside the mainstream of American religious life until its sudden resurgence during the Depression of the 1930's.

That the revival was shortly followed by a long period of subsidence is evident. In all accounts of the Pentecostal movement, the theme of revival drops out after the first few years and is replaced by that of internal dissension and institutionalization. The only subsequent revivals were those of Bosworth and Mrs. Woodworth-Etter in Dallas in 1912, and of "Sister Aimee" across the nation from about 1918–1921.[1] While the movement continued to grow after the initial revival, it did so at a slower rate. The growth shown in statistics during the second and third decades of the century was more apparent than real, since much of it reflected the absorption of formerly independent congregations by Pentecostal denominations or represented the initial reporting of groups existing from the early years.

As early as the spring of 1909, Frank Bartleman complained of the declining spirituality of the Los Angeles saints, including those at Azusa mission. The Church of God (Cleveland, Tennessee) ran a weekly series in its official periodical in early 1914 under the caption, "Pray for a Greater Outpouring of the Spirit and World-Wide Revival," which reflected that denomination's concern for the waning of the movement. The

Assemblies of God, a year after the establishment of its headquarters in St. Louis in 1915, morosely reported that "the Message of Pentecost has made practically no impression upon the minds of the people of St. Louis as a whole." In the same year, Frank Bartleman sorrowfully wrote in the Assemblies of God periodical that "the 'seven years of famine' seem to have already set in." "Another outpouring of the Spirit of God," said the editor of the *Weekly Evangel* in 1917, "is greatly needed." [2]

Frequent exhortations to pray for revival studded the pages of Pentecostal periodicals throughout the 1920's. The cry "Back to Pentecost," coupled with lamentations over the decline of the movement, was a dominant theme of numerous articles. George F. Taylor, prominent Pentecostal Holiness Church leader, was calling for a "much needed revival" in 1920. At the height of her career in the early 1920's "Sister Aimee" lamented the sad state of Pentecostals in Los Angeles, Chicago, and Baltimore. In 1925, the *Pentecostal Evangel* ruefully reported that, "Hundreds of evangelists during the past dozen years have given up." A speaker at the 1927 meeting of the Assemblies' Council declared, "A plague has broken out in the Pentecostal ranks . . . a declension, a going back from God." The remarks of others at the same convention ran in a similar vein. Looking back, it seemed to the editor of the *Latter Rain Evangel* that "in the 1920's Pentecostals began to say in their hearts, 'My Lord delayeth his coming.' " and acted accordingly. [3]

The Pentecostal movement seemed a passing fad to many non-Pentecostals. Before many years after the revival of 1906–08, references to "Pentecost," "Pentecostal services," and even "the Baptism of the Holy Ghost according to Acts 2:4" were found in Holiness literature, with no mention of speaking in tongues. The absence of any concern to avoid the use of words and phrases that may have identified them with the Pentecostals reflected their belief that the "Tongues Movement," as Holiness people called it, was already a dead issue. [4]

In the earliest years, the Pentecostal movement received considerable publicity in the secular press, but the novelty wore off. Soon, mention of it was limited to brief notices in the back pages of newspapers exposing the discreditable features of the movement: civil suits over all-night Pentecostal meetings; legal and sometimes physical battles between Pentecostals for the control of church titles and property; and the involvement of Pentecostals in crimes and immoralities that they justified on religious grounds. Lumped together indiscriminately with other, non-Pentecostal, extremists, the Pentecostals were dismissed with ridicule as "Holy Rollers," an epithet they much resented.[5]

The waning of the Pentecostal revival can be attributed in part to the natural decline of zeal following in the wake of all revivals. Yet, as compared with other revivals in American history, which lasted for the better part of a decade or more, the subsidence of Pentecostal enthusiasm came rather early.

Sudden and profound disillusion befell the Pentecostals with the collapse of their hopes for rapid world evangelization. In the earlier months of the revival scores of missionaries embarked for foreign fields expecting to preach the gospel in the languages of the natives by means of the gift of tongues. A very few missionaries claimed to have done so, but most were forced to admit failure. Some of these, believing they had been deceived by Satan, left the movement altogether, others were greatly disheartened. Nearly all had gone out "on faith," and once arriving on the mission fields with no means of support wandered into established mission stations where they were given their fare home. Some were able to secure support by correspondence with Pentecostals in the States, and stayed on to learn the language and establish mission stations of their own. Yet these early Pentecostal missionaries, on the whole, were ineffectual and often disruptive not only of the work of the established denominational missions, but of one another's work as well. J. H. King's comments on returning from a world tour of Pentecostal missions in 1910–12 represented a viewpoint that soon came to be accepted by many influential Pentecostals:

> The vast majority of Pentecostal missionaries that went out on this line [i.e., "on faith"] from 1907 to 1912 have proven failures, and their work is lost. I followed in their tracks and found it so. Yea, I found some to be real destroyers of God's work in foreign fields. Still others I found to be frauds, deceiving the people in the homeland by misrepresentation in order to secure support.[6]

The rapid waning of the Pentecostal revival was also in part a consequence of the movement's failure to attract or produce a dominant leader who might have directed the raw religious impulse of the revival into more durable channels. Pentecostals have taken great pride in the fact that their movement was not the work of any single outstanding leader, from which they conclude it must have been entirely supernatural in origin.[7]

Parham, of course, may quite properly be regarded as the founder of the Pentecostal movement, and there were other prominent leaders as well. But, because of the intensely individualistic and cliquish bent of those who believed themselves "led of the Spirit," and because of the mediocre character of the leaders, none was able to command the loyalties of American Pentecostals in the way Barratt, for example, commanded those of Norwegian Pentecostals.

Parham, the logical man to assume preeminence, was initially recognized as "Founder and Projector" of the movement in the Midwest and on the Pacific Coast. But sometime in the late fall of 1906 Parham "fell into an awful sin," and was indicted by the civil authorities in Texas. Although the charges against him were dropped, the incident had a demoralizing effect on the movement, especially in Oklahoma and Texas, where nearly all the workers left the field. The Azusa mission published a repudiation of Parham as early as December of 1906 (though with no mention of the real charges against him). In April of 1909 Parham's chief disciple, Howard Goss, and several other Pentecostals in Texas were able to reorganize the movement only after officially renouncing all connection with Parham. Within a few years Parham's name became anathema among Pentecostals nearly everywhere except in the Tri-State District where he had first established the movement. [8]

Seymour attempted to fill the void left by Parham's "fall," and organized the Pacific Coast Apostolic Faith Movement under his own leadership. But he alienated all but those in his own Azusa Street mission when he built a throne for himself and took an "unorthodox" position on the doctrine of sanctification. Florence Crawford, charging that Seymour had rejected sanctification as a second act of grace, broke with his organization, taking the Pacific Northwest wing of the movement with her. [9]

Several others, like William H. Durham and Eudorus N. Bell, were precluded from ascendancy over the movement because of their association with doctrines considered heretical by the bulk of Pentecostals. A. J. Tomlinson's efforts to gather the movement into his Church of God were unsuccessful largely because of his autocratic manner and his contention that his was the only "true church." G. B. Cashwell, the principal initiator of the movement in the Southeast, renounced Pentecostalism and returned to the Methodist Church in 1909. [10]

Perhaps most important in cutting short the initial dynamic phase of the Pentecostal revival was the near-unanimous opposition of the Christian community. Unlike most revivals, which are greeted with enthusiasm and only later spurned, the Pentecostal movement was resisted from the beginning.

The old-line denominations were little affected by the Pentecostal movement. Unlike the Holiness and Fundamentalist movements, the Pentecostal movement did not begin within the denominations, nor did it succeed in penetrating them. The movement did attract numbers of church members, but there was never a major bolt from any denomination, nor was there an identifiable Pentecostal faction within any. Such losses as were suffered by the denominations were often looked upon as beneficial. Denominational ministers tended to regard the Pentecostal movement as a convenient means for draining off the undesirable members of their congregations. Bitterly condemning the Church of God, a Southern Baptist spokesman, for example, said, "most of the folks who belong to this cult have been turned out of the churches. Not all, but most all. Those who have gone from our churches to walk this road of heresy have been worthless to the churches when they belonged."[11]

The major impact of the new movement was felt in the Holiness fellowships, and it was there that the Pentecostals found their stiffest resistance. The first issue of Azusa mission's *Apostolic Faith* said, "Many churches have been praying for Pentecost and Pentecost has come. The question is now, will they accept it?" A negative answer had already been given by some when this was printed, and would soon be given by others.[12]

At a camp meeting of the South California Holiness Association in the summer of 1906 the executive committee ruled against advocating or practicing speaking in tongues on the camp grounds. The Holiness Church of Southern California took an early stand against the movement, forcing pro-Pentecostals like Pendleton and most of his congregation out of their churches. In a short time clergymen of other Holiness groups, like the Pillar of Fire, Peniel Missions, and the Pentecostal Church of the Nazarene, who accepted the Pentecostal message were brought to trial and evicted from their posts.[13] Frank Bartleman was chased off the Methodist Episcopal camp grounds in Huntington Park for distributing Pentecostal tracts. What W. C. Dumble, correspondent for the Holiness periodical *Way of Faith,* said of the Pentecostal movement in Los Angeles could soon be said of it across the country.

> A similar gracious work of the Spirit to that in Wales is in progress here. But while that is mostly in the churches, this is outside. The churches will not

have it, or up to the present have stood aloof in a critical and condemnatory spirit.[14]

When Bartleman set forth once again to tour the country in 1908, stopping at many of the same places he had visited the previous year, he found a different reception. "It was," he said, "a harder fought battle than the year before." Bartleman met opposition at prayer conventions in Grand Rapids, Michigan, and Willmore, Kentucky, was forbidden to preach at the Christian and Missionary Alliance convention on the Old Orchard, Maine, camp grounds, and "greatly resisted" at the Nyack institute. At the Alliance church in Beaver Falls, Pennsylvania, "all hell was moved to oppose it [the Pentecostal message]."[15]

The earliest reports of the Azusa revival in the Holiness press warned against being deceived by Satanic counterfeits of the expected "Latter Rain," and called for cautious neutrality before either accepting or rejecting the new movement. In short order, however, more and more Holiness people came to accept the view held by those in California at a very early date: the "tongues movement" was "of the Devil."[16]

Holiness spokesmen who had been the mentors and idols of Pentecostals denounced the new movement with undisguised animosity. This was especially true of those Holiness leaders who were associated with the emergent Fundamentalist movement. The Pentecostal Frank Ewart compiled a collection of some of the choicer epithets hurled at the movement by its Holiness-Fundamentalist opponents.

> Most of the nominal churches branded it [the Pentecostal movement] as of the devil. The rest said emphatically, that it was not of God. . . . Dr. Campbell-Morgan said, "It was the last vomit of satan." Dr. Dixon said, "It was wicked and adulterous." Dr. Torrey said, "It was emphatically not of God, and founded by a Sodomite." Dr. Pierson said, "It was anti-Christian." Dr. Godbey, in a book called "Tongues and Demons," denounced it as "Sensual and Devilish." . . . The difficulty is to find a man with a religious reputation that has not openly declared himself its enemy.[17]

Ewart's list was by no means exhaustive. Other prominent Holiness-Fundamentalist leaders like H. A. Ironside, C. I. Scofield, and William B. Riley joined in the chorus. Even those who had taken part in the Welsh revival, which had served as an inspiration and model for the Pentecostal revival, turned against the movement. In a book written in collaboration with Jessie Penn-Lewis, Evan Roberts charged that the Pentecostal movement was a "Satanic deception" and "counterfeit" masquerading "under the guise of the Holy Spirit," which was largely responsible for hindering and checking the revival of 1904–6. In Los Angeles, Joseph Smale, who had seen the Welsh revival at first hand and left his Baptist pastorate to organize the New Testament Church dedicated to promoting a similar revival in this country, also rejected the Pentecostal movement after a period of cautious receptivity.[18]

There were a few miniscule Holiness churches that were largely won over to the Pentecostal movement, but in almost every case this was accompanied by bitter controversy and schism. The Holiness Church of North Carolina was riven with conflict over the new movement from the time that G. B. Cashwell introduced it among its membership early in 1907 until the convention of 1908. At the final showdown four of the nine ministers present, including the president, A. B. Crumpler, voted against the Pentecostal movement and left the organization in protest against the "majority" decision.[19] The Free Will Baptist Church was seriously disrupted when about half the churches of the Cape Fear Conference and all those of the Wilmington and New River Conferences (all in the Carolinas) broke away to organize the Pentecostal Free Will Baptist Church in 1911.[20] The Church of God in Christ suffered a heavy defection when its co-leaders split over the Pentecostal movement, with C. P. Jones and the majority opposed, and Charles H. Mason and a substantial minority in favor. At the 1907 general assembly in Jackson, Mississippi, the Mason faction was voted out of the church and proceeded to organize a Pentecostal church with the same name.[21]

While most Holiness groups rejected the new movement out of hand, the Christian and Missionary Alliance delayed a decision and thereby gave the Pentecostals a few years during which they were able to propagate their message from within. A closer look at the Alliance response reveals the arguments used against the movement and the process of rejection in other Holiness groups as well.

The Christian and Missionary Alliance was organized in 1897 as an interdenominational association for the promotion of "the higher life" and the support of missionary work. By 1907 the Alliance was in the process of transition to an independent Holiness denomination, but many of its adherents still held membership in the denominational churches. Because of its inter-denominational character, matters of doctrine, organization, and authority were undefined, the Alliance being held together only by an informal agreement on A. B. Simpson's Fourfold Gospel. The loose associationist structure of the Alliance left many, perhaps most, affiliated churches virtually autonomous—a condition which goes far toward explaining their difficulty in adopting a firm position on the Pentecostal movement.[22]

Revival had already broken out at the Alliance's Bible and Missionary Training Institute at Nyack, New York, when news of the Azusa Street revival was first received. Reports of people speaking in tongues in Los Angeles seemed a fulfillment of the promised restoration of the gifts of the Spirit which Simpson and the faculty at Nyack had led the students to expect.[23]

The new movement penetrated the Alliance first in Chicago, where the district superintendent, William T. MacArthur, characterized it initially as "a mixture of good and evil." But he soon found little to praise in it. "The door is . . . thrown wide open to fanaticism," wrote MacArthur; "minds have broken down under the strain and several sent to insane asylums."[24]

A. B. Simpson, in a cover editorial for the Alliance's official organ, rejoiced that the gift of tongues was apparently being restored to the Church. "But," he continued, "there have been many instances where the alleged gift of tongues led the subjects and the audiences into the wildest excesses and were accompanied with voices and actions more closely resembling wild animals than rational beings, impressing all unprejudiced observers that it was the work of the devil." And even what was the genuine work of the Holy Spirit, said Simpson, often "degenerated very soon into wildfire and fanaticism."[25]

At the May 1907 Council meeting of the Alliance at Nyack, Simpson expressed gratitude for a "year of revival, a year of the Holy Ghost," but complained that "excess," "error," and "undesirable leaders" had "led to division, fanaticism, confusion and almost every evil work." Others present, however, had no such reservations about the movement. George N. Eldridge, district superintendent of the West Central District and chairman of the Committee on Home Work (i.e., home missions), said, "There is a bursting out in many centers which is surely a visitation of God upon the earth and which may be the beginning of the final outpouring of the Holy Ghost which is to immediately precede the coming of the Lord." A number of Alliance ministers who had found the Pentecostal experience elsewhere introduced it among their colleagues in Nyack and New York City during the Council session.[26]

The outcome of the meeting was an agreement of "the brethren" to recognize the gift of tongues as genuine when exercised in "the spirit of power and of a sane mind," but to reject it when accompanied by "false teaching" and "wild excitement." "False teaching," Simpson later explained, referred primarily to the dogma that the gift of tongues was the "only proper evidence of baptism with the Holy Ghost"—a view Simpson declared "rash and wholly unscriptural."[27]

These pronouncements had slight effect in stemming the Pentecostal tide in Alliance circles. At the annual summer camp meetings in 1907, which were open to all Holiness people, numbers of converts were won to the new movement by Alliance people who claimed the Pentecostal experience and by non-Alliance Pentecostals like Bartleman and emmissaries from Azusa and elsewhere. At some camps, like the Rocky Springs Park camp near Lancaster, Pennsylvania, where Simpson preached on "True and False Fire," some restraint was exercised and relatively few converts were won by the Pentecostal faction. But elsewhere, as at the Beulah Park camp near Cleveland, Ohio, where Pentecostal champions like William Cramer and J. T. Boddy were among the officials and chief speakers, great headway was made. Among the new converts that summer were John Salmon, vice president of the Alliance in Canada, D. W. Kerr, pastor of the Alliance Tabernacle in Dayton, Ohio, and D. W. Myland, pastor of the Columbus, Ohio, church.[28]

The Alliance began to suffer defections both from the extreme pro-Pentecostals, who resented any restraints or criticisms, on the one hand, and from the anti-Pentecostals, who refused utterly to countenance the movement, on the other. Simpson hesitated to move strongly in either direction for fear of multiplying these losses, but there could be no doubt where his sympathies lay. In numerous periodical articles and tracts, Simpson and others who shared his attitude mounted a campaign to undermine the new movement without rejecting it totally.[29]

The sum of their argument was: the teaching that tongue-speaking was the only sure sign of Spirit Baptism was scripturally insupportable; the nature of the speech itself and the accompanying "manifestations" often indicated the operation of either natural or demoniacal forces; and the self-righteous and contentious spirit that led to divisions substantiated this. Moreover, in those few cases where speaking in tongues was considered to be Spirit-inspired, the speech was declared to be the "inferior" and "unintelligible" tongues of I Corinthians whose purpose was private devotion. The "missionary tongues" of Acts, whose purpose would be the evangelization of the world, were yet to be restored. Finally, it was argued that all public speaking in tongues should be subjected to the Pauline restrictions listed in I Corinthians: no more than three are to speak in tongues during any one meeting, and then in succession, and only if interpreted. Where these rules were ignored, as they were in all the early Pentecostal meetings, the speaking in tongues was to be rejected as "not of God." [30]

Just before the convening of the 11th annual Council in March of 1908, Simpson indicated the action he hoped for when he hailed the condemnation of the "Tongues Movement" in Germany by resolution of a Holiness convention in Barmen (now Wuppertal). [31] In his address to the Council, Simpson castigated those "seducing spirits and false teachers" who

> make special manifestations an evidence of the baptism of the Holy Ghost, giving to them the name of Pentecost as though none had received the spirit of Pentecost but those who had the power to speak in tongues, thus leading many sincere Christians to cast away their confidence, and plunging them in perplexity and darkness, or causing them to seek after special manifestations of other than God Himself.

The fruit of the new movement, continued Simpson, was all too often "separation . . . bitterness, and strife." [32]

Simpson's lament that "In several cases our Alliance work has been almost broken up by these diversions and distractions" was well founded. Reports to the Council by district and local superintendents revealed the loss of "fully one-half" of the Alliance people in Indianapolis, deep inroads in Chicago, and substantial defections in a number of other cities. But some, like the Portland and Nyack officials, while deploring its "evils," concluded the new movement was on the whole beneficial. [33]

Faced with strong support for the movement among some of the highest leaders in the Alliance, Simpson stayed his hand. Forcing the issue may have led to a major bolt by the pro-Pentecostal faction at a time when the Alliance was burdened with financial hardships resulting from the Panic of 1907. [34] Too pressing to be ignored, the issue was compromised by the adoption of a neutral resolution.

> Since there are great differences of opinion among the members respecting current religious movements, it would be wise to leave the question of "the Latter Rain" and related doctrines, as matters of personal liberty, just as we do the question of Baptism, Church Government, and other differences of belief among the Evangelical bodies. [35]

In a follow-up editorial, local and district superintendents and convention officials were counseled to avoid making pronouncements concerning the movement that might precipitate divisions.[36] This remained the official position of the Alliance, but unofficially sentiment was rising against the Pentecostal faction. Except for the Beulah Park camp, the Pentecostals found increased resistance in the Alliance camp meetings of 1908, especially the non-Alliance Pentecostals. Examining committees for licensing preachers, pastors, and missionaries began to weed out pro-Pentecostal candidates. Articles in Alliance periodicals became exclusively representative of the anti-Pentecostal viewpoint.[37]

Such developments led to the resignation of pro-Pentecostals, some of whom took their congregations and church property with them. Despite the deteriorating situation, decisive action was not taken until the 1912 Council meeting. A new constitution was then adopted that included a doctrinal statement which pointedly revised the earlier formula of faith in Jesus Christ as "Savior, Baptizer in the Holy Ghost, Healer and Coming King" by substituting "Sanctifier" for "Baptizer in the Holy Ghost." More importantly, the central Alliance board at New York City was given legal control over all congregational property, and the right to supply or approve all clergymen. By this action the Alliance became a Holiness denomination with clear lines of control, able to prevent the loss of property and the subversion of local churches by the Pentecostals. It was, however, much like locking the proverbial barn door, for by this time the major defections had already taken place and the appeal of the new movement was fast waning in the Alliance as it had already done in other Holiness groups.[38]

By 1912 the Holiness-Fundamentalist camp presented an almost unbroken front against the Pentecostal movement. "All our old Holiness friends rejected us," said Alfred G. Garr; "the old doors were closed."[39] In time, Holiness churches like the Pentecostal Church of the Nazarene, the Pentecostal Union Church, the Church of God (Anderson, Indiana), and the Church of God as Organized by Christ wrote specific repudiations of the "Tongues Movement" into their official creeds and minutes. Several Fundamentalist organizations officially condemned Pentecostalism in the same breath with "modernism," and Fundamentalist writers kept up a running, if intermittent, assault on the movement.[40]

Resistance from the older denominations was expected, but that the Holiness-Fundamentalist camp should denounce them far more bitterly came as a heavy blow to the Pentecostals. Yet it was the manner in which the Pentecostals presented their message and the implications of that message that largely accounted for the negative response of their fellow believers in Holiness and Fundamentalism.

Like other evangelical revivalists, the Pentecostals posed the question of personal salvation in either-or terms for the "unregenerate." But they went beyond this to present believers with a similar either-or choice, preaching that the Pentecostal movement was "the Bridal call" and that only those who accepted it would be taken up in the Rapture and receive high rewards in the coming Kingdom, while those who rejected it would suffer the terrors of the Tribulation and hold positions subordinate to the Pentecostals in the Millennium. Many Pentecostals even asserted that those who opposed the movement were, whether knowingly or not, opposing God. Like all "true believers," the Pentecostals were often completely uncompromising, belligerent, and self-righteous.[41]

It was hardly surprising that the Pentecostals most alienated those very Holiness people to whom they made their chief appeal. Holiness believers who for years had claimed to be Baptized in the Spirit now found their testimony impugned by Pentecostals who insisted that no one had received "the Baptism" except they spoke in tongues. Even those Pentecostals who regarded "tongues" as only one of several possible signs of "the Baptism" tended to disparage, if only by implication, the religious experience of those who did not speak in tongues. Moreover, by teaching that the Baptism in the Spirit was a third act of grace beyond sanctification, the Pentecostals placed themselves in the same category as the Fire Baptized people who had already been repudiated by the main body of Holiness believers for their "Third Blessing Heresy."

Rejection of the "orthodox" Holiness view of Baptism in the Spirit and acceptance of the notion of a "Third Blessing," necessarily carried with it some measure of repudiation of the Holiness movement. The Pentecostal movement came on the scene just at the point when the Holiness movement was achieving some order and stability through denominational organization. The direct challenge of the Pentecostals to the central doctrine of Holiness and their indirect challenge to the leadership of the Holiness denominations threatened to throw the Holiness movement back into the chaotic state from which it was emerging. The apparent disorder and extremely emotional character of Pentecostal meetings lent substance to Holiness fears that the Pentecostal movement would submerge and destroy the Holiness movement in a sea of chaos.

The virulence of the Holiness-Fundamentalist rejection of the Pentecostal movement was surprising to the Pentecostals, who were themselves committed both to holiness and "the fundamentals." The Pentecostals believed that their only important difference from other Fundamentalists—speaking in tongues—followed logically from a more rigorous application of the Biblical literalism that lay at the core of Fundamentalism. Their attitude was well expressed by Stanley H. Frodsham.

> A few weeks ago I heard a brother testify, "I praise God that I am a Fundamentalist, and that I am a Pentecostal Fundamentalist." That is what we all are. I do not know of a Pentecostal person anywhere who questions the inerrancy of the Scriptures, or one who doubts the virgin birth, the miracles, the physical resurrection, the Deity, or the efficacy of the blood atonement of our Lord Jesus Christ, nor one who has the slightest sympathy for the unproved theories of the evolutionists. . . . We go further and affirm that the signs and wonders that our Lord Jesus Christ said should follow "them that believe" (Mark 16:17, 18) will assuredly follow as a result of faith in Christ today. We also stand for that Fundamental of Service, the Baptism in the Holy Spirit, as that experience was originally received on the day of Pentecost. [42]

Given such wide areas of agreement, it seemed only natural to the Pentecostals that other Fundamentalists should be favorably disposed toward their movement. Yet it was precisely because the differences between themselves and other Fundamentalists were so small that the others found it necessary to maintain and even exaggerate the distinction lest they be associated with the Pentecostals in the public eye. Hence, the closer other groups stood to the Pentecostal movement in doctrine and spirit, the more vocal their dununciation of it. Alma White of the Pentecostal Union Church exemplified this trait when she launched a thoroughly vicious attack against the Pentecostals, accusing them, among other things, of practicing witchcraft, worshipping the devil, and sexual promiscuity. [43]

The opposition encountered by the Pentecostals was not verbal merely, but at times physical as well. Pentecostal meetings were mobbed by shouting, pushing men; cayenne pepper was scattered in the sawdust; rocks, decayed vegetables, and "stink bombs" were tossed through windows or into tents; tent ropes were cut, and meeting places set afire. In places where frontier traditions of violence were still strong, Pentecostals were beaten, tarred and feathered, shot at, and had their meetings broken into by galloping horsemen. In one section of Appalachia the homes and chapels of Pentecostals were dynamited. [44] Some of this abuse was because

Pentecostal preachers often supported employers against workers in strike situations.

Involvement in civil court proceedings was a common experience among Pentecostal preachers. Sometimes this resulted from the disturbances caused by mockers and scoffers, but more often from public irritation with their loud shouting and singing into the small hours of the morning, night after night. At other times their failure to obtain permits for street meetings or for pitching tents on public property brought them into court. Often the charges were dismissed after a reprimand, or token fines were imposed. But in many cases the Pentecostals refused to heed the warning or pay the fine and were imprisoned. In some instances their healing practices involved them in suits for damages, and in public prosecution for practicing medicine without a license or receiving money under false pretences. All such public restraint, the justified along with the unjustified, was regarded by Pentecostals as "persecution."[45]

Criticism and persecution spurred the Pentecostals to work more energetically, compelled them to defend and clarify their message, and helped to develop the self-image of a heroic minority struggling against overwhelming odds. It reinforced their conviction that they were the true spiritual heirs of Jesus and the Apostles, who had also been maligned and persecuted. But their exclusion from Holiness-Fundamentalist circles had a crippling effect. So long as the Pentecostals had the opportunity to confront their critics and win converts in Holiness conventions, camp meetings, and churches, opposition may well have been an asset. But once denied access to these facilities, confrontation and debate gave way to isolation. Except for an occasional polemic, non-Pentecostals soon ignored the Pentecostal movement, turning their attention to other matters like the Fundamentalist, Social Gospel, and Ecumenical movements. At an early date a wall was raised between the Pentecostals and the larger Christian community that would not be breached for half a century.

Holiness rejection of Pentecostalism can hardly be sufficiently explained by doctrinal differences. Holiness and Pentecostal people were in substantial agreement on all important points of doctrine, including the Baptism in the Spirit. True, many Pentecostals insisted that speaking in tongues was the one and indispensable sign of Spirit baptism, a position that was universally rejected by the Holiness-Fundamentalist camp, but that teaching was not universal among Pentecostals, and many Holiness people acknowledged speaking in tongues to be a legitimate evidence of "the Baptism," though not the only one.[46]

Nor do class differences in themselves explain the division among Holiness-Fundamentalist people over the Pentecostal movement. Both those who rejected and those who accepted the Pentecostal message were drawn very largely from the lower socio-economic classes, though a somewhat greater number of the faithful in the Pentecostal movement came from the very lowest social levels. Rather, the rejection of Pentecostalism by the bulk of the Holiness and Fundamentalist movements reflected the social orientation given those movements by their leadership. Middle class Holiness-Fundamentalist leaders attempted to perpetuate their values and mores by inculcating them in their lower class followers. Such values—hard work, honesty, thrift, sobriety, and self-denial—continued, indeed, to be held in high esteem by Pentecostals as well. But other values assumed greater importance, values that were in fundamental conflict with those of the middle class.

From the first, the Holiness movement was emotional in tone, at times offensively so, even to some of its adherents. But, by the time of the Pentecostal revival of 1906–8, that emotionalism was becoming muted. In time it would be transformed into an inner, sentimental pietism. The Fundamentalist movement, while cherishing sentimentalism, looked askance at overt emotionalism from its beginnings. The Pentecostals, however, came to place great emphasis on extreme emotional expression, epitomized by the speaking in tongues. Ecstasy militated against the rationalist, self-disciplinary values that were assuming prominence among Holiness people and soon found their fullest expression in the emergent Fundamentalist movement.

Holiness and Fundamentalist leaders, by rejecting the ecstatic, non-rational Pentecostal movement and reaffirming the more solid middle-class values, succeeded in holding the bulk of their followers, who aspired to middle-class status. By the time of the Pentecostal revival of 1906 many Holiness congregations were already following the mainline denominations in abandoning the inner city neighborhoods. The move registered the Holiness movement's failure to reach the immigrant poor crowding into these areas, but it also reflected the middle-class aspirations of those native-born Americans from rural backgrounds who constituted the overwhelming bulk of the movement. One by one the Holiness churches followed the example set by the Los Angeles Church of the Nazarene in 1902 when it moved out of its downtown location and into a "respectable middle-class neighborhood." By the end of the First World War the inner-city, store-front mission phase of the Holiness movement was passing rapidly and the middle-class propensities of Holiness believers were unmistakable.[47]

The Pentecostals, while by no means rejecting the more solid middle-class values, placed a higher premium upon ecstasy, and thereby directed less of their energies into the development of those characteristics more useful for rising into the middle class. Moreover, ecstatic experience, by providing a release for hostilities and anxieties, reduced the dynamic tension between reality and aspiration that underlies upward mobility. The effect of overemphasis on ecstatic religious experience was to decrease both the desire and the ability to rise into the middle class.

In a rough sort of way then, the split in the Holiness movement occasioned by the Pentecostal revival was between those who aspired to rise from lower-class status and those who sought reconciliation to it, between a prospective bourgeoisie and a despairing proletariat. The religion of the Holiness believer was often a positive asset in achieving upward mobility. For the Pentecostal, success in achieving ecstatic religious experience became in large part a surrogate for success in the social struggle.

IX

The Sanctification Schism

The Pentecostal movement was primarily a response to the massive social dislocations of the late 19th century. The old norms of belief, morality, manners, and behavior were collapsing and all social institutions were compelled to adjust to that fact. The denominations' accommodation to the thought and life of the larger society was unacceptable to the Pentecostals. So, too, was the Holiness response. Yet it was equally imperative that the Pentecostals establish clear lines of contact and separation between themselves and the larger culture, because it was precisely the need to bring order out of the chaos of their lives that led so many into the Pentecostal fold. What these converts expected was a clear set of directions through the social maze. The attempt to establish that set of directions led to an interminable series of internal controversies. The social diversity of the movement and the extreme individualism of its leaders, however, foredoomed the finding of a unified solution. Thus, the movement fragmented into a myriad of splinter organizations each with its own unique pattern of "mazeway resynthesis" and "defensive restructuring."

Extraordinary aggressiveness was a dominant characteristic of the early Pentecostal movement. This aggressiveness was generated by the enormous frustrations which the Pentecostals experienced. The major source of these frustrations was the social position of the Pentecostals. The ambiguous status of Pentecostal leaders and the very low status of the faithful exposed them to a situation in which the opportunities for frustration were great and the chances for overcoming them were few. And there were also the frustrations consequent upon the failure of Pentecostal hopes for the imminent Second Coming, their rejection by Holiness-Fundamentalist circles, and the increasing indifference of the larger society. Moreover, racial, ethnic, and personal antipathies inherent in the heterogeneous social character of the movement and glossed over in the first flush of revival constituted a latent source of frustration and, hence, aggression. As revival fires abated so too did the sense of solidarity.

A central problem for the Pentecostals, therefore, was the release of aggressive impulses. Some of these found sublimated outlets in the cathartic experience of speaking in tongues, and in the contemplation of the coming apocalypse. But speaking in tongues and prophesying the destruction of the world served also to add to the Pentecostal store of aggressiveness since, because of these practices, abuse and ridicule were heaped upon them.

Thus, it was in a continuing struggle with others that the Pentecostals found the major release for their pent-up aggressiveness. First, as Holiness adherents, they had battled against the denominations. Then, as Pentecostals they struggled against the "orthodox" Holiness legions. Finally, deprived of their opposition by their exclusion from Holiness circles, they turned to vent their hostilities against one another in internecine warfare. But no amount of such conflict could resolve the underlying frustration that sprang from their position in the social order. Therefore, aggressive hostility and controversy continued within the Pentecostal movement, issuing in a bewildering array of divisions, mergers, and redivisions. Only after World War II, when substantial numbers of Pentecostals achieved middle-class status, would there be any significant waning of the fratricidal warfare.[1]

Such combat, of course, was carried out in a religious idiom and relied upon appeals to the authority of Scripture and Spirit. Religious traditions and convictions did indeed play an important role in these controversies, but they were commingled with other elements. The internal battles of the early Pentecostal movement had social, as well as theological, sources and implications.

Controversy often arose over "truths" putatively revealed by the Holy Spirit. Such revelations were rarely claimed to be entirely new, but, rather, fresh insights into truths residing in the Bible, which had either been "lost" or had been concealed by God until the proper moment. Now, in "the end time," it was believed they would be restored or disclosed. Widespread expectations along these lines exerted considerable pressure on Pentecostal preachers to come up with novel and striking "revelations." As Howard Goss put it:

> Walking in the light of God's revelation was considered a guarantee of unbroken fellowship with God. . . . Consequently, a preacher who did not dig up some new slant on a Scripture, or get some new revelation to his own heart ever so often; a preacher who did not propagate it, defend it, and if necessary, was not prepared to lay down his life for it, was considered slow, stupid, unspiritual. . . . A familiar and most absorbing question when preachers met was: "What new revelation have you received?"[2]

Small wonder then that as Goss observed, "Many new revelations began to cause confusion." The Pentecostal movement was racked by debate and controversy over innumerable minor issues, and within a decade after the revival of 1906–8, two major struggles arose which tore the movement from top to bottom. The first concerned the doctrine of sanctification; the second arose over the water baptismal formula but came to involve the nature of the Godhead. By 1916 the Pentecostal movement was fragmented into three doctrinal segments: Second Work Trinitarians, Finished Work Trinitarians, and unitarians. Over a longer period of time, each of these segments in turn suffered still another division along racial lines.

In this chapter I shall deal briefly with those divisions of relatively minor significance, and with the first of the major doctrinal splits. In the following chapter I shall turn to the second doctrinal conflict and the racial schism.

The removal of whatever restraint their contact with other Christians had had on the Pentecostals gave freer rein to the antinomian tendencies typical of the "Spirit-led." Experience, not doctrine, was the primary interest of the early Pentecostals.[3] In fact, many regarded doctrine as divisive, and hesitated to adopt any but the vaguest statements of faith. The common experience of the Spirit, especially as expressed in speaking in tongues, bound them together and provided the basis for the rudimentary organizations initially created. Disciplinary machinery, where it existed, was rarely effective when it was used. Pentecostal pulpits were wide open to itinerant preachers with novel revelations.[4] In such circumstances heterodoxy and ultraism flourished.

The Pentecostals sought to recreate a primitive New Testament community of saints, emphasizing individual religious experience, spontaneity, and the free life of the Spirit. For them the only genuine religion was the "religion of the heart" in which one felt the immediate presence of God and lived a life under the direct guidance of the Spirit.

An important source of such guidance was speaking in tongues. "Messages" delivered by those having "the gift of tongues" and interpreted by those with "the gift of interpretation" were regarded as equivalent to prophecy, the first and highest gift of the Spirit. At times the reverential awe accorded such "messages" led to the most naive consequences. By means of tongues and interpretations Bible schools were taught, believers were instructed to sell their belongings and directed to specific mission fields, and even told whom they should marry. Resorting to those with the gifts of tongues and interpretation for personal guidance was so widespread among Pentecostals that the practice was universally known as "inquiring of the Lord."[5]

At times such use of the charismatic gifts wrought havoc in the lives of individuals, brought discredit on the movement, and sowed discord in Pentecostal ranks. Some Pentecostals, like A. J. Tomlinson, who was confirmed in office through tongues and interpretation on three occasions, found that "messages" in tongues could be used to acquire and retain authority.[6] But they learned also that the practice could as easily be turned against them. W. F. Carothers complained of the way in which "inquiring of the Lord" was used to undermine the reputations and authority of Pentecostal leaders:

> This new way of "inquiring of the Lord" promotes secret meetings, cliques and conspiracies and hence tends to division and strife. . . . No one's Christian character is safe from attack when parties of two, three or half a dozen are off together getting messages (so-called) about everything and everybody . . . you may be sure . . . there will be no secret assassination of character WHEN THE HOLY SPIRIT DOES THE WORK.[7]

Messages in tongues and interpretations were at times used to introduce or legitimize controversial doctrines and practices. A prohibition against eating pork, for example, was ostensibly endorsed by the Holy Spirit through tongues and interpretation at a Pentecostal convention in Waco, Texas, in 1907.[8] "Messages" were frequently taken down in shorthand and published with the "tongues" reproduced phonetically on one page and the English "interpretation" facing it. Tracts, pamphlets, and whole series of books of this kind were printed and widely distributed. Nor were these isloated aberrations merely. Leading Pentecostal periodicals frequently published the interpretations of such messages, though not the "tongues" from which they were derived. Because the gift of interpretation was relatively rare, messages in tongues were sometimes sent for translation to someone known to have the necessary gift. On at least one occasion an industrious Pentecostal, with phonetic transcription of tongue-speech in hand, claimed he consulted "the standard works on languages and found out what it meant."[9]

Some Pentecostal leaders attempted to curb the uninhibited and disruptive use of the charismatic gifts. They rejected the practice of "inquiring of the Lord" and the use of tongues and interpretation "as the primary method" of teaching Bible schools. They subjected all "messages" involving controversial matters to the judgment of "the elders."[10] But even to the extent that such restraints were effective they were unable to prevent dissension. Appealing to revelations based on the charismatic gifts, to the Bible, to inner illumination, and to combinations of all three, Pentecostals disputed a great variety of questions.

Pentecostals agreed that true Christians must live in a manner appropriate for those whose bodies were believed to be "temples of the Holy Ghost." All held the necessity of abstaining from liquor and tobacco. But did taboos on eating and drinking cover pork, coffee, tea, soda, and chewing gum? Did the prohibition against tobacco preclude employment that required handling it? All Pentecostals agreed that they must keep themselves "unspotted from the world," but did taboos on "worldly adornment" prohibit the wearing of all jewelry and cosmetics? What clothing and hair styles were acceptable? What entertainments and recreations, in addition to social dancing and motion pictures, were excluded by the injunction against "worldliness"?

"Be ye not unequally yoked with unbelievers" was a scriptural passage universally subscribed to by Pentecostals, but did this prohibit joining any and all organizations that included "unbelievers"? Did it also cover informal social contacts with them? "Man-made" organizational structures were unanimously denounced, but what plan of church government did God approve? How was "spiritual order" to be maintained? Were the offices of apostle and prophet to be restored to the Church? How were "scriptual" church offices to be filled?

Surely God required water baptism and partaking of the Lord's Supper. But what formula should be used in baptism? Should grape juice or wine be used in communion? Was footwashing a necessary part of the service?

Was tithing voluntary or binding? What about the handling of snakes and
fire? What regulations, if any, applied to the practice of the spiritual
gifts?

As for doctrinal matters, all believed in sanctification, but was it a second act of grace or did it commence with conversion? All believed in the
Baptism of the Spirit with speaking in tongues, but was "tongues" the
only sure sign of such Baptism? Were the Baptism in the Spirit and the
New Birth the same experience? Surely Jesus was God, but was he the
only person in the Godhead?[11]

The agitation of such questions was certain to create strong disagreements and division among people who claimed, each for himself, divine
illumination. And especially so since Pentecostals tended to consider
every thought, word, act, and belief to be of ritual significance, that is, in
and of itself either pleasing or displeasing to God. Disagreements over
seemingly minor issues, therefore, were often raised to cosmic proportions. Failure to discriminate between levels of importance, and the merg-
ing of several issues in a single controversy insured bitter debate and
schism.

Running through the controversies of the early Pentecostal movement,
and compounding their divisiveness, was the struggle for power among
individuals and among leadership groups. Although almost every con-
ceivable form of church government could be found among Pentecostals,
in actual practice all tended toward autocracy. Once in control of either
an assembly or a denomination, Pentecostal leaders were inclined to perpetuate themselves in their positions and to resist all restraint upon their
authority. Rivalry for domination, most apparent in those controversies
over church government, was often involved in schisms over other issues
as well. Given the unbridled individualism of Pentecostal leaders and the
propensity of the faithful to follow and emulate maverick personalities,
personal and clique rivalry was often an important element in fac-
tionalism and division.

Finally, the clash of ethnocentrisms stemming from the diverse social
characteristics of race, ethnic extraction, urban-rural environment,
region, and previous religious affiliation also played its role in precipita-
ting divisions. The conscious motivation of those caught up in conflict
was not necessarily other than what they professed—strictly and sincerely
religious—but other social factors operated to influence the outcome of
those struggles.

Among those Pentecostals given to extreme reliance upon Spirit guid-

ance and revelation, eccentric and cranky notions abounded. It was taught
that preachers should not waste their time preparing sermons, but simply
obey the scriptural injunction "Open your mouth and I will fill it." The
"sermon" that often came out was entirely in "tongues." Advertising
was to be avoided for "fear that the job will be taken away from the Holy
Ghost." Some zealots, determined that "man" should not usurp the leadership of the Spirit, called for "clearing the platform" of all people during worship services.[12]

Numerous pronouncements reflected a preoccupation with sexual
mores. Some held that divorced and remarried persons should leave their
families to return to their first spouse. Others taught that divorced persons
should never remarry. Some insisted that marital relations should be limited to the procreation of children once every three years; still others that
the saints should desist entirely from sexual relations. Some Pentecostals
were accused by others of believing that "sins of the flesh" glorified God
because they gave him an opportunity to manifest his grace—a belief that
allegedly led to "free love."[13]

Revelations of the Spirit became the nucleus for several new movements among Pentecostals. One such was universalism. Proponents of
"Ultimate Reconciliation" held that the death of Christ had provided salvation for all, and that ultimately all unbelievers would be reconciled to
God. It was true, according to this teaching, that Hell was a place of tor-
ment, but it was not eternal. The God of love could never accept the permanent loss of even the least of his creatures, and, therefore, at the "end
of the age" Hell would give up its inhabitants to "the New Heavens."[14]

The seed of this doctrine can be found in Parham's rejection of an eternal Hell in favor of the doctrine of the annihilation of the wicked. But
"Ultimate Reconciliation," as such, probably originated among British
Pentecostals. At least as early as 1914, however, it had been widely disseminated in America through the "Yellow Book Series" of messages in
tongues with interpretations, published in Chicago, and through a number
of publications under the caption "In School with the Holy Ghost," issuing from Chicago and Indianapolis. By 1918 the Pittsburgh Bible Institute
had become a center of the "Ultimate Reconciliation" movement under
the leadership of C. H. Pridgeon.[15]

Still another movement whose roots may have been in Britain (where it
was known as "the Spoken Word") emerged in America as the "New
Revelation" or the "set-Apostle" movement. The basis of the movement
was the belief that the only scriptural church government was by apostles,

prophets, and other church officers "set" in the church directly by the "Spoken Word" of the Holy Spirit through the gift of prophecy or its equivalent, tongues, and interpretation. Here and there an independent "Apostolic Church" like that of D. B. Rickard in Indianapolis was founded on this line. The "Gift Movement," which led to substantial defections in the Virginia Conference of the Pentecostal Holiness Church in 1916 was also committed to the "set-Apostle" theory. But, because of the extreme Spirit-centered character of such movements and their stringent anti-ecclesiasticism, little resulted from them beyond the establishment of a few autonomous congregations, Bible schools, ministerial fellowships, and publishing ventures.[16]

The effects of other dissensions are somewhat more apparent. From the earliest years the pattern of schism, merger, and fragmentation into a bewildering forest of sects was firmly fixed in the Pentecostal movement.

The break-up of Parham's Apostolic Faith Movement, as we have noted, involved the moral character of Parham, and, later, the doctrine of sanctification. Yet it was also in part a consequence of a contest, successively, for supremacy among Parham, Seymour, Goss, and Mrs. Crawford, all strong personalities with loyal followings. Seymour broke with Parham in the fall of 1906, and organized the Pacific Coast Apostolic Faith Movement. Goss left the following year with most of the Texas and Arkansas assemblies. In 1911 Mrs. Crawford repudiated Seymour and took the Pacific Northwest assemblies of the West Coast organization with her. Later, her own Apostolic Faith Movement suffered the loss of its upper Midwest affiliate, and then the defection of the group of ministers who founded the Bible Standard Conference in 1919.[17]

The Pentecostal Holiness Church was fragmented in 1918 when controversy over hair and clothing styles and over leisure time activities led to a bolt of the more puritanical faction, which then formed the Pentecostal Fire-Baptized Holiness Church. Two years later, still another schism in the Pentecostal Holiness Church resulted in the establishment of the Congregational Holiness Church. The defecting group, led by Watson Sorrow, protested the parent organization's negative stand on doctors and medicine, and its episcopal form of government. In both these schisms, and in the racial ones dealt with in the next chapter, the person and position of Joseph H. King, first and life-long overseer of the Pentecostal Holiness Church, were of more than peripheral importance.[18]

The Church of God (Cleveland, Tennessee) suffered a defection from its ranks when a group rejected the increasingly autocratic control of its general overseer, Ambrose J. Tomlinson, and his teaching on compulsory tithing. The outcome was the founding of the (Original) Church of God in 1917. Later, in 1923, Tomlinson was ejected from the Cleveland, Tennessee, denomination for misappropriation of funds. It is clear, however, that at most the charges were based on Tomlinson's poor judgment, and at worst they were trumped up. The real issue was Tomlinson's autocratic sway over the organization and the determination of a group of elders to limit his powers or, failing that, remove him. Tomlinson promptly proceeded to organize the (Tomlinson) Church of God with headquarters in the same city, Cleveland, Tennessee.[19]

The largest Pentecostal denomination, the Assemblies of God, was rent asunder during its first two years of existence (1914–16) by the unitarian controversy to be discussed in the next chapter, but minor schisms continued to plague it over the years.

In 1915, R. E. Erdman, a charter member and presbyter of the Assemblies, broke away to organize the United Pentecostal Association with congregations in western New York and Pennsylvania, and in eastern Ohio. Since this association merged in 1924 with the Pentecostal Holiness Church—a strong Second Work denomination—the schism from the Assemblies may have involved the doctrine of sanctification. The Assemblies from its founding was known to oppose the "orthodox" Second Work view of sanctification, but did not at that time adopt an official creed. Ambivalence on the issue among Erdman's followers is suggested by events following his death in 1927. At that time all but two of the congregations formerly of the old United Pentecostal Association left the Pentecostal Holiness Church in opposition to its Second Work doctrine of sanctification.[20]

As a consequence of the unitarian controversy, the Assemblies adopted its first statement of faith declaring, among other things, that:

> The baptism of believers in the Holy Ghost is witnessed by the initial physical sign of speaking with other tongues as the Spirit of God gives them utterance.[21]

The official adoption of what was called "the only evidence" position on speaking in tongues led to a schism from the Assemblies in 1918. Fred F. Bosworth, a founder and presbyter of the Assemblies and one of the most sought-after healer-evangelists in the entire Pentecostal movement, rejected as dogmatic and unscriptural the view that all who were Spirit-baptized must speak in tongues. He maintained that any of the nine gifts of the Spirit listed in I Corinthians was a valid sign of Baptism in the Spirit.[22]

The 1918 split in the Assemblies reflected a difference within the Pentecostal movement from its earlier years between what Bosworth called the "Radicals" (those who held the "only evidence" view of tongues) and the "Conservatives" (those who opposed it). Parham had held the "only evidence" position, but not all of his converts accepted it. As early as 1907, controversy over this issue arose among the lower Midwest Parhamites at a convention in Waco, Texas. The outcome was ambiguous. The "Radicals" claimed a victory, but one of their number, Howard Goss, later wrote,

> Some contended that all did not speak in tongues, while we held that all should. Thank God, it came out victorious that tongues were the evidence of the baptism in the Spirit, though not the only one.[23]

Seymour must have learned the "only evidence" teaching from Parham, but later, in answering the question "What is the real evidence that a man or woman had received the baptism with the Holy Ghost?", he replied that it was

> Divine love which is charity. . . . and the outward *manifestations;* speaking in tongues and the signs following: casting out devils, laying hands on the sick and the sick being healed, and the love of God for souls increasing in our hearts.[24]

The editor of the *Latter Rain Evangel,* William H. Piper, specifically repudiated the "only evidence" teaching in the very first issue of that periodical.

> One of the things that has hindered this great movement of God on the face of the earth, and caused many people not to seek the blessing, is the false teaching, that speaking in tongues is the only, essential and necessary evidence of the baptism in the Holy Spirit.[25]

Thomas B. Barratt declared that while speaking in tongues is "A SURE SIGN OF THE BAPTISM OF THE HOLY GHOST," "Still I believe that many have had, and that people may obtain in our day mighty Baptisms without this sign."[26]

Because the primary source of Biblical information on speaking in tongues, Paul's first letter to the church at Corinth, clearly asserts that all do not speak in tongues, the "only evidence" teaching hinged on a necessary distinction between "the sign of tongues" and "the gift of tongues." According to this theory, all speak in tongues at the moment of Spirit baptism as an outward "sign" of the inner experience, but many never again speak in tongues. Some, however, also receive the "gift" of tongues when Spirit baptized, and continue to exercise it on a permanent basis. Thus, the passage in I Corinthians refers to the gift of tongues, but not the sign of tongues.[27]

On first hearing of this distinction, Joseph H. King reacted in a way typical of many others.

> The gift could not be presented as an evidence of the baptism, for it is men-tioned as one of nine in I Corinthians, 12th chapter; and any one of the others might be as much of an evidence as this one. This the advocates of the above theory knew, and to avoid being inconsistent, they made a distinction between "speaking in tongues" and the Gift of Tongues. It was a weak, fu-tile and fanatical distinction to my mind.[28]

While the "only evidence" teaching was generally known in the early years of the movement, the distinction that King criticized was not. The first issue of Azusa Mission's periodical proclaimed that:

> About 150 people in Los Angeles, more than on the day of Pentecost, have received the gift of the Holy Ghost and the Bible evidence, the *gift* of tongues.[29]

Barratt, writing of his experience of Spirit baptism, said he had received "the full Bible evidence—the *gift* of tongues." Smith Wigglesworth ad-mitted that he knew nothing of the distinction until long after he had found the Pentecostal experience. Even the Assemblies of God statement of faith adopted in 1916 did not make the distinction.[30]

In short, until Bosworth made the question an issue in 1918, Pentecos-tals avoided separation over it because all agreed that speaking in tongues was *a* sign of Baptism in the Spirit, because it was the only sign in which they were interested, and because they were not overly concerned with the problem of reconciling their experience with I Corinthians, chapter 12.

When the 1918 Assemblies of God Council convened, Bosworth had the support of several outstanding leaders in that denomination. In the course of the debate, however, the "only evidence" faction swayed the overwhelming majority to their point of view by arguing for the necessary distinction between the sign and the gift of tongues. The notion, new to most, satisfied the more serious objections of the opposition and at the same time seemed to fit better with their own experience since most had spoken in tongues during their "Baptism in the Spirit."[31]

The 1916 statement of faith was revised to incorporate the distinction, and a resolution was passed withdrawing credentials from those who questioned "our distinctive testimony" that speaking in tongues is the only evidence of Baptism in the Spirit. Bosworth, followed by only a small faction, left the Assemblies to launch out as an independent evangelist, associating primarily with the Christian and Missionary Alliance, which at that time shared his view on the matter.[32]

Many Pentecostals believed that if the Bosworth view had prevailed it would have deprived the Pentecostal movement of its only important difference from Holiness groups like the Alliance, and thereby undermined it completely. These Pentecostals agreed with J. Roswell Flower's conclusion that:

> The question of the speaking in tongues as the sign of the baptism in the Holy Spirit is quite vital. If we, as a movement, are wrong in our position, we have no right to an existence as a body of people, as the denominational bodies would possibly take us in if we would drop this one point of contention. . . . The very life of the Pentecostal Movement hinges on this point.[33]

Tracts, pamphlets and articles streamed from Pentecostal presses in support of the official Assemblies of God position. Some Pentecostal groups had already taken that stand officially, others now fell into line behind the Assemblies.[34] Yet the controversy continued, and not all Pentecostals fully accepted the "only evidence" teaching. The second largest Pentecostal denomination, the Church of God in Christ, spoke for an indeterminable number of obscure associations and independent assemblies, as well as for itself, when it ambiguously asserted that:

> We do not presume to teach that no one has the Spirit that does not speak with tongues, yet we believe that a full baptism of Holy Ghost as was poured out on the day of Pentecost, is accompanied by speaking with other tongues.[35]

The "only evidence" controversy agitated the Pentecostal movement as a whole, yet it brought schism only in the Assemblies of God, and even there the loss was minor.

Once again, in 1919, the Assemblies suffered a loss, this time one far more serious than that of the previous year. Andrew Sinclair, another founder and presbyter of that denomination, led a number of ministers and congregations out to organize the Pentecostal Assemblies of the U.S.A. (later the Pentecostal Church of God of America). The issues involved are obscure. Assemblies of God writers allege that the defecting group held a liberal view on divorce and remarriage, and that Sinclair's associate, a "Brother Brinkman," was angered by the refusal of the Assemblies to make his periodical its official organ. The Pentecostal Church of God of America is strangely silent on its Assemblies of God origins, but Sinclair was a prominent and aggressive leader in Chicago, and may have concluded that his chances for ascendancy in the Assemblies were limited by the structural reorganization of 1916.[36]

The most renowned of all Pentecostals, Aimee Semple McPherson, held credentials in the Assemblies and conducted campaigns with their support. But fame brought independence. In a newspaper interview, she denied all connection with the Assemblies ("I am not one of the cult"), and criticized the "wildness of Pentecostal believers." The episode was publicized in the Pentecostal press, and Aimee turned in her Assemblies' credentials. In 1923 she organized the International Church of the Four-square Gospel, in large part by wooing away the members and congregations of other Pentecostal groups, including the Assemblies—many of whom had been converted to the movement through her ministry. The Assemblies of God district superintendent of the Iowa-northern Missouri district, John Goben, for example became a devotee of "Sister Aimee" and led a number of Assemblies churches in his district into her organization when he became general superintendent of the Foursquare Gospel Church in 1927.[37]

The disputes and schisms noted so far can do no more than suggest the real dimensions of internal turmoil among the Pentecostals. As Joseph H. King looked back on some thirty years of labor in overseeing sixteen conferences of the Pentecostal Holiness Church, what stood out in his mind was "the strife, contentions, divisions, judicial trials, and confusions arising and going on. . . ." The lament applied with equal force to the literally scores of other Pentecostal fellowships.[38]

As we turn to consider the major schisms in early Pentecostalism, we are able to examine more fully the social influences operating to disrupt the movement from within. Through an analysis of these major conflicts we may gain more insight into the complex, heterogeneous, and eclectic character of the Pentecostal movement in both its theological and social composition.

From the days of Wesley, it will be recalled, Holiness believers had debated whether sanctification commenced at conversion or was initiated by a distinct and subsequent second act of grace. Parham, as a Methodist minister, had accepted the latter view and made it an essential part of his "Apostolic Faith." Initially, therefore, conversion to the Pentecostal movement required that one accept the doctrine and experience of sanctification as a second act of grace before receiving the Baptism in the Spirit as a third.

But, beginning in 1908, William H. Durham, pastor of the renowned North Avenue Mission in Chicago, launched a continuing attack upon the second work theory in his periodical *The Pentecostal Testimony.* Denying that "it takes two works of grace to save and cleanse a man," Durham proposed what he called "The Finished Work of Calvary" doctrine.[39]

According to Durham, when Jesus said, "It is finished," as he died on the cross of Calvary, he meant that the work of salvation *and* sanctification was completed. Therefore, the moment a person exercised saving faith in the death of Jesus as a substitutionary atonement for his sins, the work of both salvation and sanctification was also "finished" for him.[40]

Durham and those who embraced his teaching were not at first clear about what "finished" meant. They said that "the old man, the old nature . . . is crucified with Christ," that "conversion is a complete work, not suppression of sin, but a complete eradication and removal," and also that it was "a setting apart in God which begins when we are made new creatures in Christ Jesus, and continues until we meet Him face to face."[41]

On one thing they were crystal clear. Sanctification was not a second work of grace. And, in a short time, the progressive character of sanctification came to overshadow and replace its instantaneous and eradicationist aspects. As one "Finished Work" advocate explained the doctrine in its more fully developed form:

> Everything was accomplished *for* the believer yet everything remained *to* be applied to the believer. . . . The work *for* me is done . . . the work *in* me is *being* done.[42]

In the spring of 1910, Howard Goss stayed with Durham for a three-week campaign in his Chicago mission, and invited Durham to defend his views at a camp meeting to be held in Malvern, Arkansas, that summer. There, Durham persuaded Goss and many of the former followers of Parham in the lower Midwest to his point of view.[43]

Early the following year Durham took his message to Los Angeles. He was refused admittance to Elmer Fisher's Upper Room Mission, but managed to secure the use of Azusa mission while Seymour was away on a preaching tour. There, he held continuous meetings until Seymour returned to lock him out. But, encouraged by the enthusiastic response of Pentecostals from other missions in the region, Durham opened his own work in a building at 7th and Los Angeles Streets, and his teaching spread all along the West Coast. Itinerating around the circuit of Pentecostal missions, conventions and camp meetings, Durham and other Finished Work advocates carried their message all across the country. Durham died suddenly in 1912, but his teaching outlived him and split the Pentecostal movement down the middle.[44]

Through the fall and winter of 1913–14, a call was repeatedly published in *Word and Witness* for an all-Pentecostal convention to be held the following April in Hot Springs, Arkansas. The prime mover behind this, Howard Goss, and all those who signed the call were Finished Work champions. Goss had managed to keep the Apostolic Faith Movement alive in Texas by "disfellowshipping" Parham in 1907. (Parham continued to operate under the same name). Sometime in the spring of 1912, Goss came into contact with a small group of Pentecostals in Alabama under the leadership of H. G. Rodgers. Rodgers had been associated with the Church of God (Cleveland, Tennessee), but severed those ties and, together with about a dozen others, secured ordination in C. H. Mason's black Church of God in Christ. Because Rodgers, by arrangement with Mason, had the right to issue ministerial credentials, and because he and Goss shared the "Finished Work" view, a merger was effected.[45]

Goss secured the use of the Grand Opera House in Hot Springs, and chose M. M. Pinson to deliver the opening address on "The Finished Work of Calvary." The primary purpose of the convention was to bring some stability to the movement by achieving agreement on fundamental doctrines, and cooperation in missionary ventures. Fear of "grieving the Spirit" by creating "man-made" organization, rules, and doctrines accounted for most of the vociferous outcry sounded against the convention call from numerous Pentecostal pulpits and periodicals. But many also regarded the convention as an attempt to swing the entire movement into a Finished Work organization, and opposed it for that reason as well.[46]

Several hundred Pentecostals showed up at Hot Springs, some of them to make certain the convention failed of its purposes. A new denomination, the Assemblies of God, was established by the adoption of a "Basis

Table 3. Urban-Rural Distribution of 26 Pentecostal Denominations, 1936

Denominations	Total Membership	Urban	Rural	Per Cent of Total	
				Urban	Rural
Predominantly White Denominations					
* Apostolic Faith Mission	2,288	2,154	134	94.1	5.9
Assemblies of God	148,043	92,775	55,268	62.7	37.3
Calvary Pentecostal Church	1,046	895	151	85.6	14.4
* Church of God (Cleveland, Tennessee)	44,818	18,564	26,254	41.4	58.6
* Church of God (Original)	2,269	843	1,426	37.2	62.8
* Church of God (Tomlinson)	18,351	7,759	10,592	42.3	57.7
* Congregational Holiness Church	2,167	1,072	1,095	49.5	50.5
Italian Pentecostal Assemblies of God	1,547	1,310	237	84.7	15.3
International Church of the Foursquare Gospel	16,147	13,176	2,971	81.6	18.4
* International Pentecostal Assemblies	6,333	5,091	1,242	80.4	19.6
** Pentecostal Church, Inc.	9,681	5,884	3,797	60.8	39.2
Pentecostal Church of God of America	4,296	3,197	1,099	74.4	25.6
* Pentecostal Fire-Baptized Holiness Church	1,348	429	919	31.8	68.2
* Pentecostal Holiness Church	12,955	6,201	6,754	47.9	52.1
Unorganized Italian Christian Churches of North America	9,567	9,111	456	95.2	4.8
Subtotals	280,856	168,461	112,395	56.4	43.6

of Union'' devoid of any statement of faith. Yet few could have been in doubt as to where it stood on the issue of sanctification. Only some 120 of those present signed the official register as delegates, and only 68 signed the charter of incorporation. But by the end of the year most of the white ministers of the Church of God in Christ came around to join the Assemblies, as well as many ''independents'' and those affiliated with other Pentecostal groups.[47]

The Finished Work doctrine spread widely and rapidly, coming in time to win the support of the majority of Pentecostals. By the end of the

Denominations	Total Membership	Urban	Rural	Per Cent of Total Urban	Rural
Predominantly Black Denominations					
* Apostolic Overcoming Holy Church of God	863	591	272	68.5	31.5
*Church of God in Christ	31,564	23,816	7,748	75.5	24.5
*Church of God in Christ (Pentecostal)	210	178	32	84.8	15.2
*Church of the Living God, Christian Workers Fellowship	4,525	3,243	1,282	71.7	28.3
*Church of the Living God, The Pillar and Ground of Truth	4,838	2,922	1,916	60.4	39.6
* Fire-Baptized Holiness Church of God of America	1,973	1,265	708	64.1	35.9
* House of the Lord	302	80	222	26.5	73.5
National David Spiritual Temple, Christ Church Union	1,880	1,362	518	72.4	27.6
** Pentecostal Assemblies of the World	5,713	5,306	407	92.9	7.1
* United Holy Church of America	7,535	4,232	3,303	56.2	43.8
Subtotals	59,403	42,995	16,408	72.4	27.6
Interracial					
** Pentecostal Assemblies of Jesus Christ	16,070	11,409	4,661	71.0	29.0
Totals	356,329	222,521	133,808	62.4	37.6

* "Second Work" denominations

** "Oneness" (unitarian) denominations

1920's, three of every five Pentecostals had adopted the Finished Work view of sanctification. Regionally, the Finished Work wing was strongest in the upper Midwest and the Far West, where about four of every five Pentecostals came to accept it. Only those Pentecostals in the South—the most rural-agrarian section of the nation—held strongly to the original Second Work position, with less than one in four in that region moving into the Finished Work camp.[48]

As this suggests, Finished Work Pentecostals tended to be more urban than Second Work Pentecostals. Better than two of every three Finished Work Pentecostals, but only slightly more than one in two Second Work

Table 4. Doctrinal Distribution by Region of Combined Memberships of 26 Pentecostal Denominations, 1936

Region	Total Membership	Division over Godhead				Division over Sanctification			
		Trini-tarian	"One-ness"	Per Cent of Total		Finished Work	Second Work	Per Cent of Total	
				Trini-tarian	"One-ness"			Fin-ished	Second
New England	3,532	3,439	93	97.4	2.6	2,353	1,179	66.6	33.4
Middle Atlantic	31,932	30,612	1,320	95.9	4.1	21,776	10,156	68.2	31.8
East North Central	52,105	39,692	12,413	76.2	23.8	38,380	13,725	73.7	26.3
West North Central	39,013	35,532	3,481	91.1	8.9	31,848	7,165	81.7	18.3
South Atlantic	64,585	61,990	2,595	96.9	3.1	13,730	50,855	20.9	79.1
East South Central	37,336	35,336	1,970	94.7	5.3	9,277	28,059	25.0	75.0
West South Central	75,946	69,054	6,892	90.9	9.1	51,163	24,783	67.2	32.8
Mountain	10,765	9,675	1,090	89.9	10.1	8,999	1,766	83.9	16.1
Pacific	41,115	39,605	1,510	96.3	3.6	36,374	4,741	88.4	11.6
Totals	356,329	324,865	31,464	91.2	8.8	213,900	142,429	60.1	39.9

Pentecostals, lived in urban environments. The more urban character of the Finished Work movement was somewhat more pronounced among black Pentecostals. Finished Work blacks were urban by nearly nine to one; Second Work blacks were urban by only about three to two.[49]

The Finished Work movement proved far more attractive to whites than blacks. While two of every three white Pentecostals became Finished Work believers, only one in eight blacks did so. As a consequence, the proportion of blacks in the Finished Work camp was very much less than that in the Second Work wing: about seven percent as compared to thirty percent.[50]

Region, race and social environment clearly played a role in the division of the Pentecostal movement over the issue of sanctification. Yet these were not the only factors operating in the conflict. Previous religious affiliation and conviction were also of prime importance in bringing on the schism. Those who had originally come into the Pentecostal movement from fellowships that had either never held the Second Work theory of sanctification or had repudiated it were most responsive to the Finished Work message.

Generally, Baptists and Presbyterians who had been caught up in the Holiness movement had held back from adopting the Second Work view of sanctification; no doubt because of the historic connection of their communions with Calvinism, which was anti-perfectionist and anti-Arminian.[51] Also, the Christian and Missionary Alliance and other groups in the Keswick wing of the Holiness movement, it will be recalled, had repudiated the Second Work position some time before the Pentecostal revival; again, undoubtedly because of the strong Calvinist influence in the Keswick movement.

Thus, Pentecostal converts from these fellowships—Baptist, Presbyterian, and Keswick Holiness—had no doubt felt some qualms about professing sanctification as a second act of grace, though they had done so, since the early Pentecostal movement regarded this as a necessary prerequisite for Baptism in the Spirit.

While acceptance of sanctification as a second act of grace conflicted with the earler views of these Pentecostal converts, the notion of a second act of grace did not. Most had come to believe there was a second act of grace, but that it was an enduement of power, not a cleansing from sin or purification of spirit. On the other hand, the whole notion of a third act of grace, however defined, had been overwhelmingly rejected by these same people before their conversion to the Pentecostal movement. The Fire

Baptized movement within the Holiness camp in the 1890's had preached three acts of grace, and had been labeled by most Holiness people as a "Third Blessing heresy." And nowhere had it been more thoroughly censured than in the upper Midwest, the same region where the Finished Work movement later caught on so strongly. For some Pentecostals the original Pentecostal teaching of three acts of grace was uncomfortably reminiscent of the discredited Fire-Baptized message.

Pentecostals from Calvinist and Keswick backgrounds, then, found the Finished Work doctrine more congenial because it resolved doubts raised by their earlier religious convictions, and because it fit better into the theological framework they had brought with them into the Pentecostal movement.

Those Pentecostals who had earlier encountered the Holiness movement in its Calvinist and Keswick form predominated in the Finished Work movement, especially former Baptist and Alliance people. Durham, who introduced the Finished Work teaching; Warren Fisher, Frank Ewart and Frank Bartleman, who propagated it in Southern California and elsewhere; Bell and Collins, founders of the Assemblies of God—all were former Baptist preachers. Indeed, J. Roswell Flower, another founder of the Assemblies, flatly stated that, "It was the Baptist influence which brought about the change in the doctrinal position on sanctification."[52]

Former Alliance people, however, were just as prominent in the Finished Work movement as Baptists. Flower himself had been associated with the Christian and Missionary Alliance, and soon after his conversion to the Pentecostal movement became a protegé of D. W. Myland, a former Alliance minister. J. W. Welch, D. W. Kerr, G. N. Eldridge, and many other Finished Work champions who came to hold high office in the Assemblies of God had come into the Pentecostal movement after many years of service in the Christian and Missionary Alliance.

Former Presbyterians were proportionately few in the Pentecostal movement as a whole, but three were prominent in the Finished Work movement: S. A. Jamieson of the Assemblies, Louis Franciscon, an apostle among Italian Pentecostals, and the Canadian Pentecostal leader Robert E. McAlister.[53]

Furthermore, Finished Work converts came principally from the ranks of those Pentecostals who belonged to congregations that were either completely autonomous or joined in loose associations—organizational patterns that no doubt reflected the influence of their Baptist and early Alliance background. In such circumstances the work of Finished Work proselytizers was facilitated. The Assemblies of God, for example, gathered many of these local churches and small associations into its fold. Yet numbers of Finished Work assemblies remained independent.

The Finished Work movement represented, in part, an attempt to accommodate Pentecostalism to the emergent Fundamentalist movement. With the elimination of sanctification as a second act of grace, the main body of the Pentecostal movement adopted a theological position that differed hardly at all from that preached by Torrey, Chapman, Simpson, and other Keswick-Fundamentalists in the early years of the century. If, however, the Pentecostals hoped that the Finished Work version of Pentecostalism would prove more acceptable to Keswick-Fundamentalists, they were mistaken. Leading spokesmen of the Keswick-Fundamentalists were already beginning to revise their doctrine of the Baptism in the Spirit in the same way they had revised that of sanctification. The Baptism in the Spirit, said Torrey, Ironside, and others, was not a second distinct act of grace, but was, like sanctification, a process that began at conversion and continued throughout life. There was, they said, one Baptism in the Spirit, which every believer received at the moment of conversion, but many subsequent baptisms, none of which were necessarily accompanied by any special gifts of the Spirit. Indeed, they went further, maintaining that although on rare occasions extraordinary powers might be exercised by a believer here and there, the gifts, signs, miracles, and wonders recorded in the New Testament had been granted to the Apostolic Church only for the purpose of legitimizing the new dispensation of grace, and were no longer to be expected.[54]

In contrast to the Calvinist-Keswick orientation of Finished Work Pentecostals, Second Work Pentecostals were distinctly Arminian and Wesleyan in religious background. Those who had come into the Pentecostal movement from Methodist, Wesleyan Holiness, and Free Will Baptist fellowships were strongly inclined to resist the Finished Work movement.

Several Pentecostal organizations had been founded originally as Second Work Holiness fellowships and only later came to accept the Pentecostal movement. These denominations, together with the several Apostolic Faith organizations, rejected the Finished Work teaching. Most of the leaders of these groups were former Methodist clergymen, and all had been believers in Second Work Holiness for sometime before becoming Pentecostals. In the Pentecostal Holiness Church, Joseph H. King (the overseer), F. M. Britton, George O. Goines, and Richard B. Hayes had all been Methodist ministers. While neither Ambrose J. Tomlinson nor Flavius J. Lee, early leaders of the Church of God (Cleveland, Tennessee), had been Methodist, both had been Second Work Holiness believers before embracing the Pentecostal movement. But other prominent figures in that denomination, like Watson Sorrow and E. L. Simmons, had been Methodists. The senior bishop of the Church of God in Christ, Charles H. Mason, was a former Baptist, but he had helped to found the Church of God in Christ originally as a Second Work Holiness denomination. As for the Apostolic Faith leaders, Parham, Mrs. Crawford, and Miss Minnie Hansen of Mrs. Crawford's upper Midwest affiliate, were all former Methodists, while Seymour had been a believer in sanctification as a second work of grace for some time before he met Parham.

Numbers of Free Will Baptists who had been swept into the Second Work Holiness revivals of the 1890's, and then later into the Pentecostal revival, clung to the Second Work view. Many of these had already joined the Pentecostal Holiness Church or the Church of God (Cleveland, Tennessee) before the Finished Work movement began. But three conferences of the Free Will Baptist Church in the Carolinas severed their connections with that body in 1911 over its alleged rejection of sanctification as a second act of grace, and also because of its opposition to the Pentecostal movement. The new Pentecostal Free Will Baptist fellowships growing out of this were, as might be expected, firm opponents of the Finished Work teaching.[55]

Again, in contrast with Finished Work Pentecostals, most of those who remained Second Work believers were members of established denominations like the Pentecostal Holiness Church, the Church of God, the Church of God in Christ, and the several Apostolic Faith organizations. From the preponderantly Methodist origins of their leaders, hierarchical patterns of church government were carried over into these denominations. Such structures were less vulnerable to Finished Work forays than were the autonomous congregations of other Pentecostals.

One other factor that helps explain the success of the Finished Work movement was the premium placed upon their own experience by Pentecostals. Many found that people who had never claimed sanctification came into Pentecostal services and spoke in tongues. It seemed to many that these converts had received the Baptism in the Spirit. The clear implication was that either a second work was unnecessary or that a person could receive two acts of grace simultaneously. Thus, for many the Finished Work teaching explained and legitimated experience.[56]

The Finished Work split resulted from the disruptive emergence of important sociological and theological differences within the Pentecostal movement. The Finished Work wing was predominantly Northern and Western, overwhelmingly white, considerably more urban, and reflected the Calvinist and Keswick Holiness backgrounds of its leaders in doctrine and polity. The Second Work wing, on the other hand, was largely Southern, had a very substantial black minority, and was hardly more urban than rural, while its doctrine and polity mirrored the Arminian and Wesleyan Holiness origins of its leadership—although, as we have seen, that leadership had departed from Wesleyan Holiness "orthodoxy" in adopting the "Third Blessing heresy" and the Keswick doctrines of dispensationalism and premillennialism.

As an attempt to accommodate Pentecostalism to emergent Fundamentalism, the Finished Work movement came too late, because the most articulate Fundamentalist leaders, by their redefinition of the Baptism of the Holy Spirit, were making such accommodation still less likely. But within the Pentecostal movement, the Finished Work doctrine squared better with the beliefs held by the majority before their conversion to Pentecostalism, and with their experience afterwards.

X

Trinitarian Controversy and Racial Separation

The "New Issue" arose over the proper formula to be used in administering water baptism, but developed into a debate on the nature of the Godhead that divided the movement into Trinitarian and unitarian wings. The germ of this second great controversy to rend Pentecostal ranks may be found in the early writings of Parham. It was "revealed" to Parham that the words to be used in the baptismal service were "in the name of Jesus, into the name of Father, Son and Holy Ghost." Yet, although he used this formula occasionally until at least 1912, Parham vociferously rejected the "New Issue" when it arose shortly thereafter. Appeal to Parham's authority, moreover, was not made until many years after the rise of the unitarian Pentecostal movement, by which time Parham's reputation and his teachings had been reconstructed in a more favorable light.[1]

Other influences were of greater importance in the emergence of the "Jesus Only" movement, as its opponents came to call it. The extreme literal Biblicism of the Pentecostals led them to concentrate on reproducing in detail the life of the New Testament church. Close study of the book of Acts disclosed that the Apostles baptized converts in the name of Jesus, rather than that of Father, Son and Holy Ghost. Pentecostal preachers used either formula without at first making an issue of it.[2]

Furthermore, rebaptism was fairly common among Pentecostals. New converts often regarded their previous baptism deficient because neither they nor the officiating clergymen had been Baptized in the Spirit. Then, too, some Pentecostals, like A. J. Tomlinson who was baptized in water at least three times, and his wife at least twice, believed the rite should be performed in commemoration of each new crisis experience. More than one Pentecostal had been baptized three or more times before the "New Issue" assumed prominence.[3]

The immediate origins of the new movement are to be found in the World Wide Pentecostal Camp Meeting held in the Highland Park section of Los Angeles in April 1913. Just before a baptismal service, the well-known Canadian Pentecostal, Robert E. McAlister, delivered a sermon in which he declared that, although the formula of Matthew 18:19 ("in the name of the Father, and of the Son, and of the Holy Ghost") was acceptable, the one found in Acts 2:38 ("in the name of Jesus Christ") should be preferred because it was the one used by the 1st-century Church.[4] The message was seized upon by some at the camp as a fulfillment of a "prophecy" delivered earlier, that God was about to "do a New Thing" for his people. Later, this was confirmed to one John G. Scheppe during an all-night prayer vigil when it was revealed to him that God required every true believer to be rebaptized "in the Name of Jesus" only. At first little came of the episode.[5] But, following the close of the camp meeting, McAlister, Glenn A. Cook, and Frank Ewart held a tent revival in the heart of Los Angeles, and still later they joined in the work at the Upper Room Mission. As a result of many long conversations, these three came to agree on the necessity of rebaptism "in the Name of Jesus."[6]

In the fall of 1913, McAlister, Ewart, the prominent black Pentecostal Garfield T. Haywood, and an obscure "Brother Frazee" organized the Pentecostal Assemblies of the World at Portland, Oregon. Because neither McAlister, nor Ewart, nor Cook had yet made his views public, this was not at first a distinctly "Jesus Only" fellowship. But it was soon to become such.[7]

In the spring of 1914, while McAlister and Cook were out on evangelistic tours, Ewart decided to take a public stand on what had been until then largely a matter of private speculation. On April 15, Ewart preached his first sermon on Acts 2:38 in a tent pitched just outside Los Angeles in the town of Belvedere. On Cook's return shortly afterwards, he and Ewart set up a baptismal tank in the tent, rebaptized each other "in the Name of Jesus," and called on others to follow their example. Many of the Los Angeles Pentecostals who had flocked first to Seymour in 1906 and 1907, and then to Durham in 1911 and 1912, now pressed into Ewart's tent to be rebaptized.[8]

The new message was propagated through Ewart's periodical *Meat in*

Due Season, but failed to evoke a response beyond the West Coast until Cook made a swing through Pentecostal centers in the Midwest and South in the spring of 1915. Then, numbers of individuals and congregations were swept into the new movement, especially those associated with the newly organized Assemblies of God. In St. Louis, Cook rebaptized some forty persons in Mother Moise's Rescue Home, at that time the site of the Assemblies headquarters. In Indianapolis, 469 people, an alleged majority of the Pentecostals in that city, were rebaptized, including Garfield T. Haywood. Already familiar with the new message from his acquaintance with McAlister, Cook, and Ewart, Haywood was at the time a prominent member of the Assemblies of God. His widely read paper, *A Voice Crying in the Wilderness,* became the leading unofficial mouthpiece for "the New Issue."[9]

Alarmed by what they considered a dangerous and heretical development, the presbyters of the Assemblies of God met in special session at St. Louis in May and issued a statement condemning the new movement. At several conferences, like those at Hot Springs and Little Rock, Arkansas, the faithful were warned against "the Jesus Only heresy," and pastors were advised to deny its advocates the use of their pulpits.[10] Leaders of various Pentecostal associations, like Bell, Flower, Bartleman, Garr, and Andrew Fraser, wrote against the "New Issue" in Pentecostal periodicals.[11]

But the tide could not be stemmed. At the Assemblies of God camp meeting in Jackson, Tennessee, in the summer of 1915, Eudorus N. Bell, who had been the first chairman of the Assemblies and was at the time editor of both of that denomination's official periodicals; and H. G. Rodgers, pioneer of the Pentecostal movement in the Southeast, were rebaptized "in the Name of Jesus."[12]

In the lower Midwest the movement gained a firm foothold, winning all the Assemblies' preachers in Louisiana and numbers also in Texas, Arkansas, and Oklahoma. Daniel C. O. Opperman, the second highest official of the Assemblies, and Howard Goss, principal founder of that organization, were both won over and rebaptized. Opperman's periodical, *The Blessed Truth,* trumpeted the new teaching throughout the region. By the end of the summer it seemed the Assemblies of God was about to succumb entirely to the "Jesus Only" movement, while substantial numbers of Pentecostals in other denominations as well as many "independents" were also embracing the new ritual and message.[13]

More than any other, J. Roswell Flower was responsible for organizing a reaction that eventually led to official repudiation of the new movement and eviction of its adherents from the Assemblies. As acting editor of *Word and Witness* and the *Weekly Evangel* while Bell was out rebaptizing the faithful at summer camps around the country, Flower issued a call for a meeting of the General Council in October to resolve the controversy. In preparation, Flower lined up support among the presbyters for squelching the new movement.[14]

When the General Council convened in Turner Hall, St. Louis, on October 1, neither Arch P. Collins nor Opperman (chairman and assistant chairman, respectively) was present, both being opposed to Flower's purposes. If they hoped by their absence to prevent or delay the proceedings, they had not reckoned on the determination of the Flower faction. Flower took it upon himself to open the session and appoint J. W. Welch to chair the meeting, a function he continued to perform even after Collins showed up a day or two later.[15]

Yet the Flower faction refrained from an all-out showdown. The debate on the baptismal formula made it clear that outright rejection of the new movement would lead to the defection of so many that the infant organization would perhaps be destroyed. A resolution was adopted condemning several minor notions held within the "Jesus Only" faction, but the choice of baptismal formula was left to the conscience of baptizer and baptized. All ministers were admonished against preaching on the issue in such a way as to divide "the brethren" until a final decision could be rendered at the next General Council meeting a year later.[16]

The Flower faction, however, did succeed in weeding out from positions of authority every official who showed the least sympathy for the new movement. Bell, Collins, Opperman, Goss, and Bennett F. Lawrence were all replaced by opponents of the "New Issue." Thereafter, the new leaders, believing that time was on their side, threw a blanket over the issue in hopes it would fade away by the time of the next Council session. The Assemblies' periodicals during the following year carried only a very few articles on the "New Issue," all designed to minimize its significance.[17]

But even before the 1915 Council, and increasingly so afterwards, the "New Issue" involved much more than rebaptism and the proper formula to be used. As those who administered the rite reflected on the practice, they were led to seek a theological basis for it. The consequence was a new revelation of the nature of the Godhead and the introduction of several corollary ideas and practices.[18]

The "Oneness" Pentecostals, as they soon preferred to call themselves, adopted a unitarian position. There is, they said, only one person
in the Godhead, and that person is Jesus. The reason for the use of the
Acts 2:38 baptismal formula was that "Father, Son, and Holy Ghost" are
not proper names, but rather the titles or offices of the one God whose
name is Jesus. This was, they said, clearly understood by the early
Church. When the Apostles baptized in the name of Jesus, they were not
disobeying the commandment of Jesus recorded in Matthew 28:19;
rather, they were consciously "fulfilling" that commandment, since they
knew that the name of the Father, and of the Son, and of the Holy Ghost
is "Jesus." However, concomitant with the general apostasy that led to
the formation of the Catholic Church, the truth of the "Oneness" of the
Godhead had been "lost" and replaced by the heathen, polytheistic doctrine of the Trinity. Now, at "the end time," the "true" doctrine of the
Godhead and the correct mode of water baptism, along with all the other
original truths of the "full gospel," were being restored to the "true"
Church in preparation for the Second Coming. Rebaptism in the name of
Jesus was essential because baptism in the name of Father, Son, and Holy
Ghost carried the connotation, albeit an unintended one, of belief in three
gods.[19]

Moreover, "Oneness" leaders held that salvation did not come through
faith in the substitutionary atonement of Christ alone, as Pentecostals and
indeed Fundamentalists generally maintained. Rather, Acts 2:38 clearly
set forth a three-fold "plan of salvation": faith in Christ, water baptism
in the name of Jesus, and the Baptism in the Holy Spirit with speaking in
tongues. Without fulfilling all three steps, it was argued, one could not
confidently claim "full salvation." Some Oneness spokesmen equated
the completion of the third step, Spirit Baptism, with the New Birth.[20]

Finally, the Oneness camp also claimed that the communion service
had been corrupted by those who substituted grape juice for wine. In their
insistence that wine must be used in order to fulfill the commandment of
Jesus, they were, of course, challenging one of the most universally held
Pentecostal taboos.[21]

At the time of the 1915 Council meeting of the Assemblies of God,
these additional notions were not universally entertained by those who
favored rebaptism "according to Acts 2:38." Several of these points
were condemned by a statement published in the *Weekly Evangel* just
prior to the convening of that Council. Among the signers were Goss,
Opperman, Bell, and Rodgers, all of whom had been rebaptized and were

recognized leaders of the "New Issue" movement. Submission to rebaptism at this time did not imply rejection of the Trinity. Bell, for instance, was rebaptized and administered the rite to others, but he did not at any time during his temporary association with the movement adopt either the unitarian doctrine or any of the other notions noted above. The same was true of L. V. Roberts, who was rebaptized by Cook, and subsequently rebaptized both Bell and Rodgers. Not until several years later was the "Oneness" wing of the Pentecostal movement unambiguously committed to unitarianism, and when this happened some champions of rebaptism "in Jesus' Name," like L. V. Roberts, repudiated the movement.[22]

Between the 1915 and 1916 meetings of the General Council of the Assemblies, the "Oneness" movement continued to grow, despite the news blackout imposed by most Pentecostal periodicals. And, as it grew, the unitarian theology propounded only by some of its earliest leaders became more widely accepted. The optimism of the Flower faction proved unfounded, and they braced for a showdown on the issue, which by 1916 clearly threatened to alter fundamentally the character of the Assemblies of God, if not to destroy it entirely.[23]

When the Council convened in St. Louis in October 1916, the Flower faction was determined to force the minority group to reaffirm Trinitarianism or leave the organization. The "Oneness" leaders at the session, Goss, Haywood, Opperman, and Ewart (who attended and spoke though he was not a member), were by then firmly grounded in unitarianism, but recognized that a stand on that issue would certainly meet with defeat, since not even all of their followers had as yet adopted it. They chose instead to make their stand on an issue that promised to win the support even of those who were unsympathetic to rebaptism. They would hold the Council to its original promise never to adopt a statement of doctrine that would disfellowship anyone, so long as he accepted Spirit baptism and speaking in tongues. The association, they correctly argued, had determined from the first to be a fellowship bound together by the Spirit alone, and not by "man-made" doctrines and regulations.[24]

The Flower group, however, had complete control of the proceedings. A committee composed entirely of staunch anti-Oneness people, including Bell, who had been fully reclaimed, was appointed (not elected) to draw up a "Statement of Fundamental Truths." The result came as a surprise to no one. Roughly one half of the verbiage was devoted to a reaffirmation of Trinitarianism and a thorough repudiation of Oneness theology. In the point-by-point deliberations on the statement, the Oneness faction argued and voted against each of the sixteen items, despite their agreement with all but the one on the Godhead. "You are making a creed," explained Goss, "and I am opposed to it." The tactic, however, did not work. The statement was accepted as written amid the singing of the words from an old anthem, "God in three persons, blessed Trinity."[25]

Although the "Statement of Fundamental Truths" allowed for the use of complementary baptismal formulas, it made Matthew 28:19 compulsory in all baptismal services, and also made belief in the Trinity a test of membership.[26]

The victory of the Trinitarians was a costly one in the short run. More than one fourth of the ministers affiliated with the Assemblies left, taking an indeterminate number of congregations and individuals with them. Nor were they all Oneness believers. Some left because they saw too close a similarity between the curt treatment accorded the Oneness people by Assemblies officials and what they had received at the hands of Holiness officials not many years earlier. Deeply rooted antipathies toward all organization were reawakened by the Oneness episode. In the eyes of some, the Assemblies was exposed for what those who rejected it from the first had charged: Satan's snare for bringing once more into bondage those who had been liberated by the Spirit.[27]

Yet in the long run, the ejection of the "Jesus Onlies" proved well worth the temporary decline in numbers and prestige. The Assemblies came to be regarded by many Pentecostals as the defender of orthodox, Fundamentalist Pentecostalism against heresy. Within a year the Assemblies had all but recovered its losses, and soon became by far the largest Pentecostal denomination.[28]

Goss, Opperman, and other Oneness leaders organized the General Assembly of the Apostolic Assemblies early in 1917, which before the end of the year merged into the Pentecostal Assemblies of the World. By this time, the latter organization had become unitarian under the influence of Haywood, who concentrated his efforts within that fellowship after leaving the Assemblies in 1916. Other, smaller Oneness denominations and associations were formed through the 1920's, but substantial numbers of Oneness assemblies remained aloof from all organization.[29]

The divisions over the New Issue or Oneness movement were largely restricted to the Finished Work wing of the Pentecostal movement. As we have noted, Finished Work organizations were typically rather loose associations, like the Assemblies of God until 1916. Many Finished Work

Pentecostals were affiliated with completely autonomous local assemblies. The organizational structure of that wing of the movement, therefore, facilitated the work of proselytizing Oneness evangelists. Furthermore, those who had only recently accepted Durham's revelation on sanctification were no doubt somewhat more open for new revelations than those who had not.

Some Second Work Pentecostals were won to the unitarian faith, but mostly on an individual basis. None of the established Second Work Pentecostal communions was split in the way the Assemblies had been. The more highly developed organization of Second Work denominations and their more thorough grounding in Holiness "orthodoxy" enabled them to weather this second challenge to "the Apostolic Faith" as they had the first. Oneness advocates found it difficult if not impossible to propagate their message from Second Work pulpits. Resistance to the earlier Finished Work movement, moreover, had placed Second Work Pentecostals on their guard against new revelations. Parham, Crawford, and others delighted in pointing out that persons experiencing the Pentecostal Baptism in the Spirit without first passing through a second, definite experience of sanctification had in fact received a Satanic counterfeit. That "heresies" like unitarianism should arise among such people was only to be expected; heresy was the logical and inevitable consequence of departing from the "true" doctrine of sanctification.[30]

The controversy over the New Issue within the Assemblies of God was closely linked with an internal struggle for power between two rival leadership groups. The Assemblies had come into existence at the call of the five leaders of the white ministers of the Church of God in Christ who signed the announcement of the 1914 Hot Springs convention published in *Word and Witness*—Bell, Goss, Opperman, Collins and Pinson—and H. G. Rodgers.[31]

Representatives of various Pentecostal fellowships all over the country attended the Hot Springs convention of 1914. Among them was a group of leaders from the upper Midwest and the Northeast, most of whom had been associated earlier with the Christian and Missionary Alliance. They were J. Roswell Flower (former Alliance adherent and protege of the ex-Alliance minister D. W. Myland), John W. Welch and Daniel W. Kerr (both past officials of the Alliance), and Thomas K. Leonard (sometime pastor in the Christian Church). This group had bargaining leverage in the form of publishing facilities and a Bible school at Findlay, Ohio.[32]

Rivalry between these two groups was evident from the outset. The first order of business at Hot Springs was the appointment of a committee headed by Bell and Goss to draft a resolution as a basis for organizing the new domination. At the same time, an unofficial committee headed by Leonard and Flower met secretly to draft its own resolution. The report of the secret committee was the one adopted by the Council, but the Northern, former Alliance group did not succeed in winning control of the organization. Of the four general officers chosen, three represented the Southern, former Church of God in Christ group—Bell, Collins, and Bennet F. Lawrence—while Flower was the sole representative of the rival faction. The twelve presbyters chosen included five of the Southern leadership group and four of the Northern. The authority to issue ministerial credentials for the North and East was given to Leonard; for the South and West, to Goss.[33]

In the course of the controversy over the New Issue, the leadership and organizational structure of the Assemblies were significantly altered. At the conclusion of the 1916 Council, the Northern, former Alliance group was firmly fixed in the saddle. Every one of the six Southern, former Church of God in Christ leaders who had spearheaded the creation of the Assemblies was stripped of his authority. Goss, Opperman, and Rodgers, staunch Oneness men, were forced to leave the Assemblies. Collins, who refused to join the Flower faction in evicting the Oneness advocates, remained in the Assemblies but lost his position as chairman. M. M. Pinson was more interested in missionary work than in high office, and therefore posed no real threat to the Flower party's drive for leadership. Yet, despite this, and despite his strong opposition to the Oneness teaching, Pinson was not among the presbyters chosen in 1916.[34]

Eudorus N. Bell's ambivalence throughout the controversy reflected his role as a link between the rival groups following the organization of the Assemblies in 1914. Bell had moved his printing equipment from Malvern, Arkansas, to combine it with Leonard's at Findlay, Ohio, and had taken a post on the staff of the Bible school there. When the split over the New Issue came, he finally cast his lot, somewhat reluctantly, with the Trinitarians. But he had compromised himself by being rebaptized, and he, too, was removed from his position as editor of the Assemblies' official organs.[35]

A new organizational structure also emerged as a consequence of the New Issue controversy, marking the beginning of a trend that would soon transform the Assemblies from a loose association into a centralized denomination. The number of general officers was reduced from four to two: chairman and secretary. In 1915, Welch replaced Collins in the top post, and Stanley H. Frodsham, who emerged during the dispute as a staunch supporter of the Flower faction, was elected to the second spot. The chairman and secretary constituted a new Credentials Committee, which was charged with renewing all ministerial credentials annually to insure conformity with the new Statement of Faith. They also served as members of the new, more powerful five-man Executive Presbytery; the other members were Flower, Kerr, and D. B. Rickard. A more reliable income for the national organization was assured by the charging of fees for issuing and renewing credentials, and by the adoption of a resolution charging all ministers to teach tithing.[36]

Power politics does not in itself explain the Oneness schism in the Assemblies of God, much less the split in the Pentecostal movement as a whole. Some insight into other forces operating in the division over the New Issue may be gained from an examination of the distribution and composition of the Oneness movement in relation to the other principal segments of the Pentecostal movement.

The Oneness movement fell far short of early expectations, or fears, that it might sweep the bulk of Pentecostals into its fold. By the end of the 1920's fewer than one in ten of all Pentecostals and only one of every seven Finished Work Pentecostals were unitarians. Regionally, the Oneness movement came to be limited almost entirely to the Midwest, where more than nine of every ten of their number were concentrated. In the East North Central states, nearly one of every four Pentecostals had embraced the unitarian faith by the early 1930's. The real center of their strength lay in the urban areas of Illinois, Indiana, Ohio, and Michigan.[37]

Oneness Pentecostals were even more urban than either Second Work or Finished Work Trinitarians. More than seven of every ten Oneness people resided in urban areas. In New England, where there were only a handful of unitarian Pentecostals, and in the lower Midwest, the Oneness movement was less urban than the Pentecostal movement as a whole. In the upper Midwest, where Pentecostals of all persuasions were most urban and where Oneness Pentecostals were concentrated, there was no appreciable difference between unitarians and Trinitarians. Everywhere else Oneness Pentecostals were more urban than were Trinitarian Pentecostals, with about nine out of ten of those in the Middle Atlantic, West North Central, and Pacific Coast states residing in urban areas. Black unitarians were all but entirely urban.[38]

There is no need, of course, to discuss the religious influences that held

Table 5. Urban and Racial Distributions of 3 "Oneness" Pentecostal Denominations by Region, 1936

Region	Total Member-ship	Urban	White*	Black**	Inter-racial ***	Per Cent of Total			
						Urban	White	Black	Inter-racial
New England	93	53	0	33	60	51.9	0.0	35.6	64.5
Middle Atlantic	1,320	1,194	26	735	559	90.5	1.9	55.7	42.4
East North Central	12,413	10,843	1,690	3,160	7,563	85.2	13.6	25.6	60.8
West North Central	3,481	3,115	1,347	787	1,347	89.5	38.7	22.6	38.7
South Atlantic	2,595	1,641	197	84	2,314	63.2	7.6	3.2	89.2
East South Central	1,970	630	1,327	263	380	31.9	67.3	13.3	19.4
West South Central	6,892	3,022	3,520	138	3,234	43.9	51.1	2.0	46.9
Mountain	1,090	693	705	0	385	63.5	64.7	.0	35.3
Pacific	1,510	1,308	869	413	228	86.6	57.5	27.3	15.2
Totals	31,464	22,499	9,681	5,713	16,070	71.5	30.8	18.1	51.1

*The Pentecostal Church, Inc.
**Pentecostal Assemblies of the World
***Pentecostal Assemblies of Jesus Christ

most Pentecostals firm in Trinitarianism, because all Pentecostals prided themselves on their thoroughgoing orthodoxy. Even had there been no other, social, forces operating in conjunction with the Oneness controversy, unitarianism in and of itself would have been sufficient to cause schism.

But why should some Pentecostals have turned from the orthodox doctrine of the Trinity? There is no hint of influence from historic Unitarianism. Indeed, because it denied the deity of Jesus, traditional Unitarianism was, if anything, more anathema to Oneness Pentecostals than others. There is nothing in the religious background of the most promi-

Table 6. Urban and Racial Distribution of Combined Memberships of 26 Pentecostal Denominations by Doctrinal Divisions

	% Urban	% Black
All Pentecostals	62.4	19.7*
Second Work Pentecostals	54.9	29.3
Finished Work Trinitarians	66.8	1.0
Oneness Pentecostals	71.5	43.7*

*These figures are estimates derived by dividing the interracial percentages found in Table 2 between black and white, equally.

nent Oneness leaders to differentiate them significantly in religious orientation from other Pentecostals. Goss had been raised an "infidel," but so too had Mrs. Crawford, one of the most outspoken critics of unitarian Pentecostalism. Opperman had been a leader in the somewhat eccentric Dowie sect, but Flower and numbers of others in the Assemblies of God had also been Dowie-ites at some time. Nothing is known of Haywood's earlier religious associations. Andrew Urshan, a well-known Persian-American Pentecostal who emerged as an outstanding Oneness spokesman a few years after the Assemblies of God schism, had been first a Methodist and then an Alliance adherent, as had so many of those Pentecostals who remained Trinitarians.

Nevertheless, Pentecostals who accepted the Oneness faith were more willing to break forthrightly with the evangelical Protestant theological tradition, and were more open to new revelations. Their predisposition to more radical religion may reflect a higher degree of alienation and a somewhat lower socio-economic status as compared with their fellow believers in the Finished Work who retained their Trinitarian faith.

Nearly half of the Oneness Pentecostals were black—the most ostracized, alienated and impoverished social group in America—while only a handful of blacks were to be found among Finished Work Trinitarians. Further, the per capita expenditures of the Finished Work Trinitarian denominations included in the 1936 census were fifty percent greater than those of the Oneness groups listed there.[39]

The Oneness schism cut across the Pentecostal movement, but not everywhere to the same degree. It was primarily a split within the Finished Work camp, and largely limited to the upper Midwest. The heavily black and urban character of the Oneness movement, the suggestion of a somewhat lower socio-economic level than that of other Pentecostals, and the existence of a struggle between competing leadership groups in the major Finished Work denomination—all these indicate the influence of significant social differences on what was for the Pentecostal movement a crucial theological conflict. The religious factors that predisposed some Pentecostals to unitarian theology, however, are largely obscure.

Within a decade of the initial Pentecostal Revival, the movement, aside from its fragmentation into innumerable minor factions, had split into three major doctrinal segments: Second Work Trinitarians, Finished Work Trinitarians, and unitarians (who were all of Finished Work persuasion). Within another two decades the color line had been drawn through all three segments. Unlike the principal doctrinal controversies, the race issue did not arise in the movement as a whole at any particular time. Rather, it emerged in one denomination after another, beginning early in the life of the movement and reaching a peak in the 1920's, but did not permanently split the Oneness wing until the mid-1930's.

The first racial fissure in the Pentecostal movement actually appeared during the revival of 1906. In the very year that it was swept into the Pentecostal revival, 1907, the Fire-Baptized Holiness Church suffered a schism when its black members left to organize the Fire-Baptized Holiness Church of God. Later, the white group merged in 1911 with the integrated Holiness Church of North Carolina to form the Pentecostal Holiness Church. Within two years, the blacks, already organized into a separate conference within the new denomination, were voted out by the white majority.[40]

Seymour's integrated Pacific Coast Apostolic Faith Movement became largely black when, in 1911, Mrs. Crawford's Northern wing broke away, charging Seymour had rejected the Second Work view of sanctification, and most of the white adherents of Azusa Mission left him asserting that he had rejected the Finished Work view! Seymour soon faded into obscurity, the pastor of a single congregation composed of a relatively small number of loyal blacks.[41]

A number of white Pentecostal preachers secured licensing credentials from Bishop Mason's black Church of God in Christ in the years from about 1910 to 1914. The black group was at that time one of the few legally incorporated Pentecostal denominations, so that those licensed or ordained by it could perform marriages and secure clergy rates on the railroads. The whites appear to have operated independently, using the name Church of God in Christ with no indication of its connection with the black group, and publishing their own official organ, *Word and Witness*.

While the exact relationship between the whites and blacks in the Church of God in Christ is uncertain, two things seem clear. First, the Church of God in Christ was not a fully integrated communion, and, second, the independent course taken by the whites was by mutual consent. In 1914, the leading white ministers of the Church of God in Christ were chiefly responsible for organizing the Assemblies of God at Hot Springs, Arkansas—an action that ended their connections with the black Church of God in Christ. Nevertheless, no hostility, racial or other, seems to have been involved, since Bishop Mason addressed that organizing meeting and gave his blessing to the new denomination. Although nearly all the white Church of God in Christ ministers joined the Assemblies of God, a few remained with the black group. Moreover, the Assemblies of God included a substantial number of black Pentecostals from the North and upper Midwest who had not been associated with the Church of God in Christ. During the first couple of years, integrated congregations were common among Assemblies people, especially in the North. And at least one black, Garfield T. Haywood, achieved renown, though not high office, in the Assemblies.[42]

Following the Oneness schism, however, the Assemblies became an all but "lily white" denomination. If this was fortuitous it may also have been fortunate from the standpoint of the white Trinitarian majority. For there is at least the hint of racial antipathy in the records of the 1916 Council meeting that brought the final split over the New Issue. Haywood, the black Oneness champion, was singled out for derision at the hands of the Trinitarians. In a clearly recognized allusion to Haywood and his periodical, *A Voice Crying in the Wilderness,* T. K. Leonard called the doctrines of the unitarians "hay, wood and stubble," and charged that "they are all in the wilderness and they have a voice in the wilderness." In the words of an Assemblies' chronicler:

> Haywood turned pale and started to rise to his feet, but was pulled back into his chair by those sitting near him. . . . Gilbert Sweaza, a member from Southeast Missouri, red-faced and indignant, stomped out the door. Voices from both sides were raised in protest, and it was sometime before things quieted down. . . . From that time on, the advocates of the new doctrine took little part in the discussions, having come to the conclusion that opposition would be futile: the tide had definitely turned against them.[43]

Could it have been that racial animosities had contributed to the turn of the tide? Was the emergence of the Assemblies as a *de facto* "lily white" denomination a wholly unanticipated or unwelcome consequence of the doctrinal struggle? Since 1916, except for a few black faces here and there in urban congregations of the Northeast, the Assemblies has remained a white man's church.

The Pentecostals proved unable to resist the xenophobic impulses of the 1920's. During the initial dynamic phase of the Pentecostal movement, Parham's racial prejudices, clearly apparent in his earliest writings,[44] were held in abeyance. But following his ostracism from the movement as a whole, these underlying racial hostilities, nurtured perhaps by his rejection at the hands of his black protegé, Seymour, burst forth. Looking back on the Azusa Street meetings he had attended in the fall of 1906, during which he had been asked to leave, Parham said:

> There was a beautiful outpouring of the Holy Spirit in Los Angeles. . . . Then they pulled off all the stunts common in old camp meetings among colored folks. . . . That is the way they worship God, but what makes my soul sick, and make[s] me sick at my stomach is to see white people imitating unintelligent, crude negroism of the Southland, and laying it on the Holy Ghost.[45]

By the mid-20's, Parham was writing articles for the racist, anti-Semitic, anti-Catholic periodical of Gerald B. Winrod at Wichita, Kansas. Referring to the Klansmen, for whom he preached on occasion, as "those splendid men," Parham said that personal conversion and revival were necessary before they could expect to "realize their high ideals for the betterment of mankind."[46] Aimee McPherson also preached at Klonvocations occasionally. Some dozen years after its founding, Sister Aimee's International Church of the Foursquare Gospel claimed only 25 black members, who were organized separately within the denomination.[47]

Leading Pentecostal periodicals criticized the Klan and advised their readers to avoid it, but not because of its violent nativism. The official organ of the Assemblies of God, for example, conceded that "there may be true Christians in the Klan," but went on to say "they are severely misguided" since true Christians should not join secret, oath-bound societies. Criticism of the Klan on these grounds, with no mention of its racial and religious policies, was the typical Pentecostal attitude during the 1920's.[48]

It was during the 1920's that the color line was drawn through the Church of God (Cleveland, Tennessee). Except in the state of Florida during the years 1915–17, integration was the rule in the Church of God at the state and national levels, and fairly common even at the congregational level, until 1921. At the Annual Assembly of that year, the blacks were reorganized separately from the grass roots on up to their own black overseer. "I do not like any separations between nationalities and races," explained A. J. Tomlinson somewhat apologetically, "and yet it is not always convenient, neither is it best, for different races to meet together regularly for worship." The only connection between the racial segments of the Church of God for the next four years was the attendance of the white and black overseers at one another's segregated Annual Assemblies. Following the adoption of a resolution by the whites in 1926, black congregations were granted the right to send delegates to the white Assembly each year if they so desired. Few did.[49]

Even the Oneness Pentecostals, the most bi-racial wing of the movement, succumbed eventually to the color line. The Pentecostal Assemblies of the World was a fully integrated fellowship at every level from its founding in 1913, and especially so after 1917 when the predominantly white General Assembly of the Apostolic Assemblies merged into it to create a fairly even racial balance. The blacks, however, constituted a majority in the North, while the whites bulked larger in the South. Since the national conventions, like everything else, were integrated, it proved necessary to hold them above the Mason-Dixon line. Owing to the meager financial resources of the denomination, delegates to the convention were required to provide their own fare. This meant that relatively few Southerners, who had the longest distance to travel, could afford to attend. The upshot was that the whites as a whole found themselves consistently outnumbered and outvoted at the national conventions. The blacks too became dissatisfied when the Southern whites began to follow a *de facto* policy of segregation at the local level. The whites' explanation, that the prevailing mores of the region necessitated such a policy, was unacceptable to the blacks.[50]

As early as 1921 some of the white ministers began to hold Bible conferences of their own, and at the General Convention of 1924 a clean break was made when most of them left to organize several smaller associations. None of these fellowships was notably successful, however, and they began shortly to merge together.[51]

The largest of these white groups, the Apostolic Churches of Jesus Christ, opened discussions with the Pentecostal Assemblies of the World, looking toward the restoration of an integrated Oneness body. In 1931, at St. Louis, the merger was consummated with the creation of the Pentecostal Assemblies of Jesus Christ. But once again, from the outset, the same problems arose that had plagued the Pentecostal Assemblies of the World in its earlier integrated phase. A group of blacks bolted almost immediately to renew the charter of incorporation for the Pentecostal Assemblies of the World before it expired.[52]

Dissension continued between the blacks and whites in the new Pentecostal Assemblies of Jesus Christ and led once more to disruption. The whites' announcement that the convention of 1937 would be held in Tulsa, Oklahoma—a site unacceptable to the blacks—brought about the final split. Nearly all the blacks left to rejoin the Pentecostal Assemblies of the World; none showed up as delegates to the Tulsa convention.[53]

From 1937 on, then, the Oneness Pentecostals, like the Second Work and Finished Work Trinitarians, were largely divided along racial lines, despite their greater efforts over a longer period of time to resist the segregationist impulse. The predominantly black Pentecostal Assemblies of the World, however, continued to harbor a sizable white minority in its ranks, and thereby succeeded in retaining more of the movement's original integrated character than any other important Pentecostal denomination.

Yet, while the Pentecostals were largely *organized* into racially separate fellowships, this did not mean there was no contact between the races. Pentecostals of different persuasions and affiliations have always had the custom of visiting one another's services and joining together in revival campaigns, conventions, and camp meetings. This practice of "fellowshipping" often transcended racial barriers, especially in Northern urban areas, but elsewhere as well. Integrated Pentecostal meetings continued to be common even after the organizational separation of the races.[54] Taken as a whole, Pentecostals have probably retained as much contact and friendship between racial and, it might be added, ethnic groups as have the adherents of any other religious community in America.

The survival and growth of the Pentecostal movement despite the enormity and intensity of internal controversy and its singularly fragmented character were regarded by Pentecostals as something of a miracle. Each controversial issue was viewed by some group of Pentecostals as a demonic assault aimed at destroying the new movement, and the weathering of these attacks as proof of God's determination to preserve his work. Yet it may well be that the movement survived and grew, not in spite of these fratricidal conflicts, but because of them. Without the continuing stimulus provided by such agitation, the movement may have atrophied and died. Controversy became the very life and breath of the Pentecostal movement.[55]

Each new controversy arising anywhere among Pentecostals was soon known and discussed elsewhere. Periodicals reflecting every school of Pentecostal thought and even non-Pentecostal viewpoints were avidly read and passed on, thereby reaching numbers far exceeding circulation figures. Because of the practice of "fellowshipping," even minor dissensions within a single congregation would quickly spread to others.

Constant discussion, debate, the looking up of proof-texts, the necessity of taking a stand on innumerable issues of doctrine, polity, and practice—all these aroused and engaged the interests and passions of the Pentecostals. One's response to each new revelation was seen as a matter of great, often eternal import. The act of decision, then, dignified and enhanced the sense of individual worth.

Nor were the divisions flowing from controversy entirely liabilities. While they precluded the combination of their material resources for more effective allocation, those resources were extremely meager to begin with. The greatest asset of the movement was, after all, its human resources. Division meant competition. Pentecostal preachers and laymen alike were impelled to redouble their efforts to win converts and restore fellow Pentecostals in view of the devil's success in "deceiving even the very elect." Rivalry among Pentecostals for converts gave the movement added impetus.

Moreover, because Pentecostal leaders entrenched themselves in their positions, controversy became an institutionalized method for removing pastors and denominational officials or, failing that, establishing new fellowships. Internal dissension and schism constituted a means for the upward mobility of new leaders, either within existing organizations or through the creation of new ones. The multiplicity of Pentecostal groups, and the ease with which new ones could be started provided numerous positions of authority to which the ambitious and the talented could aspire.

Finally, discord and division had the effect of accelerating the normal process of institutionalization. Official doctrinal statements, rules, regulations, norms of behavior, and hierarchical bureaucratic structures—all widely condemned in the earliest years of the movement—were increasingly adopted and extended in order to resist each new "heresy" or safeguard each new "truth." Protecting the faithful from subversion necessitated institutionalization, and with institutionalization came a higher level of stability and an increase in the likelihood of survival.

XI

The Rejection of the World

All millenarian movements contain progressive-revolutionary potential. Their criticism of the status quo may be direct or veiled, but their vision and call for a new social order is in itself a condemnation of the present one. The degree to which the revolutionary potential of a millenarian movement is realized depends upon how it views the coming Millennium. If the movement sees itself as the divine agent for building the Millennium within the present, then reform or revolution will be the likely result. If it sees the Millennium being brought in miraculously from the outside without human effort, then withdrawal and accommodation will more likely be the consequence. The choice between these conceptions is not accidental, but is determined by such things as the class character, material and intellectual resources, ideology, and psychology of the movement, as well as the structure and stability of the social order.

I have earlier noted the great store of hostility and aggressiveness of the early Pentecostals, and have maintained that it arose from the frustrations imposed by their class position. If that hostility had found its natural outlet, the Pentecostals would have struggled against those responsible for their adverse social circumstances. They would have been social reformers or social revolutionaries. But because their aggressive impulses were displaced from their rightful object, they became conservative and reactionary.

In the earliest years the Pentecostal movement did indeed evidence the revolutionary potential of all millenarian movements, but conservative elements eventually triumphed over revolutionary and progressive ones.

The most remarkable manifestation of Pentecostal progressivism was its interracial, multi-ethnic composition. This was in itself a radical criticism of prevailing race relations and a radical departure from them. But, as we have seen, in time the Pentecostals succumbed to segregation.

This same mixture of revolutionary and conservative tendencies and the developing predominance of the latter was evident in Pentecostal attitudes toward social reform, the state and the political process, capitalism, and established religion. As millenarian hopes subsided, social criticism gave way to the celebration of the American way and radical impulses were submerged in a sea of conservatism and reaction.

It will be remembered that until the closing decades of the 19th century, revivalism, holiness, and social reform were integral and mutually supporting elements within the mainstream of evangelical Protestantism. Timothy Smith corrected an older view by showing that mid-19th-century revivalism and holiness were not socially reactionary. As postmillennialists, revivalistic and holiness leaders were committed to Christianizing America and the world. They were active in establishing benevolent societies and religious institutions that ministered to social and material as well as religious needs; they threw themselves into the temperance crusade; and many of their converts became ardent champions of various reform movements.[1]

But while Smith's conclusion that "liberalism on social issues, not reaction, was the dominant note which evangelical preachers sounded before 1860"[2] is probably correct, we should recognize that the dominant note was sounded with some ambivalence. On the question of slavery— the most burning social issue of the day—some, like Phoebe Palmer, insisted that religious institutions should maintain a neutral stance, while others, like Charles G. Finney, were cautious and hesitant.[3]

This ambivalence is understandable when we realize that the holiness revivalists perceived the mission of the Church to be the regeneration and reform of individuals (salvation and sanctification). Too great an emphasis on this could, of course, lead to privatism and the neglect of Christian social obligations, but too great an emphasis on social reform could undermine the "spirituality" of the faithful and divert the Church from its central task. The latter seems to have been perceived as the greater threat. Since it was believed that individual regeneration was the chief means of social reform, it was assumed either that social reform would automatically result from the conversion of masses of individuals, or that it would be carried out by those who had a special "calling" to such work. In any event, these attitudes militated against wholehearted corporate involvement of the churches and the benevolent societies in efforts to reform social institutions, much less the whole of society.

I think that a great deal of what Smith calls social reform might more accurately be designated as social welfare or poor relief that was ancillary to individual reform. Poor relief, of course, has been an integral part of the Christian tradition throughout its history. The more ardent advocates of holiness in the mid-nineteenth century may have been somewhat more active in such work than other church members, but much of it was conducted within denominational institutions such as extension missions and institutional churches, or interdenominational ones like the American Christian Commission, the YMCA, the Evangelical Alliance, and the Convention of Christian Workers.[4] For the period during which the Holiness movement remained entirely in the churches, it is hardly possible to assert that social welfare work was the concern of the Holiness movement in contradistinction to the denominations.

When many Holiness believers left the churches to join the independent Holiness movement in the late 19th century, the social welfare aspects of denominational work suffered and the generally conservative hierarchy of the denominations cooled toward such activity. This was because workers in the city missions were often the source of independent Holiness schisms from the denominations,[5] and because the emergent Social Gospelers were pressing for church involvement in social reform that would go well beyond poor relief. Both movements represented a threat to the position and authority of the established hierarchies.

The part of the Holiness movement that embarked upon an independent course outside the established churches also evidenced a diminishing social concern and involvement, notwithstanding the notable exception of the Salvation Army and its offshoot, the Volunteers of America—which, in any event, were not indigenous developments but British imports. These organizations and to a lesser extent many other independent Holiness institutions, certainly concerned themselves with more than personal salvation and piety. They established residential shelters, distributed food and clothing, and provided job training, placement, and direct employment in industrial missions. They rendered material and moral support to the poor and the dissolute and did so without regard for the ethnic, racial, or sexual status of their clients. They frequently engaged in social criticism and occasionally became directly involved in political action to ameliorate the conditions of the poor.[6]

But it would be a mistake to conclude that the *independent* Holiness people of the *late* 19th century were incipient Social Gospelers or that their intention or achievement was social reform. More so than their forebears, the independent Holiness people saw the source of social problems in fallen human nature, which found expression in the social order through individual men. The solution was clear: men must be saved and sanctified, that is, morally regenerated as individuals. Thus, while considerable social welfare and some direct and indirect social reform accompanied Holiness efforts, these must be seen as byproducts of a movement that was essentially and increasingly individualistic, not social, in orientation. "Soul-saving" remained the basic aim of the independent Holiness movement, and its ministry to the material needs of the poor was quite simply a necessary means to that end. As the superintendent of one Holiness mission put it, "if the transients are not interested in hearing the gospel, we're not interested in feeding them."[7]

The independent Holiness movement did indeed contain progressive elements, but its overall impact was, I believe, conservative. Certainly the leading professional revivalists who preached holiness and were held in high regard by the movement were conservative on most social, economic, and political issues.[8] Some spokesmen for the Holiness movement did, however, at times engage in denunciations of men of wealth, the unjust distribution of income, and the superior rights of property over human welfare, but such criticism was very infrequently followed by action to effect social change. As Norris Alden Magnuson says, "gospel welfare leaders made their primary contribution to social concern and social justice at the point of agitation for a change *in attitude* toward the lower classes."[9]

Their influence upon the poor themselves was to inculcate honesty, sobriety, and hard work within the framework of submission to authority and acceptance of the status quo. Their belief in individual salvation and sanctification as the solution to society's problems, as Magnuson says, "obviously worked to the benefit of the established order."[10] Their generally hostile attitude toward labor unions and socialism did the same.

While the ameliorative effects of Holiness social work, limited as it was, should not be underestimated, much less denigrated, its conservative effects must be recognized as far more significant. The nature and extent of Holiness social criticism and activism was such that the existing order could respond to it with extremely modest reforms or none at all. The enthusiastic praise and support of Holiness welfare work by employers, public officials, and the formulators of public opinion show clearly that far from viewing that work as a threat to social order, they rightly saw it as a bulwark of it.[11]

By the time of the first world war, the tension between individualistic pietism and social concern in the Holiness movement was broken. Individual pietism became largely the province of the sects and the Social Gospel triumphed in the commanding heights of the mainline denominations. The independent Holiness churches began to move out of their downtown missions and into church buildings in residential middle-class neighborhoods, and in the process abandoned much of their social welfare work among the poor.[12] Within the Salvation Army and the Volunteers of America the material emphasis had by then largely overshadowed individual salvation and sanctification.[13] It is hardly coincidental that it was precisely at this time that the Church of the Nazarene switched from postmillennialism to premillennialism, following a trend that began earlier in those regional Holiness associations that bolted from the ardently postmillennialist National Holiness Association.[14]

It was from within a Holiness movement that was becoming increasingly premillennialist, withdrawn from social concern and preoccupied with personal pietism that the Pentecostal movement was born—and its original constituency came from those fringe groups that had already been repudiated by the main body of Holiness believers partly because those very trends were so much more advanced among them.

Given the poor, working class character of the Pentecostal movement, it is hardly surprising that its faith centered on an imminent Millennium to be established by divine intervention on the Apocalyptic ruins of the present world. If the world could only grow worse and would soon be destroyed, there was little point in confronting it and struggling to make it better. "There is a false theology," said the *Pentecostal Evangel*, "that tells us that the result of the influence of the Church and Christendom upon the world will be an age of peace. The Bible never teaches it." Recounting the litany of the "signs of the times"—wars, famines, pestilence, false prophets, crime, and immorality—the article concluded that the Christian's duty was "Save others! Save others! Save others!"[15] A writer for the *Latter Rain Evangel* prophesied these and greater calamities and asked, "What is the remedy for It? What can we do to arrest the downward current? Nothing! It is too late to patch up this old world.

. . . Our duty, our objective is to get men ready for the next age."[16]

Discussing the "Christian's Relation to World Reform," the English Pentecostal J. T. Boddy told his American readers,

> In the face of the appeals made to the Christian today to join hands with the world in pushing its noisy reforms (most of which, whether secular or religious, are Satan-inspired), what course should we pursue? . . . let Caesar look after his own. . . . While reforms may serve as temporary plasters upon the moral ulcers of the world, they can never reach the seat of the trouble, to effect a permanent cure. . . . The world may be satisfied with patchwork . . . but the child of God should not be unequally yoked with unbelievers and backsliders in their apparently worthy efforts for the self-betterment of the world.

To those who might object to this stance with the question, "Would you let the world go to the devil, then?", Boddy responded, "No certainly not; we don't have to, it is there already. . . . the only permanent remedy for the existing state of things . . . and the hope of this old, sin-wrecked world is the personal coming of Jesus into it."[17]

Even institutions only modestly involved in charitable endeavors fell under Pentecostal condemnation, though not so much because of their philanthropy as for their secret, "oath-bound" character, and because their memberships were composed of "unbelievers." All lodges were "unfruitful works of darkness" which would unite under Freemasonry, "the mother of them all," and "go against the religion of Jesus Christ." Parham gave up his membership in a lodge when he went Holiness and remained a critic of lodges thereafter. Lodge members were ineligible for membership in the Church of God (Cleveland, Tennessee) and probably many other Pentecostal churches, for, as Robert A. Brown asked rhetorically in a sermon against Freemasonry, "What concord hath Christ with Belial?"[18]

That one looks in vain for any glimmer of Pentecostal social activism beyond individual acts of charity at the congregational level before the second world war is hardly surprising in a movement that coupled the YMCA and the Student Volunteer Movement together with "Bolshevism" as "foreshadowings" of the reign of Antichrist.[19] The absence of all social welfare work among first generation Pentecostals and its paucity thereafter is suggested by an Assemblies of God historian's careful accounting of that denomination's "welfare activities." Nothing whatever is mentioned before the establishment in 1935 of a fund for aged ministers, which was later revised so that these ministers themselves had to contribute to it from their salaries. A children's home, founded earlier at the individual initiative of a Pentecostal woman, was incorporated into the organization in 1947, and a second one was set up in 1966. A "Home for the Aged" was established in 1948 but soon abandoned because it was "too costly to maintain." A "Retirement Center" was opened in 1960 to which an infirmary was added five years later. And disaster relief funds were distributed to rebuild several Assemblies churches that had been hard hit by a Louisiana hurricane in 1962.[20] This is the sum total of more than a half-century of "welfare activities" by the world's largest and wealthiest Pentecostal denomination. The record of other Pentecostal churches is similar, except for some black groups in recent years.

In a 1968 "Statement of Social Concern," the Assemblies continued to assert the original position that social ills were caused by man's sinful nature and that while "community-betterment projects and legislative action on social improvement . . . should be prominent in our society," these could only deal with "symptoms." The real solution could be found only in "the power of the Holy Spirit to change the lives of men." While "racism" was deplored and "equal opportunity" praised, greater emphasis was laid upon the condemnation of "rebellion," "devised confrontations," "clashes," and "revolution" and upon the support of "law enforcement." Any clear-cut institutional commitment to integration or social justice was carefully avoided.[21]

In a 1934 article entitled "The Solution to the World's Problems," the *Latter Rain Evangel* proclaimed that "These troubles, political, social, industrial, religious and otherwise can never be settled until the glorious Son of God comes back. . . . The question is now, How shall we escape the Tribulation period?"[22] As late as 1958 the general superintendent of the Assemblies of God, Ralph M. Riggs, echoed these sentiments when he said, "the human race has reached the end of the present age and is passing into a new era which will bring great tribulation to the non-Christians but great triumph to the Christians," and that the objective of the Pentecostal movement was "To give people a chance to come into the ark of safety before the storm."[23] Not society, but the individual; not reform, but escape—that has been the heart of Pentecostal social theory.[24]

The Pentecostal movement was a force for social conservatism in that it abstained from social involvement and disparaged all social ameliorative efforts by others. Reform was futile because the degeneration and dissolution of the present world system was prophesied in the Bible. Thus, by default, example, and discouragement of others, the Pentecostals contributed to the preservation of the status quo. Yet their wholesale condemnation of the world and all its works and their longing for the fulfillment of its imminent destruction constituted a radical criticism of society. The Pentecostals were asocial in practice, but antisocial and therefore potentially revolutionary in impulse.

The *Christian Evangel* expressed typical Pentecostal sentiments when it greeted the outbreak of the first world war with scarcely disguised jubilation: "War! War!! War!!!: The Nations of Europe Battle and Unconsciously Prepare the Way for the Return of the Lord Jesus to Establish His Kingdom Upon the Earth."[25] Frank Bartleman pronounced that the war was God's judgment on all nations, called on the innocent peoples of all nations to have no part in the war, and most strenuously denounced the pro-war appeals of religious leaders. "Patriotism," lamented Bartleman, "has been fanned into a flame. The religious passion has been invoked, and the national gods called upon for defense in each case. What blasphemy! . . . It is simply wholesale murder. It is nothing short of hell. And yet they glorify it."[26] The *Midnight Cry* asserted that Pentecostals could not go to war "and still retain the Spirit of God."[27]

When the United States entered the war, Pentecostal organizations everywhere voiced the view that their members should seek either conscientious objector or non-combatant status.[28] The General Council of the Assemblies of God affirmed its conviction that the Bible teaches conscientious objection, but said that its members whose consciences allowed them to bear arms were free to do so.[29] A. J. Tomlinson's Church of God was so outspoken in its criticism of combatant service that it was investigated by the United States Department of Justice for disloyalty.[30] Some Pentecostals suffered persecution for preaching against the bearing of arms.[31]

To allay suspicions that resistance to military service might contain within it the seeds of resistance to state authority in general—which indeed it did—Pentecostal leaders strenuously protested their loyalty, obedience, and subservience to the government and its laws in all other respects. Thus, the Assemblies of God adopted a resolution of "unswerving loyalty to our Government and to its Chief Executive, President Wilson" and pledged itself "to assist in every way morally possible, consistent with our faith, in bringing the present 'World War' to a successful conclusion.'' Announcing with pleasure the expression of similar sentiments by all the district councils, and the decision of the Texas District Council to cancel the ministerial credentials of anyone speaking against the government, the *Christian Evangel* told its readers, "Submit yourself to every ordinance of man *for the Lord's sake*" because " 'the powers that be are ordained of God,' and if we resist them we 'resist God.' "[32]

Submission to state authority was no mere wartime expedient, but rather a consistent orientation of the Pentecostal movement. The faithful were told to "recognize the officers of the law as God's ministers," and reminded that it was their "duty as Christian citizens" to respect, obey, and uphold all those in authority.[33] F. J. Lee preached a sermon entitled "Jesus Teaches Respect for the Law," in which he quoted with approval the assertion of Cardinal Mercier that "There is no perfect Christian who is not also a perfect patriot."[34] Donald Gee felt obliged to preface his denunciation of "unthinking patriotism" and the bearing of arms with the statement that

> It cannot be stated too emphatically that it is the duty of the Christian to be in subjection to the powers that be. . . . Absolute loyalty to the State must be the declared and actual policy of any section of the Christian church that aims at the approval of God.[35]

In time these sentiments undermined and reversed the Pentecostals' initial position on military service. In the interwar period the Church of God's strong ruling "against members going to war" was revised to read "against going to war in combatant service," and the General Conference of the Pentecostal Holiness Church rejected the Oklahoma District's motion to condemn military service and the bearing of arms.[36] During World War II, A. J. Tomlinson upheld the justice of the American cause and reassured those of his followers who chose to fight that responsibility for the bloodshed was not theirs but the government's.[37] The *Glad Tidings Herald* proclaimed that the "enemies of the Gospel of Christ must not win this war" and lauded those Pentecostals who were "nobly serving in the defense of civilization."[38] The Pentecostal Holiness Church turned away from all resistance to military service and called for "total support of the war effort," and its chief bishop, Dan T. Muse, condemned the "foolhardy," "fanatical" war protestors, saying that those who refused to register for the draft dishonored the cause of God.[39] The official position of the Church of God (Cleveland, Tennessee) continued to be conscientious objection or refusal to bear arms, but few of its members complied and at the very end of the war its stance was altered to reflect this. Members were allowed liberty of conscience to choose combatant, non-combatant, or conscientious objector status.[40] The Assemblies of God also held fast to its conscientious objection or noncombatant stand during the war, but most of its members like those of nearly all other Pentecostal denominations chose to accept combatant service. Finally, in 1967, it too adopted the Church of God position.[41]

The Pentecostal acceptance of combatant military duty signalled the death of all resistance and the near total subservence of the movement to the authority of the state. The kind of patriotism and glorification of war that Bartleman had excoriated in 1915 were embraced by an Assemblies of God historian in 1954:

> The blood of the noble youth from the ranks of the Assemblies of God flowed with that of all others on the beaches of Anzio and Kwajalein and the battle-scarred hills of Iwo Jima and the Ardennes and they wrote a like glorious page in the history of our land with those of the other great churches of America.[42]

In the Korean and Vietnam conflicts, Pentecostals who sought conscientious objector or non-combatant classification were a rarity.

On the infrequent occasions that Pentecostals took positions on public issues they almost always came down on the conservative side. Prohibition was universally approved by Pentecostals, though they were not directly active in bringing it about. Prohibition had been a goal of various reform movements down through the Progressive era, but whether it was in itself progressive is at least debatable. The primary purpose of prohibition in the eyes of its proponents, including the Pentecostals, was moral reform of the individual and restraint of what were considered the baser instincts. At any rate, by the late 1920's prohibition repeal, not prohibition, was the more usual stance of progressive forces in the nation. Pentecostals universally applauded the adoption of national prohibition, strenuously castigated efforts to repeal it, and later called for its reinstitution. In a surprising departure from their usual recommendation to avoid political participation, some Pentecostal spokesmen urged their followers to use the vote to prevent prohibition repeal.[43] Marie Brown, pastor of the largest Pentecostal church in New York City, denounced the Wets as the "worst enemies of civilization" and called on all Christians to vote for Hoover "a Christian man, level-headed and one who prays"— and one who opposed repeal.[44]

Liberal efforts to achieve world peace were disparaged by Pentecostals. The League of Nations was "preparing the way of the Beast" and would eventually establish the Antichrist at its head. The League and the Kellogg-Briand Peace Pact were futile because the world would end in death and destruction.[45]

The random pronouncements of Pentecostals on the reform administration of Franklin D. Roosevelt were for the most part negative. The repeal of prohibition was criticized and the NRA was widely regarded as "the Mark of the Beast." But Nathan Cohen Beskin was surely unique in his attempt "to prove the connection between the 'New Deal' and Jesuitism."[46] The editor of the *Latter Rain Evangel* also took a much more extreme view of the Roosevelt administration's diplomatic recognition of the Soviet Union than most Pentecostals: "The first Roosevelt made war on Spain at great cost to set the Cubans free. The second Roosevelt makes peace with Russian slave drivers to benefit from some of their blood money." In recognizing the communist government of Russia, "we have made a covenant with hell."[47]

But the reemergence of rebelliousness against the state inherent in such statements aroused fears of retaliation that some Pentecostal spokesmen sought to allay. The *Glad Tidings Herald* denounced the "wild speculation" that the NRA was the Mark of the Beast and said it placed Pentecostals "in a ridiculous position in the sight of the unbelieving world." G. F. Taylor deplored the overemphasis on the NRA as the Mark of the Beast and said that while it may be a "forerunner of the Mark," he preferred to view it as "a Christian system without Christ" that will, therefore, fail. Stanley H. Frodsham denied the implication of the *New Republic* that the Assemblies of God was anti-New Deal, protesting that "Not once have we ever criticized the President, his cabinet, his appointments, or any member of Congress." Even the writer who characterized recognition of the Soviet Union as a "covenant with hell" was quick to add, "I believe President Roosevelt is a good man but that he is dominated by a Christless and materialistic brain trust in Washington," and that Al Smith and numbers of "high brows" had pressured him into recognition.[48]

But Pentecostal political inclinations were not conservative merely; they were often outrightly antidemocratic. "The Church of God," said A. J. Tomlinson, that most autocratic of Pentecostals, "is theocratic in principle." "God's people," he went on, "must be taught submission. They must be trained to bow to authority. They must learn obedience." He condemned democracy as "a breeder of heartaches and jealousies," and a system in which "men are trained to work underhanded trickery for advantage." The Church of God, he boasted, is not, never has been and will never be a representative body. "To make it a representative body would make it more like a republic than a theocracy." Ousted from leadership, partly because he was too extreme even for those who shared his preference for theocracy, Tomlinson founded a new church in 1923 in which, "eliminating elections forever," he became general overseer for life with sole power to make all appointments in the organization.[49]

While Tomlinson's determination to impose theocratic absolutism was frowned upon by most Pentecostals, the political reality underlying the variety of organizational forms within the movement was, as we have seen, autocracy. And Tomlinson's antidemocratic views were widely shared by Pentecostals. Democracy was another of the many signs of the coming Apocalypse; it was "preparing the way for . . . Antichrist." The rise of Mussolini and Stalin was cited as proof that "democracy has gone to seed in dictatorship." Democracy is mere "human government" and therefore Christless and doomed to destruction. "It will land this world in a welter of blood and death unparalleled . . . under its last head, Antichrist."[50] When asked whether it was permissible to join lodges, E. N. Bell revealed his antipathy to the democratic principle of majority rule. Christians should not join lodges, he said, because "the majority rules, and since the majority are almost invariably sinners this puts saints to be ruled over by their own consent by the decision of the ungodly."[51]

In an article entitled "Making the World Safe for Satan" (a transparent allusion to Wilson's wartime slogan), Stanley H. Frodsham, editor of the *Pentecostal Evangel* and prominent leader in the Assemblies of God, responded to the statement in the ecumenical periodical *Interchurch World* that "the hope of America is Democracy, and the Founder of Democracy was the founder of the Church." Frodsham commented:

> Did Christ ever advocate this? No, He came preaching the Kingdom of God, a Kingdom in which God should be supreme and not man. . . . The Scriptures give one instance of the "triumph of democracy" in the life of Christ. It was when He was arraigned before Pilate and Pilate asked whether he should release unto the assembled crowd Jesus or Barabbas. And Barrabas was democracy's choice. And when Pilate asked, "What shall I do then with Jesus, which is called Christ?" they all cried out, "Let Him be crucified." This was democracy's verdict. And yet we are told that the hope of this

country and the hope of the world is "Democracy"—democracy that is just the same at heart now as then. A poor hope, indeed![52]

On rare occasions, Pentecostals even expressed support for the restriction of First Amendment liberties. "Free speech granted by the Constitution is too broad for today," said the *Glad Tidings Herald,* and should be restricted by legislation. The *Pentecostal Evangel* applauded the burning in Germany of Theodore Dreiser's books, which were caricatured as dealing with "prostitutes" and "low love affairs." "A book-burning time such as is described in Acts 19:19 would be a blessing to our land," said the author, and "our government would do well to follow the Nazi government in at least one respect."[53]

But at least one Pentecostal leader, G. F. Taylor, had some kind words for democracy. "God's ideal government," said Taylor, "is autocracy," but because of the Fall, God has permitted other governments, the best of which is democracy. The Apostle Paul taught democratic church government, the early Church practiced it, and "the church whose form of government is fashioned after that of the government of the United States is the church that has the best form of government today." While Taylor's views implied an appreciation for democracy as a general principle, his remarks were largely restricted to the subject of church government, and it should be remembered that Taylor's Pentecostal Holiness Church was episcopalian in structure and its leader was the autocratic, though moderate, J. H. King.[54]

Pentecostal inclinations toward conservatism and reaction were rarely registered in the political arena because the early Pentecostals were distinctly hostile to political participation. Charles Parham had been active in the temperance crusade in Kansas while he preached for the Methodist Episcopal Church, but there is no evidence that he was involved in that or any other social or political movement after he became an independent Holiness and, later, Pentecostal preacher. A. J. Tomlinson had been active in politics in his youth, but when his friends asked him to vote after his conversion to Holiness, he answered, "No I will only vote for Jesus," and, he reminisced years later, "I have never taken any part in politics since, nor gone to the polls and cast a ballot."[55]

Voting was only infrequently prohibited, but also only infrequently encouraged and then not, so far as I could determine, before the 1930's. It was sometimes denigrated, mostly neglected, but usually tolerated.[56] All political involvement beyond voting however was severely condemned because, as Frank Bartleman subtly remarked, "politics is rotten." [57] "I don't believe," said W. T. Gaston, who would shortly become chairman of the Assemblies of God, "any Christian is ever authorized in the Word of God to put his nose into political business. We shall never get the world converted by legislation." [58] When asked if "the saints" should vote, E. N. Bell, then chairman of the Assemblies, answered that, while he himself voted, "each is free to obey God as he sees it." But Bell surely wanted others to follow his example when he said, "I do not mix in party politics." [59] Members of the Pentecostal Holiness Church were forbidden to engage in "corrupt partisan politics," and Glad Tidings Assembly of New York City announced that it was changing its name to Glad Tidings Tabernacle because "the political organizations in this city call their respective districts 'assemblies,' and we want to have no part, not even in a name, in present day politics." [60]

The only exceptions I could find to the general avoidance of political involvement were S. Clyde Bailey, who was appointed chief of police in Marion, Illinois, in 1928 and later defeated in his campaign for mayor, and J. R. Flower, who served on the Springfield, Missouri, city council from 1953 to 1961 and on the Chamber of Commerce and the Community Chest executive committees. [61]

G. F. Taylor, who as we have seen championed democratic church organization, was nevertheless opposed to all participation in the democratic political process.

> The spirit of antiChrist pervades the world today. It is that which is keeping things going as they are. There is not a government on earth that is not controlled by this spirit. It is useless to say that the Christian people should rise up by ballot and put such a spirit out. Such a thing is impossible. The spirit will continue to gain ascendancy until it culminates in the final Antichrist of the ages. All efforts to put it down are fruitless. The only thing we can do is seek to save individuals from its power. [62]

The antidemocratic and antipolitical pronouncements of the Pentecostals were scarcely concealed attacks upon the beliefs, values and forms of the existing political system and were in that sense revolutionary, but the specific content of their radical criticism was reactionary. Since these same pronouncements reflected and inculcated attitudes that made the Pentecostals apolitical in practice, the objective effect was conservative because they presented no real challenge to the status quo. In the conflict between revolutionary and conservative elements in Pentecostal political attitudes, conservatism and reaction predominated from the earliest years. In time, radical criticism of the political process would become virtually non-existent and conservatism would prevail unalloyed.

The underlying hatred for the existing social system and their place within it that fueled Pentecostal passions in the early years sometimes found expression in surprisingly radical anticapitalist statements. Charles Parham predicted that the Second Coming would be preceded by a class conflict in which "the government, the rich and the churches will be on one side and the masses on the other. . . . Capital must exterminate and enslave the masses or be exterminated. . . . In this death struggle . . . the rich will be killed like dogs." Continuing in the same harrowing vein, Parham proclaimed,

> For a long time the voices of the masses have vainly sought for relief, by agitation and the ballot, but the governments of the world were in the hands of the rich, the nobles, and the plutocrats, who forestalled all legislative action in the interests of the masses, until the wage-slavery of the world became unbearable; until the worm, long ground under the iron heel of oppression, begins to burn with vindictive fire, under the inspiration of a new patriotism in the interests of the freedom of the working class. Therefore, would it be considered strange if the overzealous already begin to use the only means at hand for their liberty—by bombs and assassination to destroy the monsters of government and society that stand in the way of the realization of their hopes? . . . Ere long Justice with flaming sword, will step from behind the pleading form of Mercy, to punish a nation which has mingled the blood of thousands of human sacrifices upon the altar of her commercial and imperialistic expansion.[63]

Frank Bartleman echoed these anticapitalist convictions prior to American entry into the first World War. He charged that the press had "sold out to England" and that the capitalists were pressuring the government to lead the nation into war.

> Our war party, powder and ammunition manufacturers, etc., see their opportunity at this crisis with us. A fortune in war supplies and provisions await our merchants, manufacturers and capitalists. They are willing to plunge our nation even into war to get this. Our rulers dare not say no to them if they hope to retain their offices.[64]

Pentecostals generally regarded the concentration of wealth in the hands of men like J. P. Morgan and John D. Rockefeller, and the growth of the trusts as signs of the Second Coming, foreshadowings of the Beast or the Antichrist.[65] But the growth of labor unions was an equally authentic sign of the End. Despite his strong working-class sympathies, even Parham was more negative than positive on labor unions. Responding to the view of many Pentecostals that lodges and labor unions were anti-Christian, Parham said,

> While we are not personally a member of any lodge, or union, neither have we aught against them, for if the church had done its duty in feeding the hungry and clothing the naked, these institutions would not have existed, *sapping the life of the church.* . . . upon the ascension to power of the AntiChrist, a world-wide union or protective association will be organized by the fanatical patriotic followers, and one will be compelled to subscribe to this union or association, and receive a literal mark in the right hand or forehead, or he cannot buy or sell.[66]

Ambivalence toward labor unions and the working class was also evident in James McAlister's statement that,

> Whilst our sympathies are with every just claim of labor for shorter hours and better wages, and whilst we support all that is good in Socialism as against the greed of capital and the crime of profiteering, we cannot but feel that Democracy [unionism?] is intoxicated with the wine of lawlessness, and is in danger of insensate deeds of violence which will bring rivers of blood and a rain of tears [the postwar strikes?].[67]

But few other Pentecostals were either ambivalent or ambiguous in their attitudes toward labor unions. "Satan," said J. R. Flower, "has sent out into the world evil spirits which are gathering the people together in unions, labor, political, financial, religious and national, all of which will finally be united in one great union opposed to Christ and his people."[68] The postwar wave of strikes was credited by the editor of the *Pentecostal Evangel* to Bolshevist influence.[69] A writer for the *Apostolic Evangel* told of a friend who used to hold a high position in a labor union, "experience taught him that they [unions] were controlled by the spirit that is absolutely antagonistic to the Holy Spirit, and he got out. . . . If you obey Him, He will bring you out all right, in spite of all the unions in the world and the devil at the head of them."[70] C. E. Robinson, in a letter to Stanley H. Frodsham, said,

> Antichrist is in the world today in the form of labor unionism. It put up Stalin. It put up Hitler. It put up Mussolini. It has the balance of power politically in this country, and will appoint a dictator to dictate to the President

we elect as it does to the King of Italy. I have long considered the Labor Unions the most sinister thing in our government. . . .[71]

At its 1912 convention, the Church of God (Cleveland, Tennessee) adopted a resolution barring members of labor unions from church membership. Two years later this was softened to accept those who merely paid union dues but took no part in union meetings or other activities. But the year following, this was stiffened to accept as church members only those who had union dues withheld by their employers, because "such members are not responsible, but it is happened unto them according to the Scriptures, 'Behold, the hire of the laborers who have reaped down your fields, . . . is . . . kept back by fraud.' " The 1922 annual Assembly rejected a motion to return to the original position by those who argued that no member should pay dues in any way because the money was used to finance strikes and violence.[72]

The official position of the Pentecostal Holiness Church was that their members could join unions but could not hold union office, attend union meetings, or engage in labor-management conflicts. Later this was modified to permit involvement in "legal efforts on the part of labor to prevent oppression and injustice from capitalism."[73]

The wave of strikes in the cotton mills of the South during the 1930's found most Pentecostal (and Holiness) preachers standing with the operators against the strikers. In a mill at Danville-Schoolfield, Virginia, a pastor of a local Pentecostal Holiness Church encouraged his church members to cross the picket lines and go to work. When his church building was dynamited by the strikers, the mill-owners rewarded him with a plot of land and building funds for a new church.[74] Mill-owner financial support to various churches was for the express purpose of enlisting the clergy to keep the workers manageable and quiescent. Yet union organizers often found it easier to recruit Pentecostal and other sectarian church members (as distinct from pastors) into unions than members of the more established denominations.[75]

As unionism became an accepted feature of the social order after the New Deal, the attitudes of Pentecostals altered accordingly. Yet this was more the result of expediency than conviction. A deeply rooted suspicion of unions is still typical of many Pentecostals including those who hold union membership. Pentecostal preachers exhorted the faithful to be "submissive and kind in your relations with your customers, employers, work mates and neighbors," but when the chips were down, submission to employers came first.[76]

Pentecostal opposition to working-class movements more radical than unionism was outspoken and unambiguous. The IWW, anarchists, socialists, and communists all partook of the "spirit of Antichrist." Bolsheviks were terroristic, violent, and criminal; they were enemies of peace, religion, marriage, the family, and law and order. The root cause of Bolshevism was atheism, and atheism was the result of theological liberalism or Modernism, a point we shall return to. Red was the symbol of Communism, it was believed, because it was the color of sin.[77] "Our own beloved land," said the *Glad Tidings Herald,* "has been secretly invaded by the leavening enemy of Communism and other forces that are . . . working toward the overthrow of our government."[78]

Pentecostalism was a counteracting force against radicalism. Otto J. Klink had been a socialist in his native Germany and an anarchist during his first years in this country. In 1910, he said, he had been sent to assassinate President Taft in Bronx Park but the President did not show up. Following his conversion to Pentecostalism, Klink proudly proclaimed, "I still preach the general strike. . . . Not against the organized government, however, or against the rulers that are now in power, but a general strike against the old devil."[79] Thus did Pentecostalism transform anticapitalist resistance into subservience.

Nowhere were Pentecostal hostilities against established authority more fully expressed or more long-lived than in their condemnation of other religious institutions and movements. "Glancing at the religions of the world," said the *Pentecostal Holiness Advocate,* "the Pentecostal people will take most all of them to be antichristian. . . . We would put the Catholics as antichristian at once. . . . Take the branches of the Protestant Church, and we would term the most of them antichristian."[80]

The Protestant denominations, in the opinion of the Pentecostals, had turned away from true Christianity and adopted "churchianity." Formalism, liturgy, and organization had destroyed true spiritual religion in the churches. They were "cold" and "dead," "having the form of godliness but denying the power thereof." Worship was devoid of personal testimony periods, "amens," "hallelujas," and all evidence of the Spirit's presence. "The organized church," said Bartleman, "has largely proven a tremendous framework of form and ceremony built up against God."[81]

The Protestant clergy were filled with "head" knowledge in the "cemeteries" (seminaries) where they became D.D.'s (which was "invariably interpreted to mean 'Dumb Dogs' "). They were not "taught of the

Spirit'' and were therefore ignorant, even ''anti-intellectual'' because God's wisdom can never be acquired by the merely ''human'' or ''natural'' mind. ''Satan,'' said Howard Goss, ''went to work on the preachers.'' They no longer preached salvation and holiness, but delivered dull and dreary sermons on social and political matters. Some smoked and chewed tobacco, drank, swore, and told ''shady stories'' to ingratiate themselves with laymen. They were ''whitewashed sepulchres, full of dead men's bones.'' ''They are not able to bring men to Christ,'' said J. W. Welch, ''and so they are working along the line of education.''[82]

Responding to denominational criticisms of the Pentecostal movement, Elijah Clark wrote,

> I had rather worship where devils are cast out, than to go and worship where the devil reigns. . . . All you have to do to become a Christian there is shake hands with the preacher, or sign a card, or just be baptized in water, go on in your sins and go as straight to hell when you die as Lindbergh flew to France, yet they will pat you on the shoulder and call you a Christian, if you pay well.[83]

When asked if ''the saints'' could join ''sectarian churches'' (that is, the denominations), E. N. Bell replied, ''I see no way how one can be true to God, not compromise and yet stay in these churches.''[84]

It is hardly surprising, given the ''esteem'' in which they held the mainline denominations, that the Pentecostals assiduously spurned the tenor of their worship. Services were held in brush arbors, private homes, tents, the open air, or rented halls (an ''upper room'' if possible) in preference to church buildings. Organs, altars, sometimes even pulpits, trained choirs, robes, and clerical collars were ''out,'' pianos, guitars, tambourines, saxophones, trumpets, extemporaneous singing, praying, and preaching were ''in.'' Children were neither baptized at birth nor confirmed in adolescence, but ''dedicated to the Lord'' at birth and baptized only after undergoing ''the new birth'' experience. Baptism was always by immersion and took place in a lake or river, but seldom a baptistry. As Eugene N. Hastie said,

> With some workers there was a general aversion to anything resembling the nominal churches. Formality, read sermons, memorized prayers, classical singing and the use of ''big'' words were generally detested. The preachers were never called ''Reverend.'' Everybody was brother and sister so and so.[85]

There were those who "had religion" and there were those, like the Pentecostals, who "had Christ" and nothing but contempt for "religion." The Pentecostals created a kind of anti-Establishment Protestantism that was anticlerical, antitheological, antiliturgical, antisacramental, antiecclesiastical, and indeed, in a sense, antireligious. Inherent in Pentecostal scorn of the denominational clergy and the tenor of its worship were clear indications of class antagonism. Parham, with characteristic subtlety, wrote,

> with fire and sword the masses will utterly destroy the modern churches with vengeance, for they will be permitted of God to punish them for their pride, pomp, deadness, dearth and unfaithfulness.[86]

Real Christian unity, the Pentecostals believed, could be brought about only by the Spirit working in the Spirit-baptized. The ecumenical movement, therefore, was deplored as a misguided attempt to achieve unity through "man-made organizations" that compromised true Christianity and "yoked" believers together with unbelievers. Ecumenicism was "Religious Babylonianism."[87] "Satan's superman," said J. W. Welch

> is on the way; the modern church along with the nations, unconscious of what they are doing, are leading their efforts directly to the establishment of conditions for the Antichrist to take supreme control. This "get-together" idea is nothing other than that. . . . They have not only lost the vision of individual salvation, but have gone so far from the vision of the gospel that they are actually talking boastfully about saving the world through this great brotherhood of man. God help them![88]

Not just the Federal Council of Churches, but the Interchurch World Movement, the Foreign Missions Conference of North America, the International Sunday School Association, and virtually every interdenominational cooperative venture were inspired by the spirit of Antichrist, and would eventually merge with business, labor, and other conglomerates to form that one great union over which the Antichrist himself would preside.[89]

At the root of the deplorable condition of the mainline churches was apostasy. The denominations had succumbed to Modernism and abandoned "the faith once delivered to the saints." "Infidelic 'Higher Criticism' "—the historical and scientific reexamination of the Bible—denied the inerrancy of the Word of God. Evolutionary theory was diametrically opposed to the Genesis account of divine creation. "No true

Christian can believe in Evolution. If Evolution is right, then the Bible is wrong, and Christ is wrong." Modernism, the Pentecostals believed, denied the Virgin birth of Jesus and taught that salvation came through following his teachings. This was "bloodless Christianity," a rejection of the true doctrine of salvation through faith in the substitutionary atonement of Jesus' crucifixion, and in his literal, physical resurrection. The "new birth" as a crisis experience was replaced by the Modernist notion of "Christian nurture." Apocalyptic premillennialism was jettisoned for the belief of the Modernists that the Social Gospel and Ecumenicism were building the Kingdom of God on earth. And the Modernists' disbelief in miracles past and present was a denial of the power of the Holy Spirit.[90] "The religious battle of the last days," said W. T. Gaston, "is clearly drawn before this generation. It is between natural and supernatural religion."[91] The *Pentecostal Evangel* warned its readers to "Beware of the Scribes," for "The modernist pulpit today is preparing the audience, the constituency, for the Antichrist," and its message will not be " 'Crucify Him'—the Christ, but 'Enthrone him'—the Antichrist."[92]

Modernism was, they believed, a product of the German intellectuals whose teachings were responsible for the first world war. Modernism was synonymous with atheism, and atheism was the heart of Bolshevism. "The triangle of Satan is atheism, evolution and modern theology."[93] They "go hand in hand and are inseparable, and the Bolsheviks join heartily with them in their denial of the inspiration of the Holy Scriptures."[94] Otto Klink, the would-be assassin of President Taft, attributed his political radicalism to his acceptance of Modernism while studying theology at the University of Berlin.[95] N. J. Poysti, on his return from a trip to the Soviet Union, said, "I believe, if Bolsheviks will take control of the United States, all Modernist preachers and churches will be in high honor and will be recognized as the state religion for the United States."[96]

In a unique interpretation, J. C. Whalte fused Modernism, Bolshevism and Ecumenicism into a single Apocalyptic vision:

> Lenine [sic] is simply the awful shadow of the great Red king who is surely coming to reign over a great Red world. Not only will the Beast be a Red, but the Woman, the harlot, that rides and controls the Beast, will also be a Red. She will be arrayed in scarlet (Rev. 17:4). This red harlot symbolizes the coming world federation of religions. It will be a Red religion that will flaunt the red flag of communism, and drench the world with the red blood of the martyrs. Keep your eyes on the Red religion O man of God. Watch!

Its theme is communism, federation, social service and the red light of spirit seances.[97]

However severe the Pentecostals were in their assessment of other Protestant churches, they were at least willing to concede that within the denominations there were some "gospel" churches (as distinct from the "*full*" gospel" Pentecostal churches) and many true, though misguided, Christians. No such concessions were granted to Roman Catholicism.

The Christian Church, according to the Pentecostals, had fallen away from the original gospel by the time of Constantine and this "backslidden Church of God resulted in the formal coldness and scum of spirituality which collected itself together into what is now known as the Catholic Church . . . the daughter of fornication and adultery and therefore an harlot."[98] The Roman Catholic Church was the "great whore" and "mother of harlots" referred to in the Revelation of St. John. Catholicism was

Satan's great masterpiece of deception . . . a false system [with] a counterfeit god, the pope; a counterfeit savior, Mary; a counterfeit mediator, Mary; a counterfeit advocate with the Father, Mary, the priest and the saints, . . . a counterfeit priesthood of erring men.[99]

Catholicism was a resurrection of the ancient, pagan, and idolatrous "cult of Babylon" whose worship of the "Queen of Heaven" has its counterpart in the worship of the Virgin Mary.[100] Commenting on the death of Pope Pius X, the editor of the *Christian Evangel* said that although Pius had been a good man in private life, he had been "head of a gigantic religious machine that has cursed the world. . . . The Pope was behind the bloodiest wars Europe has ever known. . . . He caused the most innocent and purest souls to be tortured, maimed, murdered and burnt."[101] The Pope was the forerunner of the Antichrist and, according to their sacred numerology, the value of the inscription on his crown was 666, the Mark of the Beast. One Pentecostal spokesman held that the "Black Pope," the General of the Society of Jesus, was the Antichrist and that "the 60,000 Jesuit laymen" in America were the "secret police of the Jesuits. They control everything. They get their men into the Protestant ministry and everywhere to gain their ends."[102] The Jesuits and the capitalist class, said Frank M. Boyd, constitute a "Monarchial [sic] Party" which controlled Congress and would one day "invade the United States with armed mobs of immigrants from Europe, Asia and Africa."[103]

The Pentecostal Holiness Church adopted a resolution charging that the Pope falsely claimed the right "to dictate all the affairs of all nations and governments of the whole world," and pledged itself to "unflinching warfare against the encroachment of the Roman Catholic Church."[104]

No Roman Catholic should ever be President of the United States, said the *Pentecostal Evangel,* because of the Catholic teaching that "the pope is sovereign" and "the Church is above the State, yea, she is the State," and because "the Romanist owes allegiance to the church and its laws first." The same periodical maintained that Mussolini and Fascism were "backed by the whole strength of the Roman Church," but later, when Fascist gangs instigated anti-Catholic riots in Italy in 1931, it was declared that "Rome must reap what she has sown. . . . We are seeing a great shaking of everything that is not of God."[105] Hitler was persecuting Protestants, said the *Latter Rain Evangel,* but he signed a Concordat with the Pope and refrained from interfering in any way with Catholicism. As a result numerous Protestant ministers were appealing to the Pope for admission into the Roman Catholic Church. Commenting on the persecution of the Roman Catholic and Greek Orthodox churches in the Soviet Union, the same writer said, "The Mother of Harlots, the great whore has been judged in Russia."[106] The extreme anti-Catholicism of early Pentecostalism became much more muted in later years, but a strong undercurrent has persisted.[107]

Pentecostals were equally critical of various heterodox or quasi-Christian sects and cults, some of which, according to Norman Cohen Beskin were financed by the Jesuits.[108] Among these "False Prophets," "Lying Wonders," "delusions of Satan," and "Devil's Revivals," which, as one might expect, were preparing the way for the Antichrist, were Christian Science, New Thought, the Emmanuel Movement, Father Divine's Peace Movement, Theosophy, Spiritualism, Russellism (Jehovah's Witnesses), Unity, Mormonism, Swedenborgianism, Campbellism, Unitarianism, and Universalism. Numbers of Pentecostals were apparently being "deceived" into adhering to these movements, especially Christian Science, the Father Divine movement, and Spiritualism. Given the emphasis upon miracles generally and divine healing and Spirit-inspired speech in particular, this is quite understandable.[109]

Spiritualism was undoubtedly considered the greatest of all threats to Pentecostalism because it was "the Devil's counterfeit . . . of the gifts of the Holy Spirit." The similarities between Pentecostalism and Spiritualism explain why people found transit from one to the other fairly easy.

Pentecostals gave full credence to Spiritualist claims of healing, materializing spirits, speaking under the power of the spirits, and conversing with
the dead. But these were "Satan's lying wonders" wrought to "deceive
the very elect," and were not the work of the Holy Spirit, as was the case
in Pentecostal meetings. Spiritualists were demon-posessed. "Satan hates
God's people," said F. J. Lee, "He also abhors the works of God in this
Holy Ghost dispensation. He wants to introduce his work as being Pentecostal in order to deceive and frighten people away from the genuine."[110]

In the Pentecostal mind, nearly all religions growing out of the Christian tradition were anti-Christian, but the Jews were merely non-Christian, the "lost sheep" who would one day turn to faith in Christ. Those
who had apostacized from the faith were accountable and contemptible,
those who had never had faith were not. The Pentecostals had a feeling of
kinship toward the Jews who were, in their view, God's original "tree of
Israel" into which the Pentecostals themselves had been grafted as the
"spiritual Israel." Because they believed that the return of the Jews to
their ancient homeland in Palestine was a necessary precondition for the
Second Coming, they were actually Zionists. It is somewhat surprising
then to find the Assemblies of God (at least) swept into anti-Semitism. In
1920, that denomination's periodical reprinted an address by D. M. Pat-
ton before the 48th conference of the London Prophetical Society in
which the spurious Protocols of the Elders of Zion were given full credence. In a prefatory note, Stanley H. Frodsham wrote,

> In a recent issue of the Evangel in an article on Israel's Peril, there was a
> quotation from the London Times, "No one who knows the facts can deny
> the Jews have supplied the brains and directing power of the present Bolshe-
> vist regime so fiercely maintained by torture and massacre." The address
> given below goes to show that back of all this, fifteen years ago, there was a
> deep laid plot prepared, which had as its purpose the bringing about of a
> great world upheaval and the setting up of a great, universal Dictator, "a
> King-Despot of the blood of Zion." The events of the past six years have
> been so much on the line of the terms of the plot, as revealed by these Pro-
> tocols or secret documents of the Elders of Zion, that even worldly men are
> sitting up and taking notice, and prophetic students who are conversant with
> Daniel and Revelation, cannot but be struck with the likeness of this plot
> with the things already revealed concerning the antichrist and his plans.[111]

In subsequent articles, Frodsham denounced the "atheistic, anti-Christian Masonic Jewish Conspiracy" and referred to Trotsky and the Soviet

commissars as "apostate Jews." But by the 1930's the *Pentecostal Evangel* was publishing articles that condemned anti-Semitism and pronounced the Protocols "AntiChristian Propaganda Against the Jewish People."[112] By 1940 Frodsham, acting officially for the Assemblies of God, signed a resolution against anti-Semitism along with the editors of "all the leading Fundamentalist papers and the heads of all the leading Fundamentalist-Bible schools." Replying to an article in the *New Republic* that characterized the Assemblies of God as anti-Semitic, Frodsham said that the *Pentecostal Evangel* had published numerous articles exposing the Protocols as "a forgery and a fake" and that the official Assemblies position was "that no one can be a true Christian and at the same time hate and persecute Jews."[113]

Frodsham did not, unfortunately, acknowledge that this was a reversal of the Assemblies former stance. Nor did he mention his inability to persuade Cecil J. Lowry, then principal of the Assemblies Southwestern Bible Institute at Fort Worth, to fall in line with the new policy. Frodsham's own sincerity, however, cannot be doubted. "It certainly would be a most terrible thing," he wrote to Lowry, "if you . . . should poison the youth who attend that institute with the awful virus of anti-Semitism, which to me is the greatest menace that we have before us in America at this time."[114]

The shift away from anti-Semitism was undoubtedly facilitated by Norman Cohen Beskin, a converted Jewish Pentecostal whose articles appeared in several Pentecostal periodicals. Yet Beskin himself was not entirely free of anti-Jewish prejudice. In an exposé of the Protocols, Beskin reminded his readers that "the Jew has given you the Bible, he has given you the Gospel and the Christ, he gave you the apostles and all that is valuable and precious to you as Christians." He went on to discredit the anti-Semitic myths that said Jews owned the greatest wealth and controlled the world's money ("Is Morgan a Jew? Is the Chase National Jewish? Is Rockefeller a Jew, or Andrew Mellon?"); that they owned the biggest newspapers and the largest stores and that their manipulations had caused the Depression ("the brain-child of a crazy man"); and finally that there was an international Jewish conspiracy as outlined in the Protocols. Disappointingly, however, Beskin also said,

> The Jew has contributed much to the nations, but let me say, to my sorrow, that out of all proportion to our pecentage of population there are altogether too many Jewish socialists and anarchists. Out of all proportion, there are too many atheistic preachers and lecturers among the Jews. Columbia Uni-

versity is the most atheistic university in America. In all the history of American Congress we have had only three socialistic congressmen and all three of them were Jews. It is a shame, but it is true . . . if our Jewish leaders, instead of running around and decrying Hitler, would call upon all Jews to be true, loyal citizens, and be thankful for the priveleges we enjoy, rather than to spread socialism and communism in America much more good would be accomplished.[115]

Though perhaps unintentionally, Beskin's argument implied that the political dissent of certain Jews was somehow attributable to their Jewishness. Some lingering traces of anti-Semitism continued to plague the movement, but its record on this issue is probably about as good as most Christian communions and certainly contrasts with that of the "Apostles of Discord."[116]

The Pentecostals' nearly wholesale rejection of other religions and their perverse defiance of religious custom and sensibility must be seen not only as an expression of hostility toward religious authority, but also as a distorted expression of rebelliousness against authority in general. But this potentially revolutionary impulse was misdirected since, given the separation of state and church (such as it is) and the pluralistic structure of religion in America, an assault upon religious authority could not easily be transformed into an assault upon political and economic authority as it could in those European countries where a single church having privileged connections with the state had a virtual monopoly on religion. The effect of Pentecostal criticism was largely conservative in that it made very little impact and left the structure of American religion intact. But there was also a deeply reactionary character to Pentecostal religious criticism. Their commitment to separation of church and state and to religious freedom must be evaluated in the light of their unmistakable and gross religious intolerance.

It should be recognized, of course, that the hostility, aggressiveness and rebelliousness we have been examining were largely unconscious to the Pentecostals themselves. In their own eyes they were filled with peace, contentment, happiness, and love for all men. This was a necessary defense mechanism against the breakthrough of those contradictory urges which if expressed would arouse retaliation or fears of retaliation. When denial was inadequate in the face of the explicit content of the Pentecostal pronouncements of doom upon the world and all its works, they would rationalize. It was not, after all, the Pentecostals who wanted to destroy the world. They greatly regretted that it would happen and were doing all they could to save people from the wrath to come. Nor was their God only a God of vengeance, but also a God of love who wanted to save sinners and had sacrificed his only Son to do so. Those who rejected God's (and the Pentecostals') love were solely responsible for the coming destruction of the world and their own eternal damnation. By such means Pentecostalism provided a social and ideological environment in which the expression of hostility was legitimized and rendered free of retaliatory apprehensions.

The apparently curious mingling of revolutionary and conservative impulses in Pentecostal social attitudes reflects an underlying conflict between rebelliousness and submissiveness toward authority that is especially typical of the lower social classes in capitalist society. The natural and logical outlet for the rebellious impulses of the Pentecostals was struggle against those who were chiefly responsible for the adverse social circumstances that lay at the root of their discontent: the capitalist class and its surrogate, the state. But they were powerless to struggle, not only because of the strength and determination of their real adversaries, but also because, given their class position, they lacked the necessary perception, means and self-confidence to do so. The length and quality of their education virtually precluded perception of the structure of social relationships and their place within it. Their intellectual and material poverty sharply diminished their means of resistance. And the rebellious-submissive character structure typical of their class found its ultimate expression in submissiveness toward political and economic authority, largely because of the effects of their pietistic, Holiness upbringing and of their internalization of Pentecostal ideology.

External realities and internal psychic structure combined to compel the Pentecostals to repress their urge to rebel against those who were the real objects of that urge. Repression was an act of self-defense against the retaliation of the state and the capitalist class, and against the fears and self-condemnation that would surely accompany rebellion.

But the rebellious urge could not be successfully repressed. It broke through the repression in forms that contained both the original impulse and the repression itself. Defiance of state authority in the form of resistance to military service and condemnation of the political process were combined with absolute subservience to the state in all other matters. Castigation of the rich and the corporations went hand in hand with denunciation of labor unions, socialism, and communism. In both cases subservience prevailed because even these muted expressions of revolutionary sentiment were too threatening for the Pentecostals to sustain.

Consequently, their hostile and aggressive impulses were almost entirely displaced from the world of politics and work to the world of religion.

The Pentecostals had much justification for criticizing the established denominations, which, after all, had for the most part failed to fulfill their obligations to the poor, the immigrants, and racial and ethnic minorities. But the disproportionate and unfair character of Pentecostal deprecations of the mainline churches and of religious groups with which they had had little or no contact suggests that their hostility was fed by some source other than their legitimate religious grievances. That source was their very real political and economic grievances. The repressed hostility arising from these found partial release initially in the thinly veiled attacks on state and capital that we have examined. But much of it was released in criticism of the religious order. Here defiance could be open, unbridled, and uncompromised by the urge to submit, because religious institutions could not really punish them. But the mainline churches could and did ignore and isolate them. Thwarted of any real satisfaction by these tactics, the Pentecostals, as we have seen, turned the main thrust of their aggressive impulses against one another, while continuing, however, to castigate other religious groups as well. Only later, when Pentecostals began to experience improvement in their social circumstances and to move into the middle classes, would their intolerant assault on other religious groups and their fratricidal brawling decline. Improvement in their economic conditions and in their social relationships meant the reduction of frustration and, thus, the drying up of the springs of bitterness.

Pentecostalism was a movement born of radical social discontent, which, however, expended its revolutionary impulses in veiled, ineffectual, displaced attacks that amounted to withdrawal from the social struggle and passive acquiescence to a world they hated and wished to escape. Their aggressive hostility was in fact what Frederick Cople Jaher termed "the bitterness of those who submit to what they hate."[117] Their social powerlessness was transformed into feelings of religious powerlessness, and its solution was sought through tapping the source of all power in the Baptism in the Holy Spirit. The social consequence of the movement was diametrically opposite to its unconscious intent. Pentecostalism was an instrument forged by a segment of the working class out of protest against a social system that victimized them, but it functioned in a way that perpetuated that very system. A potential challenge to the social system was transformed into a bulwark of it.

XII

The Sources and Functions of Pentecostalism

A more systematic treatment of the questions that have guided us throughout this study is now in order. Why did the Pentecostal movement arise? What were the conditions for its emergence and survival? Why did it take the particular form that it did? Why were people attracted to it and why did they remain in it? What was its significance for Christendom and the larger American society? The evidence on which my answers to these questions are based is by now familiar to the reader, but I frankly acknowledge the interpretive character of my conclusions.

Beginning at the most general level, Pentecostalism may be viewed as one small part of a widespread, long-term protest against the whole thrust of modern urban-industrial capitalist society. That protest often took the form of a many-sided reaction against "modernity." During the past century, science and technology through the processes of industrialization and urbanization have profoundly altered all aspects of life. Revolutions in the means of production were accompanied by the growth of huge, complex, and impersonal social institutions, and by increasing social and spatial mobility. Vast hosts of people were shunted from farm to city, from continent to continent, and from one style of life to another.

Adjustment to new environments and occupations, even when it brought material benefits, levied its toll on the spiritual resources of modern man. The liberal, secular culture of the modern Western world gave rise to widespread malaise and despair. The articulation of dissatisfaction with modernity by "alienated intellectuals" has a history dating back some 150 years;[1] but such dissatisfaction was expressed by other social classes in the form of mass movements of dissent. Such movements have often displayed reactionary tendencies toward modernity, and have drawn their strongest support from those agrarian, artisan, and small entrepreneurial classes most adversely affected by urban-industrial change.[2]

Adjustment of these preindustrial classes to modern society has often taken "archaic" or "primitive" forms in which religious beliefs and customs figured prominently. Some working class groups in America drew on their religious heritage to create labor organizations, infusing them with religious values and thereby assisting in the transit from preindustrial to modern modes of thought and action.[3]

But this course was not readily available to all workers. Some held religious convictions too rigid to allow application to mundane problems and were too deeply attached to individualism to adopt collective techniques. Farm and labor organizations were often regarded as but expressions of that modernity which had disrupted their lives. At any rate, they lacked the resources to create such organizations and they were barred from joining existing ones by their unskilled and semi-skilled status, and by racial and ethnic antipathies. The response of such groups was often to withdraw from the sphere of economic and political activity to resolve their problems religiously. The Pentecostals responded in just this fashion.

Although the most severe strictures of the Pentecostals were reserved for the Church, one may discern a deeply-rooted, underlying mood of profound cultural despair. The Pentecostals' fundamental charge against the Church was that it had accommodated itself to "the world." When they protested against Higher Criticism, Darwinism, and the Social Gospel, against ecumenicism and declining morality in the Church, they were in fact protesting scientific rationalism, bureaucracy, and secularism. In short, what they deplored in the Church were those very characteristics that typify modern urban culture. Even their choice of words for all they deemed contemptible in the Church—"modernism" and "worldliness"—reflects this.

But the Pentecostal movement can hardly be explained by the overall development of capitalist society spanning the whole of American history. We must narrow our focus to the period from about 1890 to 1925 during which the movement emerged and took shape. These were years of transition from the competitive, entrepreneurial phase of capitalism to its monopolistic, bureaucratic phase. The major crisis of that transition occured in the 1890's. The general economic depression from 1893 to 1896 brought labor-capital class conflict and farmer militancy of unprecedented proportions. The period of recovery found the nation enmeshed in the problems of urbanization, mass immigration, the trusts, war with Spain, and involvement in global expansionism. The general social turmoil was accompanied by a major crisis of religious faith centering primarily upon the "Higher Criticism," evolutionary theory, and the social role of the Church.[4]

The crisis of the 90's and its aftermath gave rise to numerous protest movements, the most important of which were Populism and Progressivism. These movements contained both secular and religious elements. They brought concrete changes in society and accommodations to it. In varying degrees they were at once realistic and unrealistic, progressive, conservative, and reactionary. The Holiness and Pentecostal movements, however, were almost wholly religious, and conservative or reactionary. They not only stood aside from the more realistic efforts of other movements to improve social conditions, but condemned them.

It was during the depression of the 90's and the decade following that the Holiness movement broke from the mainline churches and developed independently. The Pentecostal movement reached a peak during the "panic" of 1907, experienced a resurgence at the time of the 1913–14 recession, and another during the post-World War I period of economic dislocation. While a purely mechanistic economic interpretation should be avoided, the coincidence of the Holiness and Pentecostal revivals with national economic decline can not have been entirely accidental.

However, if economic dislocation alone "caused " the Pentecostal movement, how could we explain its survival and growth, even at a slower rate, during years of prosperity? Widespread economic crisis did indeed contribute to spurts in Pentecostal growth, but its underlying source is not to be found in the general socio-economic conditions of national life, but rather in the specific circumstances of the working poor from whose ranks the Pentecostal movement drew the overwhelming bulk of its recruits.

The working poor included those regularly employed, sporadically employed and seldom employed.[5] They were mostly semi-skilled and unskilled workers who made up the urban and rural proletariat of industrial capitalism. They constituted the lowest base of the work force of the nation, and also a free-floating labor reserve. As a class, they were brought into being by the movement of rural Americans to the city and by the influx of masses of immigrants during the period of transition from competitive to monopoly capitalism.

The impoverished farmers of the Southern uplands and the rural migrants in urban areas—native and immigrant—who flocked to the Pentecostal standard were but a fraction of a crippled and displaced international agrarian proletariat produced by the urban-industrialization of the Western world in the latter part of the 19th century. Lines of steel were thrown out to open up vast new grain and livestock regions in Russia, Australia, Argentina, and the central Canadian-American plains, and steam-driven ships plied the oceans to link those regions to a new worldwide agrarian market. The expansion of production resulting from this transportation revolution and from the increasing use of mechanized and scientific farming techniques glutted the world market and sent agricultural prices plumeting. The farmer, largely ignorant of the operations of the new market that enmeshed him, was everywhere at bay. For farmers in marginal regions like Appalachia and the Ozarks, Southwestern Norway and Sicily, Alberta and the Mexican-American border, who hardly lived above the edge of subsistence even in the best of time, the agricultural crisis assumed catastrophic proportions.[6] Coming as they did from diverse racial and ethnic, regional and religious backgrounds, the working poor—and the Pentecostals—had at least two things in common. First, they came largely from rural-agrarian origins and experienced either the culture shock of transplantation to urban areas or, in the case of those who remained on the land, the pain of adjustment to conditions of rural decay stemming from urban-industrialization. In either case, the Pentecostals were most often found among those who suffered, both materially and spiritually, from the effects of modernity. They faced all those social and psychological problems involved in either breaking into modern urban culture or in its breaking in upon them in rural environments.

Second, their adjustment to new and changing circumstances was exacerbated by their generally low social status. For a preponderant majority of the working poor—and, again, of the Pentecostals—were either Negroes, recent immigrants, or marginal farmers of the Southern uplands. Blacks and immigrants, especially those from Southern and Eastern Europe and from Latin America, stood beyond the pale of white Anglo-Saxon Protestant American society; and the native white agrarians were hardly accorded a much higher status owing to their impoverished economic and cultural background.

The working poor generally were ill-equipped either to perceive their position in the social order or to alter it even if they had perceived it. They were educated poorly or not at all. They had little or no command of the English language. They had minimal access to the technologies and social institutions by which change could be effected. Moreover, the working poor were aided but little by the progressive reforms of the era or by periods of general prosperity. In absolute terms, the working poor as a class have no doubt experienced some improvement in their standard of living in the course of this century, but their relative social position has remained unchanged. Indeed, some have sunk into a new class of permanently unemployed welfare clients.

Because of their position on the margins of the social order and their inadequate access to the means for ameliorating their conditions of existence, many of the working poor have responded to their situation in ways that have been labeled anti-social, escapist, and unrealistic. In fact, they are at once protests against their alienated, relatively impoverished social position and attempts to alter it or, at least, temporarily ease its painful effects. Among these responses are crime, delinquency, violence, heavy drinking, drug addiction, gambling, prostitution, sexual promiscuity, and extremely other-worldly religion. Moral and ethical judgments of the difference between the last of these—religion—and the others should not be allowed to obscure its functional equivalence. Nor should the occurrence of these activities at all levels of society prevent us from recognizing their higher incidence and their prominence relative to alternative behavior patterns at the lowest levels of society. We are justified, I think, in regarding these activities as typical responses of the working poor to their social situation.

Although the working poor have constituted a near-permanent potential constituency for the Pentecostal movement, and one that was enlarged and made more receptive in periods of economic setback, only a relatively small proportion of them actually became Pentecostals. Thus, while an understanding of the conditions of the working poor as a whole moves us closer to an explanation of the Pentecostal movement, it does not in itself explain it. How were those who became Pentecostals different from those who did not?

Many, including some who were neither poor nor socially alienated, were predisposed to the movement by some personal crisis which they could not resolve, such as the death of a relative or friend, illness, marital and career failures. Such crises, as we have seen in the case of the early Pentecostal leaders, have probably been typical of converts to Pentecostalism to the present day.[7] If a Pentecostal proselytizer happened along at the appropriate moment, personal crisis alone was at times sufficient to lead one into the movement.[8] Yet, before World War II, it was unlikely that any but the socially deprived would have had the close personal contact with a Pentecostal necessary for recruitment. Thus, personal crisis was ordinarily linked to social deprivation in those who became Pentecostals. Their personal crisis grew out of problems shared by the working poor so that a Pentecostal of similar circumstances who seemed to have found a solution to his problems might gain a ready hearing. Still, personal crisis and social deprivation have characterized many more non-Pentecostals than Pentecostals.

By far the most important difference between those working poor who became Pentecostals and the much greater number who did not was the religious orientation of the former. The religious component of their cultural heritage set the Pentecostals apart and largely determined their unique response to the common problems of the working poor. Despite the variety of their former religious affiliations, those who became Pentecostals brought with them a general agreement that religion was a matter of "the heart" in which miracle and wonder held a central place. They were believers in the "religion of the Spirit" before they came into contact with Pentecostalism. Those few who were led into the movement by personal crisis alone quickly acquired the emotional, supernaturalistic outlook that had not been a part of their own religious background. But the vast majority of recruits to Pentecostalism came from the Holiness movement, from emotional, evangelical, and revivalistic Protestant backgrounds or from the more crudely superstitious forms of Catholicism.

As the Pentecostal movement became institutionalized, it drew recruits from higher levels of the class structure. But this happened only in the larger, more stable Pentecostal denominations and, even in these, not to any great extent until after World War II. Even today, it is very likely that the working poor constitute a larger proportion of Pentecostalism than they do of mainline Protestantism. Thus, the Pentecostal movement fits the classic pattern of sects that arise primarily among the socially deprived and later develop "churchly" characteristics as the deprivation of its membership is ameliorated.[9]

The contemporary neo-Pentecostal movement has apparently not drawn its constituency primarily from the same social classes as the early movement. Some regard this as undermining the validity of deprivation theory as applied to the current neo-Pentecostal movement, and, by implication, the early Pentecostal movement as well.[10]

There is no doubt, however, that material and social deprivation plus an animistic religious outlook combined to predispose most of the recruits to the early Pentecostal movement. The neo-Pentecostals do not suffer the material deprivation of the early Pentecostals, but they may suffer a real or imagined deprivation of respect and prestige. I would hazard the hypothesis that status deprivation and an anti-rationalist, anti-bureaucratic— i.e., anti-modern—temper has combined to predispose most of the recruits to the neo-Pentecostal movement. Pentecostals, old and new, have typically testified that before their conversion to Pentecostalism they felt empty and hungry for God or for something they could not articulate. In short, they felt deprived.[11]

The problems preventing the working poor generally from gaining access to the technologies and social institutions necessary for effecting social change were exacerbated in the case of the Pentecostals. The Pentecostal movement rejected the early-19th-century fusion of religious revivalism and social reform. Indeed, revivalism and social reform were set in opposition to each other in Pentecostal thought. The Salvation of individuals was the true gospel; the salvation of society—the Social Gospel— was the false gospel.

Pentecostal believers left the churches, refused to join unions, lodges, political parties, and indeed all institutions that might have been able to modify their social circumstances, because of their deeply ingrained taboo against "worldly" involvements. In short, rejecting all secular solutions to their problems, they found in Pentecostalism a religious resolution that was almost wholly other-worldly, symbolic, and psychotherapeutic.

The Pentecostal response consisted of a mixture of millenarianism and ecstasy. Either of these elements may arise at various levels of a social order undergoing some general crisis. In the upper reaches of the class structure they are likely to be attenuated and independent of one another. At lower levels they are intensified and more often combined.

Millenarianism proclaimed the existing world to be wicked and beyond redemption by any human efforts. As we have seen, this view accurately reflected the real social world of the Pentecostals. But even more generally, it reflected the real world of most of the working poor and that of many others whose lives were disrupted by the crisis of the 1890's and its aftermath. Thus, the millenarian response was prominent in the contemporaneous Adventist, Jehovah's Witness and Holiness movements, which drew their following largely from the same social base as the Pentecostals, and in the Keswick-Fundamentalist movement, which reached into the middle class.

Millenarianism also predicted the imminent destruction of this world and the creation of a new one. This answered perfectly to the psychological needs and aspirations of those whose social world was indeed collapsing and, from their standpoint, worthy of destruction. The aggressive hostilities generated by their frustrating social experience found expression and satisfaction in the rhetorical destruction of the world and of those who rejected and exploited the Pentecostals. The coming world of inverted social categories in which "the first will be last and the last will be first," would bring their final triumph and vindication, the satisfaction of their desire for respect and a better life. Pentecostalism was indeed an oblique expression of social protest.

Ecstasy was combined with millenarianism in the Pentecostal movement.[12] Yet ecstasy was waning in the Holiness movement and almost totally absent from the Adventist, Witness, and Keswick-Fundamentalist movements. These movements found the millenarian response alone sufficient, because they emphasized the cognitive and ethical dimensions of Christianity to the virtual exclusion of the emotional. Since ecstasy and millenarianism have, more often than not, been combined in lower-class religious movements in societies undergoing severe crisis, it was Pentecostalism, rather than these, which conformed to the norm.[13] For the Pentecostals, the problems arising from a social milieu substantially similar to that of the adherents of these other movements, could only be resolved by a millenarianism of emotional power and ecstatic dimensions.

The predisposition to ecstasy, then, is directly related to the relative emphasis given to the emotional component of religion. Where cultural tradition defines religion as primarily "of the heart" or "of the Spirit," ecstasy is implicit and struggles to become explicit. Ecstasy was present in virtually every American revival movement from the Great Awakening to the Pentecostal movement. All taught a crisis experience of salvation which brought forth the ecstatic response in many converts. Ecstasy was perhaps even more frequent and more intense in those revival movements that fostered still a second crisis experience called sanctification. Even today the psychological effects of ecstasy, though rarely the physical, may be found among those converts to evangelical and fundamentalist groups that teach a crisis salvation experience in which "Christ comes into your heart" and one is "born again of the Spirit." What we find in Pentecostalism are simply the more extreme psychological and physical phenomena springing from a very full development of the ecstatic potentiality of all religion "of the heart" and "of the Spirit."

Once present, ecstasy, like millenarianism, fluctuates in relation to the socio-economic fortunes of its devotees. The poorer, more dislocated and despised, the more marginal and highly mobile such people are in the social order, the more extreme will be their ecstatic response.

This certainly was the case with the Pentecostals in relation to all other religious groups in which ecstasy and millenarianism can be found. But it was also true within the Pentecostal movement itself. Those Pentecostal groups, like the Assemblies of God, that first achieved a modicum of stability and realized some improvement in their social circumstances, were the first in which ecstasy began to subside. On the other hand, less stable and newer groups, like the Oneness organizations, that were composed almost entirely of the most impoverished and socially ostracized Pentecostals, were characterized by a higher degree of ecstasy. Also, the degree of ecstasy in the parent Church of God (Cleveland, Tennessee) was lower than that in each of its schismatic offspring at the time they broke away. Then, too, the Pentecostal movement as a whole experienced a new wave of ecstasy during the Depression when masses of new converts were recruited into it from the lowest social classes. Today, ecstasy is most pronounced in independent storefront Pentecostal missions among blacks and recent Hispanic immigrants.

For the Pentecostals, as for many adherents of similar religious movements, ecstasy was a mode of adjustment to highly unstable social circumstances over which they had little or no control. When men cannot adjust to their environment by reason and action, they fall back upon symbolic manipulation and the inner world of desire and imagination. The most extreme form of this is ecstasy—being "outside one's self" and one's real world.[14] In the dissociated experience of "the Baptism" the Pentecostals symbolically expressed their disorganized, chaotic social circumstances, and were thus better able to accommodate to them.

Millenarian and ecstatic elements, in however diluted forms, were present in the evangelical Protestant consensus of the 19th century from which the Pentecostal movement emerged by way of the Holiness movement. Yet, while the Pentecostals were influenced by this tradition, their main inspiration came from the fountainhead of Christian ecstatic millenarianism: the Bible, and, in particular, the Acts of the Apostles, the First Epistle to the Corinthians, the Revelation of St. John and, to a lesser extent, Daniel.

The Pentecostals were a people of "the Book," avidly reading it over and over in a crudely literal manner. They also read Pentecostal, Holiness, and other Fundamentalist literature that confirmed their naive understanding of the Bible. The Pentecostals used Acts and I Corinthians as their guides to the present, and Revelation and Daniel as their guides to the future.

There is little that can be found in early Pentecostal ecstatic-millenarianism that cannot be found in these Biblical writings. Ecstatic-millenarianism was a central feature of early Christianity and of early Pentecostalism. Yet in the early Church rational and ethical elements soon predominated, while those features were distinctly minimal in early Pentecostalism. Ecstatic-millenarianism was central to early Pentecostalism because the Pentecostals self-consciously sought to duplicate that aspect of the life of the early Church, but also because the early Pentecostals stood in much the same relationship to their society as the Apostolic Church had to its. The similarity between the social circumstances of the early Christians and those of the early Pentecostals goes a long way toward explaining their common preoccupation with the cultivation of ecstasy and of millenarian fantasies.

Non-Pentecostal Christendom has found it extremely difficult to accept this. Part of the difficulty arises from an implicit agreement with the Pentecostal view that the Church today *should* be a replica of the original—an ahistorical approach that ignores the inevitability of social change and demeans the ability of Christianity to adapt to it. That resistance has also reflected the vested interests of the mainline clergy. But of at least equal importance is that the middle-class clergy and laity of most established Protestant churches cannot "see" the ecstatic-millenarianism that permeates the New Testament because, unlike the Pentecostals, they do not have a position in the social order similar to that of the early Christians. A frank acknowledgment that the ecstatic-millenarianism of the early Church is hardly appropriate for those who have more effective means for relating to their world would be far more meritorious than misguided attempts to explain away the obvious ecstatic-millenarian content of the New Testament writings.

The New Testament and Christian history provide examples of a great many manifestations of ecstasy other than speaking in tongues. Indeed, historically, speaking in tongues has been one of the least common of ecstatic phenomena. Why then was it singled out for emphasis by the Pentecostals? The answer lies partly in the preoccupation of the Holiness movement with the doctrine of Baptism in the Spirit. Once this presumed act of grace was redefined by the Keswick wing of Holiness as a baptism of power, rather than of purity, and once external physical evidence of it was sought, the stage was set for focusing on speaking in tongues.

Most Keswick-Holiness leaders, like Torrey, abandoned the search for incontrovertable physical evidence of "the Baptism," resting instead on the evidences of faith and works. But those who did not, like Parham and the students at Bethel College, could not help but "discover" the conjunction of speaking in tongues and the presence of the Spirit in the Book of Acts, as Torrey had earlier done. The doctrine of "the Baptism in the Spirit with the initial physical evidence of speaking in tongues" is not in the New Testament, and was not adopted by the bulk of Pentecostals until some time after the Los Angeles revival of 1906. But the germs of that doctrine, the elements from which it was made, may indeed be found in Acts and I Corinthians.

The early Christians had a much more amorphous view of the Spirit than the Pentecostals. The Church as described in the New Testament was continually "surprised" by the Spirit. No one could tell when the Spirit might "fall," but when it did, its presence could be seen. What could be seen, of course, were the physical automatisms resulting from mental dissociation. Among the variety of "manifestations," however, speaking in tongues was clearly regarded as proof positive that one was "filled with the Spirit."[15] There is no suggestion that this was considered the only proof, nor that the early Christians believed in a second or third act of grace called "the Baptism in the Holy Spirit." Nevertheless, the *conjunction* of speaking in tongues and the presence of the Spirit, rare as it may be in the New Testament, is found more often than that of any other manifestation and the Spirit. Indeed, if one were to search the New Testament only for a single specific physical sign of the Spirit's presence, it would be difficult not to find it in speaking in tongues.

While the Biblical basis for speaking in tongues among Pentecostals is fairly clear, the social basis for this specific practice is not. As modern society has become more complex and interdependent, a standardized but rapidly changing mode of verbal communication has become increasingly important in coordinating society's activities. For the individual, verbal facility in the use of the argot appropriate for a given situation has become a crucial factor in finding a way through the social maze. But those who became Pentecostals were lacking in verbal skills because of their minimal access to education and to other social institutions that produce and distribute culture. Here again, their Holiness heritage exacerbated their problem by demeaning education and inculcating rigid taboos against "worldly" literature, plays, movies, and, later, radio and television. Indeed, participation in any social or cultural activities that might have ameliorated their verbal inadequacy was discouraged if not prohibited. More importantly, most of those who became Pentecostals were handicapped by regional, ethnic, racial, and foreign accents, and many who were recent immigrants could hardly speak English at all. Minimal command of the major means of communication in modern urban culture was a concomitant of their social position, a means by which they were kept there, and a symbol of their social marginality.

Those who became Pentecostals could no doubt work on reducing or eliminating some of the putatively adverse characteristics of their racial, ethnic, regional, and cultural heritage such as clothing and eating styles, and norms of behavior and belief, but language was more intractable. Southern whites and blacks could not readily overcome their accents and dialects, nor could recent European and Latin American immigrants hope to achieve flawless English. In short, language was a central problem in the day-to-day lives of many of those who were drawn to the Pentecostal movement. Virtually powerless and speechless in the larger society, they found in Pentecostalism power and speech, however illusory, beyond their fondest dreams.

Speaking in tongues is a form of regressive speech.[16] It most closely resembles the earlier stages of speech development in infants. Some degree of regression is not only normal, but realistic for anyone undergoing great stress. When current patterns of behavior prove inadequate, people search backward into their experience in the hope of finding some more effective response to their environment. The diverse social stresses under which the Pentecostals labored and their specific language problem propelled them back in the experience of speaking in tongues to that infant stage of maturation where the first crude attempts at speech had indeed been an effective response to their milieu. The gods of childhood applauded their first incoherent utterances. The cries and babblings of infancy gave them power over their environment, and the feeling of well-being. That such feelings of power and happiness are recaptured in the experience of speaking in tongues is confirmed by the universal testimony of Pentecostals and neo-Pentecostals alike. The presumed approval of God, the praise of fellow believers and the awe of many non-believers created feelings of self-worth in those denied it in their day-to-day lives.

Even hatred and ridicule are rewards for those who are normally accorded no attention whatever. Thus, the powerless, voiceless position of the Pentecostals and the anxieties arising from that position provided a social basis for speaking in tongues.

Needless to say, speaking in tongues contributed little to solving the Pentecostals' real problem of communication in the larger society except, perhaps, in inspiring a new self-confidence that had some carry over to speech. For the most part, speaking in tongues, by assuaging the psychological effects of their social experience without appreciably changing it, contributed to the perpetuation of the Pentecostals in their social position and, hence, the perpetuation of the social basis for Pentecostalism.

Speaking in tongues also constituted a common Pentecostal "language," bridging the gaps between the many accents, dialects, and languages of the Pentecostals, and providing a "linguistic" basis for a new community of the Spirit. Speaking in tongues has been for the Pentecostals what Latin once was for the Roman Catholic laity: a means for communicating attitudes and emotions, but not thought, an expression of communal solidarity.[17]

The Pentecostal movement arose and survived because it served a number of functions for the Pentecostals, for American Protestantism, and for the wider social order.

The Pentecostal believer, it is clear, derived considerable psychic gain from his religion. By fostering the experience of "Baptism in the Holy Spirit," Pentecostalism provided a catharsis for the troubled; by creating close-knit, primary religious fellowships, it restored a sense of community to the displaced and ostracized; by holding forth the promise of an imminent Kingdom, it offered hope and solace for the despairing. These benefits were not unalloyed. The gains accruing from "the Baptism" tended to preclude adjustments at a psychological level that may have done greater service to the total personality. Yet there were many Pentecostals who achieved a new sense of well-being, self-respect, and self-confidence, and some whose psychic gains were translated into secular gains, however modest.

Perhaps the chief benefits of the movement went to the Pentecostal leaders. They were, for the most part, actual or prospective preachers whose careers were blocked by the increasing bureaucratization and higher educational requirements in the mainline Protestant denominations and, to some extent, even in the Holiness churches. The Pentecostal movement gave such men and women the opportunity for the realization of their career aspirations. The unorganized character of the movement initially, its later crystallization into myriad organizations, and its disdain for any but charismatic qualifications for leadership, created numerous positions of prestige with easy access to the ambitious and modestly talented.

To those outside the movement the positive aspects of Pentecostalism were often obscured by its severely negative evaluation of other Christian groups and of American culture generally. The Pentecostals assaulted not only the more extreme Modernists of their day, but all who made the slightest attempt to readjust the faith to recent scientific and historical findings; anything short of total rejection of Darwinism and Higher Criticism received unequivocal condemnation. They bewailed the abandonment of old-time, camp meeting revivalism as the standard technique for evangelization and bitterly condemned the Social Gospel as a perversion of the true gospel of individual salvation. They deplored any relaxation of the mores of an older, rural-agrarian society. The tone more than the substance of such Pentecostal criticisms was especially disconcerting to those outside the movement. The intemperate and indiscriminate nature of so much of what the Pentecostals said and wrote seemed to belie their claim to superior Christian experience and character.

It is hardly surprising that Christendom as a whole chose to ignore the Pentecostal movement in quiet disdain for half a century, or that some Holiness and hard-core Fundamentalists kept up an intermittent assault upon it as a heretical or anti-Christian cult.

Yet Pentecostalism, along with other emotional and fundamentalist movements, inadvertently served the interests of the mainline denominations. The Pentecostal movement opposed the trend toward increasing bureaucratization in the major denominations—a trend that paralleled the secular movement toward monopoly capitalism. It is not too fanciful, I think, to suggest that the relationship between the sects and the mainline denominations has been similar to that between small entrepreneurial businesses and the giant corporations; between competitive capitalism and monopoly capitalism. During the late 19th and early 20th centuries the larger Protestant denominations were moving toward greater collaboration, inspired by the dream of unity embodied in the Federal Council of Churches.[18] The reality, however, was oligopolistic predominance of the hierarchies of the half dozen or so largest churches over the whole of Protestantism. At the same time, the churches were beset by schismatic movements and the proliferation of small sects that were vehemently opposed to this monopolistic trend. These smaller groups, including the Pentecostals, constituted a religious petit-bourgeois sector vis-à-vis the monopoly-capitalist denominational sector.

Just as business monopolists accept, even encourage, a small entrepreneurial sector that does not really participate in capital accumulation but serves certain necessary social functions, so have the religious monopolists accepted a sectarian sector. So long as these sects remain small and divided, it is possible for mainline church leaders to actually idealize and romanticize them, since they pose no real threat to the established church order.[19] Moreover, the sects have assumed the "unprofitable" burden of Christianizing the poor. They have moved into the church buildings abandoned by the major churches in decaying rural and central-city areas, and have thereby freed the denominations to concentrate on the more "profitable" urban middle and upper classes.

The sects minister to those marginal regions, neighborhoods, and social classes from which no significant economic or prestigious benefit can be derived. Hence, the large denominations are perfectly content to allow the sects to compete fiercely among themselves for a share of what may be a sizeable, but nevertheless "unprofitable" religious "market."

The small sects, including the Pentecostals, jealously guard their independence. Their struggle against the major denominations is a struggle to avoid submergence into the religious "proletariat" of the monopolists, that is, relegation to church membership or an obscure position in the major churches. The sectarian leaders fear the loss of the rewards, however modest, of leadership in a small religious group. The petit-bourgeois fears and aspirations of the sectarians are reflected in the constant schisms and mergers that typify the sects. From this perspective, for example, the Pentecostal schisms may be seen as entrepreneurial competition for a share of the market, while mergers are business expedients to avoid dissolution or to dominate a larger share of that market.

The sects, including Pentecostalism, have also acted as a "safety valve" for discontent in the major churches, draining-off their "undesirable" church members. The effectual exportation of discontent freed the mainline denominations from the need to compromise in their headlong accommodation to emergent monopoly-capitalist society. By recruiting substantial numbers of the more conservative, fundamentalist and pietistic members out of the larger churches, the Pentecostals and other sectarians hastened the dominance of "culture religion" within mainline Protestantism. The only other significant opposition to that dominance came from those few seminaries where the Social Gospel had triumphed. The come-outer sectarians, lacking any socially responsive prophetic vision or leadership, became increasingly reactionary and irrelevant. The faculty and students of the Social Gospel seminaries, lacking any mass social base, became increasingly radical and irrelevant. Both developments enabled the major churches to become more nearly the dispensers of the ideology of the dominant monopoly-capitalist class: individualism, nationalism, free enterprise, the rights of capital, and the duty of labor to be honest, work hard, sacrifice, and worship Mammon and Success. The gospel of conformity to things as they are has been effectively internalized by masses of Americans in no small part through the influence of mainstream Protestantism.[20]

Again, as the business monopolists often profit from innovations developed in the petit-bourgeois sector, the major churches sometimes capitalize upon the innovations of the sects. Pentecostalism, for example, was rejected until, with the end of the "revival" of the 1950's and the impact of the anxieties of the 60's, some in the denominations, despite some reluctance, recognized in neo-Pentecostalism an opportunity to enhance their waning influence and membership.[21] The innovations of tongue-speaking, healing, and exorcism have, of course, been modified within the churches. They may be practiced only in the "proper" or "Biblical" manner, which is to say only in ways that do not greatly offend middle-class sensibilities or that do not challenge the existing church order.

The effects of the Pentecostal movement on the larger social order, while certainly not very extensive, have been of some significance. Pentecostalism eased the transit from rural to urban environments of a portion of those masses of displaced agrarians from here and abroad who have flowed sporadically but continuously into the cities since the late 19th century. Pentecostalism was a means of acculturation, providing a buffer against the chaotic impact of the urban-industrial milieu upon these migrants. The community of the Spirit was a haven to which the Pentecostals could repair from the buffetings of their daily experience. By the repeated ritual renewal of their ties with an older rural-agrarian religious tradition of emotional revivalism, and by the cathartic effects of ecstasy, Pentecostalism made it easier for them to function in their new environment. Moreover, Pentecostalism's rejection and condemnation of "the world" in rhetoric and symbol, in effect, liberated the Pentecostals to adapt to that world in practice.[22]

Pentecostalism has internalized in its adherents those characteristics and moral values that the society as a whole subscribes to, but only the lower classes are expected to live up to: passivity, obedience, honesty, hard work, thrift, self-denial, and sobriety. In short, Pentecostalism has served the social function of developing the ideal proletariat for urban-industrial capitalism—just as other sectarian movements have.[23] And it has probably succeeded in doing this among those who had the most difficulty in acculturating. Religious crisis experiences often involve a reorganization of personality, values, and behaviors that enable someone to adjust better to the imperatives of his situation. That Pentecostals found it necessary to pass through two, three, and sometimes more crisis experiences before they could feel at peace, suggests that, in their case, acculturation to urban-industrial society was acutely painful.

Most significantly for the larger society, Pentecostalism has not seriously challenged the social order or appreciably changed the *relative* position of Pentecostals within it. Their sporadic clashes with local authorities over the holding of religious meetings, and their initial opposition to bearing arms in World War I should not obscure their overall respect and subservience to "the powers that be." Aside from these early, modest challenges to secular authority, the Pentecostals have been ideal workers and citizens in every respect except for their cultivation of ecstasy. In the early years, by deploring all political and economic activism, Pentecostalism deflected social protest from effective expression, and channeled it into the harmless backwaters of religious ideology. Thus, Pentecostalism has been a conservative bulwark of the status quo.

In recent years Pentecostal conservatism has become even more apparent. With Pentecostals voting and joining unions, especially since World War II, their preachers, editorialists and church authorities with few exceptions have endorsed the most conservative political, social, and economic policies. Such endorsement is rarely stated explicitly in print, since, in public, Pentecostal and neo-Pentecostal spokesmen have either been utterly silent or "neutral" on the great social issues of our day. Nevertheless, from their conversation and from reading between the lines it is clear that the Pentecostals have been decidedly negative on union militancy and strikes, mass demonstrations, the anti-war movement, anti-racist activism, student protest, movements to end sex discrimination, and countercultural life styles.[24]

Even the presumed "radical" or "extremist" practices of tongues, exorcism, and healing are conservative in effect, because they have kept the

Pentecostals busily engaged in activities which have no impact whatever on the fundamental political economy or social relations of American society, and because they serve to reconcile the Pentecostals to things as they are. Because these practices are so "different" they have appeared to challenge the status quo, but they have been mere rituals of rebellion, cathartic mechanisms which in fact stabilize the social order.

The world of the early Pentecostals was one of share-cropping and tenant-farming, of backwoods cabins and ghetto tenements, of poverty and unemployment, of crime and vice, of racism and discrimination, of grinding, monotonous labor and fatigue, of material squalor and spiritual despair. Encumbered with racial and ethnic characteristics that constituted ineradicable handicaps in American society, faced with near-insuperable social and economic obstacles, restricted by background and opportunity from direct assault on the fundamental sources of their unhappy state, the Pentecostals found in Pentecostalism not only solace, but meaning and purpose for their lives. Rejected by the world, the Pentecostals in turn rejected the world. Lacking the skills and opportunities to improve their fortunes in this world, they renounced worldly success and developed their talents within the limits of the community of the Spirit. Denied the satisfaction of social relationships devoid of prejudice and condescension, they found salvation in a sublime experience of union with the Divine that carried them above their grueling, insipid lives, and in the fantastic contemplation of an imminent reversal of social roles and rewards. Like so many other dissenting religious movements in history, the early Pentecostal movement weighed church and society in the balance and found them wanting.

The root source of the Pentecostal movement was social discontent. Its initial millenarian vision contained within it a rejection of the social order and a hope for a new, more just society, but the belief that the Millennium would come without human effort was inimical to the real life interests of the Pentecostals. The radical social impulse inherent in the vision of the disinherited was transformed into social passivity, ecstatic escape, and, finally, a most conservative conformity.

Notes

Introduction

1. "Closely Guarded Secret," *Living Church,* July 10, 1960, pp. 5+; "Speaking in Tongues," *Time,* Aug. 15, 1960, pp. 53ff.; Donavan Bess, " 'Speaking in Tongues': The High Church Heresy," *The Nation,* Sept. 28, 1963, pp. 173–7; John G. Sherrill, *They Speak with Other Tongues* (New York: McGraw-Hill, 1964), pp. 64–6; Dennis J. Bennett, *Nine O'Clock in the Morning* (Plainfield, N.J.: Logos, 1970).

2. "Hidden Revival," *Time,* Feb. 1, 1963, pp. 64f.; F. Farell, "Outburst of Tongues: The New Penetration," *Christianity Today,* Sept. 13, 1963, pp. 3–7; McCandlish Phillips, "And There Appeared unto Them Tongues of Fire," *Saturday Evening Post,* May 16, 1964, pp. 30–32; W. M. Horn, "Speaking in Tongues: A Retrospective Appraisal," *Lutheran Quarterly,* XVII (Nov. 1965), pp. 316–29; Edward D. O'Connor, "Pentecost and Catholicism," *The Ecumenist,* VI (July–Aug. 1968), pp. 161–4. Besides the book by Sherrill cited in note 1, two others on the neo-Pentecostal movement are: Morton T. Kelsey, *Tongue-Speaking: An Experiment in Spiritual Experience* (Garden City: Doubleday, 1964), and David J. duPlessis, *Pentecost Outside Pentecost* (Dallas: the author, 1960).

3. Assemblies of God, General Council. *Minutes of the Annual Meeting of the Assemblies of God in the U.S.A., Canada and Foreign Lands,* Vol. 4, 1916, pp. 12f.

4. I refer to the adherents of the movement as "Pentecostals" throughout this study because the more grammatically correct "Pentecostalists" is rarely used by rank and file Pentecostals in referring to themselves. For similar reasons, and because of certain problems that I deal with in the next chapter, I use "speaking in tongues" rather than "glossolalia" (from the Greek *glossais lalein*).

5. Martin E. Marty, *A Nation of Behavers* (Chicago: Univ. of Chicago Press, 1976), pp. 106–25.

6. Walter J. Hollenweger, "Handbuch der Pfingstbewegung," 7 vols., unpublished Th.D. diss., Univ. of Zurich, 1965, I, lxvi–lxxvi, lists 149 different Pentecostal denominations and associations in the United States. The Pentecostal denominations listed in H. Jacquet, Jr. (ed.), *The Yearbook of American and Canadian Churches, 1975* (Nash-

ville: Abingdon, 1975), have a total of 1,953,338 members, but several denominations failed to report their statistics, including the largest black group, The Church of God in Christ. On the basis of my survey of Pentecostal congregations in New York City, I would estimate that at least 20 per cent of Pentecostals are not reported in any census.

7. For a survey of the historiography of Fundamentalism see Ernest R. Sandeen, "Toward a Historical Interpretation of the Origins of Fundamentalism," *Church History,* XXXVI (March 1967), 66–83, and "Another Look at Fundamentalism: A Response to Ernest R. Sandeen," *Church History,* XXXVII (June 1968), 195–202. See also Sandeen's superb study of the millenarian origins of the Fundamentalist movement, *The Roots of American Fundamentalism* (Chicago: Univ. of Chicago Press, 1970).

8. Most Pentecostals believe the "new birth" to be a single experience of conversion; some believe it consists of both the conversion experience and the "Baptism in the Holy Spirit"; the "Oneness" or unitarian Pentecostals add still a third requirement, water baptism "in Jesus' name," i.e., not in the name of the Father, Son, and Holy Ghost.

9. Or the seven or fourteen points noted by Sandeen (*Roots,* pp. xiv–xv, 192, 273–7), which do not, I think, differ very much in substance from the five points: the verbal inerrancy of the Bible, the Virgin Birth, substitutionary atonement and physical resurrection of Jesus, and the literal, physical Second Coming of Christ.

10. Sandeen, *Roots,* pp. xiii, *et passim.*

Chapter I

1. *The Idea of the Holy* (New York: Oxford Univ. Press, 1961), *passim.* Otto's views have been contested, of course, but these remarks certainly apply to Pentecostalism and similar ecstatic movements.

2. P. G. S. Hopwood, *The Religious Experience of the Primitive Church* (New York: Charles Scribner's Sons, 1937), pp. 145–206.

3. Ernst Troeltsch, *The Social Teachings of the Christian Churches,* 2 vols. (New York: Harper & Bros., 1960), *passim,* esp. II, pp. 691–802.

4. Of the substantial literature on the subject see, for example, I. M. Lewis, *Ecstatic Religion* (Baltimore: Penguin, 1971); Raymond Prince (ed.), *Trance and Possession States* (Montreal: R. M. Bucke Memorial Society, 1968); George Barton Cutten, *The Psychological Phenomena of Christianity* (New York: Charles Scribner's Sons, 1908); James B. Pratt, *The Religious Consciousness* (New York: Macmillan, 1920); Frederick M. Davenport, *Primitive Traits in Religious Revivals* (New York: Macmillan, 1905).

An excellent professional psychological treatment of tongues and related phenomena may be found in the classic work of Pierre Janet, *The Major Symptoms of Hysteria* (New York: Hafner Publishing Co., 1965), 1st ed. 1907. A more recent work that incorporates newer psychological concepts is Henry P. Laughlin, *The Neurosis in Clinical Practice* (Philadelphia: W. B. Saunders, 1956), esp. pp. 241–372. Anyone may display hysterical symptoms under certain conditions; this does not mean, necessarily, that he or she is suffering from the disease clinically defined as hysteria.

5. For the history of possession see the monumental work of T. K. Oesterreich, *Possession: Demoniacal and Other* (Secaucus, N.J.: Lyle Stuart, 1966), 1st German ed. 1921.

6. A convenient summary of the body of opinion may be found in William J. Samarin,

Tongues of Men and Angels (New York: Macmillan, 1972), pp. 19–24. Samarin, however, rejects this view.

7. Lewis, *Ecstatic Religion*, pp. 45f.; Erika Bourguignon, "World Distribution and Patterns of Possession States," in Prince, *Trance and Possession States*, pp. 3–34.

8. *Apostolic Faith* (Los Angeles), II, p. 13 (May 1908).

9. Ralph M. Riggs, *The Spirit Himself* (Springfield, Mo.: Gospel Publishing House, 1949), p. 94.

10. "Symposium on Speaking in Tongues," *Dialogue*, 2 (Spring 1963), 152–9.

11. Arnold M. Ludwig, a recognized authority on altered states, defines them as "mental states . . . which can be recognized subjectively by the individual himself (or by an objective observer of the individual) as representing a sufficient deviation in terms of subjective experience or psychological functioning, from certain general norms as determined by the subjective experience and psychological functioning of that individual during alert, waking consciousness." "Altered States of Consciousness," in Prince, *Trance and Possession States*, pp. 69f.

   It may be that altered states represent the *constriction* of consciousness and not, as some would have it, its expansion. Peter H. Van Der Walde, "Trance States and Ego Psychology," in Prince, *Trance and Possession States*, pp. 57–68. See also William Sargant's introduction to the Perennial Library edition of his *Battle for the Mind* (New York: Harper & Row, 1971), in which he affirms the similar effects of sensory deprivation and sensory bombardment on the brain and on thought.

12. Samarin's position is that tongues are "most often independent of dissociative behavior" (*Tongues of Men and Angels*, p. 33), but as he himself acknowledges, this runs counter to the observations of nearly all other scholars (including my own over a period of 30 years). The internal evidence of the very Pentecostal testimonies that he quotes is incompatible with Samarin's view (*Tongues of Men and Angels*, pp. 22–33, 70, *et passim*).

   Others who share Samarin's view on this point include former Pentecostal Walter J. Hollenweger, *The Pentecostals: The Charismatic Movement in the Churches* (Minneapolis: Augsburg, 1972), p. 344, and D. Moody Smith, "Glossolalia and Other Spiritual Gifts in a New Testament Perspective," *Interpretation*, 28 (1974):307–20.

13. Felicitas Goodman, "Phonetic Analysis of Glossolalia in Four Cultural Settings," *Journal for the Scientific Study of Religion*, 8 (1969): 227–39.

14. George Barton Cutten, *Speaking with Tongues: Historically and Psychologically Considered* (New Haven: Yale Univ. Press, 1927); Sargant, *Battle for the Mind*. Sargant's more recent work is *The Mind Possessed: A Physiology of Possession, Mysticism and Faith Healing* (New York: J. B. Lippincott, 1974).

15. Raymond Prince, "Can the EEG Be Used in the Study of Possession States?" in Prince, *Trance and Possession States*, pp. 121–37; Peter H. Van Der Walde, "Trance States and Ego Psychology," *ibid.*, pp. 57–68. "Hypnosis," says Van Der Walde, "is the presence of an induced trance or altered state."

16. Lewis, *Ecstatic Religion*, p. 46.

17. John P. Kildahl, *The Psychology of Speaking in Tongues* (New York: Harper & Row, 1972), pp. 48–56. The research done up to 1968 on the psychological health of tongue-speakers is summarized by E. Mansell Pattison, "Behavioral Science Research on the Nature of Glossolalia," *Journal of the American Scientific Affiliation*, 20 (Sept. 1968), 73–86.

18. Ames T. Richardson, "Psychological Interpretations of Glossolalia: A Reexamination of Research," *Journal for the Scientific Study of Religion,* 12 (1973): 199–207.

19. Lewis, *Ecstatic Religion,* p. 185.

20. Carl Brumback, *What Meaneth This?* (Springfield, Mo.: Gospel Publishing House, 1947), pp. 109–15; Harold Horton, *The Gifts of the Spirit* (Bedfordshire, Eng.: Redemption Tidings Bookroom, 1946), p. 104; Donald Gee, *Concerning Spiritual Gifts* (Springfield, Mo.: Gospel Pub. House, 1947), p. 57; Charles W. Conn, *Pillars of Pentecost* (Cleveland, Tenn.: Pathway Press, 1956), p. 57; Elijah C. Clark, *The Baptism of the Holy Ghost "and More"* (Cleveland, Tenn.: Church of God Pub. House, 1931), pp. 105, 117–19; Robert Chandler Dalton, *Tongues Like as of Fire: A Critical Study of Modern Tongues Movements in the Light of Apostolic and Patristic Times* (Springfield, Mo.: Gospel Pub. House, 1945), pp. 103–6; Steve Durasoff, *Bright Wind of the Spirit* (Englewood Cliffs, N.J.: Prentice-Hall, 1972), pp. 1, 4, 7f., *et passim.*

    For innumerable cases of alleged xenoglossy see Ralph W. Harris, *Spoken by the Spirit* (Springfield, Mo.: Gospel Pub. House, 1973).

21. *Word and Witness,* March 20, 1913, p. 4. See also *Midnight Cry,* 3 (May 1915), pp. 1–3; and "Gibberish or Real Languages?", *Weekly Evangel,* Nov. 13, 1915, p. 1.

22. *Pentecostal Evangel,* July 17, 1926, pp. 5f.; Sept. 18, 1926, pp. 6f.; July 30, 1927, pp. 4ff.

23. "The Truth about the Pentecostal Revival," pamphlet (London, 1908), pp. 10f., 34.

24. Polman, "As the Spirit Gave Them Utterance," *Weekly Evangel,* Feb. 24, 1917, pp. 5f.; Donald Gee, "Interpretation of Tongues," *Pentecostal Evangel,* May 22, 1926, pp. 6f.

25. Samarin, *Tongues of Men and Angels,* p. 107.

26. Cutten, *Speaking with Tongues,* pp. 178–81. Hollenweger is one of the few who accept the claims of Pentecostals to speak in languages they have never learned.

27. Conversation with Paul Qualben, psychiatrist at Brooklyn Medical Center who has studied tongue-speech for at least a decade; *Christianity Today,* Nov. 8, 1963, pp. 17–20; F. Farrell, "Outburst of Tongues: The New Penetration," *Christianity Today,* Sept. 3, 1963, pp. 3–7; *New York Times,* May 17, 1964, p. 86; John L. Sherrill, *They Speak with Other Tongues* (N.Y.: McGraw-Hill, 1964), pp. 112–13.

28. Samarin, *Tongues of Men and Angels,* pp. 2, 69, 103–28.

29. Samarin himself acknowledges that vocalizations other than those that fit his definition are indeed considered speaking in tongues among Pentecostals, *Tongues of Men and Angels,* pp. 11ff., 37f.

30. Cutten, *Speaking with Tongues,* pp. 178–81; Samarin, *Tongues of Men and Angels,* pp. 112ff. My own experience corroborates this.

31. Hollenweger, *The Pentecostals,* p. 344. Numerous contemporary comedians like Danny Kaye, Jerry Lewis, and Buddy Hackett have demonstrated this talent, but I have never heard a Pentecostal tongue-speaker who could.

32. Cutten, *Speaking with Tongues,* pp. 176ff.

33. Thomas Flournoy, *From India to the Planet Mars: A Study of a Case of Somnambulism with Glossolalia* (New York: Harper & Bros., 1900).

34. Ian Stevenson, *Xenoglossy* (Charlottesville, Va.: University Press of Virginia, 1975).

35. L. Carlyle May, "A Survey of Glossolalia and Related Phenomena in Non-Christian Religions," *American Anthropologist,* 58 (Feb. 1956): 75–96; G. J. Jennings, "An Ethnological Study of Glossolalia," *Journal of the American Scientific Affiliation,* 20

(1968): 5–16; Oesterreich, *Possession,* pp. 236–375; J. W. Westgarth, *The Holy Spirit and the Primitive Mind* (London: Victory Press, 1946); M. Van Der Kroef, "Messianic Movements in the Celebes, Sumatra and Borneo," in Sylvia Thrupp (ed.), *Millennial Dreams in Action* (New York: Schocken, 1970), pp. 101f., 116.

36. Eduard Lohse, *The New Testament Environment* (Nashville: Abingdon, 1971), p. 163.

37. William Foxwell Albright, *From the Stone Age to Christianity* (Garden City, N.Y.: Doubleday Anchor, 1957), pp. 300–306, *et passim.*

38. Lohse, *New Testament Environment,* pp. 222–43; Johannes Behm, "Glossa," in Gerhard Kittel and Gerhard Friedrich (eds.), *Theological Dictionary of the New Testament,* 10 vols. (Grand Rapids, Mich.: Wm. B. Eerdmans, 1964–76), I, pp. 719–27; Hans Lietzmann, *The Beginnings of the Christian Church* (New York: Meridian, 1963), pp. 168–70; Hans Jonas, *The Gnostic Religion,* 2nd ed. rev. (Boston: Beacon, 1963), pp. 284f.; S. Angus, *The Mystery Religions and Christianity* (New York: Charles Scribner's Sons, 1925), pp. 1–38, *et passim.*

39. Eduard Schweizer, "Pneuma," in *Theological Dictionary of the New Testament,* VI, pp. 332–454.

40. Hans Conzelmann, *I Corinthians: A Commentary on the First Epistle to the Corinthians* (Philadelphia: Fortress, 1975), p. 65.

41. Ernst Käsemann, *Essays on New Testament Themes* (Naperville, Ill.: Alec R. Allenson, 1964), p. 138.

42. Schweizer, "Pneuma"; Behm, "Glossa"; Ernst Käsemann, *New Testament Questions Today* (Philadelphia: Fortress, 1969), pp. 126f. (see also p. 116 and fn. p. 109). See also Lietzmann, *Beginnings,* pp. 122–7, 142–9; Hans Lietzmann, *The Founding of the Church Universal* (New York: Meridian, 1963), pp. 54–7; Hans Conzelmann, *History of Primitive Christianity* (Nashville, Tenn.: Abingdon, 1973), p. 49; Hans Conzelmann, *Outline of the Theology of the New Testament* (New York: Harper & Row, 1969), pp. 37f.; Conzelmann, *I Corinthians,* p. 234; Ernst Käsemann, *Perspectives on Paul* (Philadelphia: Fortress, 1971), pp. 15, 122, 130f.; Käsemann, *Essays on New Testament Themes,* p. 138; Ferdinand Hahn, *The Worship of the Early Church* (Philadelphia: Fortress, 1973), pp. 44–6, 67, 70f.; John C. Hurd, *The Origin of I Corinthians* (Naperville, Ill.: Alec R. Allenson, 1965), p. 192; Rudolf Bultmann, *Primitive Christianity in Its Contemporary Setting* (New York: Meridian, 1956), pp. 175–7, 203f.; Karl Kundsin, "Primitive Christianity in the Light of Gospel Research," in Rudolf Bultmann and Karl Kundsin, *Form Criticism* (New York: Harper & Row, 1962), pp. 127f.; F. F. Bruce, *New Testament History* (Garden City, N.Y.: Doubleday, 1971), pp. 320f.; Maurice Goguel, *The Primitive Church* (New York: Macmillan, 1964), pp. 263–70; Philip Schaff, *Apostolic Christianity, A.D. 1–100* (New York: Charles Scribner's Sons, 1910), pp. 230–40; Hopwood, *The Religious Experience,* pp. 145–51.

43. Conzelmann, *History of Primitive Christianity,* p. 51; Arthur Darby Nock, *Early Gentile Christianity and Its Hellenistic Background* (New York: Harper & Row, 1964), pp. 88f.; Lietzmann, *Beginnings,* p. 148; Walter Schmithals, *Gnosticism in Corinth* (Nashville: Abingdon, 1971). p. 175n.

44. Behm, "Glossa," lists I Thes. 5:19ff.; II Cor. 12:2ff. Käsemann, *Perspectives on Paul,* lists Rom. 8:26f.; II Cor. 12:4ff.; Eph. 6:18; Jude 20; and Rev. 22:17. D. Moody Smith, "Glossolalia and Other Spiritual Gifts in a New Testament Perspective," *Interpretation,* 28 (1974), 307–20, lists Rom. 8:26f.; I Thes. 5:19f.; Eph. 5:18f. Cutten,

Speaking with Tongues, pp. 19f., lists I Thes. 5:19f.; Eph. 5:18f.; and Col. 3:1–6.
Even such a prominent Pentecostal as Donald Gee has confessed that "the scriptural basis for the practice is admittedly slender," "Movement Without a Man," *Christian Life*, July 1966, p. 52.

45. Stuart D. Currie, " 'Speaking in Tongues': Early Evidence Outside the New Testament Bearing on 'Glossais Lalein'," *Interpretation*, 19 (July 1965), 274–94.

46. Werner George Kümmel, ed., *Introduction to the New Testament*, rev. ed. (Nashville: Abingdon, 1973), p. 279.

47. Behm, "Glossa."

48. Ernst Haenchen, *The Acts of the Apostles: A Commentary* (Philadelphia: Fortress, 1971), pp. 304–8, 354, 445, 554.

49. Currie, " 'Speaking in Tongues'."

50. Robert H. Gundry, " 'Ecstatic Utterance' (N.E.B.)?'' *Journal of Theological Studies*, 17 (1966): 299–307; J. G. Davies, "Pentecost and Glossolalia," *Journal of Theological Studies*, 3 (1952): 228–31.

51. Haenchen, *Acts*, p. 175. Hermann W. Beyer, "Heteros," in *Theological Dictionary of the New Testament*, II, pp. 702–4, takes the same neutral stance.

52. Behm, "Glossa"; Krister Stendahl, "The New Testament Evidence," in Michael P. Hamilton (ed.), *The Charismatic Movement* (Grand Rapids: Eerdmans, 1975). This position is also taken by Conzelmann, *History of Primitive Christianity*, p. 36; Gerhard Krodel, "An Exegetical Examination," in "Symposium on Speaking in Tongues," *Dialogue*, 2 (Sept. 1963): 152–9; Leonhard Goppelt, *Apostolic and Post-Apostolic Times* (New York: Harper & Row, 1970), p. 22; Eduard Lohse, "Pentecost," *Theological Dictionary of the New Testament*, IV, pp. 44–53 (who cites Martin Dibelius); Frank W. Beare, "Speaking with Tongues: A Critical Survey of the New Testament Evidence," *Journal of Biblical Literature*, 83 (Sept. 1964): 229–46; S. McL. Gilmour, "Easter and Pentecost," *Journal of Biblical Literature*, 81 (Jan. 1962): 62–66; D. Moody Smith, "Glossolalia and . . ."; C. G. Williams, "Glossolalia as a Religious Phenomenon: 'Tongues' at Corinth and Pentecost," *Religion*, 5 (Jan. 1975): 16–32; Doremus Almy Hayes, *The Gift of Tongues* (New York: Eaton & Main, 1913), pp. 29–48 (who cites Schmeidel, Zeller, Meyer, Ramsey, and Bartlet); Joseph Klausner, *From Jesus to Paul* (Boston: Beacon, 1943), p. 275 (who cites Foakes-Jackson); and Haenchen, pp. 172f., (who does not agree, but cites as those who do: Bauernfeind, Lohse, Trocme, and Harnack).

53. Kümmel, *Introduction to the New Testament*, p. 186.

54. Conzelmann, *I Corinthians*, pp. 208f., 237ff., 221; Käsemann, *Perspectives on Paul*, p. 134; Hahn, pp. 70–73; Hans von Campenhausen, *Ecclesiastical Authority and Spiritual Power in the Church of the First Three Centuries* (Stanford: Stanford Univ. Press, 1969), p. 60.

55. Conzelmann, *I Corinthians*, pp. 233f.

56. Kümmel, *Introduction to the New Testament*, p. 272; Schmithals, *Gnosticism in Corinth*, pp. 174f., 193f.

57. *Ibid.*, pp. 174f., 193f.

58. Conzelmann, *I Corinthians*, p. 214.

59. Käsemann, *Perspectives on Paul*, p. 123, and *Essays on New Testament Themes*, pp. 83f.

Paul also fought a second-front war against legalistic Judaising tendencies which threatened to make of Christianity just another Jewish sect.

60. Käsemann, *Perspectives on Paul,* p. 152, and *Essays on New Testament Themes,* pp. 63-7, 74f., 83f.; Schmithals, *Gnosticism in Corinth,* pp. 172ff.

61. Campenhausen, *Ecclesiastical Authority,* pp. 55-75; Hans von Campenhausen, *Tradition and Life in the Church* (Philadelphia: Fortress, 1968), pp. 123-33; Lietzmann, *Beginnings,* pp. 142-9; Conzelmann, *History,* pp. 77, 106f.; Hahn, *Worship,* pp. 44f.

62. Käsemann, *Perspectives on Paul,* p. 123; see also Conzelmann, *History,* p. 106.

63. Schmithals, *Gnosticism in Corinth,* pp. 275-79; Lietzmann, *Founding,* pp. 56f.

64. Käsemann, *Essays,* pp. 88, 188; Campenhausen, *Ecclesiastical Authority,* pp. 76f.; Conzelmann, *History,* pp. 115-18; Lietzmann, *Founding,* pp. 54-68.

65. Lietzmann, *Founding,* pp. 54-61, 193-202; Hahn, *Worship,* pp. 79-98; Campenhausen, *Ecclesiastical Authority,* pp. 76ff.; Conzelmann, *History,* pp. 116-18. The quote is from Lietzmann, *Founding,* p. 59.

66. Cutten, *Speaking with Tongues,* pp. 32-47.

67. This position was officially adopted about the year 1000. Philip T. Weller (ed.), *The Roman Ritual* (Milwaukee: Bruce Publishing, 1952), II, p. 169. See the numerous examples of "demon possession" evidenced by speaking in tongues in Leon Cristiani, *Evidence of Satan in the Modern World* (New York: Macmillan, 1962), and in Oesterreich, *Possession, passim.*

68. Bernard L. Bresson, *Studies in Ecstasy* (New York: Vantage Press, 1966), *passim;* Stanley H. Frodsham, *With Signs Following* (Springfield, Mo.: Gospel Pub. House, 1941), pp. 153-62; Dalton, pp. 15-30, 107-13; Riggs, *The Spirit Himself,* pp. 90-100; Brumback, *What Meaneth This?,* pp. 89-96; Gee, *Pentecostal Movement,* pp. 9-10; Elijah Clark, *Baptism of the Holy Ghost,* pp. 113-15; Fred J. Foster, *Think It Not Strange: A History of the Oneness Movement* (St. Louis, Mo.: Pentecostal Pub. House, 1965), pp. 22f.; Steve Durasoff, *Bright Wind,* pp. 31-60.

There is currently a widely circulated but baseless rumor among Pentecostals that Billy Graham speaks in tongues, in private devotions at least.

69. Klaude Kendrick, *The Promise Fulfilled: A History of the Modern Pentecostal Movement* (Springfield, Mo.: Gospel Pub. House, 1961), p. 20; Nichol, *Pentecostalism,* p. 21.

70. For post-Los Angeles revival reports of tongue-speaking alleged to have taken place before that revival see Francis M. Britton, *Pentecostal Truth* (Royston, Ga.: Publishing House of the Pentecostal Holiness Church, 1919), pp. 234-9; Daniel Awry, *c.* 1891, *Apostolic Faith* (Los Angeles), I (Oct. 1906), p. 4; Martha J. Lewis, 1898, *The Upper Room,* I (Sept. 1909), pp. 1f.; A. P. Dennis, 1887, *Weekly Evangel* (May 1916); C. E. Preson, *c.* 1874, *Latter Rain Evangel,* v. 1-5 (1909), pp. 22f.; H. L. Christopher, in Sweden, 1899 (Christopher to Stanley E. Frodsham, Sept. 1, 1926, letter in the files of the *Pentecostal Evangel,* Springfield, Missouri); Mrs. Michael Baxter (wife of the founder of *Christian Herald*), *c.* 1885, *Pentecostal Evangel,* April 10, 1926, p. 3; Paul Bettex at Princeton Theological Seminary, 1890, Stanley H. Frodsham, *Wholly for God* (Springfield, Mo.: Gospel Pub. House, n.d.), p. 15; among Holiness people in Tennessee and North Carolina, 1899-1900, *Weekly Evangel,* Jan. 29, 1916, pp. 4f., Feb. 5, 1916, pp. 4f., Feb. 17, 1916, pp. 2f.; among Holiness Baptists in Georgia and South Carolina, mid-1890's, *Weekly Evangel,* May 6, 1916, pp. 4f.; among the "Gift Peo-

ple" of New England, beginning in 1854 and continuing to 1906, R. B. Swan, *Weekly Evangel*, Feb. 12, 1916, p. 4; A. J. Rawson, *The Apostolic Faith* (Los Angeles), I (Dec. 1906), p. 3; and V. P. Simmons, "History of Tongues," *The Bridegroom's Messenger*, I (Dec. 1907), pp. 2f.; in Armenia and south Russia in the mid-19th century, Kelsey, *Tongue-Speaking*, pp. 59, 65–8; see also Frodsham, *With Signs Following*, pp. 7–17.

See, as an example of this kind of "history," George H. Williams and Edith Waldvogel, "A History of Speaking in Tongues *and Related Gifts*" (my italics), in Hamilton, *The Charismatic Movement*.

71. On the Camisards see Cutten, *Speaking with Tongues*, pp. 48–66; on the Irvingites see P. E. Shaw, *The Catholic Apostolic Church* (New York: King's Crown Press, 1946), and Andrew L. Drummond, *Edward Irving and His Circle* (London: James Clarke & Co., 1935); on the Mormons see Thomas F. O'Dea, *The Mormons* (Chicago: Univ. of Chicago Press, 1957), pp. 158–60. As recently as 1941 the Mormon leader Heber Grant asserted that all the gifts of the Spirit were present in his denomination, G. Homer Durham (ed.), *Gospel Standards* (Salt Lake City: Deseret New Press, 1941), pp. 10ff. On the Spiritualists see Charles W. Ferguson, *The Confusion of Tongues* (Garden City, N.Y.: Doubleday, Doran & Co., 1928), pp. 29–32.

Chapter II

1. See Appendix I.
2. For a study of Wesley's shifting ideas on sanctification see Harold Lindstrom, *Wesley and Sanctification* (London: Epworth Press, 1956). For the historical development of those ideas in American Methodism see John Leland Peters, *Christian Perfectionism and American Methodism* (Nashville: Abingdon Press, 1956).
3. Timothy L. Smith, *Revivalism and Social Reform* (New York: Harper & Row, 1965), pp. 45–62; Sidney E. Mead, *The Lively Experiment* (New York: Harper & Row, 1963), pp. 29–35, 55–6, 121–2; Winthrop Hudson, *The Great Tradition of the American Churches* (New York: Harper, 1963), pp. 65–78.
4. Smith, *Revivalism*, pp. 103–13; Charles G. Finney, *Lectures on Revivals of Religion* (New York, 1898), pp. 415–16; Charles G. Finney, *Lectures on Systematic Theology* (Oberlin, 1846), pp. 550–53.
5. Smith, *Revivalism, passim*. For the view that holiness declined in the two decades before the Civil War, see Merrill E. Gaddis, "Christian Perfectionism in America," unpublished Ph.D. dissertation, University of Chicago, 1929, pp. 268–84.
6. Mead, *The Lively Experiment*, pp. 134–68; Smith, *Revivalism*, pp. 15–44, 80–102.
7. Gaddis, "Christian Perfectionism in America," pp. 311–20; Timothy L. Smith, "The Holiness Crusade," *The History of American Methodism*, ed. Emory S. Bucke, 3 vols. (Nashville, Tenn.: Abingdon Press, 1964), II, 608–27; Timothy L. Smith, *Called Unto Holiness: The Story of the Nazarenes* (Kansas City, Mo.: Nazarene Publishing House, 1962), pp. 21–6; Peters, *Christian Perfectionism and American Methodism*, pp. 133–9.
8. Henry F. May, *Protestant Churches and Industrial America* (New York: Harper & Bros., 1949), pp. 39–44.
9. U.S. Bureau of Census, *Historical Statistics of the United States* (Washington, D.C.: Government Printing Office, 1960), pp. 228–9.
10. H. Richard Niebuhr, *The Social Sources of Denominationalism* (Cleveland: World

Publishing Co., 1962), pp. 34–9, 77–80, 104–5, *et passim;* Aaron I. Abell, *The Urban Impact on American Protestantism, 1865–1900* (London, 1962), pp. 5–7, 62, 246; Mead, *The Lively Experiment,* pp. 161–2.

In a religious census of Pittsburgh and Allegheny in 1886 it was found that business, professional, and salaried men comprised less than 10% of the population, but over 60% of Protestant church membership (Abell, p. 62).

11. Abell, *Urban Impact,* pp. 5–7, 246; Mead, *The Lively Experiment,* pp. 160–62, 172–3; Paul Carter, *The Decline and Rise of the Social Gospel* (Ithaca, N.Y.: Cornell Univ. Press, 1956), pp. 54–6, 63–8; William Warren Sweet, *The Story of Religion in America* (New York: Harper & Bros., 1939), p. 505; Hudson, *The Great Tradition,* pp. 161–2.

12. F.N. Zabriskie, *And the Poor Have the Gospel Preached to Them* (New York, n.d.), pp. 14–15, quoted in Abell, *Urban Impact,* pp. 6–7; see also Henry F. May, *Protestant Churches,* pp. 61–2; and Paul A. Carter, *The Spiritual Crisis of the Gilded Age* (De-Kalb: Northern Ill. Univ. Press, 1971), pp. 9–13.

13. Hudson, *The Great Tradition,* pp. 198–202; Carter, *Spiritual Crisis,* pp. 9–10; Franklin Hamlin Littell, *From State Church to Pluralism* (Garden City, N.Y.: Doubleday, 1962), pp. 69, 72, 80, 93, 125.

14. Henry F. May, *Protestant Churches, passim,* esp. pp. 170–204; Charles H. Hopkins, *The Rise of the Social Gospel in American Protestantism, 1865–1900* (New Haven: Yale Univ. Press, 1940), *passim.*

15. Peters, *Christian Perfectionism and American Methodism,* pp. 143–4.

16. *Ibid.,* pp. 133–48.

17. Smith, "Holiness Crusade"; Gerald O. McCulloh, "The Changing Theological Emphases," *The History of American Methodism,* ed. Bucke, Vol. II, 594–9.

18. The most thorough treatment of the separatist phase of the late 19th-century Holiness movement as a whole is Charles Edwin Jones, "Perfectionist Persuasion: A Social Profile of the National Holiness Movement, 1867–1936," unpub. Ph.D. diss., Univ. of Wisconsin, 1968.

19. *Ibid.,* pp. 141ff., 150, 176ff.

20. Peters, *Christian Perfectionism and American Methodism,* pp. 139–42; *The Central Christian Advocate,* Jan. 18, 1882, quoted in Smith, "Holiness Crusade."

21. *Journal of the General Conference, Methodist Episcopal Church, 1894* (Nashville, 1894), p. 25, quoted in Smith, "Holiness Crusade."

22. Peters, *Christian Perfectionism and American Methodism,* pp. 148–80; Smith, "Holiness Crusade"; Gaddis, "Christian Perfectionism in America," pp. 321–53; Smith, *Called,* pp. 11–53.

23. See references in fn. 21 above.

24. Mary B. Woodworth-Etter, *Signs and Wonders God Wrought in the Ministry for Forty Years* (Chicago: the author, 1916), pp. 48–9, 63–4, 70.

25. *Ibid.,* p. 76.

26. *Ibid.,* pp. 44–5, 118.

27. *Ibid.,* pp. 145–7, 152–3. These incidents of speaking in tongues before the Los Angeles revival are suspect, since I was not able to corroborate them and they were all reported after 1906.

28. The fullest account of the Fire-Baptized movement is in Synan, *Holiness-Pentecostal Movement,* pp. 55–76. Joseph E. Campbell, *The Pentecostal Holiness Church, 1898–1948* (Franklin Springs, Ga.: The Publishing House of the Pentecostal Holiness

Church, 1951), pp. 193–205; F. M. Britton, *Pentecostal Truth* (Royston, Ga.: Publishing House of the Pentecostal Holiness Church, 1919), p. 232. Neither Campbell nor Synan nor Britton explains Irwin's additional "baptisms," and the only reference I could find to them in the sources was in a letter from W. E. Fuller, the overseer of the black churches of the Fire-Baptized Church, to the editor of *Live Coals,* January 11, 1905, in which Fuller says, "I praise God for the blood that cleans up, the Holy Ghost that fills up, the fire that burns up, and the dynamite that blows up, so I am above sin, the flesh and the devil, and in this holy war to stand till Jesus comes."

29. A. J. Tomlinson, *The Last Great Conflict* (Cleveland, Tenn.: Press of Walter E. Rodgers, 1913), pp. 189–198; L. Howard Juillerate, *Brief History of the Church of God* (Cleveland, Tenn.: Church of God Publishing House, 1922), pp. 7–8; Homer A. Tomlinson (ed.), *Diary of A. J. Tomlinson,* 3 vols. (New York: Church of God, World Headquarters, 1949–55), I, 25–6. The claims of having spoken in tongues before the Los Angeles revival are suspect because they post-date that revival.

30. Frank Bartleman, *How Pentecost Came to Los Angeles* (Los Angeles: the author, 1925), pp. 21–31, 79–81.

31. Conn, *Pillars of Pentecost,* p. 42; Juillerate, *Brief History,* p. 12; Campbell, *The Pentecostal Holiness Church,* pp. 204–5; Woodworth-Etter, *Signs and Wonders,* pp. 122–5; Smith, *Called,* pp. 124–8.

32. Woodworth-Etter, *Signs and Wonders,* pp. 103–4, 108–19, *et passim;* Smith, *Called,* p. 120; Campbell, *The Pentecostal Holiness Church,* pp. 205, 233; A. J. Tomlinson, *Last Great Conflict,* pp. 190–93; Charles Edwin Jones, *Guide,* pp. 176f.

33. Campbell, *The Pentecostal Holiness Church,* pp. 201–2; Conn, *Pillars of Pentecost,* pp. 44–6; Smith, *Called,* pp. 122–3; Gaddis, "Christian Perfectionism in America," p. 329; Charles Edwin Jones, *Guide,* pp. 324–30.

34. The accounts of the Spirit baptisms of Moody by his son, and of Torrey and Chapman by themselves are quoted in John R. Rice, *The Power of Pentecost* (Wheaton, Ill.: Sword of the Lord Publishers, 1949), pp. 146–9. See also Dwight L. Moody, *Secret Power* (Chicago: Fleming H. Revell, 1881); Reuben A. Torrey, *The Baptism with the Holy Spirit* (New York: Fleming H. Revell, 1895); J. Wilbur Chapman, *Received Ye the Holy Ghost?* (New York: Fleming H. Revell, 1894); and Adoniram J. Gordon, *The Ministry of the Spirit* (New York: Fleming H. Revell, 1894).

35. William G. McLoughlin, Jr., *Modern Revivalism: Charles G. Finney to Billy Graham* (New York: Ronald Press, 1959), pp. 193–4; Bernard A. Weisberger, *They Gathered at the River* (Chicago: Qudadrangle Books, 1966), pp. 208, 218; W. R. Moody, *D.L. Moody* (New York: Fleming H. Revell, 1930), pp. 159, 224.

36. McLoughlin, *Modern Revivalism,* pp. 122–3, 126, 160–61; 433–4, 523; Weisberger, *They Gathered,* pp. 230–37.

37. McLoughlin, *Modern Revivalism,* pp. 244–9, 400; Weisberger, *They Gathered,* pp. 171–3, 239–40.

38. McLoughlin, *Modern Revivalism,* pp. 221–33; Weisberger, *They Gathered,* pp. 207–10, 229–31.

39. McLoughlin concurs in this judgment, *Modern Revivalism,* pp. 193–4.

40. *Ibid.,* pp. 285–93, 301–305.

41. Smith, *Called,* pp. 35–7.

42. S. B. Shaw (ed.), *Echoes of the General Holiness Assembly* (Chicago: S. B. Shaw, 1901), pp. 29–30.

43. Henry A. Ironside, *A Historical Sketch of the Brethren Movement* (Grand Rapids: Zondervan, 1942), *passim;* Ernest R. Sandeen, "Toward a Historical Interpretation of the Origins of Fundamentalism," *Church History,* XXXVI (March 1967), 66–83; Sandeen, *Roots,* pp. 59–80.

44. See references in fn. 42.

45. Weisberger, *They Gathered,* pp. 194–97; for Moody's Brethren and Keswick connections see Sandeen, *Roots,* pp. 172–87.

46. Sandeen, *Church History,* XXXVI (March 1967); Sandeen, *Roots,* pp. 176–87.

47. *Ibid.*

48. Andrew Murray, *The Spirit of Christ* (London: Nisbet & Co., 1888), pp. 24–32, 313–25.

49. Smith, *Called,* pp. 24–5; Sandeen, *Church History,* XXXVI (March 1967), Sandeen, *Roots,* pp. 172–87.

50. The works of the Keswick writers cited in fn. 33 and others often mention or quote Asa Mahan, *Baptism of the Holy Ghost* (London, 1872), and Charles G. Finney, *Enduement of Power* (London, 1872).

51. Sandeen, *Church History,* XXXVI (March 1967); Sandeen, *Roots,* pp. 132–61.

52. In addition to the works cited in fn. 33 above, see Adoniram J. Gordon, *Ministry of Healing* (Harrisburg, Pa.: Christian Publications, 1882); Arthur T. Pierson, *The Acts of the Holy Spirit* (New York: Gospel Pub. House, 1895); Amzi C. Dixon (ed.), *The Holy Spirit in Life and Service* (New York: Fleming H. Revell, 1895); James E. Cumming, *Through the Eternal Spirit* (New York: Fleming H. Revell, 1896); and William Arthur, *The Tongue of Fire* (New York: Harper & Bros., 1905). Torrey preached on the Baptism of the Holy Spirit at the turn of the century in the Sandwich Islands, Australia, New Zealand, China, Japan, India, Germany, France, Switzerland, and throughout the British Isles, besides, of course, all over the United States, Torrey, *Baptism with the Holy Spirit,* p. 208, *et passim.*

53. C. I. Scofield, *Plain Papers on the Doctrine of the Holy Spirit* (New York: Fleming H. Revell, 1899), pp. 9, 11. See also the comment made to the same effect by F. B. Meyer in the introduction to Gordon, *Ministry of the Spirit,* p. ix. The abundance of literature on the Holy Spirit by Holiness-revivalist leaders in this period contrasts with the neglect of that subject "until recent years" by theologians and theological schools (perhaps the two trends are related). See Henry P. VanDusen's Foreword to Lindsay Dewar, *The Holy Spirit and Modern Thought* (New York: Harper & Bros., 1959), p. vii.

54. See, e.g., Shaw, *Echoes,* p. 59; Cumming, *Through the Eternal Spirit,* pp. 133–4; Pierson, *Acts of the Holy Spirit,* pp. 88–9, 135–7, 141; Gordon, *Ministry of Healing,* p. 249; Gordon, *Ministry of Spirit,* pp. 71–2, 210–12; Arthur, pp. 292–3.

55. Torrey, *Baptism with the Holy Spirit,* pp. 10–15.

56. *Ibid.,* p. 18.

57. *Ibid.,* pp. 37–62.

58. Premillennialism is the doctrine that the Second Coming of Christ will occur *before* the Millennium (a thousand-year era of peace and happiness). Ordinarily this belief leads to extreme pessimism about the course of human history and man's ability to build a better world. Withdrawal from social involvements in hatred and despair is the logical consequence of this belief. However, premillennialism is often combined with apocalypticism—the belief that the Second Coming will be accompanied by the total and vio-

lent destruction of the extant social order. Premillennialists who believe that they are the divine instruments for the Apocalypse are likely to engage in extreme revolutionary activity.

Postmillennialism is the doctrine that Christ will return only *after* mankind has achieved the Millennium. The consequences of this belief are usually optimism, reformism, and a self-confidence that often degenerates into complacency.

The movement from post- to premillennialism in the Holiness movement as a whole is exemplified by the Nazarenes, who were strongly postmillennialist in the formative years, but just as strongly premillennialist by the time of the first world war. Smith, *Called,* pp. 194f., 309–17.

59. See chapter 6, "Apostles and Prophets."

60. *The Holiness-Pentecostal Movement,* p. 8, *et passim.*

61. See chapter 9, "The Sanctification Schism."

62. *Homiletic Review,* XXXIII (January 1897), pp. 20–24, 93–6; (February 1897), pp. 116–20; (March 1897), pp. 210–18.

63. Frederick G. Henke, "The Gift of Tongues and Related Phenomena," *American Journal of Theology,* XIII (April 1909), pp. 193–206; *Missionary Review,* May 1906, pp. 322–3.

64. Mary N. Garrard, *Mrs. Penn-Lewis: A Memoir* (Bournemouth, Eng.: Overcomer Book Room, 1947), pp. 221–2.

65. R. B. Jones, *Rent Heavens: The Revival of 1904* (London: Pioneer Mission, 1948); Jessie Penn-Lewis, *The Awakening in Wales, 1904–05* (Leicester, Eng.: Overcomer Book Room, 1922). A collection of eyewitness accounts and contemporary news reports may be found in S. B. Shaw (ed.), *The Great Revival in Wales* (Chicago: the author, 1905). For an unfriendly treatment see J. Vyrnwy Morgan, *The Welsh Revival, 1904–05* (London: Chapman & Hall, 1909).

66. Shaw, *Great Revival,* p. 93.

67. *Ibid.,* pp. 83–4.

68. *Ibid.,* pp. 95–7, 111–17, 153.

69. One such report was in the *Yorkshire Post,* Dec. 27, 1904, Cutten, *Speaking with Tongues,* p. 114.

   Later, the Pentecostal movement recruited some of Roberts's converts in Wales, Gee, *Pentecostal Movement,* pp. 34–6. Roberts, Mrs. Penn-Lewis, F. B. Meyer, and other leaders of the Welsh Revival condemned the Pentecostal movement as a "counterfeit" of the true work of the Holy Spirit. See, e.g., Garrard, pp. 27–30, 233–4, 310; Jessie Penn-Lewis and Evan Roberts, *War on the Saints* (Dorset, Eng.: Overcomer Literature Trust, n.d.), *passim.*

70. E. Cynolwyn Pugh. "The Welsh Revival of 1904–05," *Theology Today,* XII (July 1955), 226–35; for examples of the Welsh dialect used in the "hywl" see Shaw, *Great Revival,* pp. 107, 140.

71. Shaw, *Great Revival,* pp. 64, 166–7; Gee, *Pentecostal Movement,* pp. 5–6.

72. Henke, *American Journal of Theology,* XIII (April 1909): Pugh, *Theology Today,* XII (July 1955); *Missionary Review,* XXIX (April 1906), 310; (May 1906), 322–3.

Chapter III

1. Parham, as we shall see, "fell from grace" in the eyes of all but a few of his followers while the Los Angeles revival of 1906–7 was still in progress, and his role in the origin

of the Pentecostal movement was all but completely obscured for nearly fifty years. Parham's name does not appear in any Pentecostal history of the movement before that of Klaude Kendrick. In the periodical literature after 1906 Parham is either totally ignored, alluded to without name, or only briefly mentioned, and then in sorrow or admonition. Those Pentecostals like Synan, Kendrick, Brumback, and Nichol, who have belatedly acknowledged Parham's place in Pentecostal history, have been sketchy in their treatment of him.

The general silence concerning Parham's pivotal part in initiating the movement left a vacuum that Homer A. Tomlinson, "World Bishop of the Church of God, the Pentecostal and Holiness Movement" (The Church of God, Aug. 1, 1967, p. 1), attempted to fill by asserting that his father, Ambrose J. Tomlinson, was in fact the founder of the original Pentecostal group from which all others in the world have developed. Homer A. Tomlinson visited Elmer T. Clark after reading the first edition of Clark's Small Sects in America (Nashville: Cokesbury Press, 1937) in which neither Parham nor Tomlinson was mentioned. Tomlinson claims to have convinced Clark that the Pentecostal movement began with the small Christian Union group in southern Appalachia in the 1890's—the group his father served as general overseer for some twenty years (The Church of God, April 1, 1967, p. 4). In the revised edition of Small Sects (1949, p. 101) Clark stated that "most of the [Pentecostal] churches raised up were the direct or indirect creations of A. J. Tomlinson."

Homer A. Tomlinson says that, after speaking in tongues broke out among the Appalachian group, his grandmother, who lived next door to Parham in Abilene, Kansas, in 1899, told Parham about it, and that Parham's representatives visited the work and carried the message and practice of "tongues" back to Parham who then claimed credit for the movement (H. A. Tomlinson to R. M. Anderson, Sept. 12, 1967). But Parham was living in Topeka in 1899, and, at any rate, he had witnessed speaking in tongues many years prior to 1899, Charles F. Parham, A Voice Crying in the Wilderness, (Baxter Springs, Kansas: Joplin Printing Co., 1944 (1st ed. 1902), p. 29.

It is clear, however, that the Appalachian group was a typical "Second Blessing" Holiness body until the Pentecostal message was introduced among them from Los Angeles. While incidental speaking in tongues may have occurred among those mountain people in the 1890's, Tomlinson was not a member of the group until 1903 (when it was known as the Holiness Church at Camp Creek) although he had been acquainted with its leaders from the time of the revival of 1896. But there is no mention of speaking in tongues in Tomlinson's diary, nor in the minutes, doctrinal statements, or periodicals of that body (it changed its name again in 1906 to The Church of God) until Tomlinson's diary entry for June 14, 1907 when he attended a meeting in Birmingham, Alabama, at which M. M. Pinson brought the Pentecostal message from the Azusa Street mission in Los Angeles, Homer A. Tomlinson (ed.), Diary of A. J. Tomlinson (3 vols., New York: The Church of God, World Headquarters, 1949–55) III, 49. Tomlinson did not speak in tongues until the Church of God annual assembly at Cleveland, Tennessee, in January 1908, when he reached the experience under the ministry of G. B. Cashwell, who had in turn gained it at Azusa Street mission in Los Angeles and was invited by Tomlinson for the express purpose of introducing the belief and practice of speaking in tongues to that assembly, Tomlinson, Diary, I, 17–18. The Church of God (Cleveland, Tennessee) first officially adopted a doctrinal statement on speaking in tongues at the 1911 annual assembly, The Church of God, Book of Minutes (Cleveland, Tennessee: Church of God Publishing House, 1922), pp. 45–7.

2. Parham, *Voice,* pp. 11–14; William E. Connally, *History of Kansas State and People* (3 vols., Chicago: American Historical Society, 1928), III, 1324.

3. Sarah Thistlethwaite Parham (comp.), *The Life of Charles F. Parham: Founder of the Apostolic Faith Movement* (Joplin, Mo.: Tri-State Printing Co., 1930), p. 5.

4. William F. Zornow, *Kansas: A History of the Jayhawk State* (Norman, Okla.: Oklahoma University Press, 1957), pp. 190–208; Charles B. Driscoll, "Major Prophets of Holy Kansas," *American Mercury,* VIII (May, 1926), 18–26.

5. Parham, *Voice,* pp. 15–18; Parham, *Life,* pp. 6–10.

6. See references in fn. 5 above.

7. Connally, *History of Kansas,* III, 1324.

8. Parham, *Voice,* pp. 19–20; Parham, *Life,* pp. 10–26.

9. See references in fn. 8.

10. Parham, *Life,* pp. 29–32.

11. *Ibid.,* pp. 33–48.

12. *Ibid.,* pp. 48f.; Parham, *Voice,* pp. 30f.; *Topeka State Journal,* Oct. 20, 1900; *Welcome to Shiloh,* tract (n.p., n.d.). Parham mistakenly gives the name as "Charles Sanford" and all subsequent writers have repeated his error.

13. See references in fn. 12 above.

14. Ethel E. Goss, *The Winds of God: The Story of the Early Pentecostal Days (1901–1914) in the Life of Howard Goss* (New York: Comet Press, 1958), pp. 18–19.

15. *Topeka State Journal,* Oct. 20, 1900; see the photo of Stone's mansion in Parham, *Voice,* p. 32; Parham, *Life,* pp. 55–8.

16. Parham, *Voice,* p. 32.

17. Agnes N. Ozman LaBerge, *What God Hath Wrought,* tract (Chicago: n.p., 1919); A. N. O. LaBerge, "History of the Pentecostal Movement from January 1, 1901," (typescript, attached to letter of A. N. O. LaBerge to E. N. Bell, Feb. 28, 1922, in the files of the *Pentecostal Evangel,* Springfield, Missouri (cited hereafter as PEF); A. N. O. LaBerge to editor, *Weekly Evangel,* March 4, 1916, p. 5; Bloch-Hoell, *Pentecostal Movement,* p. 23.

18. Parham, *Voice,* pp. 32–3; Parham, *Life,* pp. 51–8; *Topeka State Journal,* Oct. 20, 1900; LaBerge, "History"; "Mother" Dobson to E. N. Bell, Nov. 12, 1921, *PEF.*

19. Parham, *Life,* pp. 2, 31; *Topeka State Journal,* Jan. 9, 1901; *Cincinnati Inquirer* (dateline Galena, Kansas, Jan. 27, 1904), quoted in Parham, *Life,* p. 97.

20. *The Lawrence World* (n.d.), quoted in Parham, *Life,* p. 76.

21. Goss, *Winds of God,* p. 17.

22. Kendrick, *Promise,* pp. 50–54; Brumback, *Suddenly,* pp. 21–5; Nichol, *Pentecostalism,* pp. 27–9; J. Roswell Flower, "Birth of the Pentecostal Movement," *Pentecostal Evangel,* Nov. 26, 1950, pp. 3, 12–14.

23. LaBerge, "History."

24. Parham, *Life,* pp. 58–9.

25. *Ibid.,* p. 52.

26. LaBerge, "History,"

27. *Ibid.*

28. Parham, *Life,* pp. 52–3, 60–61; Parham, *Voice,* p. 34; LaBerge, "History."

29. Howard D. Stanley to J. Roswell Flower, Feb. 18, 1949, and May 17, 1954, *PEF;* LaBerge, "History."

30. Parham, *Life,* pp. 53–4.

31. *Ibid.,* pp. 51–2.

32. Parham, *Voice*, p. 31.

33. LaBerge, "History."

34. Stanley to Flower, Feb. 18, 1946, *PEF*.

35. *Latter Rain Evangel*, Jan. 1909, p. 2; Parham, *Life*, p. 59; *Topeka State Journal*, Jan. 9, 1901.

36. *Topeka State Journal*, Jan. 8, 1901; Jan. 9, 1901. Among the languages claimed by those at Bethel, and allegedly spoken for the benefit of this reporter were: German, Swedish, Hindoo and Zulu. The reporter also witnessed Miss Ozman engaged in automatic writing.

37. Parham, *Life*, pp. 55, 71–5; *The Harvester: Kansas District of the Assemblies of God, 1913–1915* (n.p., 1955); *Topeka State Journal*, Jan. 8, 9, 14, and 15, 1901. See other newspaper accounts quoted in Parham, *Life*, pp. 70–76.

38. Parham, *Life*, pp. 75–86.

39. Stanley to Flower, Feb. 18, 1946, *PEF*.

40. Miss Ozman later said, "Notwithstanding God's dealings with me, I got into the flesh and was under a cloud spiritually, and was willing to lay down the baptism because of criticism and censure." (Woodworth-Etter, p. 432). See also LaBerge, "History," and Bloch-Hoell, *Pentecostal Movement*, p. 23.

   Miss Ozman married and became a minister in the Fire Baptized Holiness Conference of Oklahoma (at the time, still a Holiness group). By 1913 she was a minister of the Church of God in Christ (then a Pentecostal group), (Brumback, *Suddenly*, pp. 154–5). During a revival in Topeka in 1915, Mrs. Woodworth-Etter prayed over Mrs. Ozman LaBerge for the healing of her consumption—successfully according to Mrs. Woodworth-Etter (Woodworth-Etter, p. 431).

41. Charles F. Parham, "The Latter Rain," *The Apostolic Faith* (Baxter Springs, Kans.), 3 (July 1926), p. 3.

42. Parham, *Life*, pp. 86–7.

43. 4th edition, Baxter Springs, Kans.: Joplin Printing Co., 1944.

44. Parham at this time was called "The Divine Healer," *Cincinnati Inquirer*, dateline Galena, Kans., Jan. 27, 1904, quoted in Parham, *Life*, p. 96; Mrs. Mary A. Arthur to E. N. Bell, Dec. 7, 1921, *PEF*.

45. Arrell M. Gibson, "Lead Mining in Southwest Missouri after 1865," *Missouri Historical Review*, LIII (July 1959), 315–28; WPA Writers Project, *Kansas: A Guide to the Sunflower State* (New York: Hastings House, 1939), pp. 87–8; Goss, *Winds of God*, pp. 9f.; Marie G. Windell, "The Camp Meeting in Missouri," *Missouri Historical Review*, XXXVIII (April 1943), 253–70.

46. Parham had turned away from his short-lived rejection of water baptism to triune immersion and then single immersion "in the name of Jesus, into the name of the Father, Son and Holy Ghost." Parham, *Voice*, p. 24; Parham, *Life*, pp. 88–101; Goss, pp. 9–14.

47. Howard A. Goss to J. Roswell Flower, March 10, 1950, *PEF*; Parham, *Life*, p. 102; Goss, *Winds of God*, p. 29.

48. WPA Writers Project, *Texas*, pp. 50f., 58f.; *Weekly Evangel*, Feb. 19, 1916, p. 4; Feb. 26, 1916, pp. 4f.; March 4, 1916, pp. 4f.

49. Parham, *Life*, pp. 104–15; Goss, *Winds of God*, pp. 29–35.

50. *Houston Suburbanite*, Aug. 12, 1905, quoted in Kendrick, *Promise*, p. 62; *Weekly Evangel*, Feb. 19, 26, and March 4, 1916.

51. Parham, *Life*, pp. 124–35; Goss, *Winds of God* pp. 29–40.

52. Frank J. Ewart, *The Phenomenon of Pentecost* (St. Louis: Pentecostal Publishing House, 1947), pp. 36f.; Goss, *Winds of God*, p. 36; *The Apostolic Faith* (Los Angeles), I (September 1906), p. 1; Glenn A. Cook, *The Azusa Street Meeting*, tract (Los Angeles: n.p., n.d.); Bartleman, *How Pentecost*, p. 43; Parham, *Life*, p. 37; *Weekly Evangel*, Feb. 19, March 4, 1916; Alma White, *Demons and Tongues* (Zarephath, N.J.: Pillar of Fire Publishers, 1919), pp. 55f.

53. Parham, *Life*, p. 137; Bartleman, *How Pentecost*, p. 43.

54. Oscar Osterberg, "I Was There," *Full Gospel Business Men's Voice*, XIV (May 1966), pp. 4–7+; Frodsham, *With Signs*, (1941), pp. 31f.; *Los Angeles Daily Times*, April 18, 1906, p. 1. Hollenweger erroneously identifies "Nelly Terry" [sic] as the pastor of the Santa Fe mission. *The Pentecostals*, p. 22.

55. Parham, *Life*, pp. 137f.; *Weekly Evangel*, March 4, 1916, p. 4; Bartleman, *How Pentecost*, pp. 43f.

Chapter IV

1. Robert M. Fogelson, *The Fragmented Metropolis: Los Angeles, 1850–1930* (Cambridge, Mass.: Harvard Univ. Press, 1967), pp. 77–9, 123–5; Christopher Rand, *Los Angeles; The Ultimate City* (New York: Oxford Univ. Press, 1967), pp. 163–70.

2. Fogelson, *Fragmented Metropolis*, pp. 67, 72f., 186–204; John E. Bauer, "Los Angeles in the Health Rush, 1870–1900," *California Historical Society Quarterly*, XXXI (March 1952), 13–31.

3. Fogelson, *Fragmented Metropolis*, pp. 75–7, 146f.

4. *RB, 1916*, p. 125; Christian and Missionary Alliance, *10th Annual Report (1907)* (Nyack, N.Y.: 1907), pp. 68f.; Smith, *Called*, pp. 96–112, 137–40; Bartleman, *How Pentecost, passim.* "Full gospel" was a term widely used by Holiness people to distinguish their doctrine from that of non-Holiness people, which they characterized as a partial or false gospel.

5. Quoted in Fogelson, *Fragmented Metropolis*, pp. 190f.

6. Bartleman, *How Pentecost*, pp. 6–27. The quotation is from Frodsham, *Signs Following* (1946), pp. 34f.

7. Bartleman, *How Pentecost*, pp. 1–23.

8. *Ibid.*, pp. 37–41.

9. *Apostolic Faith* (Los Angeles), I (Sept. 1906); Osterberg, "I Was There."

10 *Apostolic Faith* (Los Angeles), I (Sept., Dec. 1906); Frank Ewart, *The Phenomenon of Pentecost* (St. Louis, Mo.: Pentecostal Publishing House, 1947), pp. 37–8; Glenn A. Cook, "The Azusa Street Meeting," tract (Los Angeles, n.p., n.d.).

11. Zelma Argue, "Memories of Fifty Years Ago," *Pentecostal Evangel*, April 22, 1956, pp. 6–7, 29; Mrs. C. M. McGowan, "Another Echo from Azusa," typescript, *PEF;* Bartleman, *How Pentecost*, p. 43; Osterberg, *FGBM Voice*, May 1966.

12. Parham, *Life*, pp. 154–5; *Apostolic Faith* (Los Angeles), I (Sept., Dec. 1906); Howard A. Goss, "Reminiscences of an Eyewitness," *Weekly Evangel*, March 4, 1916, p. 4. Hollenweger errs in saying that Seymour was accompanied by Lucy Farrow and J. A. Warren when he arrived in Los Angeles. Also, he mistakenly identifies Warren as a woman, *The Pentecostals*, p. 22.

13. Bartleman, *How Pentecost*, pp. 44–8; *Apostolic Faith* (Los Angeles), I (Sept. 1906).

14. Rachel Sizelove, "The Sparkling Fountain," tract (n.p., n.d.); *Apostolic Faith* (Los

Angeles), I (Sept., Oct. 1906), Bartleman, *How Pentecost,* pp. 47–8; see photo of the mission in Brumback, *Suddenly,* p. 49.

15. Brumback, *Suddenly,* p. 36; Frodsham, *Signs Following* (1946), p. 32; Nichol, *Pentecostalism,* pp. 33–4; Kendrick, *Promise Fulfilled,* pp. 65–6; Synan, *Holiness-Pentecostal Movement,* pp. 106–10; Ewart, *Phenomenon of Pentecost,* pp. 40–43; *Pentecostal Evangel,* April 6, 1946, pp. 6–7.

Walter J. Hollenweger, in *The Pentecostals,* states that "the origins of the Pentecostal movement go back to a revival amongst the negroes of North America at the beginning of the present century" (p. xvii). This is inaccurate. The movement originated among a group of whites at the turn of the century and was not introduced among blacks until six years later when a black convert (Seymour) of the white originator (Parham) brought it to Los Angeles. After a few weeks at most (and possibly only days) during which Seymour's flock was all black, whites began to attend the meetings at Bonnie Brae. Whites and blacks together secured and prepared the premises at Azusa Street, and the meetings there were integrated from the very first day. By 1908 the Azusa mission was all black (except for occasional visitors), but the Pentecostal movement in Los Angeles was predominantly white. Indeed, before, during, and after the Los Angeles revival, and from its beginning until the present day, the Pentecostal movement in America has been predominantly white, although the proportion of the total black population that became Pentecostals has probably been greater than the proportion of the total white population that did so in America.

Hollenweger also asserts that "important . . . for the growth of the Pentecostal movement was its ability to make use of the North American negro's faculties of understanding and communicating by way of enthusiastic spiritual manifestations to build up a community and fellowship." (p. xvii). But this ignores the fact that it was by means of "enthusiastic spiritual manifestations" that the Apostolic Church was built up and that such manifestations were also prominent in white European Christendom for centuries before there was any important contact with blacks. Indeed, these "manifestations" among black Americans have probably been due as much to the religious influence of whites as to that of the African heritage.

Hollenweger errs when he says that Parham was "the leader of the Azusa Street revival" (*ibid.,* p. 23). It is true that Azusa's letterhead stationery listed Parham as "Projector" (and also that the first issues of its periodical *The Apostolic Faith* (Los Angeles) named him in its editorial masthead as "Founder and Projector"). However, Parham made only one visit to Azusa Street, in October or November of 1906 when the revival was already underway. At that time he was asked to leave, and, thereafter, Azusa's literature ceased to mention his name and Parham had no contact whatever with the work of the mission.

16. Bartleman, *How Pentecost,* p. 48. Bartleman's statement is corroborated by *Apostolic Faith* (Los Angeles), I (Sept. 1906), and Cook, "Azusa Street Meeting"; *The Los Angeles Daily Times,* April 18, 1906.

17. *The Baptist Herald,* April 28, 1906, quoted in Kenneth K. Bailey, *Southern White Protestantism in the Twentieth Century* (New York: Harper & Row, 1964), p. 3.

18. Bartleman, *How Pentecost,* pp. 47–53.

19. Cook, "Azusa Street Meeting"; Sizelove, "Sparkling Fountain"; Bartleman, *How Pentecost,* p. 48; *Way of Faith,* August 1, 1906, quoted by Bartleman, *How Pentecost,* p. 63.

20. Ewart, *Phenomenon*, p. 41; Bartleman, *How Pentecost*, pp. 67–8.
21. Bartleman, *How Pentecost*, pp. 49, 61–64; *Los Angeles Times*, Sept. 9, 1956; *Apostolic Faith* (Los Angeles), I (Sept. 1906).
22. Bartleman, *How Pentecost*, p. 53.
23. *Apostolic Faith* (Los Angeles), I (Sept., Oct., Dec. 1906); Cook, "Azusa Street Meeting"; Bartleman, *How Pentecost*, p. 58.
24. Bartleman, *How Pentecost*, pp. 58–9.
25. *Ibid.*, p. 60.
26. *Ibid.*, pp. 61, 70, *et passim*; *Apostolic Faith* (Baxter Springs, Kans.), 3 (April 1925); Frodsham, *Signs Following* (1946), pp. 31–40. Cf. Bartleman's description and those of all other eyewitnesses with Morton T. Kelsey's fanciful statement that, "In the converted livery stable in Los Angeles the experience of speaking in tongues took hold and became an alternative to emotional revivalism . . . many people who shied away from camp meetings were able to find a lasting fulfillment in the Pentecostal experience of tongues. . . . a continuing religious value which the indiscriminate emotionalism of the camp meeting did not have." Kelsey, *Tongue-Speaking*, p. 74.
27. *Apostolic Faith* (Los Angeles), I (Sept. 1906); Cook, "Azusa Street Meeting"; A. W. Orwig, "My First Visit to the Azuzu [sic] Street Pentecostal Mission, Los Angeles, California," *Weekly Evangel*, March 18 and April 8, 1916; Frodsham, *Signs Following* (1946), p. 34.
28. Cook, "Azusa Street Meeting"; *Apostolic Faith* (Los Angeles), I (Sept., Oct. 1906); Bartleman, *How Pentecost*, pp. 54–5, 70.
29. Cook, "Azusa Street Meeting"; *Word and Work* (Framingham, Mass.), March 1935, pp. 1–2. Both of these sources carry the same photo of the twelve. One of the unidentified persons was probably Phoebe Sargent, whose name appeared with those of some of the others on the Azusa mission's stationery in October 1908, Bloch-Hoell, *Pentecostal Movement*, p. 48. I have not been able to identify the twelfth person, a man.
30. Bartleman, *How Pentecost*, pp. 67–8; Brumback, *Suddenly*, p. 58.
31. Bartleman, *How Pentecost*, pp. 82–4; *Way of Faith* (Columbia, S.C.), Sept. 1906.
32. *Apostolic Faith* (Los Angeles), I (Sept., Oct. 1906); Osterberg, *FGBM Voice*, May 1966; Bartleman, *How Pentecost*, pp. 93–5.
33. *Apostolic Faith* (Los Angeles), I (Sept. 1906); *Los Angeles Times*, Sept. 9, 1956; *Weekly Evangel*, March 11 and 25, 1916; Bartleman, *How Pentecost*, pp. 54, 67–8.
34. *Weekly Evangel*, April 29 and May 13, 1916; Frodsham, *Signs Following* (1926), pp. 43–6; Sizelove, "Sparkling Fountain"; Alice R. Flower, *Grace for Grace* (Springfield, Mo.: the author, 1961), pp. 31–4; J. Roswell Flower, "Church Orientation," mimeo, *PEF*; *Apostolic Faith* (Los Angeles), I (Dec. 1906).
35. On the Azusa correspondence see Thomas B. Barratt, *When the Fire Fell and an Outline of My Life* (Larvik, Norway: Alfons Hansen and Soner, 1927), pp. 109–10; and Bloch-Hoell, *Pentecostal Movement*, pp. 66, 136; for the rest J. R. Flower, "Church Orientation," *PEF*.
    The most detailed account of the spread of the Pentecostal movement in the Southeast is Synan, *Holiness-Pentecostal Movement*, pp. 117–39.
36. Bartleman, *How Pentecost*, pp. 97–112.
37. *Apostolic Faith* (Los Angeles), I (Oct. 1906); Cook, "Azusa Street Meeting"; *Word and Work*, March 1936, pp. 1–2.
38. *Apostolic Faith* (Los Angeles), I (Sept., Oct., Dec. 1906); The Apostolic Faith, *A His-*

torical Account of the Apostolic Faith (Portland, Ore.: Apostolic Faith Pub. House, 1965), pp. 64–8.

39. *Apostolic Faith* (Los Angeles), I (Sept., Oct., Dec. 1906); Barratt, *When the Fire*, pp. 104–40.

40. *Apostolic Faith* (Houston, Tex.), II (Oct. 1908); Parham, *Life*, pp. 155–9; *New York Times*, April 2 and 3, Sept. 27, 1906; Mrs. Robert A. Brown (née Burgess) to E. N. Bell, April 5, 1922, *PEF*.

41. *The Upper Room* (Los Angeles), I (Sept. 1909); J. T. Boddy to E. N. Bell, n.d., *PEF*; Bartleman, *How Pentecost*, pp. 105–6, 109–10; J. H. King, *Yet Speaketh*, pp. 125–39; Hattie Duncan to E. N. Bell, Jan. 19, 1922, *PEF*; George H. Paul, "The Religious Frontier in Oklahoma: Dan T. Muse and the Pentecostal Holiness Church" (unpublished Ph.D. diss., University of Oklahoma, 1965), pp. 66–7; Campbell, *Pentecostal Holiness Church*, pp. 480–81; Nickels John Holmes, *Life Sketches and Sermons* (Royston, Ga.: Press of the Pentecostal Holiness Church, 1920), pp. 137–8. In Great Britain, the annual Holiness conventions at Sunderland from 1908–14 occupied "The supreme place of importance" in the history of the Pentecostal movement, Gee, *Pentecostal Movement*, p. 37.

42. *Way of Faith*, 1906, *passim*; Holmes, *Life Sketches*, pp. 136–7; *Apostolic Faith* (Los Angeles), I (Dec. 1906); Campbell, *Pentecostal Holiness Church*, pp. 208–12, 140–43; *The Christian & Missionary Alliance* (Nyack, N.Y.), 1906–9, *passim*; Woodworth-Etter, *Signs and Wonders*, pp. 145–7; *Gospel Witness* (Louisville, Ky.), Sept. 1906; *Herald of Light* (Indianapolis), 1906; *passim*; Bartleman, *How Pentecost*, pp. 127–8.

43. At least two other periodicals of the same name were being published at the same time: one by Parham at Zion City, Illinois, and elsewhere, and one by E. N. Bell and others at Houston and elsewhere (Parham, *Life*, p. 339); *Apostolic Faith* (Baxter Springs, Kans.), 5 (June 1928); J. R. Flower, "Historic Record of the Birth of the Assemblies of God," mimeo, 1950, *PEF*.

44. *Apostolic Faith* (Los Angeles), I (Sept., Oct., Dec. 1906); *Apostolic Faith* (Portland, Ore.), 18 (Jan. 1909); *Christian Missionary Alliance*, Nov. 3, 1906; Brumback, *Suddenly*, p. 85; *Weekly Evangel*, April 29, 1916; King, *Yet Speaketh*, pp. 111–12.

45. See, for example, the account in the *New York American*, Dec. 3, 1906, repr. in Bloch-Hoell, *Pentecostal Movement*, pp. 49–51; Bartleman, *How Pentecost*, p. 116.

46. *Apostolic Faith* (Los Angeles), II (May 1908); *Apostolic Faith* (Portland, Ore.), 18 (Jan. 1909).

47. Z. Argue, *What Meaneth This?*, p. 12; *Pentecostal Holiness Advocate* (Franklin Springs, Ga.), May 6, 1937; *Latter Rain Evangel*, Dec. 1934, p. 12; A. Flower, *Grace for Grace*, p. 81; *Weekly Evangel*, April 29, 1916; Gee, *Pentecostal Movement*, p. 13; Hollenweger, "Handbuch," II, 496–7; *Apostolic Faith* (Los Angeles), II (May 1908); S. Clyde Bailey, *Pioneer Marvels of Faith* (Morristown, Tenn.: the author, 1958), p. 45. My list numbers 74 periodicals.

48. *Latter Rain Evangel*, April 1909; June 1910; April, June, July 1911; May 1912; *Word and Witness* (Malvern, Ark.), Aug. 20, 1912; Eugene N. Hastie, *History of the West Central District* (Ft. Dodge, Ia.: the author, 1948), pp. 42–3, 48–9; Apostolic Faith, *Historical Account*, pp. 73–80, 124; *Christian Evangel* (Findlay, Ohio), July 11, 1914.

49. *Latter Rain Evangel*, June 1909; Oct. 1911; *Midnight Cry* (New York), March 1919.

50. Hastie, *History*, pp. 31–2; King, *Yet Speaketh*, *passim*; *Evening Light and Church of God Evangel* (Cleveland, Tenn.), Aug. 15, 1910.

51. *Word and Witness*, Sept. 1915; A. Flower, *Grace for Grace*, pp. 56–8; *Latter Rain Evangel* (July 1912); Assemblies of God *Minutes* (1914), p. 7; *ibid.* (1919), p. 23; Kendrick, *Promise Fulfilled*, p. 128.

52. Hastie, *History*, pp. 66–74; Georgia Bond (ed.), *Life Story of O. H. Bond* (Oakgrove, Ark.: the editor, 1958), p. 142; S. C. Bailey, *Pioneer Marvels*, p. 2; Kulbeck, *What God Hath Wrought*, p. 182; Paul "Religious Frontier," pp. 60–61; Goss, *Winds of God*, p. 34; Aimee Semple McPherson, *This Is That* (Los Angeles: Echo Park Evangelistic Assoc., 1923), pp. 151–2, 102, 124, 184–7, 347–50; W. F. Bryant, "Work in the Mountains of Tennessee," *Evening Light and Church of God Evangel*, March 1, 1910.

53. Assemblies of God, *Early History of the Assemblies of God* (Springfield, Mo., 1959), pp. 5–6; Bartleman, *How Pentecost, passim;* Hastie, *History*, pp. 70–71; Goss, *Winds of God*, p. 35.

54. Brumback, *Suddenly*, pp. 107–9; Hastie, *History*, pp. 123–4; Apostolic Faith, *Historical Account*, pp. 86–9; interview with Ozro T. Jones, Sept. 14, 1966.

55. Hastie, *History*, pp. 66–74; Bartleman, *How Pentecost*, p. 85; Brumback, *Suddenly*, p. 129.

56. Walter J. Higgins, *Pioneering in Pentecost* (El Cajon, Calif.: the author, 1958), pp. 20–24; Hastie, *History*, p. 70.

57. Frank Bartleman, *From Plow to Pulpit* (Los Angeles: the author, 1924), pp. 22–3.

Chapter V

1. Assemblies of God, *Combined Minutes, 1st Gen. Council (1914)*, p. 2.

2. Donald Gee said of the early Pentecostals, "Above all things, their hearts glowed with the expectation and conviction that this was destined to be the last revival before the coming of the Lord, and that, for them, all earthly history would soon be consummated by the 'Rapture'." *Pentecostal Movement*, p. 2. Elijah C. Clark wrote, "This mighty Pentecostal revival is designed to conquer and to prepare the Church of God for the translation." *The Baptism of the Holy Ghost, "And More,"* p. 42. David H. McDowell, an early figure in the Assemblies of God, summed up the predominant view of the early Pentecostals when he specifically discarded the notion that the Second Coming was but one feature of a program that included salvation, Baptism in the Spirit, healing, spiritual gifts and the Second Coming, saying rather that the Second Coming "is THE program and all the rest peripheral." "The Purpose of the Coming of the Lord," *Pentecostal Evangel*, May 5, 1925, pp. 2–3. When I asked Marie Burgess Brown, who was primarily responsible for establishing the Pentecostal movement in the greater New York region, what the central message of the movement was, she answered without hesitation, "The Coming of the Lord Jesus." Interview Nov. 5, 1965.

Cf. Bloch-Hoell, *Pentecostal Movement*, pp. 87–8, who rejects this view, and says "eschatology in itself does not appear to have assumed any unusual importance. It looks more as though the eschatological element in the Pentecostal preaching is included in order to intensify the appeal to conversion or to home and foreign mission work." To the contrary, I have found eschatology to be a central theme of all the early Pentecostal literature. I hope to show that tongues and healing, which Bloch-Hoell and other non-Pentecostal writers have held to be the primary emphases of the movement, derived their meaning and importance from the Second Coming theme. Moreover, I hold that the proselyting activities of the movement were in part ritualistic—that is, were believed to be pleasing to God whether successful or not—and in part means toward the end of hastening the Second Coming. Only after 1911 or so, when eschatological hopes began to diminish (though they were again aroused temporarily by World War I), were tongues and healing split off from their original eschatological roots to assume an independent importance.

3. *Apostolic Faith* (Los Angeles), I (Sept. 1906; Jan. 1908), II (Jan. 1909); G. B. Studd, "My Convictions," *Jesus is Coming,* April 9, 1919, repr. in *Weekly Evangel,* July 15, 1916.

4. Bartleman, *How Pentecost,* p. 116; Tomlinson, *Diary,* I, 50; see also Woodworth-Etter, *Signs and Wonders,* pp. 387–8; Sizelove, "Sparkling Fountain."

5. *Latter Rain Evangel,* I (April 1909), pp. 13–14. Robert A. Brown, editor of *Midnight Cry* (New York), justified the publication of that periodical on the grounds that "this is our last chance to warn the people to prepare to meet the Bridegroom." I (March, April 1911), p. 4.

6. *Weekly Evangel,* March 18, 1916.

7. I use the word "myth" in the sense in which Mark Schorer used it in *William Blake* (New York: Henry Holt & Co., 1946), quoted in Henry A. Murray (ed.), *Myth and Mythmaking* (New York: George Braziller, 1960), pp. 354–5, "The term denotes . . . neither the negation nor the contrary of ideas, but their basis and their structure, the element by which they are activated. . . . the instruments by which we continually struggle to make our experience intelligible to ourselves. . . . a large, controlling image that gives meaning to the facts of ordinary life."

8. See for example "Latter Rain Lectures," *Latter Rain Evangel,* I (May–Oct. 1909); "Special Second Coming Edition," *Weekly Evangel,* April 10, 1917; "Second Coming," *Pentecostal Holiness Advocate, Feb. 28, 1918; and sermons on the Second Coming in Woodworth-Etter, Signs and Wonders,* pp. 223–41, and Lee, *Life Sketches,* pp. 38–50, 199–203, 228–33, 251–5, 260–64.

9. The following survey of Parham's thought is based primarily on Parham, *Voice,* and Parham, *Everlasting Gospel, passim.*

10. See the chart in Parham, *Everlasting Gospel,* p. 124.

11. Parham, *Voice,* p. 83.

12. *Loc. cit.*

13. *Ibid.,* pp. 105–6. The sceptre of David, says Parham, was carried by Jeremiah to Ireland and from there to Scotland, and eventually England, symbolizing the geneological connection by which Parham, to *his* satisfaction, traces the ancestry of Queen Victoria right back to Adam by way of Abraham, Isaac, and Jacob. Also, the stone on which all the kings of Israel were crowned was carried over the same route as the sceptre, and lies today embedded beneath the coronation chair in Westminster Abbey. *Voice,* pp. 94–9.

14. Parham, *Voice,* pp. 106–7.

15. Parham does not use the word "dispensation," but clearly means the same thing.

16. Yet, paradoxically, Parham also says, "no one who has not Israelitish blood in their veins will have any part or lot in the [b?] ride of Christ (there seemingly will be people of all races). In Jesus there flowed in His veins the blood of all races, so by the intermarriage of the Israelitish nations, Israel's blood has found its way among the races. In the Body and Bride of Christ there seemingly will be people from all races in whose veins flow the blood of Abraham." *Voice,* p. 86.

17. Parham, *Voice*, p. 28.

18. Parham, *Everlasting Gospel*, p. 69.

19. *Ibid.*, pp. 19, 26–8.

20. *Ibid.*, p. 30.

21. Parham, *Voice*, p. 90.

22. *Ibid.*, pp. 70–79.

23. *Ibid.*, p. 138.

24. Sandeen, *Roots*, pp. 132–61, *et passim*. Sandeen's focus is specifically on the millenarian roots of what later became known as the Fundamentalist movement. Because of this, and despite his own disclaimer in the introduction to his book, Sandeen tends to equate the Darbyite wing of the millenarian movement with the whole. He chooses to ignore the continuing Millerite and Irvingite traditions, explicitly excludes the Jehovah's Witnesses, and erroneously states that "the millenarian movement did not appeal to the members of the . . . Pentecostal groups." In fact, as I hope I have succeeded in demonstrating, the Pentecostal movement was initially a predominantly millenarian movement. These comments are not intended to detract from Sandeen's scholarship, which is superb within the limits he set for himself.

25. Gilbert Seldes, *The Stammering Century* (New York: John Day, 1928); Charles W. Ferguson, *The Confusion of Tongues: A Review of Modern Isms* (Garden City, N.Y.: Doubleday, Doran & Co., 1928), *passim.*; J. Stillson Judah, *The History and Philosophy of Metaphysical Movements* (Philadelphia: Westminster Press, 1967), pp. 60–61, 68–71, *et passim*.

26. Parham, *Voice*, pp. 26, 79.

27. George E. Mowrey, *The Era of Theodore Roosevelt* (New York: Harper & Row, 1962), pp. 92–105; Richard Hofstadter, *Age of Reform* (New York: Vintage Books, 1955), pp. 131–48.

28. Hofstadter, *Age of Reform*, pp. 60–93, 131–214; Frederick C. Jaher, *Doubters and Dissenters: Cataclysmic Thought in America, 1885–1918* (New York: Free Press of Glencoe, 1964), *passim*.

29. Many years after formulating his doctrine Parham maintained that "The foundation of all our theology is built on the basic doctrine of Conditional Immortality and Destruction of the Wicked." *Apostolic Faith* (Baxter Springs, Kans.), 3 (April 1925), p. 4.

30. See fn. 8; and *Apostolic Faith* (Portland, Ore.), 18 (Jan. 1909), which carried the headline "JESUS IS COMING SOON."

31. *Latter Rain Evangel*, I (Sept. 1909), p. 13.

32. *Evening Light and Church of God Evangel*, March 1, 1910, p. 1.

33. *Latter Rain Evangel*, II (Oct. 1901), pp. 17–23.

34. *Apostolic Faith* (Los Angeles), I (Sept. 1906).

35. *Ibid.*, I (Sept., Oct. 1906; Jan. 1908); *Apostolic Faith* (Portland, Ore.), 18 (Jan. 1909); Ewart, *Phenomenon*, p. 47; A. E. Seddon, "Edward Irving and Unknown Tongues," *Homiletic Review*, LVII (1909), 103–9; Christian and Missionary Alliance, *11th Annual Report* (1907/08), pp. 11–12; Cutten, *Speaking in Tongues*, pp. 124–5; Bloch-Hoell, *Pentecostal Movement*, p. 196, fn. 99, and p. 431; Oskar Pfister, *Die Psychologische Enträtselung der Religiösen Glossolalie und der Automatischen Kryptographie* (Leipzig and Vienna: Franz Deuticke, 1912), pp. 38–41, cited in Samarin, *Tongues of Men and Angels*, pp. 90f.

36. Seddon, *Homiletic Review*, LVII.

37. *Apostolic Faith* (Baxter Springs, Kans.), 5 (June 1925), pp. 2–6.

38. Herman L. Harvey, "The Gift of Tongues," *Pentecostal Power*, repr. in *Bridal Call* (Los Angeles), II (April 1919), pp. 7–9.

39. *Latter Rain Evangel*, I (Sept. 1909), pp. 9–11; *Pentecostal Herald*, IV (Sept. 1918), pp. 1–2; *Grace and Truth* (Memphis, Tenn.), Sept. 1918, pp. 1, 3; Goss, *Winds of God*, pp. 108–9; Brumback, *Suddenly*, p. 112; Gee, *Pentecostal Movement*.

40. Balls, streaks, and pillars of fire were seen so often that they were known as "the 'like as of fire' " (Tomlinson, *Diary*, I, 167–8; III, 59; Woodworth-Etter, *Signs and Wonders*, p. 171. Tomlinson's *Diary*, Woodworth-Etter's *Signs and Wonders*, and P. D. Smith's (Mr. & Mrs.), *He Is Just the Same Today* (Springfield, Mo.: Gospel Pub. House, 1931), are mines of information on all of the phenomena mentioned above.

41. "Back to Pentecost," *Weekly Evangel*, Jan. 1, 1916, pp. 4–5.

42. For a study emphasizing the psychological aspects of snake handling see Weston LaBarre, *They Shall Take Up Serpents* (Minneapolis: Univ. of Minn. Press, 1962). There are numerous examples of snake handling in Tomlinson's *Diary*. Some Church of God preachers taught snake handling as necessary for salvation, though this was officially repudiated. Church of God, *Minutes, 13th Annual Assembly* (1917), p. 297. As late as 1930, A. J. Tomlinson still maintained: "The Church stands for the whole Bible rightly divided, and it is wrongly dividing to cut out the tongues and serpents." *White Wing Messenger*, Oct. 11, 1930, quoted in Duggar, *Tomlinson*, p. 53. The Assemblies of God condemned snake handling as a ritual practice, but asserted that believers accidentally handling snakes were immune to any harm. *Pentecostal Evangel*, April 17, 1920, p. 1; April 5, 1924, pp. 2–3. The Pentecostal Holiness Church took the same position. *Pentecostal Holiness Advocate*, Aug. 1, 1918, pp. 8–9, 12. In time this became the position of nearly all Pentecostal groups, including most Church of God groups. George Hensley broke away from the Church of God (Cleveland, Tenn.) to organize "The Church of God with Signs Following After," which insisted that all the signs of Mark 16:17–18 should be performed by every true believer, and were tests of the validity of one's faith. Archie Robertson, *That Old-Time Religion* (Boston: Houghton-Mifflin Co., 1950), pp. 169–71.

    On handling fire see *Pentecostal Holiness Advocate*, Oct. 11, 1917, pp. 2–3; Ernest Buckles, "A Brief History of the Church of God [of the Apostolic Faith]," pamphlet (n.p., n.d.).

43. See fn. 40 above.

44. For a compendium of healing sermons and testimonials based on the *Church of God Evangel* and the Church of God (Cleveland, Tenn.) *Minutes* from 1910 to 1960, see James A. Cross (ed.), *Healing in the Church* (Cleveland, Tenn.: Pathway Press, 1962). On healing in the Atonement see, for example, *Latter Rain Evangel*, I (March 1909), pp. 18–22; *Grace and Truth* (Memphis, Tenn.), Oct. 1915, pp. 1–2. On laying on of hands see for example Woodworth-Etter, *Signs and Wonders*, pp. 280, 383, 424. On anointing with oil, *Church of God Evangel*, July 15, 1910. On prayer handkerchiefs and aprons, Tomlinson, *Diary*, III, 56; *Pentecostal Evangel*, Feb. 23, 1924; *Glad Tidings Herald*, 18 (June 1929), p. 5. On applying Pentecostal periodicals for healing (which was exceptional), Duncan Aikman, "The Holy Rollers," *American Mercury*, XV (Oct. 1928), 180–91.

45. *Latter Rain Evangel,* Jan., 1926, p. 11.

46. Ewart, *Phenomenon,* pp. 49, 90–93; *Pentecostal Evangel,* Feb. 6, 1926, p. 6; Jan. 5, 1924, p. 8.

47. Woodworth-Etter, *Signs and Wonders,* p. 275; Gee, *Pentecostal Movement,* pp. 147–8.

48. *Latter Rain Evangel,* 18 (Jan. 1925), pp. 8–11.

49. *Word and Witness,* Oct. 20, 1913, p. 3; Dec. 20, 1913, p. 1; *Church of God Evangel,* March 4, 1914.

50. *Pentecostal Evangel,* June 10, 1922, p. 4.

51. Gee, *Pentecostal Movement,* p. 148.

52. Woodworth-Etter, *Signs and Wonders,* pp. 250–57, 380–84, 396–8; interviews with Marie Burgess Brown.

53. *Church of God Evangel,* March 28, 1914.

54. *Pentecostal Evangel,* Nov. 3, 1923.

55. Lee, *Life Sketches,* pp. 368–73; Woodworth-Etter, *Signs and Wonders,* pp. 144, *et passim.*

56. Woodworth-Etter, *Signs and Wonders,* p. 386. See also Tomlinson, *Diary,* III, 61, *et passim; Latter Rain Evangel,* Aug. 1927, pp. 2–4.

57. Jan. 3, 1931.

58. See, for example, "How To Cast Out Demons," *Pentecostal Evangel,* Aug. 6, 1927; and Robert Thom, *The Holy Spirit and the Name* (n.p., n.d.), pp. 89–99.

59. This development is explained more fully below in chapter 9.

Chapter VI

1. See Appendix II. I have included Smith Wigglesworth and Thomas B. Barratt in what purports to be a sample of American Pentecostal leaders. Wigglesworth was closely associated with the English Pentecostal movement, and Barrett with the Norwegian; both were more nearly international leaders. I decided to include them because they were universally recognized as leaders by American Pentecostals and spent much time in this country, Wigglesworth as a resident for long periods of time, and Barratt on several extensive evangelistic tours.

2. Barratt was born in England and returned there as a student during his adolescence; the rest of his childhood and youth was spent in Norway. I have listed him as Norwegian because his cultural orientation was thoroughly Norwegian.

3. These terms are explained below in chapters 9 and 10.

4. McPherson, *This is That, passim;* Goss, *passim;* "J. Roswell Flower," data sheet, mimeo, *PEF;* the quotation is from Goss, *Winds of God,* pp. 147–8.

5. Computed from United States Bureau of the Census, *Historical Statistics of the United States* (Washington, D.C.: Government printing Office, 1960), Series A 195–209, p. 14. The censuses of 1870 and 1880 underestimated the urban population since they included only towns of 8,000 and more. Beginning with the 1900 census, "urban" has meant towns of 2,500 and more.

6. The blue collar occupations were weaver, carpenter, lumberjack, and riverman. On Barratt see Bloch-Hoell, *Pentecostal Movement,* pp. 178–9; Holmes, *Life Sketches,* pp. 7–8.

7. Tomlinson, *Diary,* I, 14; Bartleman, *Plow to Pulpit,* pp. 5–6; Eunice M. Perkins, *Fred*

Francis Bosworth (2nd ed.; Detroit: the author, 1927), pp. 15–22; Watson Sorrow, *Some of My Experiences* (Atlanta: the author, 1954), pp. 6–9; Z. Argue, *What Meaneth This?*, p. 3; George N. Eldridge, *Personal Reminiscences* (Los Angeles: West Coast Publishing Co., n.d.), pp. 7–8; W. M. Hayes (ed.), *Memoirs of Richard Baxter Hayes* (Philadelphia: the editor, 1945), pp. 1, 11; Flower, *Grace for Grace*, pp. 41–5.

8. Stanley H. Frodsham, *Smith Wigglesworth: Apostle of Faith* (Springfield, Mo.: Gospel Publishing House, 1949), pp. 11–12; Bartleman, *Plow to Pulpit*, p. 5; King, *Yet Speaketh*, pp. 13–17; Woodworth-Etter, *Signs and Wonders*, pp. 19–20; Goss, *Winds of God*, p. 2.

9. Homer, A. Tomlinson, for example, called his father a college graduate, but the Quaker school he is said to have attended, Westfield Academy in Westfield, Indiana, did not even pretend to be a college at that time, and, furthermore, has no record of A. J. Tomlinson having been enrolled there. H. A. Tomlinson implied his father's name was deliberately removed from the records, Homer A. Tomlinson to R. M. Anderson, September 12, 1967.

10. On Wigglesworth see Gee, *Pentecostal Movement*, p. 224, and Brumback, *Suddenly*, p. 272; Woodworth-Etter, *Signs and Wonders*, p. 20; on Brown see *Glad Tidings Herald* (New York), XXVII (May 1948); on Piper, *Latter Rain Evangel*, Jan. 1912, p. 2; Flower, *Grace for Grace*, p. 41.

11. On Moody's Chicago school, which served as a prototype for others, see J. Wilbur Chapman, *The Life and Work of Dwight Lyman Moody* (London: James Nisbet & Co., 1900), pp. 229–44.

12. J. H. King, "My Experience," *Pentecostal Holiness Advocate*, May 23, 1946, pp. 6–7, 11–16; Eldridge, *Reminiscences*, pp. 15, 23–4.

13. On Parham see *supra*, p. 48; on Mason, Interview with Ozro T. Jones, September 14, 1966; Bartleman, *Plow to Pulpit*, p. 22; on Daniel Awrey, *Latter Rain Evangel* (Mar. 1910), p. 19.

14. Taylor returned to the University of North Carolina after many years in the Pentecostal movement to take his bachelor's degree at the age of 47, and his master's three years later, Campbell, pp. 479–82; Holmes, *Life Sketches*, pp. 41–58; on Collins, *Christian Evangel*, Jan. 23, 1915; on Barratt, Bloch-Hoell, *Pentecostal Movement*, p. 178.

15. *Pentecostal Evangel*, June 30, 1923.

16. Bucke, *History*, II, 651; Luther C. Fry, *The U. S. Looks at Its Churches* (New York: Institute for Social and Religious Research, 1930), pp. 63, 144.

17. On Mrs. Crawford, The Apostolic Faith, *Historical Account*, p. 54; Goss, *Winds of God*, p. 10.

18. Flower, pp. 25–6, 42–5; on Vogler, *Harvester* (publication of the Kansas District of the Assemblies of God, n.d.), pp. 54–5.

19. Bartleman, *Plow to Pulpit*, pp. 6–12.

20. On the grim characteristics of working-class families see Urie Bronfenbrenner, "Socialization and Social Class Through Time and Space," in E. E. Maccoby, et al. (eds.), *Readings in Social Psychology* (New York: Henry Holt, 1958). Authoritarian parental influences are suggested by Alice Flower's statement that, "The matter of obedience was paramount with Mother, any disobedience being firmly dealt with" (*Grace For Grace*, p. 22); and by Aimee S. McPherson's comment concerning her mother: "the one absorbing, all important business of her life became bringing up the baby [i.e.

Aimee] in the way she should go'' (*This Is That*, p. 18). On cruelty and the authoritarian personality type see Saul M. Siegel, ''The Relationship of Hostility to Authoritarianism,'' *Journal of Abnormal and Social Psychology*, LII (1956), 368-72.

21. On Bell, *Pentecostal Evangel*, June 30, 1923; on Collins, *Christian Evangel*, Jan. 23, 1915; Eldridge, pp. 7-8; S. Clyde Bailey, *Pioneer Marvels*, p. 2; Interview with Marie Burgess Brown, Nov. 5, 1965; on Mrs. Crawford, The Apostolic Faith, *Historical Account*, pp. 59-61; on Taylor, Campbell, *Pentecostal Holiness Church*, p. 479; on Pinson, Brumback, *Suddenly*, p. 168.

22. Woodworth-Etter, *Signs and Wonders*, pp. 19-36.

23. McPherson, *This Is That*, pp. 63-79.

24. King, *Yet Speaketh, passim*.

25. Barratt, *When the Fire Fell*, pp. 90, 100-101; the quotation is from an article by Barratt in *Christian and Missionary Alliance*, Nov. 3, 1906, p. 275.

26. W. M. Hayes, *Memoirs of R. B. Hayes*, pp. 56-81, 93-4; Goss, *Winds of God*, p. 10; on Muse see Paul, ''Religious Frontier,'' p. 73.

27. On Marie Burgess Brown, *Midnight Cry*, I (March-April 1911), 1-2; on Bell, *Pentecostal Evangel*, June 30, 1923; Barratt, *When the Fire Fell, passim;* on Mason, Interview with Ozro T. Jones, Sept. 14, 1966; Tomlinson, *Diary, passim;* King, *Yet Speaketh, passim*.

28. Bartleman, *Plow to Pulpit, passim*.

29. Perkins, *passim*.

30. H. Richard Niebuhr and Daniel D. Williams (eds.), *The Ministry in Historical Perspectives* (New York: Harper and Bros., 1956), pp. 277-80; American Academy of Political and Social Sciences, *Annals* (March 1948), pp. 84-91.

   Insofar as his social origins went, the Pentecostal leader was very similar to the run-of-the-mill Protestant clergyman. As late as 1935 it was said, ''responses to the call of the ministry are strongly skewed in favor of candidates from small communities, from relatively humble antecedents, both educationally and economically, and from the less well-established racial elements of the population.'' H. Paul Douglass and Edmund deS. Brunner, *The Protestant Church as a Social Institution* (New York: Harper and Bros., 1935), p. 107. But again we must remind ourselves that a comparison of our forty-five Pentecostals with other Protestant *leadership* groups would show them to differ significantly in social origins.

31. Harold U. Faulkner, *Politics, Reform and Expansion* (New York: Harper and Row, 1963), pp. 70-71.

32. Goss, *Winds of God*, pp. 10-14; on Mrs. Crawford, The Apostolic Faith, *Historical Account*, pp. 54-8.

33. Carolina Evangelistic Association, ''Twentieth Anniversary of the Garr Auditorium, 1930-50,'' booklet (Charlotte, N.C., 1950).

34. Eric Booth-Clibbum, the grandson of the founder of the Salvation Army, died while serving as a Pentecostal missionary to French West Africa, *Pentecostal Evangel*, Jan. 2, 1926, pp. 12-14, 20.

35. On Olazabal, *Pentecostal Evangel*, Oct. 16, 1920, p. 3; on Franciscon, Joseph Fiorentino, ''In the Power of His Spirit,'' pamphlet published by the Christian Church of North America, n.d., pp. 7-9. I have not been able to find a single prominent Pentecostal of Roman Catholic upbringing who went directly into the Pentecostal movement. The Italian-American Joseph Petrelli and the Mexican-American ''Bro.'' Feliciano, for

example, went from Roman Catholic to Baptist and Methodist as preachers, respectively, before becoming Pentecostals, *Pentecostal Evangel,* Aug. 6, 1932, pp. 2–3; *Christian Evangel,* June 1, 1918, p. 10.

36. Interview with Marie Burgess Brown; Holmes, *Life Sketches,* pp. 65, 97–8.

37. Since King made the change only after rejection as a candidate for the M. E., So. ministry it might be argued that the decision was dictated by expediency. But King's rejection was largely owing to his advocacy of Holiness views before the examining committee of the anti-Holiness North Georgia Conference (King, *Yet Speaketh,* pp. 42–49); F. M. Britton, *Pentecostal Truth* (Royston, Ga.: Publishing House of the Pentecostal Holiness Church, 1919), pp. 217–23; W. M. Hayes, *Memoirs of R. B. Hayes,* pp. 12–16; Z. Argue, *What Meaneth This?* pp. 3–8.

38. Frodsham, *Smith Wigglesworth,* p. 117.

39. Smith, *Called Unto Holiness,* pp. 35–7.

40. Barratt, *When the Fire Fell,* pp. 31–4; Eldridge, *Reminiscences,* p. 39; Z. Argue, *What Meaneth This?* p. 6; Stanley H. Frodsham to David J. Fant, Aug. 30, 1943, *PEF.*

41. On Olazabal, *Pentecostal Evangel,* Oct. 16, 1920, p. 3; interview with Marie Burgess Brown, Nov. 5, 1965; on Urshan, Foster, *Think It Not Strange,* pp. 39–40; Bartleman, *Plow to Pulpit,* pp. 28–9, 32, 39; Woodworth-Etter, *Signs and Wonders,* p. 78; Tomlinson, *Diary,* I, 23; Holmes, *Life Sketches,* pp. 68–71, 74, 88, 99–101, 305.

42. See e.g., *Live Coals* (Royston, Ga.), Jan. 11, 1905, p. 3; *Pentecostal Holiness Advocate,* Oct. 11, 1917, p. 9.

43. On the predominant role of former Alliance adherents in the Assemblies of God see Brumback, *Suddenly,* pp. 94–5, *et passim;* Eldridge was successively chairman of the Committee on Home [Missionary] Work, district superintendent of the West Central District, and then, simultaneously, district superintendent of Calif., Ariz., Utah, and Nev., and superintendent of southern California, Christian and Missionary Alliance, *10th Annual Report* (1907), pp. 166–7; *ibid., 11th Annual Report* (1907/08), pp. 6–7. Welch was superintendent of Oklahoma, *ibid., 14th Annual Report* (1911), p. 33. Kerr was Chairman of the Committee on Divine Healing, and a featured speaker at Alliance conventions, *ibid., 8th Annual Report* (1905), pp. 150–52; Frodsham, *Signs Following* (1926), pp. 42–7; *Christian and Missionary Alliance,* March 14, 1908, p. 405. On the Assemblies Reading Course, *Pentecostal Evangel,* Jan. 5, 1924, p. 8; on the use of the Scofield Bible in Assemblies Bible schools, Frank C. Masserano, "A Study of Worship Forms in the Assemblies of God Denomination," unpublished Th.M. thesis, Princeton Theological Seminary, 1966, pp. 34–5.

44. Cf. Aimee S. McPherson, *The Foursquare Gospel* (Los Angeles: Echo Park Evangelistic Association, 1946), pp. 21–3, where Mrs. McPherson says her gospel "came to her by inspiration" in 1922, with Albert B. Simpson, *The Four-Fold Gospel* (Harrisburg, Pa.: Christian Publications, Inc., 1925), p. 4, where Simpson tells of preaching his gospel "more than forty years ago."

45. E.g., *Bridal Call,* II (Nov. 1918), p. 17; *The Apostolic Evangel,* 17 (April 25, 1925), p. 2; and *Pentecostal Evangel,* Oct. 14, 1922, p. 22. The last of these periodicals contained more than 300 separate such advertisements in the years 1924–8, according to the content analysis of Masserano (p. 52). The number of ads in any other given four year period would probably be greater, since Scofield Bible ads were banned from that periodical by the Executive Presbytery of the Assemblies of God from 1924–6, *Pentecostal Evangel,* May 1, 1926. On the popularity of the Scofield Bible and Keswick

writings among Pentecostals, see Hastie, *History*, pp. 128–9 and Masserano, "Study of Worship Forms," pp. 54–5, whose assertions have been substantiated by other Pentecostals to whom I have spoken.

Chapter VII

1. Culbreth to Corvin, n.d., quoted in R. O. Corvin, "History of the Educational Institutions of the Pentecostal Holiness Church" (unpublished Ph.D. dissertation, Southwestern Baptist Theological Seminary, 1956), pp. 20–21; Hastie, *History*, pp. 71–2; see also Brumback, *Suddenly*, pp. 100–101, 118–20, and Synan, *Holiness-Pentecostal Movement*, pp. 177f.

2. The statistical tables are compiled from U.S. Bureau of the Census, *Religious Bodies, 1936*, 3 vols. (Washington, D.C.: Government Printing Office, 1941).

   The census statistics of most religious groups have probably always been distorted upward because of the pressure to show a pattern of growth. The case of the Pentecostals, however, is complicated by a number of factors, especially in the earlier years of the movement, which is why I have chosen to rely mostly upon the 1936 census, rather than that of 1926, which was more accurate for most denominations. The Pentecostal statistics of the 1916 and 1926 censuses were almost certainly grossly underestimated because of the large proportion in completely autonomous congregations, because of the refusal of many Pentecostal groups to keep or report statistics (it was a sin to "number" the people), and because of the practice of some denominations that did report of counting only "saved" adults (since no others could be full members).

   On the other hand, some Pentecostal denominations, especially the larger ones, were infected very early with the fever to show success statistically, and tended to inflate their membership figures. The reliability, for example, of all Church of God in Christ statistics is highly suspect. The late Bishop Ozro T. Jones, its principal official at the time, and his successor, Bishop Ozro T. Jones, Jr., told me in 1966 that they had no statistical data, past or current, concerning either the number of congregations or the membership of their denomination. Interview, Sept. 14, 1966.

   Nevertheless, while the statistics I have used are incomplete and distorted in different directions, they are the best available and, hopefully, have at least some rough correspondence to the actual proportionate distribution of Pentecostals by the various social characteristics measured.

   The regional divisions may be found in Appendix III.

3. I include in "the South" the South Atlantic and the East and West South Central States. The national statistics are computed from U.S. Bureau of the Census, *Historical Statistics*, Series A 123–180, pp. 12–13.

4. Tomlinson, *Diary*, I, 25–8; III, 49; Conn, *Like a Mighty Army*, pp. 52–3, 79; Church of God, *Minutes, 4th Annual Assembly (1909)*, pp. 31–2.

5. Tomlinson, *Diary*, July 2, 1907 entry quoted in Duggar, *Tomlinson*, p. 47.

6. Duggar, p. 52; *Evening Light and Church of God Evangel*, March 1, 1910, p. 8.

7. *White Wing Messenger*, Dec. 7, 1929.

8. Tomlinson, *Diary*, I, 60–63.

9. *Ibid., passim;* Table 1.

10. Campbell, *Pentecostal Holiness Church*, pp. 239–51; Synan, *Holiness-Pentecostal*

Movement, pp. 117–39; Table 1. The major schisms from the Church of God were the (Original) Church of God and the (Tomlinson) Church of God; those from the Pentecostal Holiness Church were the Pentecostal Fire-Baptized Holiness Church, and the Congregational Holiness Church. See Chapters 9 and 10.

11. See Table 1; the West South Central region includes the greater Ozarks.

12. The groups growing out of the Assemblies of God were the Pentecostal Church of God of America, the Pentecostal Assemblies of Jesus Christ, and the Pentecostal Church, Inc. See chapters 9 and 10; Table 1.

13. Gaddis, "Christian Perfectionism in America," p. 392.

14. Edward C. Kirkland, *A History of American Economic Life* (New York: F. C. Crofts & Co., 1932), p. 562; Shannon, *Farmer's Last Frontier,* p. 40; Pope, *Millhands,* pp. 101, 129.

15. *RB 1936,* II, 400–403; Conn, *Like a Mighty Army,* p. 321.

16. See, e.g., "Reports from the Field" section in each weekly issue of the *Pentecostal Evangel* during this period.

17. Goss, *Winds of God,* pp. 30–42; Tomlinson, *Diary, passim;* McPherson, *That Is That,* pp. 110–21.

18. *RB 1926* and *1936, passim.*

19. *Loc. cit.*

20. *Pentecostal Evangel,* Dec. 15, 1928, pp. 2–3.

21. Brumback, *Suddenly,* p. 84.

22. *Upper Room* (Los Angeles), I (Sept. 1909), p. 4.

23. Parham, *Life,* p. 302.

24. *Apostolic Faith* (Los Angeles), I (Dec. 1906), pp. 1–2; (Jan. 1908), p. 1.

25. Apostolic Faith, *Historical Account,* pp. 87–8, 102; see also pp. 73–93.

26. Parham, *Life,* pp. 246, 302.

27. Paul, "Religious Frontier," pp. 77–81, 146.

28. *Pentecostal Evangel,* March 22, 1924, pp. 6–7.

29. Perkins, *Bosworth,* pp. 69–70; Sorrow, *Experiences,* p. 91.

30. Woodworth-Etter, *Signs and Wonders,* pp. 359–61, 406–16, 436–7.

31. McPherson, *This Is That,* pp. 99, 114–15, 117; *Bridal Call* (Montwait, Mass.), I (March 1918), pp. 7, 15.

32. McPherson, *This Is That,* pp. 159–61, 215–19.

33. *Ibid.,* pp. 381–3, 437–43, 526; *Bridal Call* (Los Angeles), VI (June 1922), 6–18.

34. McPherson, *This Is That,* pp. 169–84, 219–39, 324–58.

35. Tables 2 and 3: Interview with O. T. Jones, Sr. and Jr.
    The proportion of blacks in the national population in 1930 was about 12%. U.S. Bureau of the Census, *Historical Statistics,* Series A 22–3, p. 8.

36. Table 2.

37. Tables 1 and 3.

38. *Weekly Evangel,* April 22, 1916, p. 11; April 20, 1918, p. 11; *Christian Evangel,* June 15, 1918, p. 11; July 27, 1918, p. 8; *Pentecostal Herald* (Chicago), IV (Aug. 1918), p. 3; *Pentecostal Evangel,* Jan. 24, 1920, p. 11; Sept. 1, 1923, p. 13; Assemblies of God, *Reports and Financial Statements, 1925–27* (Springfield, Mo., 1927), p. 13.

39. *Pentecostal Evangel,* March 3, 1928, pp. 6–7.

40. *Weekly Evangel,* Nov. 11, 1916, p. 13.

41. H. C. Ball and Alice E. Luce, *Glimpses of Our Latin American Work in the United States and Mexico* (Springfield, Mo.: Gospel Pub. House, 1940), *passim; Weekly Evangel,* Oct. 6, 1917, p. 4.

42. *Weekly Evangel,* Oct. 20, 1917, p. 9; Nov. 10, 1917, p. 12; Assemblies of God, *Minutes, 1919,* pp. 22–3; *Pentecostal Evangel,* March 4, 1922, p. 13; *RB, 1936,* II, 63–72; Assemblies of God, *Reports and Financial Statements, 1925–27,* p. 13; *Pentecostal Evangel,* April 30, 1938, pp. 1, 10.

43. *Weekly Evangel,* Oct. 6, 1917, p. 4; Nov. 10, 1917, p. 12; *Pentecostal Evangel,* June 12, 1920, pp. 10–11.

44. Assemblies of God, *Minutes, 1929,* p. 94; *Pentecostal Herald* (St. Louis, Mo.), March 1967, p. 4; King, *Yet Speaketh,* p. 340.

45. Goss, *Winds of God,* p. 11–12; Woodworth-Etter, *Signs and Wonders,* pp. 376–8; Hastie, *History,* pp. 77–9; *Pentecostal Evangel,* Aug. 6, 1927, p. 20; April 5, 1930, p. 12.

46. *Apostolic Faith* (Portland, Oregon), 18 (Jan. 1909), p. 1; *Christian Evangel,* Sept. 5, 1914, p. 13; *Pentecostal Evangel,* March 10, 1928, p. 13; Oct. 6, 1928, p. 13; Assemblies of God, *Minutes, 1923,* p. 69.

47. Joseph Fiorentino, "In the Power of His Spirit," (pamphlet published by the Christian Church of North America, n.d.); *RB 1936,* II, 748–9.

48. *Pentecostal Evangel,* Sept. 15, 1928, p. 5; Aug. 3, 1929, p. 5; Duggar, *Tomlinson,* p. 426; A. Flower, *Grace for Grace,* pp. 91–3.

49. H. Paul Douglass, *One Thousand City Churches* (New York: Geo. H. Doran Co., 1926), pp. 135–40.

50. *New York Times,* April 2, 1906, p. 1; April 3, 1906, p. 4; April 5, 1906, p. 1; Sept. 27, 1906, p. 7; Parham, *Life,* pp. 155–9; Hollenweger lists thirty-nine prominent Assemblies of God leaders alone as former followers of Dowie, *"Handbuch,"* II, 459–60.

51. John C. Sinclair to E. N. Bell, Jan. 3, 1922, *PEF: Latter Rain Evangel,* I (Oct. 1908), pp. 2–6; Frodsham, *With Signs* (1926), pp. 35–6; Irvine J. Harrison, "A History of the Assemblies of God" (unpublished Th.D. diss., Berkeley Baptist Divinity School, 1954), p. 131.

52. *Weekly Evangel,* Oct. 7, 1927, pp. 5, 8; *Christian Evangel,* June 29, 1918, p. 14.

53. Frederick Link to the Editor of the *Pentecostal Evangel,* March 9, 1951, *PEF;* Frodsham, *With Signs* (1926), pp. 39–40; Fiorentino, *passim; RB, 1936,* II, 752–5.

54. *Apostolic Faith* (Portland, Ore.), 18 (Jan. 1909), p. 1; Frodsham, *With Signs* (1926), p. 42; Link to Editor, March 9, 1951, *PEF.*

55. *Apostolic Faith* (Los Angeles), II (May 1908), p. 4; *Pentecostal Herald* (Chicago), II (March 1917), 4; VI (June 1920), 1.

56. *RB, 1926,* I, 389–91; *RB, 1936,* II, 480–82; St. Clair Drake and Horace H. Clayton, *Black Metropolis* (2 vols., New York: Harper & Row, 1962), II, 414.

57. Frederick G. Henke, "The Gift of Tongues and Related Phenomena at the Present Day," *American Journal of Theology,* XIII (1909), 196ff.; Seddon, *Homiletic Review,* LVII (1909); Pratt, *Religious Consciousness,* p. 187; D. A. Hayes, *Gift of Tongues,* pp. 85–91.

58. Thomas B. Barratt, "How I Obtained My Pentecost," *Christian and Missionary Alliance,* Nov. 3, 1906, pp. 275–6; Barratt, *When the Fire Fell,* pp. 104–40; *Apostolic Faith* (Baxter Springs, Kans.), 3 (March 1927), p. 7.

59. *Apostolic Faith* (Los Angeles), I (Oct. 1906), p. 2; (Dec. 1906), p. 1; *New York American*, Dec. 3, 1906, repr. in Bloch-Hoell, *Pentecostal Movement*, pp. 49–51; Mrs. Robert A. Brown to E. N. Bell, April 5, 1922, *PEF*.

60. *Apostolic Faith* (Baxter Springs, Kans.), 3 (March 1927), p. 7; Brown to Bell, April 5, 1922, *PEF*; *Midnight Cry* (New York), (March–April 1911).

61. *Midnight Cry* (New York), I (March–April 1911); Brown to Bell, April 5, 1922, *PEF*; Gordon F. Gardiner and Marie E. Brown, *The Origin of Glad Tidings Tabernacle* (N.Y.: n.p., 1955), *passim*. Synan erroneously credits Sturdevant with introducing the movement in New York City, *Holiness-Pentecostal Movement*, pp. 113f.

62. Gardiner and Brown, *Origin, passim*; *Apostolic Faith* (Zion City, Ill.), April 1907, quoted in Parham, *Life*, pp. 191–4.

63. Gardiner and Brown, *Origin*, pp. 23–7, 33–4; Brown to Bell, April 5, 1922, *PEF*; Glad Tidings Tabernacle, *Golden Jubilee* (pamph. New York, 1957).

64. Homer A. Tomlinson to Robert M. Anderson, Sept. 12, 1967; Historical Records Survey, *Guide to Vital Statistics in the City of New York* (New York: Works Project Admin., 1942), *passim*; *Apostolic Faith* (Portland, Ore.), 18 (Jan. 1909), p. 1; *Midnight Cry* (New York), I (Dec. 1911), p. 6.

65. Gilbert Osofsky, *Harlem: the Making of a Ghetto* (New York: Harper & Row, 1966), pp. 145–6; Hist. Rec. Survey, *Guide to Vital Statistics in the City of New York*, pp. 49, 55; *Midnight Cry* (New York), IV (Aug. 1971), pp. 7, 8.

66. *Midnight Cry* (New York), I (Dec. 1911), p. 6; *Salem Gospel Tabernacle, 1926–1956* (Anniversary Booklet); *Herald of Pentecost* (Chicago), VI (March 1956), pp. 1, 5.

67. Fiorentino, "In the Power of His Spirit," p. 9; Joseph Demola to Robert M. Anderson, May 18, 1966.

68. *RB, 1936*, II, 604–14; Antonio Callazo, Overseer, Eastern Spanish District of the Church of God to Robert M. Anderson, May 18, 1966.

69. Woodward, *Origins*, pp. 448–55; K. Bailey, *Southern White Protestantism*, pp. 3–24.

70. See references in fn. 69 above; and Furniss, *Fundamentalist Controversy*, pp. 119, 142, 156–8.

71. Furniss, *Fundamentalist Controversy*, pp. 76–95; Woodward, *Origins*, pp. 389–90; McLoughlin, *Modern Revivalism*, pp. 293–6.

72. Woodward, *Origins*, pp. 450–51.

73. Robert S. Lynd and Helen Merrell Lynd, *Middletown* (New York: Harcourt, Brace & World, 1956), pp. 315–409; Gaddis, "Christian Perfectionism in America," pp. 395–404; Smith, *Called*, pp. 145–7, 224–7.

74. Bailey, *Southern White Protestantism*, pp. 42–3; McLoughlin, *Modern Revivalism*, pp. 293–6, 454, 462.

75. Woodward, *Origins*, pp. 142–79; McLoughlin, *Modern Revivalism*, pp. 293–6.

76. Eugene L. Fevold, *The Lutheran Free Church* (Minneapolis: Augsburg Publishing House, 1969); *Christian Century*, Jan. 30, 1952, pp. 127–9.

77. Fiorentino, "In the Power of His Spirit," p. 11.

78. Osofsky, *Harlem*, pp. 143f.

79. James Mooney, *The Ghost Dance Religion and the Sioux Outbreak of 1890* (Chicago: University of Chicago Press, 1965).

80. There is an excellent discussion of animism and spiritism as elements of peasant religion in William I. Thomas and Florian Znaniecki, *The Polish Peasant in Europe and America* (Chicago: University of Chicago Press, 1918), I, 205ff.; see also Max Weber,

The Sociology of Religion (Boston: Beacon Press, 1962), pp. 80–84. Weber also maintained that artisan classes generally share the same religious notions, *ibid.*, pp. 97–8, 101.

Chapter VIII

1. Frodsham, *With Signs* (1941), pp. 41–52 *et passim;* Kendrick, *Promise Fulfilled*, pp. 66–72 *et passim;* Brumback, *Suddenly*, pp. 64–87 *et passim;* Bloch-Hoell, *Pentecostal Movement*, pp. 53–6.

2. Bartleman, *How Pentecost*, pp. 139–40; *Church of God Evangel*, Jan. 24, 1914, through Feb. 14, 1914; *Weekly Evangel*, April 15, 1916, p. 9; *Weekly Evangel*, March 11, 1916; *Weekly Evangel*, Feb. 17, 1917, p. 1.

3. *Pentecostal Holiness Advocate*, June 3, 1920; McPherson, *This Is That*, pp. 156–7, 164, 169; *Pentecostal Evangel*, July 11, 1925, p. 4; report on 1927 Council is in *Pentecostal Evangel*, Oct. 22, 1927, pp. 4–5 and Oct. 29, 1927, pp. 4–5, 17; *Latter Rain Evangel*, Jan. 1932, p. 2. See also the series "Back to Pentecost," throughout the fall and winter issues of the *Pentecostal Evangel*, 1920–21, and again in the summer of 1924.

4. See, e.g., *Christian Witness and Advocate of Bible Holiness* (Chicago), March 16, 1916, p. 6; *Pentecostal Herald* (Louisville, Ky.), Jan. 20, 1915, p. 1; July 24, 1918, pp. 1, 8.

5. See, e.g., *New York Times*, June 28, 1914, III, p. 3; Sept. 24, 1919, p. 20; March 7, 1921, p. 11; March 21, 1921, p. 23; *Christian Evangel*, Aug. 29, 1914, p. 3; Church of God, *Minutes, 11th Annual Assembly* (1915), quoted in Conn, *Like a Mighty Army*, pp. 130–31; G. Bond, *Life Story of Rev. O. H. Bond*, p. 62.

6. The quote is from King, *Yet Speaketh*, p. 192. See also Christian and Missionary Alliance, *Minutes of the 11th Annual Assembly* (1907/08), pp. 11–12; *Word and Witness*, Sept. 20, 1913, p. 1; Jan. 20, 1914, p. 2; *Midnight Cry* (New York), March 1916, p. 4; Pentecostal World Conference, *Minutes of the 2nd . . . . . Paris*, May 21–9, 1949 (Cleveland, Tenn., 1949), pp. 44–45; Ewart, *Phenomenon*, p. 47; Bloch-Hoell, *Pinsebevegelsen*, p. 431.

7. Donald Gee, "Movement Without a Man," *Christian Life*, July 1966, pp. 27–9; Brumback, *Suddenly*, pp. 48–63.

8. Thomas B. Barratt to Mrs. I. May Throop, Sept. 28, 1906, quoted in Barratt, *When the Fire Fell*, pp. 109–110; Barratt to Clara C. Lunn, Nov. 22, 1906, cited in Bloch-Hoell, *Pentecostal Movement*, p. 136; *Apostolic Faith* (Los Angeles), I (Dec. 1906), p. 1; "Notice About Parham," *Word and Witness*, Oct. 20, 1912, p. 3; "The Work Greatly Hindered," *Weekly Evangel*, March 4, 1916, p. 4; Pentecostal Evangel, Jan. 7, 1922, p. 8; J. R. Flower, "Church Orientation," p. 17; Goss, pp. 78–9; Parham, *Life*, pp. 163–6, 184–5, 198–201, 260–61; W. T. Dixon to S. H. Frodsham, Jan. 10, 1941, *PEF;* Howard Goss to J. R. Flower, March 10, 1950, *PEF.*

Critics and apologists of Parham agree on the sexual nature of his offense, but not on its exact character. Parham's wife says he was unjustly accused of deserting his wife and children, and clearly implies he was believed to be guilty of adultery. Parham, *Life*, pp. 198–201. E. N. Bell said Parham's sins are described in the first chapter of Romans. "What the General Council Stands For," *Pentecostal Evangel*, Jan. 7, 1922, p. 8. Bloch-Hoell, following the anti-Pentecostal writers H. J. Stolee and O. H. Haavik, interprets this as meaning Parham was a homosexual (though this is only one of several "sins" described in Romans I). Bloch-Hoell, *Pentecostal Movement*, pp. 19–21. The Pentecostal Irvine J. Harrison says Parham was "observed . . . through the keyhole of his door misconducting himself while alone in his room." But Harrison cites an article in the *Weekly Evangel*, March 4, 1916, p. 4, that in no way supports this assertion, "A History of the Assemblies of God," p. 97.

9. Brumback, *Suddenly,* pp. 61–62; Apostolic Faith, *Historical Account,* p. 70.

10. See chapters 9 and 10 on Durham, Bell, and Tomlinson; on Cashwell see Synan, *Holiness-Pentecostal Movement,* pp. 138f.

11. *Pentecostal Evangel,* June 12, 1926, pp. 8–9, 12; Sweet, *Revivalism,* p. 177; the quotation is from the *Florida Baptist Advocate,* May 13, 1915, repr. in *Church of God Evangel,* Aug. 7, 1915.

12. *Apostolic Faith* (Los Angeles), I (Sept. 1906), p. 1.

13. McGowen, *PEF;* Bartleman, *How Pentecost,* pp. 67–8, 82, 86–7; *Apostolic Faith* (Los Angeles), I (Oct. 1906), pp. 3, 4; Ewart, *Phenomenon,* pp. 4–7.

14. *Way of Faith* (Columbia, S. C.), Sept. 6, 1906, quoted in Bartleman, *How Pentecost,* pp. 86–7.

15. Bartleman, *How Pentecost,* pp. 105–25.

16. *Gospel Witness* (Louisville, Ky.), Sept. 1906, p. 30; *Christian and Missionary Alliance,* Sept. 22, 1906, p. 177; *Herald of Light* (Indianapolis, Ind.), Dec. 29, 1906, p. 13; *Apostolic Faith* (Los Angeles), I (Oct. 1906), p. 2; *The Bridegroom's Messenger* (Atlanta), I (Dec. 1907), p. 3; *God's Revivalist,* Dec. 12, 1907, p. 1; *Missionary Review,* XXXI (Jan. 1908), 60–61; (July 1908), 531–3.

17. Ewart, p. 85.

18. H. A. Ironside, *Holiness: The False and the True* (New York: Loizeaux Bros., [1912]); C. I. Scofield, *Christian Sanity* (Chicago: Moody Bible Institute Bookstore, n.d.); C. I. Scofield, Introduction to A. E. Bishop, *Tongues, Signs and Visions Not God's Order for Today* (Chicago: Moody Bible Institute Bookstore n.d.). See Barratt's rebuttal to Bishop in *Pentecostal Evangel,* Dec. 8, 1926, p. 6. William B. Riley, *Speaking with Tongues* (n.p., n.d.). See Arch P. Collins' rebuttal to Riley in *Pentecostal Evangel,* April 17, 1920, p. 4; Jessie Penn-Lewis and Evan Roberts, *War on the Saints* (Dorset, Eng.: Overcomer Literary Trust, n.d.), pp. 33–4, 144–9, *et passim;* Joseph Smale, "The Latter Rain," *Living Truth,* Jan. 1907; see also the articles in the religious periodical press cited in Cutten, *Psychological Phenomenon,* pp. 57–8, and in Pratt, pp. 180–87.

19. *Pentecostal Holiness Advocate,* March 17, 1921, pp. 8–9; March 24, 1921, pp. 8–9; Campbell, *Pentecostal Holiness Church,* pp. 239–51.

20. Pentecostal Free Will Baptist Church, *Discipline of the Pentecostal Free Will Baptist Church* (n.p., n.d.), pp. 5–12; "History of the Pentecostal Free Will Baptist Church," *The Messenger,* Oct. 1965, pp. 4.

21. Church of God in Christ, *Manual,* pp. 7–9; interview with O. T. Jones, Sr. and Jr.

22. *RB, 1936,* II, 364–5; Aiden W. Tozer, *Wingspread* (Harrisburg, Pa.: Christian Publications, 1943), *passim.*

23. *Christian and Missionary Alliance,* Nov. 12, 1906, p. 305; Nov. 17, 1906, pp. 316, 318; Dec. 1, 1906, pp. 338–9; Christian and Missionary Alliance, *10th Annual Report* (*1907*), p. 77; Brumback, *Suddenly,* pp. 88–9.

24. *Christian and Missionary Alliance,* Jan. 26, 1907, p. 40; Feb. 9, 1907, p. 64.

25. *Ibid.,* Feb. 2, 1907, p. 49.

26. Christian and Missionary Alliance, *10th Annual Report (1907),* pp. 5–6, 166–7.

27. *Christian and Missionary Alliance,* June 8, 1907, p. 205; June 29, 1907, pp. 302–3.

28. *Ibid.,* July 27, 1907, p. 37; Aug. 17, 1907, p. 73; Sept. 17, 1907, p. 116; Frodsham, *With Signs* (1926), pp. 46–7.

29. See references in fn. 28 above.

30. *Christian and Missionary Alliance,* July 6, 1907, p. 313; July 13, 1907, p. 13; July 27, 1907, p. 44; Oct. 5, 1907, p. 17; Oct. 19, 1907, pp. 38, 50; Mabette Anderson, *The Latter Rain and Its Counterfeit* (New York: n.p., 1907).

31. *Christian and Missionary Alliance,* Feb. 29, 1908, p. 366; March 7, 1908, pp. 385–6.

32. Christian and Missionary Alliance, *11th Annual Report* (1907/08), pp. 10–11.

33. *Ibid.,* pp. 11, 67–76.

34. *Ibid.,* pp. 5–6.

35. *Ibid.,* p. 13.

36. *Christian and Missionary Alliance,* March 28, 1908, p. 432.

37. *Ibid.,* July 11, 1908, p. 250; Sept. 12, 1908, pp. 402–3; David McDowell to R. M. Anderson, March 16, 1967; *Christian and Missionary Alliance,* April 4, 1908, pp. 7–9, 17; April 11, 1908, p. 25; April 18, 1908, p. 40; Oct. 31, 1908, pp. 72–3; July 31, 1909, pp. 297–8, 302.

38. Christian and Missionary Alliance, *12th Annual Report (1909),* p. 58; *15th Annual Report (1912),* pp. 39–50; Tozer, *Wingspread,* pp. 133–4.

39. *Weekly Evangel,* March 25, 1916, p. 4.

40. Gaddis, "Christian Perfectionism in America," p. 488; Clark, *Small Sects* (1949), pp. 75–81. The Pentecostal Church of the Nazarene dropped the word "Pentecostal" in 1919. Edwin Scott Gaustod, *Historical Atlas of Religion in America* (New York: Harper & Row, 1962), p. 125. The Pentecostal Union Church changed its name to The Pillar of Fire in 1917. *R.B. 1936,* II, 677–9. The Pentecostal Bands of the World became the Missionary Bands of the World in 1925. *R.B. 1926,* II, 578.

   On anti-Pentecostal writings of Fundamentalists see, e.g., *Pentecostal Evangel,* Nov. 26, 1921, p. 4; July 9, 1927, pp. 4–5; July 23, 1927, pp. 2–3; Sept. 27, 1930, p. 4; William C. Irvine, *Heresies Exposed* (New York: Loizeaux Bros., 1917); Russell R. Byrum, *Holy Spirit Baptism and the Second Cleansing* (Anderson, Ind.: Gospel Trumpet Co., 1923); John Matthews, *Speaking in Tongues* (Kansas City, Mo.: the author, 1925); T. J. McCrossan, *Speaking with Other Tongues* (Harrisburg, Pa.: Christian Publications, n.d.); B. P. Neely, *The Bible Versus the Tongues Theory* (Kansas City, Mo.: Beacon Hill Press, 1930).

41. See, e.g., Woodworth-Etter, *Signs and Wonders,* pp. 544–51; Bartleman, *How Pentecost,* pp. 88–9. All Pentecostal writers acknowledge the presence of such characteristics; see, e.g., John T. Nichol, "The Role of the Pentecostal Movement in American Church History," *The Gordon Review,* II (Dec. 1956); Nichol, *Pentecostalism,* pp. 79–80; Brumback, *Suddenly,* pp. 114–15; Gee, *Pentecostal Movement,* pp. 18–19.

42. *Pentecostal Evangel,* April 5, 1925, p. 15.

43. Alma White, *Demons and Tongues* (Zarephath, N.J.: Pillar of Fire Pub., 1919).

44. Woodworth-Etter, *Signs and Wonders,* pp. 179–84; McPherson, *This Is That,* pp. 105–6, 131–7; Tomlinson, *Diary,* I, 110–14; Ewart, *Phenomenon,* pp. 20, 50–51; Goss, *Winds of God* pp. 87–89. See also Brumback, *Suddenly,* pp. 282–93; Conn, *Like a Mighty Army,* pp. 108–9; Nichol, *Pentecostalism,* pp. 70–80.

45. Tomlinson, *Diary*, I, 108–9, 112, 115; *Word and Witness*, Oct. 20, 1913, p. 1; *Church of God Evangel*, Oct. 21, 1916; Woodworth-Etter, *Signs and Wonders*, pp. 305–28; S. C. Bailey, *Pioneer Marvels*, p. 13; *Pentecostal Herald* (Chicago), II (March 1917), 4; Ewart, *Phenomenon*, pp. 51–3; McPherson, *This Is That*, pp. 105–6, 121–2; *Pentecostal Evangel*, Dec. 13, 1914, p. 12; *Church of God Evangel*, July 11, 1914, and Oct. 24, 1914.

46. See chapter 9 on the "only evidence" controversy.

47. Charles Edwin Jones, "Perfectionist Persuasion," pp. 332, 350–54, 364–8.

Chapter IX

1. The first substantial indication of this was the organization in 1948 of the Pentecostal Fellowship of North America, which included about half of all American Pentecostals. *Pentecostal Fellowship of North America* (Toronto: Pentecostal Fellowship of North America, n.d.). Attempts at the World Pentecostal Conferences of 1947 and 1949 to create a world organization caused such bitter controversy that they were abandoned. Hollenweger, *The Pentecostals*, pp. 67f.

2. Goss, *Winds of God*, pp. 155–6.

3. Atter, *Third Force*, pp. 3–6; Gee, *Pentecostal Movement*, p. 30; J. R. Flower, "Origin & Development of the Assemblies of God," p. 17.

4. Assemblies of God, *Minutes, 1918*, p. 12 *Minutes, 1919*, p. 13; Gee, *Pentecostal Movement*, p. 58.

5. Christian and Missionary Alliance, *11th Annual Report* (1907/08), p. 12; *Apostolic Faith* (Houston, Texas), n.d., repr. in *Latter Rain Evangel*, Oct. 1910, pp. 7–10; Goss, *Winds of God*, pp. 105–6; *Word and Witness*, Dec. 20, 1913, p. 2; Woodworth-Etter, *Signs and Wonders*, pp. 488–93; *Weekly Evangel*, July 10, 1915, p. 1; *Pentecostal Evangel*, June 2, 1928, pp. 4–5; March 3, 1928, pp. 6–7; Brumback, *Suddenly*, pp. 109, 112.

6. Church of God (Cleveland, Tenn.), *Minutes, 8th Annual Assembly (1913)*, p. 101; *Minutes, 9th Annual Assembly (1913)*, p. 145; *Minutes, 10th Annual Assembly (1914)*, pp. 172–4.

7. *Latter Rain Evangel*, Oct. 1910, pp. 7–10.

8. Goss, *Winds of God*, p. 102.

9. On the shorthand transcription and publication of tongues and interpretation see *Apostolic Faith* (Los Angeles), I (Oct. 1906), 2; *Christian and Missionary Alliance*, Oct. 31, 1908, pp. 72–3; *Word and Witness*, April 20, 1914, p. 3; Parham, *Everlasting Gospel*, pp. 96–7; King *Yet Speaketh*, p. 131. For English "translations" of "messages" in tongues and interpretation see *Apostolic Faith* (Los Angeles), I (Sept., Oct., Dec. 1906), *passim; Latter Rain Evangel*, Oct. 1908, pp. 1, 7–13; Feb. 1909, p. 2; *Weekly Evangel*, all issues from October through December 1915; *Bridal Call* (Los Angeles) II (Apr. 1919), pp. 11–14. On sending tongues transcriptions to interpreters see Holmes, pp. 180–84. The quotation is from *Apostolic Faith* (Los Angeles), I (Oct. 1906), p. 2.

10. *Apostolic Faith* (Houston), n.d., repr. in *Latter Rain Evangel*, Oct. 1910, pp. 7–10; *Word and Witness*, Dec. 20, 1913, p. 2; Goss, *Winds of God*, pp. 101–2; *Weekly Evangel*, July 10, 1915, p. 1; *Pentecostal Evangel*, Nov. 25, 1922, p. 6; March 3, 1928, pp. 6–7.

11. One or more of the questions in this and the preceding paragraphs are discussed in al-

most any issue of any Pentecostal periodical during the years from the beginning of the movement to the end of the 1920's. Some of these questions are further dealt with below.

12. Goss, *Winds of God*, pp. 45–6; *Apostolic Faith* (Los Angeles) I (Dec. 1906) p. 3; *Weekly Evangel*, July 10, 1915, p. 1; interview with O. T. Jones, Sr. and Jr.

13. Brumback, *Suddenly*, pp. 109–10; *Word and Witness*, Jan. 20, 1914, p. 2; Atter, *Third Force*, pp. 145–6; see also the allusion to the "Social and Marital Purity Teaching," Assemblies of God, *Minutes, 1925*, p. 38.

14. See the series of "Reconciliation Tracts," by A. E. Saxby and A. E. Knoch in *PEF;* A. E. Knoch, *The Exact Truth Regarding an Eternal Hell: A Reply* (Los Angeles: Concordat Publishing Concern, 1922). The reply is to R. A. Torrey, *The Exact Truth Regarding an Eternal Hell* (Los Angeles: Biola Book Room, n.d.). *Weekly Evangel*. April 10, 1915, p. 3; *Pentecostal Evangel*, Feb. 14, 1925, pp. 6–7; Dec. 10, 1927, pp. 2–3, 7; *Pentecostal Testimony* (Toronto), X (Jan. 1929), pp. 11–16; A. E. Saxby to S. H. Frodsham, Sept. 16, 1927, and Jan. 16, 1928, *PEF.*

15. On the British origins of "Ultimate Reconciliation" see Gee, *Pentecostal Movement*, pp. 124–5; Atter, *Third Force*, pp. 138–9. On the "Yellow Book Series" see *Word and Witness*, April 20, 1914, p. 3. On the "In School with the Holy Ghost" series see Parham, *Everlasting Gospel*, pp. 96–7. On the Pittsburgh Bible Institute see Rachel Craig to S. H. Frodsham, Dec. 19, 1927, *PEF;* see also the allusion to "Pridgeonism" as a condemned "heresy" in Assemblies of God, *Minutes, 1925*, p. 38.

16 *Pentecostal Holiness Advocate*, Aug. 3, 1922, pp. 8–10;; Sept. 28, 1922, pp. 8–10; Gee, *Pentecostal Movement*, pp. 73, 125–6; Atter, *Third Force*, pp. 136–7; Campbell, *Pentecostal Holiness Church*, pp. 267–8; Hastie, *History*, p. 86; King, *Yet Speaketh*, p. 309.

17. See Chapter 8 and Hastie, *History*, p. 164.

18. Moore, *Handbook*, pp. 236–7; King, *Yet Speaketh*, p. 316; Campbell, *Pentecostal Holiness Church*, p. 277; B. L. Cox, *History and Doctrine of the Congregational Holiness Church* (n.p., 1959), pp. 7–9.

19. Tomlinson, *Diary*, I, 262–3; II, 13–39; Duggar, *Tomlinson*, p. 176.

20. Assemblies of God, *Early History*, p. 9; Campbell, *Pentecostal Holiness Church*, pp. 282–4.

21. Assemblies of God, *Minutes, 1916*, pp. 12–13.

22. F. F. Bosworth, "Do All Speak with Tongues?" (tract), *PEF; Pentecostal Evangel*, May 5, 1928, pp. 4–5; Brumback, *Suddenly*, pp. 216–25.

23. Bosworth, "Do All Speak with Tongues?", *PEF; Pentecostal Evangel*, May 5, 1928, pp. 4–5; Goss, *Winds of God*, pp. 57–9; the quote is from *Weekly Evangel*, May 4, 1916.

24. *Apostolic Faith* (Los Angeles), I (Jan. 1908) p. 2. Italics added.

25. *Latter Rain Evangel*, Oct. 1908, pp. 15–20; Mar. 1909, pp. 22–3.

26. Thomas B. Barratt, *The Truth About the Pentecostal Revival* (London: n.p., 1908), p. 12. Barratt later accepted the "only evidence" viewpoint, *Pentecostal Evangel*, May 5, 1928, pp. 4–5.

27. See the special issue on "the distinctive testimony of the Pentecostal Movement," *Pentecostal Evangel*, Sept. 2, 1922; T. B. Barratt, "The Baptism of the Holy Ghost and Fire," a series of articles in the *Pentecostal Evangel*, May 5, 1928, pp. 4–5; May 12, 1928, pp. 6–7; May 19, 1928, pp. 4–5; May 26, 1928, pp. 4–5. Brumback, *Suddenly*,

pp. 216–25; Brumback, *What Meaneth This?, passim;* Goss, *Winds of God,* pp. 48–55.

28. Excerpt from J. H. King, *Passover to Pentecost* (n.p., 1914), repr. in *Pentecostal Holiness Advocate,* May 23, 1946, p. 11. Nevertheless, King soon came to accept the distinction and the Pentecostal Holiness Church adopted ''the only evidence'' position.

29. *Apostolic Faith* (Los Angeles), I (Sept. 1906). Italics added.

30. Barratt's statement is in *Apostolic Faith* (Los Angeles), I (Dec. 1906) p. 3, italics added. Assemblies of God, *Minutes, 1916,* pp. 10–13. See also Barratt, *When the Fire Fell,* p. 125; Smith Wigglesworth, *Ever-Increasing Faith* (n.p., n.d.), quoted in *Pentecostal Evangel,* Sept. 13, 1924, pp. 2–3, 5; Goss, *Winds of God,* pp. 48–55.

31. Assemblies of God, *Minutes, 1918; Christian Evangel,* Oct. 5, 1918, pp. 2–3; Brumback, *Suddenly,* pp. 216–25. Among those who first supported and then deserted Bosworth at the Council were Arch P. Collins, a founder and past Chairman of the Assemblies, W. T. Gaston, who became Chairman from 1925–9, and M. M. Pinson, another founder and a Presbyter. *Christian Evangel,* March 22, 1919, p. 9.

32. See references in fn. 31 above.

33. *Pentecostal Evangel,* April 17, 1920, p. 2.

34. *Christian Evangel,* June 15, 1918, pp. 6–7; Aug. 24, 1918, p. 6; *Pentecostal Evangel,* Dec. 27, 1919, pp. 8–9, Sept. 2, 1918, entire issue; June 16, 1928, pp. 6–7; *Pentecostal Herald* (Chicago), IV (Aug. 1918) p. 4; *Pentecostal Holiness Advocate,* Jan. 17, 1918, pp. 8–9; Jan. 24, 1918, pp. 4–5; Church of God (Cleveland, Tenn.), *Minutes, 8th Annual Assembly* (1913); The Pentecostal Fellowship of North America, *Constitution and By-Laws* (Toronto: Testimony Press, n.d.); Apostolic Faith (Portland, Ore.), *The Apostolic Faith: Its Origins, Functions and Doctrines* (n.p., n.d.) pp. 3–4; Pentecostal Church of God of America, Inc., *General Constitution and By-Laws* (Joplin, Mo., 1966), p. 17; United Pentecostal Church, *Manual of the United Pentecostal Church* (St. Louis, Mo., 1967), pp. 18–19; Bible Way Churches of Our Lord Jesus Christ World Wide, *Brief History and Doctrine of the Bible Way Churches of Our Lord Jesus Christ World Wide* (Washington, D.C., n.d.), p. 8; The Christian Church of North America, *Who We Are* (Pittsburgh, n.d.), p. 11.

35. Church of God in Christ, *Manual of the Church of God in Christ* (Memphis, Tenn., 1951), pp. 56–7; interview with O. T. Jones, Sr. and Jr. The ''only evidence'' doctrine is rejected by the Elim Pentecostal Churches in England, the Pentecostal Mission in Switzerland, the Apostolic Faith Mission in South Africa, and nearly all German and Chilean Pentecsotals. Hollenweger, *The Pentecostals,* pp. 332, 334f. It is also rejected by the Apostolic Church in England, some Scandinavian and many ''independent'' American Pentecostals.

36. Hastie, *History,* pp. 156–8; Kendrick, *Promise Fulfilled,* pp. 145–7; Pentecostal Church of God of America, Inc., *General Constitution and By-Laws,* pp. 13–15.

37. *Pentecostal Evangel,* June 10, 1922, p. 9; Hastie, *History,* pp. 158–61.

38. King, *Yet Speaketh,* p. 333.

39. *Pentecostal Testimony* (Chicago), n.d. quoted in Brumback, *Suddenly,* pp. 99; J. R. Flower to Elmer T. Clark, Nov. 17, 1944, *PEF.*

40. See references in fn. 39, and Brumback, *Suddenly,* pp. 98–103.

41. Durham is quoted in Brumback, *Suddenly,* p. 99. The seemingly contradictory statements are both by Robert A. Brown in an article in *Midnight Cry* (New York), I (Dec. 1911), pp. 1–2.

42. *Latter Rain Evangel,* Aug. 1912, pp. 2–3.

43. Goss, *Winds of God,* pp. 126–7.

44. Bartleman, *How Pentecost,* pp. 145–53; Goss, *Winds of God,* pp. 135–6.

45. Goss, *Winds of God,* pp. 126–7, 155–6; *Weekly Evangel,* March 4, 1916. Assemblies of God writers have explicitly denied that Rodgers was associated with Tomlinson's Church of God (Cleveland, Tenn.) and even that Rodgers had any knowledge that such a church existed. Assemblies of God *Early History,* p. 6; Brumback, *Suddenly,* pp. 154f. But Rodgers' reports of the work of the Church of God in Anniston, Newton, and Slocumb, Alabama, and at the Interstate Camp Meeting in Ft. Worth, published in that church's official organ in 1910, show that Rodgers was an active worker for the Church of God (Cleveland, Tenn.). *Church of God Evangel,* June 1, July 1, and July 15, 1910.

46. *Pentecostal Evangel* April 5, 1964, pp. 7, 26–7. J. R. Flower to Richard Crayne, n.d., repr. in Richard Crayne, *Early 20th Century Pentecost* (Morristown, Tenn.: the author, 1960), pp. 56–8; Tomlinson, *Diary,* I, 238–9; *Church of God Evangel,* June 20, 1914.

47. *Pentecostal Evangel,* Oct. 10, 1925; Moore, "Handbook," pp. 25–6; Assemblies of God, *Early History,* pp. 9, 13–15.

48. See Table 4.

49. See Table 3.

50. *Loc. cit.*

51. Smith, *Revivalism and Social Reform,* pp. 139–41.

52. J. R. Flower to E. T. Clark, Nov. 17, 1944, *PEF.*

53. See Appendix II for references to each person named.

54. R. A. Torrey, *The Person and Work of the Holy Spirit* (New York: Fleming H. Revell Co., 1910); H. A. Ironside, *Holiness: The False and the True* (Neptune, N.J.: Loizeaux Bros., 1964, 1st ed. 1912). A recent, full statement of the non-Pentecostal Fundamentalist position may be found in Merrill F. Unger, *The Baptizing Work of the Holy Spirit* (Findlay, Ohio: The Dunham Publishing Co., 1962).

55. Pentecostal Free Will Baptist Church, *Discipline* pp. 5–16.

56. *Pentecostal Herald* (Chicago), IV (Sept. 1918), pp. 1–2; Higgins, *Pioneering,* p. 17.

Chapter X

1. Parham, *Voice,* pp. 23–24; Parham, *Life,* p. 242; Foster, *Think It Not Strange,* pp. 69–71.

2. *Christian Evangel,* Sept. 6, 1919, pp. 6–7; *Latter Rain Evangel,* May 1915, pp. 2–9; *Word and Witness,* June 1915, pp. 2–3.

3. Tomlinson, *Diary,* I, 180–82, 234; III, 13, 31; *Weekly Evangel,* March 27, 1915, pp. 1–3.

4. Ewart, *Phenomenon,* pp. 50–51, 75–6; Brumback, *Suddenly,* p. 191; Foster, *Think It Not Strange,* pp. 9, 51–2.

5. See references in fn. 4.

6. See references in fn. 4.

7. *Word and Witness,* March 20, 1914, pp. 2–3. McAlister denied any connection with the group soon after its founding. *Word and Witness,* May 20, 1914, p. 2.

8. Ewart, *Phenomenon,* pp. 51–4; Foster, *Think It Not Strange,* pp. 53–4.

9. Ewart, *Phenomenon,* p. 53; Glenn A. Cook, "The Truth About E. N. Bell," *Herald of Truth* (Houston), Aug. 1947, p. 3; *Weekly Evangel,* July 17, 1915, pp. 1–2; Foster,

Think It Not Strange, pp. 54–7, 61–2; Brumback, *Suddenly,* pp. 192–6. It is not certain whether Haywood was associated with both groups simultaneously or left the Pentecostal Assemblies of the World to join the Assemblies of God and only later returned to the former organization.

10. *Weekly Evangel,* May 29, 1915, pp. 3–4; *Word and Witness* June 1915, pp. 1–3; Oct. 1915, p. 4; Foster, *Think It Not Strange,* pp. 54–5, 65–7; Oliver F. Fauss, *Buy the Truth and Sell It Not* (St. Louis, Mo.: Pentecostal Pub. House, 1965), pp. 33–4.

11. *Weekly Evangel,* June 5, 1915, pp. 1, 3; July 17, 1915, pp. 1–2; *Midnight Cry* (New York), May 1915, p. 7; *The Victorious Gospel* (Los Angeles), early spring 1915, p. 4; *Latter Rain Evangel,* May 1915, pp. 2–9.

12. Ewart, *Phenomenon,* p. 99; Foster, *Think It Not Strange,* pp. 55–6; Brumback, *Suddenly,* pp. 195–6.

13. Foster, *Think It Not Strange,* pp. 56–7, 60–63; Fauss, *Buy the Truth,* pp. 7–8, 17–20, 24; Brumback, *Suddenly,* pp. 197–9.

14. *Word and Witness,* Sept. 1915, p. 4; Brumback, *Suddenly,* pp. 197–8.

15. Assemblies of God, *Minutes, 1915,* pp. 4–9; Brumback, *Suddenly,* pp. 200–203.

16. See references in fn. 15 above, and *Weekly Evangel,* Oct. 16, 1915, pp. 1–2.

17. Assemblies of God, *Minutes, 1915,* pp. 4–9; Brumback, *Suddenly,* pp. 202–4; *Weekly Evangel,* Nov. 6, 1915, p. 1; March 4, 1916, pp. 6–7.

18. *Weekly Evangel,* June 12, 1915, pp. 1, 3; Ewart, *Phenomenon,* p. 95; Foster, *Think It Not Strange,* pp. 52–3; interview with O. T. Jones, Sr. and Jr.; Brumback, *Suddenly,* pp. 192, 202.

19. Ewart, *Phenomenon,* pp. 95–9; Foster, *Think It Not Strange,* pp. 15–21; Fauss, *Buy the Truth,* pp. 4–6, 25–31, 65–70; *Latter Rain Evangel,* May 1915, pp. 2–9.

20. See references in fn. 19 above and also Pentecostal Assemblies of the World, *Ministerial Record* (Indianapolis, 1919), p. 26; S. C. Johnson, *Twenty One Burning Subjects* (Philadelphia: Church of the Lord Jesus Christ of the Apostolic Faith, n.d.); *Word and Witness,* Jan. 20, 1914, p. 3; *Christian Evangel,* June 28, 1919, pp. 1–2; July 12, 1919, pp. 1–2, 9; Foster, *Think It Not Strange,* p. 85.

21. *Midnight Cry* (New York), May 1915, p. 7; *Word and Witness,* Oct. 1915, p. 4.

22. *Word and Witness,* Sept. 1915, p. 4; Oct. 1915, pp. 1, 4; *Christian Evangel,* Sept. 16, 1919, pp. 6–7; *Pentecostal Evangel,* Feb. 19, 1921, p. 23.

23. Foster, *Think It Not Strange,* pp. 65–7; Brumback, *Suddenly,* pp. 202–4.

24. Assemblies of God, *Minutes, 1916,* pp. 8–14; *Weekly Evangel,* Oct. 21, 1916, p. 4; Ewart, *Phenomenon,* p. 34; Brumback, *Suddenly,* pp. 203–7; Foster, *Think It Not Strange,* pp. 67–8.

Hollenweger erroneously dates the eviction of the "Oneness" faction from the Assemblies of God in 1915. *The Pentecostals,* p. 32.

25 Assemblies of God, *Minutes, 1916,* pp. 8–14; *Weekly Evangel,* Oct. 21, 1916, p. 4; Brumback, *Suddenly,* pp. 204–10.

26. Assemblies of God, *Minutes, 1916,* pp. 8–14.

27. Brumback, *Suddenly,* pp. 209–10; Foster, *Think It Not Strange,* pp. 67–8; Fauss, *Buy the Truth,* pp. 33–4.

28. Brumback, *Suddenly,* pp. 209–10.

29. *Weekly Evangel,* Jan. 20, 1917, p. 15; Foster, *Think It Not Strange,* pp. 73–9; Fauss, *Buy the Truth,* p. 35.

30. Ernest A. Buckles, *A Brief History: The Church of God* (of the Apostolic Faith),

(Drumright, Okla.: the author, 1935); *Pentecostal Holiness Advocate,* July 31, 1919, pp. 3–5; Parham, *Everlasting Gospel,* pp. 118–20; "The Pentecostal Movement," tract (Portland, Ore.: The Apostolic Faith n.d.).

31. *Word and Witness,* Dec. 20, 1913, p. 1; Assemblies of God, *Early History,* pp. 4–8.

32. Brumback, *Suddenly,* pp. 162–71, 187; Cook, *Herald of Truth* (Houston), Aug. 1947, p. 3.

33. Brumback, *Suddenly,* pp. 172–80, 186–90.

34. Assemblies of God, *Minutes, 1916;* Brumback, *Suddenly,* p. 201.

35. Assemblies of God, *Early History,* pp. 16–18; Assemblies of God, *Minutes, 1916.*

36. Assemblies of God, *Minutes, 1916.*

37. See Tables 4 and 5.

38. Table 6.

39. $18.00 as compared with $12.00. *RB, 1936,* II.

40. King, *Yet Speaketh,* pp. 125–5; Campbell, *Pentecostal Holiness Church,* p. 259.

41. Bloch-Hoell, *Pentecostal Movement,* pp. 53–4; Apostolic Faith, *Historical Account,* p. 70.

42. Goss, *Winds of God,* pp. 126f., 155f., 163; Assemblies of God, *Early History,* pp. 8–10.

43. Assemblies of God, *Minutes, 1916;* the quote is from Brumback, *Suddenly,* p. 208.
    Synan is mistaken when he says that "no Negroes were invited" and that "none of Mason's group appeared" at the Hot Springs convention. Synan, *Holiness-Pentecostal Movement,* p. 170.

44. See *supra,* pp. 82–3.

45. *Apostolic Faith* (Baxter Springs, Kans.), 3 (April 1925) pp. 9–10.

46. Parham, *Life,* p. 276; *Apostolic Faith* (Baxter Springs, Kans.), III (March 1927), 5.

47. *Bridal Call* (Los Angeles).

48. *Pentecostal Evangel,* Aug. 16, 1924, pp. 8–9; *Latter Rain Evangel,* Nov. 1928, pp. 2–5.

49. Church of God (Cleveland, Tenn.), *Minutes, 14th Annual Assembly (1919),* p. 13; *16th Annual Assembly (1921),* pp. 25–6; *21st Annual Assembly (1926),* pp. 44–5; Tomlinson, *Diary,* II, 27; Simmons, *History,* pp. 85–8; Conn, *Like A Mighty Army,* pp. 133, 202–3. The quotation is from Church of God, *Minutes, 16th Annual Assembly (1921),* pp. 25–6.

50. Foster, *Think It Not Strange,* pp. 73–5.

51. *Ibid.,* pp. 75–9.

52. *Ibid.,* pp. 79–80.

53. *Loc. cit.*

54. Anton T. Boison, "Economic Distress and Religious Experience: A Study of the Holy Rollers," *Psychiatry,* II (May 1939), 185–94; Archie Robertson, *That Old-Time Religion* (Boston: Houghton Mifflin Co., 1950), pp. 167, 176–81; interview with O. T. Jones, Sr. and Jr.

55. For insight into the integrative function of conflict I am indebted to Malcolm J. Calley, *God's People: West Indian Pentecostal Sects in England* (New York: Oxford Univ. Press, 1965).

Chapter XI

1. Smith, *Revivalism and Social Reform*.
2. *Ibid.*, p. 151.
3. *Ibid.*, pp. 211f.; Charles C. Cole, Jr., *The Social Ideas of the Northern Evangelists, 1826–1860* (New York: Octagon Books, 1966), pp. 204–8.
4. Abell, *Urban Impact of American Protestantism*, pp. 35f., 88, 137–65.
5. Smith, *Called Unto Holiness*, p. 48.
6. Norris Alden Magnuson, "Salvation in the Slums: Evangelical Social Welfare Work, 1865–1920." Ph.D. diss., Univ. of Minnesota, 1968. My conclusions differ from Magnuson's.
7. *Ibid.*, p. 165n.; see also pp. 80, 88.
8. McLoughlin, *Modern Revivalism*, pp. 167, 310–12, 435–44.
9. Magnuson, "Salvation in the Slums," p. 457, italics added.
10. *Ibid.*, pp. 437f.
11. *Ibid.*, pp. 188, 439f., 306.
12. Jones, "Perfectionist Persuasion," pp. 350–54, 364f., 374f.
13. Abell, *Urban Impact of American Protestantism*, pp. 118–36.
14. Smith, *Called Unto Holiness*, pp. 309–17; Jones, "Perfectionist Persuasion," pp. 149f., 175.
15. *Pentecostal Evangel*, March 3, 1923, pp. 2f., 8.
16. "The Doom of Civilization," *Latter Rain Evangel*, v. 24, 10 (July 1932), p. 3.
17. *Pentecostal Evangel*, Jan. 24, 1920, p. 4.
18. *Pentecostal Evangel*, Oct. 14, 1922, p. 5; *Latter Rain Evangel*, v. 20, no. 3 (Nov. 1928), pp. 2–5, v. 4, no. 1 (Oct. 1911), pp. 2–6; Parham, *Life*, p. 32; Church of God (Cleveland, Tenn.), *Minutes*, 1908, p. 26; *Pentecostal Evangel*, Nov. 3, 1923, p. 1.
19. *Pentecostal Evangel*, Feb. 7, 1920, pp. 2f.
20. William M. Menzies, *Anointed to Serve: The Story of the Assemblies of God* (Springfield, Mo.: Gospel Pub. House, 1971), pp. 283–6.
21. Assemblies of God, General Presbytery, *Minutes*, Aug. 21, 1968, pp. 24ff., repr. in Menzies, *Anointed to Serve*, pp. 394f.
22. *Latter Rain Evangel*, v. 26, no. 2 (Nov. 1934), pp. 16f., 22f.
23. Irwin Winehouse, *The Assemblies of God: A Popular Survey* (New York: Vantage Press, 1959), pp. 191–3.
24. Pentecostal historians generally concede that the movement was almost totally disinterested and uninvolved in social and political activism until fairly recent times. Nichol, *Pentecostalism*, pp. 232ff.; Menzies, *Anointed to Serve*, p. 369; Synan, *Old Time Power*, pp. 186f., 190, 251; Synan, *Pentecostal-Holiness Movement*, p. 185; see also J. R. Flower to N. J. Tavani, Jan. 13, 1950, *PEF*. Walter Hollenweger shows that, with some important exceptions, social conservatism is still typical of Pentecostals around the world, *The Pentecostals*, pp. 467–72.
25. *Christian Evangel*, Aug. 15, 1914, p. 1 headline.
26. *Weekly Evangel*, Aug. 10, 1915, p. 3.
27. *Midnight Cry*, Aug. 1915, p. 8.
28. *Weekly Evangel*, Apr. 28, 1917, pp. 5, 7, Aug. 4, 1917, pp. 6f.; Parham, *Life*, pp. 272ff.; Conn., *Like a Mighty Army*, p. 150; Hastie, *History*, pp. 94f.; Menzies, *Anointed to Serve*, pp. 326f.

29. *Weekly Evangel,* May 19, 1917, p. 8.

30. Tomlinson, *Diary,* I, pp. 248f.

31. Hastie, *History,* pp. 96f.

32. Assemblies of God, *Minutes,* 1917, p. 17; *Minutes,* 1918, p. 9; *Christian Evangel,* June 1, 1918, p. 8.

33. Church of God (Cleveland, Tenn.), *Minutes,* 1908; *Pentecostal Evangel,* Nov. 28, 1936, pp. 1, 3.

34. Lee, *Life Sketches,* pp. 72–7.

35. "War, the Bible and the Christian," *Pentecostal Evangel,* Nov. 15, 1930, pp. 2f.; see also Nov. 28, 1936, pp. 1, 3.

36. Conn, *Like a Mighty Army,* p. 15n.; Paul, "Religious Frontier," p. 94.

37. *White Wing Messenger,* March 7, 1942.

38. *Glad Tidings Herald,* v. 32, no. 1 (May 1943), p. 4.

39. Synan, *Old Time Power,* p. 206; Paul, "Religious Frontier," p. 142.

40. Church of God (Cleveland, Tenn.), *Minutes,* 1945, p. 31.

41. J. R. Flower to Frank S. Mean, December 13, 1947, *PEF ;* Hastie, *History,* pp. 101f.; Menzies, *Anointed to Serve,* p. 328.

42. Harrison, "History of the Assemblies of God," pp. 156f.

43. *Glad Tidings Herald,* v. 19, no. 5 (Oct. 1930), p. 3; *Pentecostal Holiness Advocate,* July 17, 1930, pp. 1–8, Jan. 18, 1940, entire issue.

44. *Glad Tidings Herald,* v. 20, no. 4 (Nov. 1931), p. 4; v. 21, no. 4 (Nov. 1932), p. 4.

45. *Midnight Cry,* v. 5, no. 3 (Oct. 1918), pp. 1f.; *Christian Evangel,* March 18, 1919, p. 2; *Pentecostal Evangel,* July 10, 1920, p. 1, Sept. 22, 1928, p. 8.

46. One of the "proofs" of this charming contention was that Cardinal Gibbons called Roosevelt "my boy." "Roosevelt and the Jesuits: Will the Jew Accept a Jesuit-Jew for His Messiah?", *Latter Rain Evangel,* v. 26, no. 12 (Sept. 1934), pp. 10–12.

47. *Latter Rain Evangel,* v. 26, no. 3 (Dec. 1933), p. 13, v. 26, no. 5 (Feb. 1934), pp. 14f., v. 26, no. 6 (March 1934), p. 12. The U. S. ambassador to the Soviet Union was identified as "Bolshevist Bullit."

48. *Glad Tidings Herald,* v. 25, no. 2 (May 1936), pp. 7f.; *Pentecostal Holiness Advocate,* Sept. 21, 1933, p. 2; Stanley H. Frodsham to the editor, *New Republic,* April 12, 1941, *PEF; Latter Rain Evangel,* v. 26, no. 5 (Feb. 1934), pp. 14f.

49. Church of God (Cleveland, Tenn.), *Minutes,* 1917, pp. 268f.; Tomlinson, *Diary,* III, p. 9; Church of God (Cleveland, Tenn.), *Minutes,* 1919, p. 17; Tomlinson, *Diary,* III, pp. 41f.

50. *Word and Witness,* May 1915, p. 5; *Pentecostal Evangel,* May 15, 1920, p. 8, May 29, 1920, p. 4, July 10, 1920, p. 1; *Latter Rain Evangel,* v. 18, no. 11 (Aug. 1926), pp. 2–6, v. 19, no. 7 (May 1927), pp. 4–8; D. B. Rickard, "New Revelation and New Crisis," pamphlet (Indianapolis: Apostolic Church, n.d.).

51. *Pentecostal Evangel,* Nov. 26, 1921, p. 2.

52. *Pentecostal Evangel,* May 15, 1920.

53. *Glad Tidings Herald,* v. 24, no. 3 (July 1935), p. 4; "Book Burning Needed," *Pentecostal Evangel,* May 4, 1935, p. 7. Bryan Wilson noted the absence of democratic beliefs and the prevalence of autocracy among British Pentecostals in "The Pentecostalist Minister," *American Journal of Sociology,* 64 (1959), pp. 494–504.

54. *Pentecostal Holiness Advocate,* Sept. 21, 1922, pp. 4f., Sept. 28, 1922, pp. 8f., Oct. 12, 1922, pp. 4f.

55. Parham, *Life*, p. 25; Tomlinson, "Answering the Call of God," p. 9.

56. Church of God (Cleveland, Tenn.), *Minutes*, 1908, p. 26; *Pentecostal Evangel*, Oct. 14, 1922, p. 5; *Pentecostal Holiness Advocate*, June 28, 1917, pp. 8f.; George Thayer, *The Farther Shores of Politics* (New York: Simon & Schuster, 1967), pp. 520f. Thayer quotes Homer Tomlinson as saying that when he announced he was running for President on the Theocratic Party ticket in 1952, his followers thought he had backslidden because they would neither vote nor hold a government job. In 1966 Tomlinson's Theocratic Party merged with the National Hamiltonian Party whose slogans were "Rule by the Aristocrats," and "Your People Sir Are a Great Beast." *Ibid.*, pp. 525f.

57. *Weekly Evangel*, Aug. 17, 1915, p. 2.

58. *Pentecostal Evangel*, Feb. 4, 1922, p. 6.

59. *Pentecostal Evangel*, Oct. 14, 1922, p. 4.

60. Pentecostal Holiness Church, *Discipline*, 1925, p. 39; *Midnight Cry*, v. 7, no. 4 (Oct. 1921), p. 7.

61. Bailey, *Pioneer Marvels*, pp. 14f.; Flower, *Grace for Grace*, p. 162.

62. *Pentecostal Holiness Advocate*, June 28, 1917, pp. 8f.

63. Parham, *Everlasting Gospel*, pp. 28–30.

64. *Weekly Evangel*, Aug. 17, 1915, pp. 1f. Bartleman unwittingly echoed the German socialists' view that Germany was "more civilized and liberty-loving" than Russia and, therefore, her victory over Russia would be "a step forward." *Weekly Evangel*, July 10, 1915, p. 3, Aug. 7, 1915, p. 1.

65. *Pentecostal Holiness Advocate*, July 15, 1917, pp. 3f.; *Pentecostal Evangel*, Dec. 15, 1930, p. 3, June 6, 1931, pp. 4f.; *Latter Rain Evangel*, v. 24, no. 10 (July 1932); Lee, *Life Sketches*, pp. 251–5; Church of God (Cleveland, Tenn.), *Minutes*, 1913, pp. 149f.; *Word and Witness*, May 1915, p. 1.

66. Parham, *Everlasting Gospel*, pp. 33–5, italics added.

67. *Pentecostal Evangel*, July 10, 1920, p. 1.

68. *Word and Witness*, May 1915, p. 1.

69. *Pentecostal Evangel*, Nov. 29, 1919, p. 6.

70. *Apostolic Evangel*, n.d., repr. in *Pentecostal Evangel*, Dec. 25, 1920, p. 3.

71. C. E. Robinson to Stanley H. Frodsham, n.d. (c. April 1941), *PEF*.

72. Church of God (Cleveland, Tenn.), *Minutes*, 1913, pp. 125f., *Minutes*, 1914, p. 177, *Minutes*, 1922, p. 24.

73. Pentecostal Holiness Church, *Minutes*, 1921, cited in Paul, "Religious Frontier," p. 94; Pentecostal Holiness Church, *Discipline*, 1929, cited in Synan, *Old Time Power*, p. 191.

74. Synan, *Old Time Power*, p. 191.

75. Pope, *Millhands and Preachers*, pp. 140, 147, 164f. The variance between Pentecostal clergy and laity on unions may account for the reluctant shift of the leadership from its strong anti-union bias.

76. *Pentecostal Evangel*, Sept. 12, 1931, p. 3.

77. *Pentecostal Evangel*, Feb. 7, 1920, pp. 2f., Jan. 28, 1928, p. 9, Feb. 2, 1924, p. 2, series on "What is Bolshevism," Feb. 1, 1936 to March 28, 1936; Lee, *Life Sketches*, pp. 233–7.

78. *Glad Tidings Herald*, v. 24, no. 3 (July 1935), p. 4.

79. Otto J. Klink, "From Soap Box to Pulpit," *Pentecostal Evangel*, April 4, 1931, pp. 2f., 7.

80. *Pentecostal Holiness Advocate,* June 28, 1917, p. 2.

81. Bartleman, *How Pentecost,* p. 158.

82. Hastie, *History,* p. 68; Goss, *Winds of God,* p. 150; *Pentecostal Evangel,* Sept. 17, 1927, pp. 2f., Nov. 11, 1923, p. 2; Brumback, *Suddenly,* pp. 119f.; *Pentecostal Evangel,* March 28, 1925, p. 9.

83. E. Clark, *Baptism of the Holy Ghost,* pp. 125f.

84. *Weekly Evangel,* Jan. 20, 1917, p. 9.

85. Hastie, *History,* p. 68.

86. Parham, *Everlasting Gospel,* p. 32.

87. *Pentecostal Evangel,* March 6, 1920, pp. 8f.

88. "The Present Great World Crisis," *Pentecostal Evangel,* March 28, 1925, pp. 2f., 8f.

89. *Weekly Evangel,* April 10, 1915, p. 1; *Pentecostal Evangel,* March 6, 1920, pp. 8f., April 3, 1920, March 28, 1925, pp. 2f., 8f., Oct. 18, 1930, pp. 4f., Dec. 5, 1936, pp. 1f., Dec. 12, 1936, pp. 4f.

90. *Latter Rain Evangel,* v. 1, no. 7 (April 1909), pp. 13–19; *Pentecostal Evangel,* Jan. 10, 1920, p. 4, Sept. 8, 1923, p. 4, Feb. 23, 1924, p. 1, May 2, 1925, p. 5, June 13, 1925, p. 8, Sept. 19, 1925, p. 3, Jan. 28, 1928, pp. 1, 8f., March 3, 1928, pp. 1, 5, Oct. 12, 1929, pp. 6f., 13, Feb. 21, 1931, p. 3; *Pentecostal Holiness Advocate,* June 5, 1924, pp. 5–7, Dec. 24, 1925, pp. 8f.

91. *Pentecostal Evangel,* Oct. 12, 1929, p. 6.

92. *Pentecostal Evangel,* Sept. 19, 1925, p. 3.

93. *Pentecostal Evangel,* Nov. 26, 1927, p. 1.

94. J. N. Hoover, "Bible Bolshevists," *Pentecostal Evangel,* March 3, 1928, p. 1.

95. *Pentecostal Evangel,* April 4, 1931, pp. 2f., 7.

96. *Pentecostal Evangel,* Feb. 15, 1936, p. 2; see also *Latter Rain Evangel,* v. 22, no. 9 (June 1930), p. 3.

97. "The Red Terror," *Pentecostal Evangel,* Feb. 2, 1924, p. 5; see also, Hastie, *History,* p. 206.

98. E. Clark, *Baptism of the Holy Ghost,* pp. 93ff.

99. *Apostolic Evangel,* June 1, 1917, pp. 4f., 14.

100. *Pentecostal Evangel,* June 20, 1931, pp. 4f.

101. *Christian Evangel,* Aug. 29, 1914, p. 2.

102. *Latter Rain Evangel,* v. 23, no. 6 (Mar. 1931), pp. 3–7; see also E. Clark, *Baptism of the Holy Ghost,* p. 93.

103. *Christian Evangel,* Oct. 10, 1914, p. 2; see the series by Boyd, "Romanism: What Is Its Place in the Last Days?" *Pentecostal Evangel,* July 26, 1924, pp. 6f., Aug. 2, 1924, pp. 6f., Aug. 16, 1924, pp. 8f.

104. Pentecostal Holiness Church, *Discipline,* 1925, pp. 92f.

105. *Pentecostal Evangel,* July 26, 1924, pp. 6f., Jan. 5, 1924, Oct. 9, 1926, pp. 1f., 7, June 20, 1931, pp. 4f.

106. *Latter Rain Evangel,* v. 26, no. 1 (Oct. 1934), p. 3.

107. In a book widely read by Pentecostals, Carl Brumback said as late as 1947 that, "For one thousand years Christendom was under the darkness of the perverted teachings and pagan practices of Papal Rome, and very few rays of light were able to penetrate that gross darkness." *What Meaneth This?,* p. 277. During the Presidential campaign of 1960 the Pentecostal Holiness Church took an official stand against the election of a Roman Catholic and ran a series of articles on the subject in its official organ. Synan,

Old Time Power, p. 254. I knew several Pentecostals who turned out to vote for the first time in their lives in order to defeat J. F. Kennedy in 1960.

108. Cohen named the Father Divine movement, the Seventh Day Adventists and the Oxford movement as such, *Latter Rain Evangel*, v. 26, no. 1 (Oct. 1934), p. 3.

109. *Midnight Cry*, v. 1, no. 7 (April 1909), pp. 13-19, v. 2, no. 1 (Aug. 1912), pp. 2f., 8; *Pentecostal Holiness Advocate*, March 21, 1918, p. 2, April 18, 1918, pp. 4f., April 25, 1918, p. 4, May 2, 1918, p. 3, May 16, 1918, pp. 6f., June 6, 1918, pp. 4f., June 20, 1918, p. 4, Jan. 20, 1920, p. 10; *Pentecostal Evangel*, Oct. 14, 1922, p. 1, April 26, 1924, pp. 4f., Nov. 22, 1924, pp. 6f., Sept. 19, 1925, p. 5, Dec. 11, 1926, pp. 6f., Oct. 18, 1930, pp. 4f., Feb. 3, 1934, p. 5; *Latter Rain Evangel*, v. 26, no. 1 (Oct. 1934), p. 3.

110. *Pentecostal Holiness Advocate*, April 25, 1918, p. 4; *Pentecostal Herald*, v. 8, no. 9 (Jan. 1922), pp. 1f.; *Apostolic Faith* (Baxter Springs, Kans.), v. 4, no. 12 (Dec. 1938), v. 5, no. 1 (Jan. 1929); *Pentecostal Evangel*, Feb. 7, 1920, pp. 8f., March 6, 1929, pp. 3, 6f., Feb. 23, 1924, p. 6, April 26, 1924, pp. 4f., May 10, 1924, pp. 4f., Aug. 2, 1924, pp. 8f., Aug. 30, 1924, pp. 6f., Sept. 6, 1924, p. 8, Sept. 20, 1924, p. 10, Dec. 12, 1927, pp. 6f., April 21, 1928, p. 4, Oct. 29, 1929, p. 13; Church of God (Cleveland, Tenn.), *Minutes*, 1917, p. 296; F. J. Lee, "Spiritualism, A Reality: Spiritualism of the Spirit, But Not of the Holy Ghost," *Life Sketches*, pp. 325-32.

111. *Pentecostal Evangel*, Sept. 4, 1920, pp. 6f.

112. *Pentecostal Evangel*, Nov. 22, 1930, pp. 6f., Jan. 31, 1931, pp. 6f., May 18, 1935, pp. 1, 9, May 25, 1935, pp. 6f.

113. Stanley H. Frodsham to the editor, *New Republic*, April 12, 1941, *PEF*.

114. Stanley H. Frodsham to Cecil J. Lowry, May 22, 1942, *PEF*. By 1950 Lowry was the editor of the anti-Semitic, Red-baiting *Christian Vanguard* (Oakland, Calif.) and had apparently left the Assemblies of God. *Christian Vanguard*, v. 2, no. 2 (March 1950).

115. Norman Cohen Beskin, "The Truth About the Protocols," *Latter Rain Evangel*, v. 26, no. 1 (Oct. 1933), p. 3.

116. Ralph Lord Roy, *Apostles of Discord* (Boston: Beacon, 1953).

117. Frederic Cople Jaher, *Doubters and Dissenters: Catacylsmic Thought in America, 1885-1918* (New York: Free Press of Glencoe, 1964), p. 18.

Chapter XII

1. Antimodernity as a general current in the Western world, and the cultural crisis of Western civilization at the turn of the century are discussed in Fritz Stern, *The Politics of Cultural Despair* (New York: Doubleday Anchor, 1965), pp. 5-15, 326-8; and Gerhard Masur, *Prophets of Yesterday* (New York: Harper & Row, 1966), esp. pp. 1-21. The antimodern aspects of American evangelical religion in the early 20th century are discussed in Richard Hofstadter, *Anti-intellectualism in American Life* (New York: Vintage Books, 1966), pp. 117-44.

2. Socio-religious protest movements as response to modernity in other lands (which throw light on Pentecostalism indirectly) are dealt with by Eric J. Hobsbawm, *Primitive Rebels: Studies in Archaic Forms of Social Movements in the 19th and 20th Centuries* (New York: W. E. Norton & Co., 1959), and Vittorio Lanternari, *The Religions of the Oppressed: A Study of Modern Messianic Cults* (New York: New American Library, 1963).

3. Herbert Gutman, "Protestantism and American Labor," *American Historical Review,* LXXXII (October 1966), 74–101.

4. See Richard Hofstadter's incisive discussion of "the psychic crisis of the 90's in "Manifest Destiny and the Phillipines," Daniel Aaron (ed.), *America in Crisis* (New York: Alfred A. Knopf, 1952).

   For the crisis in religious thought see Paul A. Carter, *The Spiritual Crisis of the Gilded Age* (DeKalb: Northern Illinois Univ. Press, 1971).

5. In the absence of very much in the way of welfare services before 1933, there were few permanently unemployed.

6. Earl W. Hayter, *The Troubled Farmer, 1850–1900: Rural Adjustment to Industrialism* (DeKalb, Ill.: Northern Illinois University Press, 1968); Fred A. Shannon, *The Farmer's Last Frontier* (New York: Holt, Rinehart & Winston, 1945); Richard Hofstadter, *Age of Reform* (New York: Vintage Books, 1955), pp. 23–59.

7. The psychiatrist Dr. Paul Qualben found, on the basis of in-depth interviewing of 26 contemporary tongue-speakers, that 85% "had experienced a clearly defined anxiety crisis preceding their speaking in tongues". Kildahl, *The Psychology of Speaking in Tongues,* pp. 39–41, 57. Virginia Hine's conclusion that "only 16% of her sample reported that they were experiencing any sort of crisis just prior to their . . . glossolalic experience" cannot be accepted since it is based upon the explicit statements of Pentecostals after the fact. "Non-pathological Pentecostal Glossolalia: A Summary of Relevant Psychological Literature," *Journal for the Scientific Study of Religion,* 8 (1969): 211–26. The biographical facts and/or examination of what is implicit in Pentecostal testimonies constitute the only reliable data.

8. Such persons could just as well have been recruited into any other "salvationist" movement. In the 1930's, German youth of similar backgrounds and circumstances were found in roughly equal proportions among street-fighting Nazis and Communists. On the importance of personal contact in recruitment to the neo-Pentecostal movement, which applies equally to the early Pentecostal movement, see Gerlach and Hine, *People, Power, Change,* pp. 79–97.

9. See, e.g., the works of Troeltsch, *Social Teachings;* Niebuhr, *Social Sources,* and Vittorio Lanternari, *The Religions of the Opressed, passim.*

10. Virginia Hine, "Deprivation and Disorganization Theories of Social Movements," unpublished paper on file at Univ. of Minnesota, Minneapolis; Gerlach and Hine, *People, Power, Change,* pp. xxl f.

11. For an analysis of deprivation theory that is not bound to the simplistic notion that the deprived are always at the bottom of the social order, see David F. Aberle, "A Note on Relative Deprivation Theory as Applied to Millenarian and Other Cult Movements," in Thrupp, *Millennial Dreams,* pp. 108–14.

12. It will be remembered that ecstasy is a state of mental dissociation that produces psychological and physical effects which, since they are dissociated from full consciousness, are attributed to an external supernatural power.

13. Examples would be early Christianity as a whole, many "heretical" movements throughout Christian history, and numerous non-Christian movements of recent times. See, e.g. Lanternari, *Religions of the Oppressed,* and Sylvia L. Thrupp (ed.), *Millennial Dreams in Action* (New York: Schocken Books, 1970), *passim.*

14. See, e.g., Lewis, *Ecstatic Religion, passim.* On religion itself as a mechanism by

which man adapts to his environment, see the superb study of Weston La Barre, *The Ghost Dance: The Origins of Religion* (New York: Dell Pub. Co., 1970).

15. It is ironic that what was an infallible sign of Holy Spirit possession in the early Church has been an infallible sign of demon possession from Medieval times to the very recent past.

16. Wayne E. Oates, "A Socio-Psychological Study of Glossolalia," in Frank E. Stagg, E. Glenn Hinson, and Wayne E. Oates, *Glossolalia* (Nashville: Abingdon Press, 1967); John B. Oman, "On 'Speaking in Tongues': A Psychological Analysis," *Pastoral Psychology*, V. 14, no. 139 (1963): 48–51. Samarin rejects this view, but he himself says "glossolalia can be called regressive because the most common sounds of any speaker appear to be the ones that are learned earliest by a child," *Tongues and Angels*, p. 42 and *passim*.

17. Latin is, of course, unlike tongues in that it is comprehensible to the clergy and in itself, but it is, like tongues, incomprehensible to the laity. For examples of tongues as a conveyor of emotional meanings, see Samarin, *Tongues of Men and Angels*, pp. 88–98, 162–8.

18. Now the National Council of Churches, which is affiliated with the World Council of Churches.

19. William G. McLoughlin, "Is There a Third Force in Christendom?", in Wm. G. McLoughlin and Robert N. Bellah, *Religion in America* (Boston: Beacon Press, 1968).

20. Not that Roman Catholicism and Judaism have been much less effective in producing the same result.

21. The attachment of mainline clergy to the anti-racist and anti-war movements of the 60's may also be seen as a response to their increasing irrelevance in the real functioning of American society. Unlike the Pentecostals, the mainline clergy abhor social irrelevance.

22. On Pentecostal acceptance of dominant social values, see Marion Dearman, "Christ and Conformity: A Study of Pentecostal Values," *Journal for the Scientific Study of Religion*, 13 (Dec. 1974): 437–53.

23. The Pentecostal movement has also had the effect of inculcating patterns of thought, values, and behavior that are ideally compatible with industrial capitalism in, for example, Mexico, Chile, Brazil and among West Indians in Britain. Gerlach & Hine, *People, Power, Change*, pp. 108 f.

24. A typical conversion story in Pentecostal and neo-Pentecostal literature is of the stereotypical young man, deeply involved in such activities, who gets "the Baptism," and becomes a conscientious, law-abiding, responsible citizen dedicated to helping others find "the experience" so that they too can give up all that "fleshly" or "worldly" activity and be sublimely happy. Conversions of policemen and members of the armed forces are prominently featured.

Appendix I

Acts of Grace

Differing views were held concerning the number of acts of grace ("blessings"), the terms used to refer to them, and their meanings. The following somewhat oversimplified scheme, in roughly chronological order, may help to minimize the confusion:

1. All Holiness, Keswick, Pentecostal, and Fundamentalist believers held to a first act of grace called "Salvation" or the "New Birth," which meant the forgiveness of sins through faith in the propitiatory death of Jesus, and the acquisition of a new, divine nature.

2. Wesleyan Holiness believers held to a second act of grace ("the Second Blessing") called "Baptism in the Spirit" or "Sanctification," which meant the elimination or minimization of sin in the believer (that is, moral purification).

3. Keswick Holiness believers held to a second act of grace and also called it "Baptism in the Spirit," but for them it meant a divine "enduement of power" for Christian service, especially for "soul-winning." They rejected the Wesleyan view of sanctification that moral purification was an act of grace, and held that it was a gradual process. (Later, they also rejected the whole notion of a second act of grace, and maintained that the "enduement of power," like sanctification, was a continuing aspect of the Christian life.)

4. Fire-Baptized Holiness believers held the Wesleyan view and terminology on the second act of grace, and introduced a third act of grace called "Baptism in (or of) Fire" which meant an "enduement of power." (That is, what the Keswick movement had considered to be the second act of grace became, under a different name, a third act of grace for the Fire-Baptized people.)

5. The Pentecostals initially held the Wesleyan view on the second act of grace but called it "Sanctification" exclusively, and reserved the term "Baptism in the Spirit" for a third act of grace which meant "enduement of power" evidenced by some gift of the Spirit (in practice, almost always speaking in tongues).

6. A majority of Pentecostals later (c. 1912–14) rejected the Wesleyan position on sanctification in favor of the Keswick position, so that what had been the third act of grace for Pentecostals became the second act with the same terminology and meaning (that is, "Baptism in the Spirit" as an "enduement of power" evidenced by spiritual gifts). A minority of Pentecostals continued to hold to the original position stated in number 5 above. (These are called "Second Work Pentecostals" in distinction from the "Finished Work" majority.)

7. Still later (c. 1916–20) most *American* Pentecostals (as distinct from others in the world) adopted the view that Baptism in the Spirit was *always* evidenced by speaking in tongues, rather than by any one of the several gifts of the Spirit.

Appendix II

The Forty-five Pentecostal Leaders of Chapter VI and the Sources for Biographical Information Concerning Each

Argue, A. H.
>Argue, Zelma. *What Meaneth This?* Winnipeg: the author, 1924.

Awrey, Daniel
>*Latter Rain Evangel.* Vol. 2 (March 1910).
>Campbell, Joseph E. *The Pentecostal Holiness Church, 1898–1948.* Franklin Springs, Ga.: Publishing House of the Pentecostal Holiness Church, 1951, p. 199.

Bailey, S. Clyde
>Bailey, S. Clyde. *Pioneer Marvels of Faith.* Morristown, Tenn.: the author, 1958.

Barratt, Thomas Ball
>Barratt, Thomas Ball. *When the Fire Fell and an Outline of My Life.* Larvik, Norway: Alfons Hansen and Soner, 1927.
>Bloch-Hoell, Nils. *The Pentecostal Movement.* Oslo: Universitetsforlaget, 1964, pp. 178–9.

Bartleman, Frank
>Bartleman, Frank. *From Plow to Pulpit.* Los Angeles: the author, 1924.
>Bartleman, Frank. *How Pentecost Came to Los Angeles.* Los Angeles: the author, 1925.

Bell, Eudorus N.
>*Pentecostal Evangel,* June 30, 1923.
>*Pentecostal Evangel,* Sept. 13, 1923.

Bosworth, Fred F.

> Perkins, Eunice M. *Fred Francis Bosworth: His Life Story*. Detroit: the author, 1927.

Britton, Francis M.

> Britton, Francis M. *Pentecostal Truth*. Royston, Ga.: Publishing House of the Pentecostal Holiness Church, 1919.
>
> Campbell, Joseph E. *The Pentecostal Holiness Church, 1898–1948*. Franklin Springs, Ga.: Publishing House of the Pentecostal Holiness Church, 1951, pp. 328–30.

Brown, (Mrs.) Marie Burgess

> Gardiner, Gordon P., and Brown, Marie E. *The Origin of Glad Tidings Tabernacle*. New York: n.p., 1955.
>
> *Midnight Cry*, I (March–April 1911).
>
> *Pentecostal Evangel*, March 12, 1927, pp. 1, 8–9.

Brown, Robert A.

> *Glad Tidings Herald*, XXVII (May 1948).
>
> *Midnight Cry*, VII (Aug. 1917), pp. 4–5.

Collins, Arch P.

> *Christian Evangel*, Jan. 23, 1915.
>
> *Pentecostal Evangel*, July 9, 1921.

Crawford, (Mrs.) Florence L.

> The Apostolic Faith. *A Historical Account of the Apostolic Faith*. Portland, Ore.: Apostolic Faith Publishing House, 1965.

Durham, William H.

> Atter, Gordon. *The Third Force*. Petersborough, Ont.: The College Press, 1962, p. 59.
>
> Hayes, Doremus A. *The Gift of Tongues*. New York: Eaton & Main, 1913, pp. 85–9.

Eldridge, George N.

> Eldridge, George N. *Personal Reminiscences*. Los Angeles: the author, n.d.
>
> *Pentecostal Evangel*, Feb. 22, 1930.
>
> Christian and Missionary Alliance. *Annual Report of the President, 11th (1907/08)*. Nyack, N.Y., 1908, pp. 6–7.

Ewart, Frank J.

> Ewart, Frank J. *The Phenomenon of Pentecost*. St. Louis: Pentecostal Publishing House, 1947.

Flower, J. Roswell

> Flower, Alice Reynolds. *Grace for Grace*. Springfield, Mo.: the author, 1961.
>
> Brumback, Carl. *Suddenly . . . from Heaven*. Springfield, Mo.: Gospel Pub. House, 1961, pp. 72–4.
>
> "Personal Data." mimeo. Files of the *Pentecostal Evangel* (cited as *PEF*).

Franciscon, Louis
>Fiorentino, Joseph. *In the Power of His Spirit* (Christian Churches of North America publication, n.p., n.d.).

Frodsham, Stanley H.
>Frodsham, Stanley H. *With Signs Following.* Springfield, Mo.: Gospel Publishing House, 1941, p. 7.
>*Pentecostal Evangel,* Dec. 8, 1928.

Garr, Alfred G.
>Carolina Evangelistic Association. *Twentieth Anniversary of the Garr Auditorium, 1930–50.* Charlotte, N.C., 1950.
>Bartleman, Frank. *How Pentecost Came to Los Angeles,* Los Angeles: the author, 1925.

Goines, George O.
>*Pentecostal Holiness Advocate,* Sept. 19, 1918.

Goss, Howard A.
>Goss, Ethel E. *The Winds of God: The Story of the Early Pentecostal Days (1901–1914) in the Life of Howard A. Goss.* New York: Comet Press, 1958.

Hayes, Richard Baxter
>Hayes, W. M. (ed.). *Memoirs of Richard Baxter Hayes.* Philadelphia: the author, 1945.

Holmes, Nickels John
>Holmes, Nickels John. *Life Sketches and Sermons.* Royston, Ga.: Press of the Pentecostal Holiness Church, 1920.
>*Pentecostal Holiness Advocate,* Jan. 22, 1930.

Jones, Ozro T., Sr.
>Interview, Sept. 7, 1966.

Kerr, Daniel W.
>*Pentecostal Evangel,* April 16, 1927.

King, Joseph H.
>King, Joseph H. *Yet Speaketh: The Memoirs of the Late Bishop Joseph H. King.* Franklin Springs, Ga.: Pentecostal Holiness Publishing House, 1949.
>King, Joseph H. *From Passover to Pentecost.* Franklin Springs, Ga.: Pentecostal Holiness Publishing House, 1914.

LaBerge, Agnes N. Ozman
>LaBerge, Agnes N. Ozman. "History of the Pentecostal Movement from January 1, 1901" (typescript), *PEF.*

Lee, Flavius J.
>Lee, (Mrs.) Flavius J. (ed.). *Life Sketches and Sermons of F. J. Lee.* Cleveland, Tenn.: Church of God Publishing House, n.d.

Mason, Charles H.
>Church of God in Christ. *Manual of the Church of God in Christ.* 5th ed. rev., n.p., 1951.

Atter, Gordon. *Third Force*. Petersborough, Ont.: The College Press, 1962, p. 61.

Interview with O. T. Jones, Sr. and Jr., Sept. 7, 1966.

McAlister, Robert Edward

Kulbeck, Gloria G. *What God Hath Wrought*. Toronto: Pentecostal Assemblies of Canada, 1958, pp. 29–30.

McPherson, Aimee Semple

McPherson, Aimee Semple. *This Is That: Personal Experiences, Sermons and Writings*. Los Angeles, Echo Park Evangelistic Association, Inc., 1923.

Muse, Dan T.

Paul, George H. "The Religious Frontier in Oklahoma: Dan T. Muse and the Pentecostal Holiness Church," unpublished Ph.D. diss., Univ. of Oklahoma, 1965.

Olazabal, Fransisco

Pentecostal Evangel, Oct. 16, 1920.

Tomlinson, Homer A. (ed.). *Diary of A. J. Tomlinson* 3 vols., New York: The Church of God, World Headquarters, 1949–55, Vol. 1, pp. 70–71.

Parham, Charles Fox

Parham, Sarah T. (comp.). *The Life of Charles F. Parham: Founder of the Apostolic Faith Movement*. Joplin, Mo.: Tri-State Printing Co., 1930.

Parham, Charles F. *A Voice Crying in the Wilderness*. Baxter Springs, Kans.: Joplin Printing Co., 1944.

Parham, Charles F. *The Everlasting Gospel*. Baxter Springs, Kans.: privately printed, 1942.

Piper, William H.

Latter Rain Evangel, Jan. 1912.

Simmons, E. L.

Simmons, E. L. *History of the Church of God*. Cleveland, Tenn.: Church of God Publishing House, 1938, pp. 7–8.

Simpson, W. W.

Atter, Gordon. *Third Force*. Petersborough, Ont.: The College Press, 1962, pp. 64–5.

Sorrow, Watson

Sorrow, Watson. *Some of My Experiences*. Atlanta: the author, 1954.

Taylor, George F.

Campbell, Joseph E. *The Pentecostal Holiness Church, 1898–1948*. Franklin Springs, Ga.: Publishing House of the Pentecostal Holiness Church, 1951, pp. 479–82.

Tomlinson, Ambrose Jessup

Tomlinson, Homer A. (ed.). *Diary of A. J. Tomlinson*. 3 vols. New York: The Church of God, World Headquarters, 1949–55.

Tomlinson, A. J. *Answering the Call of God*. Cleveland, Tenn.: n.p., n.d.

Duggar, Lillie. *A. J. Tomlinson: Former General Overseer of the Church of God*. Cleveland, Tenn.: White Wing Publishing House, 1964.

Urshan, Andrew D.

Pentecostal Evangel, Oct. 7, 1916.

Foster, Fred. *Think It Not Strange: A History of the Oneness Movement.* St. Louis: Pentecostal Publishing House, 1965, pp. 39–40.

Vogler, Fred

Harvester: Kansas District of the Assemblies of God, 1913–1915. n.p. 1915.

Brumback, Carl. *Suddenly . . . from Heaven*. Springfield, Mo.: Gospel Publishing House, 1961, p. 72.

Welch, John W.

Pentecostal Evangel, July 29, 1939.

Wigglesworth, Smith

Frodsham, Stanley H. *Smith Wigglesworth: Apostle of Faith*. Springfield, Mo.: Gospel Publishing House, 1949.

Woodworth-Etter, Mary B.

Woodworth-Etter, Mary B. *Signs and Wonders God Wrought in the Ministry for Forty Years*. Chicago: Hamond Press, W. B. Conkey Co., 1916.

Appendix III

Regional Divisions of the United States, Bureau of the Census

New England: Maine, New Hampshire, Vermont, Massachusetts, Rhode Island, and Connecticut.

Middle Atlantic: New York, New Jersey, and Pennsylvania.

East North Central: Ohio, Indiana, Illinois, Michigan, and Wisconsin.

West North Central: Minnesota, Iowa, Missouri, North Dakota, South Dakota, Nebraska, and Kansas.

South Atlantic: Delaware, Maryland, District of Columbia, Virginia, West Virginia, North Carolina, South Carolina, Georgia, and Florida.

East South Central: Kentucky, Tennessee, Alabama, and Mississippi.

West South Central: Arkansas, Louisiana, Oklahoma, and Texas.

Mountain: Montana, Idaho, Wyoming, Colorado, New Mexico, Arizona, Utah, and Nevada.

Pacific: Washington, Oregon, and California.

Selective Bibliography

I *Depositories* (by order of volume and extent of their holdings).
Oral Roberts University. Pentecostal Collection. Tulsa, Okla.
Assemblies of God. Headquarters. Springfield, Mo.
Church of God (Cleveland, Tenn.). Headquarters. Cleveland, Tenn.
Pentecostal Holiness Church. Headquarters. Franklin Springs, Ga.
Union Theological Seminary. Library. New York, N.Y.
Glad Tidings Tabernacle. New York, N.Y.
Church of God of Prophecy. Headquarters. Cleveland, Tenn.

II *Bibliographical Guides*
Burr, Nelson R., et al. *A Critical Bibliography of Religion in America.* Vol. IV,
    Religion in American Life. Princeton: Princeton Univ. Press, 1961.
Dayton, Donald W. *The American Holiness Movement: A Bibliographical In-
    troduction.* Wilmore, Ky.: B. L. Fisher Library, Asbury Theological Sem-
    inary, 1971.
Faupel, David W. *The American Pentecostal Movement: A Bibliographical
    Essay.* Wilmore, Ky.: B. L. Fisher Library and Society for Pentecostal
    Studies, 1972.
Hollenweger, Walter J. "Handbuch der Pfingstbewegung," Part III, 4 vols., Th.D.
    diss., Univ. of Zurich, 1965.
———. "Literatur von und uber die Pfingstbewegung," *Nederlands Theologisch
    Tijdschrift,* 18 (April 1964): 289–306.
Jones, Charles Edwin. *A Guide to the Study of the Holiness Movement.* Me-
    tuchen, N.J.: Scarecrow Press & American Theological Library Assoc.,
    1974.
Martin, Ira J. *Glossolalia, The Gift of Tongues: A Bibliography.* Cleveland,
    Tenn.: Pathway Press, 1970.

Mills, Watson E. "Literature on Glossolalia," *Journal of the American Scientific Affiliate,* 26 (no. 4, 1974): 169–73.

Mills, Watson E. *Speaking in Tongues: A Classified Bibliography.* Franklin Springs, Ga.: Society for Pentecostal Studies, 1974.

Oral Roberts University Library. *Divine Healing.* Tulsa, 1973.

———. *General—On Baptism of the Holy Spirit.* Tulsa, 1973.

———. *Gifts of the Holy Spirit.* Tulsa, 1973.

———. *Pentecostal Periodicals.* Tulsa, 1971.

Pattison, E. Mansell. "Behavioral Science Research on the Nature of Glossolalia," *Journal of the American Scientific Affiliate,* 20 (Sept. 1968): 73–86.

Raskopf, R.W. "Recent Literature on the Pentecostal Movement," *Anglican Theological Review,* sup. ser. no. 2 (1973): 113–18.

Richardson, James T. "Psychological Interpretations of Glossolalia: A Reexamination of Research," *Journal for the Scientific Study of Religion,* 12 (1973): 199–207.

III *Speaking in Tongues*

A. *New Testament and Early Church*

Angus, S. *The Mystery Religions and Christianity.* New York: Charles Scribner's Sons, 1925.

Beare, Frank W. "Speaking with Tongues: A Critical Survey of the New Testament Evidence," *Journal of Biblical Literature,* 83 (Sept. 1964): 229–46.

Behm, Johannes, "Glossa," in Gerhard Kittel and Gerhard Friedrich (eds.), *Theological Dictionary of the New Testament.* Grand Rapids: Eerdmans, 1964, vol. I, pp. 719–27.

Beyer, Hermann W. "Heteros," in Gerhard Kittel and Gerhard Friedrich (eds.), *Theological Dictionary of the New Testament.* Grand Rapids: Eerdmans, 1964, vol. II, pp. 702–4.

Bruce, F. F. *New Testament History.* Garden City, N.Y.: Doubleday, 1971.

Bultmann, Rudolf. *Primitive Christianity in Its Contemporary Setting.* New York: Meridian, 1956.

———. *Theology of the New Testament.* New York: Charles Scribner's Sons, 1955.

Campenhausen, Hans von. *Ecclesiastical Authority and Spiritual Power in the Church of the First Three Centuries.* Stanford: Stanford Univ. Press, 1969.

———. *Tradition and Life in the Church.* Philadelphia: Fortress Press, 1968.

Conzelmann, Hans. *I Corinthians: A Commentary on the First Epistle to the Corinthians.* Philadelphia: Fortress, 1975.

———. *History of Primitive Christianity.* Nashville: Abingdon, 1973.

————. *An Outline of the Theology of the New Testament*. New York: Harper & Row, 1969.

————. *The Theology of St. Luke*. New York: Harper & Row, 1960.

Currie, Stuart D. " 'Speaking in Tongues': Early Evidence Outside the New Testament Bearing on 'Glossais Lalein'," *Interpretation*, 19 (July 1965): 274–94.

Dalton, Robert Chandler. *Tongues Like as of Fire: A Critical Study of Modern Tongues Movements in the Light of Apostolic and Patristic Times*. Springfield, Mo.: Gospel Pub. House, 1945.

Davies, J. G. "Pentecost and Glossolalia," *Journal of Theological Studies*, 3 (1952): 228–31.

Ellis, E. Earle. " 'Spiritual Gifts' in the Pauline Community," *New Testament Studies*, 20 (1974): 128–44.

Foakes-Jackson, F. J. *The Acts of the Apostles*. New York: Harper & Bros., 1931.

————. *The History of the Christian Church: From Earliest Times to A.D. 461*. New York: George H. Doran, 1924.

Gilmour, S. MacL. "Easter and Pentecost," *Journal of Biblical Literature*, 81 (no. 1, 1962): 62–6.

Goguel, Maurice. *The Primitive Church*. New York: Macmillan, 1964.

Goppelt, Leonhard. *Apostolic and Post-Apostolic Times*. New York: Harper & Row, 1970.

Grant, R. M. *Gnosticism and Early Christianity*. New York: Columbia Univ., 1966.

Green, William M. "Glossolalia in the Second Century," *Restoration Quarterly*, 16 (1973): 231–9.

Gundry, Robert H. " 'Ecstatic Utterance' (NEB)?" *Journal of Theological Studies*, 17 (1966): 299–307.

————. *A Survey of the New Testament*. Grand Rapids: Zondervan, 1970.

Haardt, Robert. *Gnosis: Character and Testimony*. Leiden: E. J. Brill, 1971.

Haenchen, Ernst. *The Acts of the Apostles: A Commentary*. Philadelphia: Fortress, 1971.

Hahn, Ferdinand. *The Worship of the Early Church*. Philadelphia: Fortress, 1973.

Hopwood, P. G. S. *The Religious Experience of the Primitive Church*. New York: Charles Scribner's Sons, 1937.

Hurd, John C. *The Origins of I Corinthians*. Naperville, Ill.: Alec R. Allenson, 1965.

Jonas, Hans. *The Gnostic Religion*, 2nd ed. rev. Boston: Beacon, 1963.

Käsemann, Ernst. *Essays on New Testament Themes*. Naperville, Ill.: Alec R. Allenson, 1954.

————. *Jesus Means Freedom*. Philadelphia: Fortress, 1970.

————. *New Testament Questions Today*. Philadelphia: Fortress, 1969.

Käsemann, Ernst. *Perspectives on Paul.* Philadelphia: Fortress, 1971.

Klausner, Joseph. *From Jesus to Paul.* Boston: Beacon, 1943.

Krodel, Gerhard. "An Exegetical Examination," in "Symposium on Speaking in Tongues," *Dialog,* 2 (Sept. 1963): 152–9.

Kümmel, Werner George (ed.). *Introduction to the New Testament,* rev. ed. Nashville: Abingdon, 1973.

Kundsin, Karl. "Primitive Christianity in the Light of Gospel Research," in Rudolf Bultmann and Karl Kundsin. *Form Criticism.* New York: Harper & Row, 1962.

Lietzmann, Hans. *The Beginnings of the Christian Church.* New York: Meridian, 1963.

———. *The Founding of the Church Universal.* New York: Meridian, 1963.

Lohse, Eduard. *The New Testament Environment.* Nashville: Abingdon, 1971.

———. "Pentecost," in Kittel and Friedrich (eds.), *Theological Dictionary of the New Testament,* vol. VI, pp. 44–53.

Martin, Ira J. *Glossolalia in the Apostolic Church.* Berea, Ky.: Berea College Press, 1960.

Ness, William H. "Glossolalia in the New Testament," *Concordia Theological Monthly,* 32 (Apr. 1961): 221–3.

Nock, Arthur Darby. *Early Gentile Christianity and Its Hellenistic Background.* New York: Harper & Row, 1964.

Rogers, C. L. "The Gift of Tongues in the Post Apostolic Church (AD 100–400)," *Bibliotheca Sacra,* 122 (1965): 134–43.

Schaff, Philip. *Apostolic Christianity, A.D. 1–100.* New York: Charles Scribner's Sons, 1910.

Schmithals, Walter. *Gnosticism in Corinth.* Nashville: Abingdon, 1971.

Schweizer, Eduard. "Pneuma," in Kittel and Friedrich (eds.), *Theological Dictionary of the New Testament,* vol. VI, pp. 332–454.

Smalley, S. S. "Spiritual Gifts and I Corinthians 12:12," *Journal of Biblical Literature,* 87 (Dec. 1968): 427–33.

Smith, D. Moody. "Glossolalia and Other Spiritual Gifts in a New Testament Perspective," *Interpretation,* 28 (1974): 307–20.

Stendahl, Krister. "The New Testament Evidence," in Michael P. Hamilton (ed.), *The Charismatic Movement.* Grand Rapids: Eerdmans, 1975.

Sweet, J. P. M. "A Sign for Unbelievers: Paul's Attitude to Glossolalia," *New Testament Studies,* 13 (1967): 240–57.

Williams, C. G. "Glossolalia as a Religious Phenomenon: 'Tongues' at Corinth and Pentecost," *Religion,* 5 (no. 1, 1975): 16–32.

B. *Psychological and Socio-linguistic Character*

Alland, Alexander, Jr. "Possession in a Revivalistic Negro Church," *Journal for the Scientific Study of Religion,* 1 (Spring 1962): 204–13.

Beckmann, David M. "Trance: From Africa to Pentecostalism," *Concordia Theological Monthly,* 45 (Jan. 1974): 11–26.

Boison, Anton T. "Economic Distress and Religious Experience: A Study of the Holy Rollers," *Psychiatry,* 2 (May 1939): 185–94.

―――. "Religion and Hard Times: A Study of the Holy Rollers," *Social Action,* March 1939, pp. 8–35.

Cristiani, Leon. *Evidence of Satan in the Modern World.* New York: Macmillan, 1962.

Cutten, George Barton. *The Psychological Phenomena of Christianity.* New York: Charles Scribner's Sons, 1908.

―――. *Speaking with Tongues: Historically and Psychologically Considered.* New Haven: Yale Univ. Press, 1927.

Flournoy, Thomas. *From India to the Planet Mars: A Study of a Case of Somnambulism With Glossolalia.* New York: Harper & Bros., 1900.

Goodman, Felicitas D. "Altered Mental States vs. 'Style of Discourse': Reply to Samarin," *Journal for the Scientific Study of Religion,* 11 (1972): 197–9.

―――. "Phonetic Analysis of Glossolalia in Four Cultural Settings," *Journal for the Scientific Study of Religion,* 8 (1969): 227–39.

―――. *Speaking in Tongues: A Cross-Cultural Study of Glossolalia.* Chicago: Univ. of Chicago Press, 1972.

―――, et al. *Trance, Healing and Hallucination.* New York: John Wiley & Sons, 1974.

Hine, Virginia H. "Pentecostal Glossolalia: Toward a Functional Interpretation," *Journal for the Scientific Study of Religion,* 8 (1968): 211–26.

―――, "Non-pathological Pentecostal Glossolalia: A Summary of Relevant Psychological Literature," *Journal for the Scientific Study of Religion,* 8 (1969): 211–26.

Janet, Pierre. *The Major Symptoms of Hysteria.* New York: Hafner, 1965. (1st ed., 1907, rev. ed., 1920).

Jennings, G. J. "An Ethnological Study of Glossolalia," *Journal of the American Scientific Affiliate,* 20 (1968): 5–16.

Kildahl, John P. and Paul Qualben. "Final Progress Report: Glossolalia and Mental Health," mimeo, Brooklyn, N.Y., n.d.

Kildahl, John P. *The Psychology of Speaking in Tongues.* New York: Harper & Row, 1972.

Laffal, Julius, et al. "Communication of Meaning in Glossolalia," *Journal of Social Psychology,* 92 (April 1974): 277–91.

Laughlin, Henry P. *The Neurosis in Clinical Practice.* Philadelphia: W. B. Saunders, 1956.

May, L. Carlyle. "A Survey of Glossolalia and Related Phenomena in Non-Christian Religions," *American Anthropologist,* 58 (Feb. 1956): 75–96.

Mosimann, Eddison. *Das Zungenreden Geschichtlich und Psychologisch Untersucht.* Tübingen: J. C. B. Mohr, 1911.

Oesterreich, T. K. *Possession: Demoniacal and Other.* Secaucus, N.J.: Lyle
    Stuart, 1966. (1st German ed., 1921).
Oates, Wayne E. "A Socio-Psychological Study of Glossolalia," in Frank E.
    Stagg, et al., *Glossolalia.* Nashville: Abingdon, 1967.
Oman, John B. "On 'Speaking in Tongues': A Psychological Analysis," *Pastoral Psychology,* 14 (1963): 48–51.
Pratt, James B. *The Religious Consciousness.* New York: Macmillan, 1920.
Prince, Raymond (ed.). *Trance and Possession States.* Montreal: R. M. Bucke
    Memorial Society, 1968.
Samarin, William J. "Glossolalia as Regressive Speech," *Language and Speech,*
    16 (1973): 77–89.
———. "The Linguisticality of Glossolalia," *The Hartford Quarterly,* 8 (1968):
    49–75.
———. "Sociolinguistic vs. Neurophysiological Explanations for Glossolalia:
    Comment on Goodman's Paper," *Journal for the Scientific Study of Religion,* 11 (1972): 293–6.
———. *Tongues of Men and Angels.* New York: Macmillan, 1972.
Stevenson, Ian. *Xenoglossy.* Charlottesville, Va.: Univ. Press of Virginia, 1974.
Thurston, Herbert S. J. *The Physical Phenomena of Mysticism.* Chicago: Henry
    Regnery, 1952.
Vivier, Lincoln Morse Van Eetveldt. "Glossolalia," M.D. thesis, Department of
    Psychiatry and Mental Health, University of Witwatersrand, South Africa,
    1960.
Wood, William W. "Cultural and Personality Aspects of the Pentecostal Holiness
    Religion," Ph.D. diss., University of North Carolina, 1961.

IV   *American Religion*

A. *Reference Works*

Clark, Elmer T. *The Small Sects in America.* Nashville: Cokesbury, 1937.
———. *The Small Sects in America.* Rev. ed. New York: Harper & Row, 1968.
Douglass, H. Paul. *1000 City Churches.* New York: George H. Doran, 1926.
Fry, Luther C. *The U.S. Looks at Its Churches.* New York: Institute for Social
    and Religious Research, 1930.
Gaustad, Edwin Scott. *Historical Atlas of Religion in America.* New York:
    Harper & Row, 1962.
Jacquet, H., Jr. (ed.). *The Yearbook of American and Canadian Churches,* 1975.
    Nashville: Abingdon, 1975.
Landis, Benson Y. "A Guide to the Literature on Statistics of Religious Affiliation," *Information Service* (National Council of Churches), 42, no. 20
    (1963).
———. *Yearbook of American Churches, 1967.* New York: Dept. of Public Services, National Council of Churches of Christ in the U.S.A., 1968.

Mayer, F. E. *The Religious Bodies of America*. 4th ed., rev. St. Louis: Concordia, 1961.

United States, Bureau of the Census. *Census of Religious Bodies, 1916*. Washington D.C.: Government Printing Office, 1919.

———. *Census of Religious Bodies, 1926*. Washington, D.C.: Government Printing Office, 1929.

———. *Census of Religious Bodies, 1936*. Washington, D.C.: Government Printing Office, 1939.

United States, Works Project Administration. Historical Records Survey, New York. *Guide to Vital Statistics in the City of New York . . . Churches.* 5 vols., New York: Works Project Admin., 1942.

B. *General History*

Ahlstrom, Sydney E. *A Religious History of the American People*. New Haven: Yale Univ. Press, 1972.

Handy, Robert T. *A History of the Churches in the United States and Canada*. New York: Oxford Univ. Press, 1977.

C. *Historical Interpretation and Analysis*

American Academy of Political and Social Science. *The Annals, 256 (March 1948). "Organized Religion in the U.S."*

———. *Not Many Wise: A Reader on Religion in American Society*. Boston: Pilgrim Press, 1962.

Brauer, Jerald (ed.). *Reinterpretation in American Church History*. Chicago: Univ. of Chicago Press, 1968.

Clebsch, William A. *From Sacred to Profane America: The Role of Religion in American History*. New York: Harper & Row, 1968.

Davies, Horton. *Christian Deviations: The Challenge of the New Spiritual Movements*. Philadelphia: Westminster, 1965.

Ferguson, Charles W. *The Confusion of Tongues: A Review of Modern Isms*. Garden City, N.Y.: Doubleday, Doran, 1928.

Handy, Robert T. *A Christian America: Protestant Hopes and Historical Realities* New York: Oxford Univ. Press, 1971.

Hudson, Winthrop S. *The Great Tradition of the American Churches*. New York: Harper & Row, 1963.

Littell, Franklin Hamlin. *From State Church to Pluralism: A Protestant Interpretation of Religion in American History*. Garden City, N.Y.: Anchor, 1962.

McLoughlin, William G., and Robert N. Bellah (eds.). *Religion in America*. Boston: Beacon, 1968.

Marty, Martin E. *A Nation of Behavers*. Chicago: Univ. of Chicago Press, 1976.

———. *The New Shape of American Religion*. New York: Harper & Row, 1959.

———. *Righteous Empire: The Protestant Experience in America*. New York: Dial, 1970.

Mead, Sidney E. *The Lively Experiment: The Shaping of Christianity in America*. New York: Harper & Row, 1963.

Newbigin, James Edward Leslie. *The Household of God*. New York: Friendship Press, 1954.

Niebuhr, H. Richard. *The Kingdom of God in America*. New York: Harper & Bros., 1959.

Smith, James Ward, and A. Leland Jamison (eds.). *The Shaping of American Religion*. Princeton: Princeton Univ. Press, 1961.

Van Dusen, Henry P. "Third Force in Christendom: Gospel-Singing, Doomsday-Preaching Sects," *Life,* 44 (June 9, 1958): 113–22+.

Zaretsky, Irving I. and Mark P. Leone (eds.). *Religious Movements in Contemporary America*. Princeton: Princeton Univ. Press, 1975.

D. *19th and 20th Century History*

Alexander, Thomas G. "Wilford Woodruff and the Changing Nature of Mormon Religious Experience," *Church History,* 45 (1976): 56–69.

Andrews, Edward Deming. *The People Called Shakers: A Search for the Perfect Society*. New York: Oxford Univ. Press, 1953.

Abell, Aaron I. *The Urban Impact on American Protestantism, 1865–1900*. Hamden, Conn.: Archor, 1962.

Bailey, Kenneth K. *Southern White Protestantism in the Twentieth Century*. New York: Harper & Row, 1964.

Beardsley, Frank Grenville. *A History of American Revivals*. Boston: American Tract Society, 1904.

Bucke, Emory S. *The History of American Methodism*. 3 vols. Nashville: Abingdon, 1964.

Carter, Paul A. *The Decline and Revival of the Social Gospel*. Ithaca: Cornell Univ. Press, 1956.

———. *The Spiritual Crisis of the Gilded Age*. DeKalb: Northern Illinois Univ. Press, 1971.

Cole, Charles C., Jr. *The Social Ideas of the Northern Evangelists, 1826–1860*. New York: Octagon, 1966.

Cross, Robert D. *The Emergence of Liberal Catholicism in America*. Cambridge, Mass.: Harvard Univ. Press, 1958.

———. *The Church and the City, 1865–1910*. Indianapolis: Bobbs-Merrill, 1967.

Driscoll, Charles B. "Major Prophets of Holy Kansas," *American Mercury,* 8 (May 1926): 18–26.

Drummond, Andrew Landale. *Edward Irving and His Circle*. London: James Clarke, 1935.

Farish, Hunter Dickenson. *The Circuit Rider Dismounts: A Social History of Southern Methodism*. Richmond, Va.: Dietz, 1938.

Fevold, Eugene L. *The Lutheran Free Church*. Minneapolis: Augsburg, 1969.

Gaustad, Edwin Scott (ed.). *The Rise of Adventism: Religion and Society in Mid-19th Century America.* New York: Harper & Row, 1974.

Gutman, Herbert G. "Protestantism and American Labor," *American Historical Review,* 72 (Oct. 1966): 74–101.

Harrell, David Edwin, Jr. *White Sects and Black Men in the Recent South.* Nashville: Vanderbilt Univ. Press, 1971.

Hopkins, Charles Howard. *The Rise of the Social Gospel in American Protestantism, 1865–1900.* New Haven: Yale Univ. Press, 1940.

Judah, J. Stillson. *The History and Philosophy of Metaphysical Movements.* Philadelphia: Westminster, 1967.

Loud, Grover C. *Evangelized America.* New York: Dial, 1928.

McLoughlin, William G., Jr. *Modern Revivalism: Charles Grandison Finney to Billy Graham.* New York: Ronald Press, 1959.

May, Henry F. *Protestant Churches and Industrial America.* New York: Harper & Bros. 1949.

Mooney, James. *The Ghost Dance Religion and the Sioux Outbreak of 1890.* Chicago: Univ. of Chicago Press, 1965.

Newmark, Marco R. "The Story of Religion in Los Angeles, 1781-1900," *Quarterly of the Historical Society of Southern California,* 28 (March 1946): 35–50.

Niebuhr, H. Richard, and Daniel D. Williams (eds.). *The Ministry in Historical Perspective.* New York: Harper & Bros., 1956.

O'Dea, Thomas F. *The Mormons.* Chicago: Univ. of Chicago Press, 1957.

Perry, H. Francis. "The Workingman's Alienation from the Church," *American Journal of Sociology,* 4 (1898–99):

Robertson, Archie. *That Old-Time Religion.* Boston: Houghton Mifflin, 1950.

Schlesinger, Arthur M. "A Critical Period in American Religion, 1875–1900," *Massachusetts Hist. Soc. Proceedings,* 64 (1930-32): 523–48.

Sechler, Earl T. *Our Religious Heritage: Church History of the Ozarks, 1806–1906.* Springfield, Mo.: Westport Press, 1961.

Seldes, Gilbert, *The Stammering Century.* New York: John Day, 1928.

Shaw, P.E. *The Catholic Apostolic Church, Sometimes Called Irvingites.* New York: King's Crown Press, 1946.

Spain, Rufus B. *At Ease in Zion: Social History of Southern Baptists, 1865–1900.* Nashville: Vanderbilt Univ., 1967.

Sweet, William Warren. *Revivalism in America.* New York: Charles Scribner's Sons, 1944.

Weisberger, Bernard A. *They Gathered at the River: The Story of the Great Revivalists and Their Impact Upon Religion in America.* Chicago: Quadrangle, 1966.

Windell, Marie G. "The Camp Meeting in Missouri," *Missouri Historical Review,* 38 (April 1943): 253–70.

V *The Holiness, Keswick, and Fundamentalist Movements*
A. *History*

Chapman, J. Wilbur. *The Life and Work of Dwight Lyman Moody.* London: James Nisbet, 1900.

Cross, Whitney R. *The Burned-Over District.* New York: Harper & Row, 1965.

Cunningham, Raymond J. "From Holiness to Healing: The Faith Cure in America, 1872–1892," *Church History,* 43 (Dec. 1974): 499–513.

Furniss, Norman F. *The Fundamentalist Controversy, 1918–1931.* New Haven: Yale Univ. Press, 1954.

Gaddis, Merrill Elmer. "Christian Perfectionism in America." Ph.D. diss., Univ. of Chicago, 1929.

Garrard, Mary N. *Mrs. Penn-Lewis: A Memoir.* Bournemouth, Eng.: Overcomer Book Room, 1947.

Hopkins, Evan, et al. *The Story of the Welsh Revival as Told by Eyewitnesses, Together with a Sketch of Evan Roberts and His Message to the World.* New York: Fleming H. Revell, 1905.

Ironside, Henry A. *A History of the Brethren Movement.* Grand Rapids: Zondervan, 1942.

Jones, Charles Edwin. "Perfectionist Persuasion: A Social Profile of the National Holiness Movement Within Methodism, 1867–1936." Ph.D. diss., Univ. of Wisconsin, 1968.

Jones, R. B. *Rent Heavens: The Revival of 1904.* London: Pioneer Mission, 1948. 1st ed., 1931.

Lindsay, Gordon. *The Life of John Alexander Dowie.* Shreveport, La.: Voice of Healing Pub., 1951.

Lindstrom, Harold. *Wesley and Sanctification.* London: Epworth Press, 1956.

Magnuson, Norris. "Salvation in the Slums: Evangelical Social Welfare Work, 1865–1920." Ph.D. diss., Univ. of Minnesota, 1968.

Moody, W. R. *The Life of D. L. Moody.* London: Morgan & Scott (*c.* 1900).

Moore, L. "Another Look at Fundamentalism: A Response to Ernest R. Sandeen," *Church History,* 37 (1968): 195–202.

Morgan, John Vyrnwy. *The Welsh Religious Revival, 1904–1905.* London: Chapman & Hall, 1909.

Penn-Lewis, Jessie. *The Awakening in Wales, 1904–05.* Leicester: Overcomer Book Room, 1922.

Peters, John Leland. *Christian Perfectionism and American Methodism.* New York: Abingdon, 1956.

Pugh, E. Cynolwyn. "The Welsh Revival of 1904–05," *Theology Today,* 12 (1955): 226–35.

Sandeen, Ernest R. *The Roots of Fundamentalism: British and American Millenarianism, 1800–1930.* Chicago: Univ. of Chicago Press, 1970.

———. "Toward a Historical Interpretation of the Origins of Fundamentalism," *Church History,* 36 (1967): 66–83.

Shaw, S. B. *The Great Revival in Wales*. Chicago: the author, 1905.

————. *Echoes of the General Holiness Assembly Held in Chicago, May 3–13, 1901*. Chicago: the author, 1901.

Smith, Timothy L. *Called Unto Holiness: The Story of the Nazarenes: The Formative Years*. Kansas City, Mo.: Nazarene Publishing House, 1962.

————. "The Holiness Crusade," in Emory S. Bucke (ed.), *The History of American Methodism*. 3 vols. New York: Abingdon, 1964. vol. II, pp. 608–27.

————. *Revivalism and Social Reform: American Protestantism on the Eve of the Civil War*. New York: Harper & Row, 1965.

Tozer, Alden Wilson. *Wingspread*. Harrisburg, Pa.: Christian Publications, 1943.

Warfield, Benjamin B. *Perfectionism*. Nutley, N.J.: Presbyterian and Reformed Publications, 1974. 1st ed., 1886.

B. *Doctrinal Literature*

Anderson, Mabette. *The Latter Rain and Its Counterfeit*. pamph. New York: n.p., 1907.

Arthur, William. *The Tongue of Fire*. New York: Harper & Bros., 1905.

Blackstone, William E. *Jesus Is Coming*. New York: Fleming H. Revell, 2nd ed., 1886.

Byrum, Russel R. *Holy Spirit Baptism and the Second Cleansing*. Anderson, Ind.: Gospel Trumpet Co., 1923.

Chapman, J. Wilbur. *Received Ye the Holy Ghost?* New York: Fleming H. Revell, 1894.

Cumming, James Elder. *Through the Eternal Spirit*. New York: Fleming H. Revell, 1896.

Dixon, Amzi C. (ed.). *The Holy Spirit in Life and Service: Addresses Delivered Before the Conference on the Ministry of the Holy Spirit, Brooklyn, 1894*. New York: Fleming H. Revell, 1895.

Finney, Charles Grandison. *Lectures on Revivals of Religion*. New York: Fleming H. Revell, 1898.

————. *Lectures on Systematic Theology*. Oberlin, Ohio: Oberlin College, 1846.

Gordon, Adoniram J. *The Ministry of Healing*. New York: Fleming H. Revell, 1882.

————. *The Ministry of the Spirit*. Chicago: Fleming H. Revell, 1894.

Ironside, Henry A. *Apostolic Faith Missions and the So-Called Second Pentecost*, pamph. New York: Loizeaux Bros., n.d. (c. 1914–1916).

Ironside, Henry A. *Holiness: The False and the True*. Neptune, N.J.: Loizeaux Bros., 1964. 1st ed., 1912.

Irvine, William C. *Heresies Exposed*. New York: Loizeaux Bros., 1946. 1st ed. 1917.

McCrossan, T. J. *Speaking with Tongues: Sign or Gift, Which?* Harrisburg, Pa.: Christian Publications, n.d.

Matthews, John. *Speaking in Tongues*. Kansas City, Mo.: the author, 1925.

Moody, Dwight L. *Secret Power*. Chicago: Fleming H. Revell, 1881.

Murray, Andrew. *The Spirit of Christ*. London: Nisbet, 1888.

Panton, D. M. *Irvingism, Tongues and the Gifts of the Holy Ghost*. n.p., n.d., pamph.

Penn-Lewis, Jessie, and Evan Roberts. *War on the Saints*. Dorset, Eng.: Overcomer Literature Trust, n.d.

Pierson, Arthur T. *Acts of the Holy Spirit*. New York: Fleming H. Revell, 1896.

Riley, William B. *Speaking with Tongues*. n.p., n.d., pamph.

Scofield, C. I. *Christian Sanity*. n.p., n.d., pamph.

―――. *Plain Papers on the Doctrine of the Holy Spirit*. Chicago: Fleming H. Revell, 1899.

Simpson, Albert B. *The Four-Fold Gospel*. Harrisburg, Pa.: Christian Publications, 1925.

―――.*The Gospel of the Kingdom: A Series of Discourses on the Lord's Coming*. New York: Christian Publishing Co., n.d.

―――. *The Holy Spirit, or Power From on High*. New York: Christian Alliance Publication Co., 1924.

―――. *When the Comforter Came*. Harrisburg, Pa.: Christian Publications, 1911.

Torrey, Reuben A. *The Exact Truth Regarding an Eternal Hell*. Los Angeles: Biola Book Room, n.d., pamph.

―――. *How To Obtain Fullness of Power*. Wheaton, Ill.: Sword of the Lord Publishers, n.d. (1st ed. 1897).

―――. *The Baptism with the Holy Spirit*. New York: Fleming H. Revell, 1895.

―――. *The Person and Work of the Holy Spirit*. New York: Fleming H. Revell, 1910.

White, Alma. *Demons and Tongues*. Zarephath, N.J.: Pillar of Fire Publications, 1919.

VI *The Pentecostal Movement*

A. *Original Sources*

1. *Official Pentecostal Publications*

Apostolic Bible Institute. *Line upon Line: Church History Periods Illustrated*. St. Paul:, 1957, pamph.

Apostolic Faith. *The Apostolic Faith: Its Origins, Functions and Doctrines*. Portland, Ore.: n.d.

Assemblies of God, General Council. Minutes of the Annual Meeting of the Assemblies of God in the U.S.A., Canada and Foreign Lands, vols. 1–9 (1914–1921).

―――. Minutes of the Biennial Meeting . . . , vols. 10–17 (1923–1937).

―――. Minutes of the Executive Presbyters, 1946.

————. *50th Anniversary*. Springfield, Mo.: Gospel Publishing House, 1964. booklet.

Bible Way Churches of Our Lord Jesus Christ World Wide. *Brief History and Doctrine of the* ————. Washington, D.C.; n.d.

Carolina Evangelistic Assoc. *Twentieth Anniversary of the Garr Auditorium, 1930–1950*. Charlotte, N.C., 1950. pamph.

Christian Churches of North America. *Who We Are*. Pittsburgh: n.d. pamph.

————. *In the Power of His Spirit*. n.p., n.d. pamph.

Christian and Missionary Alliance. Annual Report. Nyack, N.Y.: 1905–1912.

Church of God (Cleveland, Tenn.). Book of Minutes, 1906–1922. Cleveland, Tenn.: Pathway Press, 1923.

————. Minutes of the General Assemblies. Cleveland, Tenn.: Pathway Press, 1906–1966.

————. Report of Investigation: Proceedings of Elders Council and Correspondence, convened at Cleveland, Tenn.; June 12–21, 1923.

Church of God of Prophecy. Cyclopedic Index of Assembly Minutes (1906–1949) of the Church of God Over Which A. J. Tomlinson Was General Overseer and M. A. Tomlinson Is Now General Overseer. Cleveland, Tenn.: White Wing Publishing House, 1950.

————. Minutes, 64th Annual Assembly. Chatanooga, 1969.

Church of God of Prophecy. *These Necessary Things: The Doctrine and Practices of the Church of God of Prophecy*. 3rd ed., Cleveland, Tenn., 1968.

Church of God of the Apostolic Faith. Minutes of the Annual Conference. Mulberry, Kans., 1919, 1924, 1937.

Church of God in Christ. Manual of the ————. Memphis, 1951.

Church of the Living God. Discipline and Articles of Faith. Winston-Salem, n.d.

Full Gospel Evangelistic Association. Constitution and By-Laws for Churches Associated with the ————. n.p., n.d.

International Church of the Foursquare Gospel. Annual Convention Report. Los Angeles, 1931.

————. *Aimee Semple McPherson: Declaration of Faith*. comp. by A. S. McPherson. Los Angeles, n.d. pamph.

————. *The Four Square Gospel*. Los Angeles: Raymond L. Cox for the Heritage Committee of the Foursquare Gospel Church, 1969.

————. *History of Foursquaredom*. Los Angeles, n.d. mimeo.

Glad Tidings Tabernacle. *Golden Jubilee*. New York, 1957. pamph.

(Original) Church of God. Manual of the ————. Chattanooga, 1952.

Pentecostal Assemblies of the World. Ministerial Record. Indianapolis, 1919.

Pentecostal Church of God of America. General Constitution and By-laws. Joplin, Mo.: 1966.

————. *This We Believe*. Joplin, Mo.; n.d., pamph.

Pentecostal Fellowship of North America. Constitution and By-laws. Toronto, n.d.

Pentecostal Fellowship of North America. *The Pentecostal Fellowship of North America,* n.p., n.d. pamph.

Pentecostal Fire Baptized Holiness Church. Discipline and General Rules of the —————. Toccoa, Ga., 1919.

Pentecostal Free Will Baptist Church. Discipline of the —————, n.p., n.d.

—————. Minutes of the —————. Dunn, N.C., 1966.

Pentecostal Full Gospel Church, Inc. General Principles, Discipline and By-laws. Baltimore, n.d.

Pentecostal Holiness Church. Discipline of the —————. Falcon, N.C.; 1917. Royston, Ga., 1921. Franklin Springs, Ga., 1925.

—————. Minutes of the General Conference. 1925, 1929, 1933, 1945.

—————. Manual. Franklin Springs, Ga., 1965.

—————. Yearbook. Franklin Springs, Ga., 1930.

Pentecostal World Conference. Minutes. Cleveland, Tenn., 1949.

Salem Gospel Tabernacle. *Salem Gospel Tabernacle, 1926–1956.* Brooklyn, N.Y., 1956. booklet.

—————. *Salem Gospel Tabernacle, 1926–1966.* Brooklyn, N.Y., 1966. booklet.

United Pentecostal Church. Manual of the —————. St. Louis, 1967.

—————. *United We Stand.* Hazelwood, Mo.: Pentecostal Publishing House, 1970.

—————. *What We Believe and Teach: Articles of Faith.* St. Louis, n.d. pamph.

2. *Memoirs and Other First-Hand Accounts*

Anderson, Robert Mapes. Correspondence with various Pentecostal leaders and organizations. Possession of the author.

Argue, A. H. *Is Speaking in Tongues an Essential Sign?* Chicago: The Pentecostal Herald, 1919. pamph.

Argue, Zelma. *What Meaneth This? The Story of Our Personal Experiences and Evangelistic Campaigns: The Argue Evangelistic Party.* Winnipeg: the author, 1924.

Bailey, S. Clyde. *Pioneer Marvels of Faith: Wonderful 46 Years Experience.* Morristown, Tenn.: the author, 1958.

Ball, H. C. and Alice E. Luce. *Glimpses of Our Latin American Work in the United States and Mexico.* Springfield, Mo.: Gospel Publishing House, 1940.

Barrat, Thomas Ball. *The Truth about the Pentecostal Revival.* London, 1908. pamph.

—————. *When the Fire Fell and an Outline of My Life.* Larvik, Norway: Alfons Hansen and Soner, 1927.

Bartleman, Frank. *From Plow to Pulpit: From Maine to California.* Los Angeles: the author, 1924.

—————. *How Pentecost Came to Los Angeles: As It Was in the Beginning.* Los Angeles: the author, 1925.

Bell, Eudorus N. Correspondence of ————. Files of the Pentecostal Evangel, Springfield, Mo. (cited as PEF).

Bond, Georgia. (comp.). *Life Story of the Rev. O. H. Bond.* Oakgrove, Ark.: the compiler, 1958.

Bosworth, Fred F. *Do All Speak with Tongues?* n.p., n.d. pamph.

Britton, Francis M. *Pentecostal Truth.* Royston, Ga.: Publishing House of the Pentecostal Holiness Church, 1919.

Gardiner, Gordon P. and Marie E. Brown. *The Origin of Glad Tidings Tabernacle.* New York, 1955, pamph.

Brown, Marie E. Burgess. Interview, Robert Mapes Anderson, New York, N.Y., Nov. 5, 1965. Typescript in the possession of the author.

Bryant, William F. and M. S. Lemons. Interview, "Brother" Chesser, March 17, 1954. Typescript, Doc. no. 27A, in the files of the library of Pathway Press, Cleveland, Tenn.

Bryant, William F. Interview by unnamed person, 1949. Typescript in the files of the library of Pathway Press, Cleveland, Tenn.

Bryant, (Mrs.) William F. Interview by unnamed person, Feb. 8, 1954. Typescript, Doc. no. 8A, in the files of the library of Pathway Press, Cleveland, Tenn.

Clark, Elijah C. *The Baptism of the Holy Ghost "And More."* Cleveland, Tenn.: Church of God Publishing House, 1931.

Cook, Glenn A. *The Azusa Street Meeting.* Los Angeles, n.p., n.d. (c. 1920). pamph.

————. "The Truth About E. N. Bell," *Herald of Truth,* Aug. 1947, p. 3.

Eldridge, George N. *Personal Reminiscences.* Los Angeles: West Coast Publishing Co., n.d.

Ewart, Frank J. *The Phenomenon of Pentecost: A History of the Latter Rain.* St. Louis: Pentecostal Publishing House, 1947.

————. *The Revelation of Jesus Christ.* St. Louis: Pentecostal Publishing House, n.d. pamph.

Flower, Alice Reynolds. *Grace for Grace: Some Highlights of God's Grace in the Daily Life of the Flower Family.* Springfield, Mo.: the author, 1961.

Flower, J. Roswell. *Church Orientation.* PEF. mimeo.

————. Correspondence. PEF.

————. *Historic Record of the Growth of the Assemblies of God.* PEF. mimeo.

Frodsham, Stanley H. Correspondence. PEF.

————. *The Life of Joy.* Springfield, Mo.: Gospel Publishing House, n.d.

————. *Wholly for God.* Springfield, Mo.: Gospel Publishing House, n.d.

————. *With Signs Following.* Springfield, Mo.: Gospel Publishing House, 1926.

————. *With Signs Following.* Springfield, Mo.: Gospel Publishing House, 1941.

Goss, Ethel E. (ed.). *The Winds of God: The Story of the Early Pentecostal Days (1901–1914) in the Life of Howard Goss.* New York: Comet Press, 1958.

Hansen, Michael. *My Life.* New York, n.d. (c. 1965). mimeo.

———. Interview, Robert Mapes Anderson, New York, 1967.

Hayes, W. M. (ed.). *Memoirs of Richard Baxter Hayes.* Philadelphia: the editor, 1945.

Higgins, Walter J. *Pioneering in Pentecost: My Experiences of 46 Years in the Ministry.* El Cajon, Calif.: the author, 1958.

Holmes, Nickels John. *Life Sketches and Sermons.* Royston, Ga.: Press of the Pentecostal Holiness Church, 1920.

Jensen, Fred. Interviews, Robert M. Anderson. New York, 1967–73.

Jones, Ozro T., Sr. & Jr. Interview, Robert M. Anderson, Philadelphia, Sept. 14, 1966.

King, Joseph H. "History of the Fire Baptized Holiness Church," *Pentecostal Holiness Advocate,* March 21, through April 21, 1921.

———. *From Passover to Pentecost.* Franklin Springs, Ga.: Pentecostal Publishing House, 1914.

King, Joseph H. and Blanche L. *Yet Speaketh, Memoirs of the Late Bishop Joseph H. King.* Franklin Springs, Ga.: Pentecostal Publishing House, 1949.

Knoch, A. E. *All in All: The Goal of the Universe.* Los Angeles: Concordat Publishing Concern, n.d.

LaBerge, Agnes N. Ozman. "History of the Pentecostal Movement from Jan 1, 1901". PEF. typescript.

———. *What God Hath Wrought.* Chicago, 1919. pamph.

Lawrence, Bennet F. *The Apostolic Faith Restored.* Springfield, Mo.: Gospel Publishing House, 1916.

Lee, Flavius J. Correspondence, 1924–26. Files of the library of Pathway Press, Cleveland, Tenn.

———. Diary and Account Books, 1914–19. Files of the Headquarters of the Church of God (Cleveland, Tenn.)

Lee, (Mrs.) Flavius J. (comp.). *Life Sketches and Sermons of F. J. Lee.* Cleveland, Tenn.: Church of God Publishing House, n.d.

McGowan, (Mrs.) C. M. *Another Echo from Azusa.* PEF. mimeo.

McPherson, Aimee Semple. *The Foursquare Gospel.* Los Angeles: Echo Park Evangelistic Assoc., 1946.

———. *This Is That: Personal Experiences, Sermons and Writings.* Los Angeles: Echo Park Evangelistic Assoc., 1923.

Morehead, H. R. Interview by unnamed person. Doc. no. 9A in the files of the library of Pathway Press, Cleveland, Tenn., n.d.

Osterberg, A. G. "Azusa's 50th Anniversary," *The Foursquare Magazine,* Oct. 1956, pp. 16–18.

Osterberg, Oscar. "I Was There," *Full Gospel Businessmen's Voice,* 14 (May 1966): 4–7+.

Parham, Charles Fox. *The Everlasting Gospel*. Baxter Springs, Kans.: the author, 1942.

——. *Kol Kare Bomidbar: A Voice Crying in the Wilderness*. Baxter Springs, Kans.: Joplin Printing Co., 1944.

Parham, Sarah Thistlethwaite (comp.). *The Life of Charles F. Parham: Founder of the Apostolic Faith Movement*. Joplin, Mo.: Tri-State Printing Co., 1930.

Perkins, Eunice M. *Fred Francis Bosworth: His Life Story*. Detroit: the author, 1927.

Price, Charles S. *The Story of My Life*. Pasadena: the author, 1935.

Simmons, E. L. "Reminiscences of ——". Doc. no. 19A. in the files of the library of Pathway Press, Cleveland, Tenn., March 2, 1954. typescript.

Sizelove, Rachel. *The Sparkling Fountain*. n.p., n.d. pamph.

Sorrow, Watson. *Some of My Experiences*. Atlanta: the author, 1954.

Sumrall, Lester F. *"All for Jesus": The Life Story of Wesley Rowland Steelberg*. Springfield, Mo.: Gospel Publishing House, 1955.

Taylor, G. F. "Our Church History," *Pentecostal Holiness Advocate,* Jan. 20 through Apr. 21, 1921.

Tomlinson, Ambrose J. *A. J. Tomlinson: Former General Overseer of the Church of God*. Comp. by Lillie Duggar. Cleveland, Tenn.: White Wing Publishing House, 1964.

——. *Answering the Call of God*. Cleveland, Tenn.: White Wing Publishing House, n.d. pamph.

——. *Diary of* ——. 3 vols. ed. by Homer A. Tomlinson. New York: The Church of God, World Headquarters, 1949–55.

——. *God's Annointed Prophet of Wisdom: Choice Writings of A. J. Tomlinson in Times of His Greatest Anointings*. 2nd. ed. Cleveland, Tenn.: White Wing Publishing House, 1970.

——. *God's Twentieth Century Pioneer: A Compilation of Some of the Writings of A. J. Tomlinson*. Cleveland, Tenn.: White Wing Publishing House, 1962.

——. *Historical Annual Addresses*. Cleveland, Tenn.: White Wing Publishing House, 1970.

——. "Journal of Happenings: The Diary of A. J. Tomlinson, March 7, 1901–Nov. 3, 1923." Files of the Church of God (Cleveland, Tenn.), n.d. typescript.

——. *The Last Great Conflict*. Cleveland, Tenn.: Walter E. Rodgers, 1913.

Tomlinson, Homer A. *The Shout of a King*. Queens Village, N.Y.: The Church of God, U.S.A. Hdqtrs., 1968.

——. Interview, Robert Mapes Anderson. Queens Village, N.Y., April 14, 1967.

Wigglesworth, Smith. *Ever-Increasing Faith*. n.p., n.d.

Frodsham, Stanley H. *Smith Wigglesworth: Apostle of Faith*. Springfield, Mo.: Gospel Publishing House, 1949.

Woodworth-Etter, (Mrs.) M. B. *Signs and Wonders God Wrought in the Ministry for Forty Years*. Chicago: Hammond Press, W. B. Conkey Co., 1916.

3. *Periodicals*

Apostolic Faith. There were at least four different periodicals published under this title. The first was that of Charles F. Parham, published in Topeka, Houston, Zion City, Ill., and possibly other places until about 1909, when it began to issue from Baxter Springs, Kansas. It has been issued irregularly from 1897 to the present.

A second paper with the same name was published by E. N. Bell, F. W. Carothers and others in Houston from about 1907 (when they broke with Parham) until 1913 when it was absorbed into *Word and Witness*.

A third paper of the same name was published by the Azusa Street mission from 1906 until at least 1908, and perhaps afterwards.

The fourth was published by Florence Crawford at Portland, Oregon beginning in 1908 or 1909 and still exists under the name *Herald of Light*.

I have consulted scattered issues of all but those of the Houston paper for the years 1905–09, and Parham's Baxter Springs paper for the years from 1925 through 1929.

Apostolic Herald. Seattle, 1909.

Apostolic Messenger. Winnipeg, 1908.

Apostolic Witness & Missionary Herald. Dallas, Ore., 1909.

Assembly Friend. Chicago, 1951.

Bible Friend. Minneapolis, 1921.

Bible Study. Philadelphia, vol. 1, n.d.

Bridal Call. Los Angeles, 1918–23.

Bridegroom Echo. Los Angeles, 1949.

Bridegroom's Messenger. Atlanta, 1907.

Christian & Missionary Alliance. Nyack, N.Y., 1905–09.

Christian Evangel. Various places, 1913–15, 1918–19.

Christian Witness & Advocate of Bible Holiness. Chicago, 1916.

Church of God Evangel. Title varies. Cleveland, Tenn., 1906–29.

Elim Pentecostal Herald. Hornell, N.Y., 1935.

Evening Light & Church of God Evangel. (See *Church of God Evangel*.)

Foursquare Magazine. Los Angeles, 1944.

Full Gospel Business Men's Voice. Santa Ana, Calif., 1965–76.

Glad Tidings Herald. Title varies. New York, 1918–43.

God's Revivalist & Bible Advocate. Cincinnati, 1901, 1906–08.

Gospel Witness. Los Angeles, 1914.

Gospel Witness. Louisville, Ky., 1906.

Grace and Truth. Memphis, 1914–16, 1918.

Herald of Faith. Chicago, 1935.

Herald of Light. Indianapolis, 1905–06, 1910.

Herald of Pentecost. Chicago, 1956.

Herald of Pentecost. Duluth, 1953–56.

Homiletic Review. Chicago, 1896–1909.

Latter Rain Evangel. Chicago, 1908–12, 1915–16, 1925–34.

Live Coals. Royston, Ga., 1905–06.

Los Angeles Times. Los Angeles, 1906, 1956.

The Midnight Cry. New York, 1911–18.

Missionary Review of the World. 1904–06, 1908.

New York Times. New York, 1906–28, 1961–65.

Peniel Herald. Los Angeles, 1907–09, 1911.

Pentecost. London, 1947.

Pentecostal Evangel. Springfield, Mo., 1919–32.

Pentecostal Herald. Chicago, 1917–18, 1920, 1922.

Pentecostal Herald. Louisville, 1915–20.

Pentecostal Herald. St. Louis, 1967.

Pentecostal Holiness Advocate. Franklin Springs, Ga., 1905–06, 1916–25, 1937, 1946, 1950.

Pentecostal Testimony. Winnipeg, 1928–30.

Things New and Old. London, 1924.

Time. 1960–1965.

Topeka State Journal. Topeka, 1900–1901.

Upper Room. Los Angeles, 1909.

Victorious Gospel. Los Angeles, 1915.

Victory. Bournemouth, Eng., 1912.

Way of Faith. Columbia, S.C., 1901, 1906, 1918, 1921.

Weekly Evangel. St. Louis, 1915–18.

Word and Witness. Malvern, Ark., 1912–15.

Word and Work. Framingham, Mass., 1935.

B. *History and Analysis*

Aikman, Duncan. "The Holy Rollers," *American Mercury*, 15 (Oct. 1928): 180–91.

Apostolic Faith. *A Historical Account of the* ————. Portland, Ore.: Apostolic Faith Publishing House, 1965.

Assemblies of God, Kansas District Council. *The Harvester: History of the Kansas District Council, 1913–1955*. n.p.: Kansas District Council of the Assemblies of God, n.d. (c. 1955).

Assemblies of God, Public Relations Department. *Early History of the Assemblies of God*. Springfield, Mo.: Assemblies of God, International Headquarters, 1959. pamph.

Atter, Gordon. *The Third Force*. Peterborough, Ont.: The College Press, 1962.

Bloch-Hoell, Nils. *The Pentecostal Movement.* New York: Humanities Press, 1964.

———. *Pinsebevegelsen.* Oslo: University of Oslo Press, 1956.

Boisen, Anton T. *Religion in Crisis and Custom.* New York: Harper & Bros., 1945.

Brumback, Carl. *Suddenly . . . from Heaven: A History of the Assemblies of God.* Springfield, Mo.: Gospel Publishing House, 1961.

Bresson, Bernard L. *Studies in Ecstasy.* New York: Vantage Press, 1966.

Buckles, Ernest A. *A Brief History: The Church of God* [of the Apostolic Faith]. Drumright, Okla.: the author, 1935. pamph.

Campbell, Joseph E. *The Pentecostal Holiness Church, 1898–1948.* Franklin Springs, Ga.: The Publishing House of the Pentecostal Holiness Church, 1951.

Carter, Herbert F., and Mrs. Ruth K. Moore. "History of the Pentecostal Free Will Baptist Church, Inc.," *The Messenger* (Oct. 1965): 4+.

Cintron, Pedro. "American Denominational Revivalism and the Pentecostal Movement: A Comparative Study." S.T.M. thesis, Union Theological Seminary, 1963.

Conn, Charles W. *Like a Mighty Army Moves the Church of God, 1886–1955.* Cleveland, Tenn.: Church of God Publishing House, 1955.

Corvin, R. O. "History of the Educational Institutions of the Pentecostal Holiness Church. Ph.D. diss., Southwestern Baptist Theological Seminary, 1956.

Cox, B. L. *History and Doctrine of the Congregational Holiness Church.* n.p., 1959.

Crayne, Richard. *Early Twentieth Century Pentecost.* Morristown, Tenn.: the author, n.d. booklet.

———. *Pentecostal Handbook.* Morristown, Tenn.: the author, n.d. (c. 1963). booklet.

Davis, A. S. "Pentecostal Movement in Black Christianity," *The Black Church,* 2 (1972): 65–88.

Dearman, Marion. "Christ and Conformity: A Study of Pentecostal Values," *Journal for the Scientific Study of Religion,* 13 (1974): 437–53.

Durasoff, Steve. *Bright Wind of the Spirit: Pentecostalism Today.* Englewood Cliffs, N.J.: Prentice-Hall, 1972.

Elinson, Howard. "The Implications of Pentecostal Religion for Intellectualism, Politics and Race Relations," *American Journal of Sociology,* 70 (1965): 403–15.

Fauss, Oliver F. *"Buy the Truth and Sell It Not": The History of the Revelation of Baptism in the Name of Jesus, and of the Fullness of God in Christ.* St. Louis: Pentecostal Publishing House, 1965.

Fidler, R. L. "Historical Review of the Pentecostal Outpouring in Los Angeles at the Azusa Street Mission in 1906," *The International Outlook,* Jan.– March 1963, pp. 3–14.

Flora, C. B. "Social Dislocation and Pentecostalism: A Multivariate Analysis," *Sociological Analysis,* 34 (Winter, 1973): 296–304.

Foster, Fred J. *Think It Not Strange: A History of the Oneness Movement.* St. Louis: Pentecostal Publishing House, 1965.

Gee, Donald. *The Pentecostal Movement.* London: Elim Publishing Co., 1949.

———. "Movement Without a Man," *Christian Life,* 28 (July 1966): 52+.

Gerlach, Luther P., and Virginia H. Hine. "Five Factors Crucial to the Growth and Spread of a Modern Religious Movement," *Journal for the Scientific Study of Religion,* 7 (1968): 23–40.

——— and ———. *People, Power, Change: Movements of Social Transformation.* Indianapolis: Bobbs-Merrill, 1970.

Gibson, Luther. *History of the Church of God,* Mountain Assembly. n.p., 1954. booklet.

Hamilton, Michael P. (ed.). *The Charismatic Movement.* Grand Rapids: Eerdmans, 1975.

Harper, Michael. *As at the Beginning: The 20th Century Pentecostal Revival.* London: Hodder & Stoughton, 1965.

Harrison, Irvine John. "A History of the Assemblies of God." Th.D. diss., Berkeley Baptist Divinity School, 1954.

Hastie, Eugene N. *History of the West Central District* [of the Assemblies of God]. Fort Dodge, Ia.: the author, 1948.

Henke, Frederick. "The Gift of Tongues and Related Phenomena at the Present Day," *American Journal of Theology,* 13 (1909): 193–206.

Hollenweger, Walter J. "A Black Pentecostal Concept: A Forgotten Chapter of Black History," *Concept,* Special Issue no. 30, June 1970.

Hollenweger, Walter J. "Handbuch der Pfingstbewegung." 7 vols. Th.D. diss., Univ. of Zurich, 1965.

———. "Pentecostalism and Black Power," *Theology Today,* 30 (Oct. 1973): 228–38.

———. *The Pentecostals: The Charismatic Movement in the Churches.* Minneapolis: Augsburg, 1972.

Hoover, Mario G. "Origin and Structural Development of the Assemblies of God." M.A. thesis, Missouri State Univ., 1970.

Jauhiainan, Henry H. "Independent Pentecostal Church Movement," *Conviction,* 6 (March 1968): 6–7.

Johnson, Elva M. *Mission U.S.A.: A Study of Home Missions.* Springfield, Mo.: Gospel Publishing House, 1957.

Juillerate, L. Howard. *Brief History of the Church of God.* Cleveland, Tenn.: Church of God Publishing House, 1922.

Kampmeier, A. "Recent Parallels to the Miracle of Pentecost," *Open Court,* 22 (Aug. 1908): 492–98.

Kendrick, Klaude. "The Pentecostal Movement: Hopes and Hazards," *Christian Century,* 80 (1963): 608–10.

Kendrick, Klaude. *The Promise Fulfilled: A History of the Modern Pentecostal Movement*. Springfield, Mo.: Gospel Publishing House, 1961.

La Barre, Weston. *They Shall Take Up Serpents: Psychology of Southern Snake Handling Cult*. Minneapolis: Univ. of Minnesota Press, 1962.

Lovett, Leonard. "Perspective on the Black Origins of the Contemporary Pentecostal Movement," *Journal of the Interdenominational Center*, 1 (Fall 1973): 36–49.

McDonnell, Kilian. "New Dimensions in Research on Pentecostalism," *Worship*, 45 (April 1971): 214–19.

McWilliams, Carey. "Aimee Semple McPherson: 'Sunlight in My Soul,' " in Isabel Leighton (ed.), *The Aspirin Age: 1919–1941*. New York: Simon & Schuster, 1949.

Madsen, Darrel D. "The Origin and Development of the Pentecostal Evangel," PEF.

Masserano, Frank C. "A Study of the Worship Forms of the Assemblies of God Denomination." Th.M. thesis, Princeton Theological Seminary, 1966.

Mavity, Nancy Barr. *Sister Aimee*. Garden City, N.Y.: Doubleday, Doran & Co., 1931.

Menzies, William W. *Anointed To Serve: The Story of the Assemblies of God*. Springfield, Mo.: Gospel Publishing House, 1971.

Moore, Everett LeRoy. "Handbook of Pentecostal Denominations in the U.S." M.A. thesis, Pasadena College, 1954.

Muelder, W. G. "From Sect to Church: Rural Pentecostal Sects and the Church of the Nazarene," *Christendom*, 10 (1945): 450–62.

Nichol, John T. *Pentecostalism*. New York: Harper & Row, 1966.

———. "The Role of the Pentecostal Movement in American Church History," *The Gordon Review*, II (Dec. 1956).

O'Dea, Thomas F., and Renato Poblete. "Anomie and the 'Quest for Community': the Formation of Sects Among the Puerto Ricans of New York," *American Catholic Sociological Review*, 21 (Spring 1960): 18–36.

Oliver, Bernard John, Jr. "Some Newer Religious Groups in the U.S.: Twelve Case Studies." Ph.D. diss., Yale Univ., 1946.

Parkes, William. "Pentecostalism: Its History, Background and Recent Trends," *London Quarterly & Holborn Review*, 35 (1966): 147–53.

Paul, George Harold. "The Religious Frontier in Oklahoma: Dan T. Muse and the Pentecostal Holiness Church." Ph.D. diss., Univ. of Oklahoma, 1965.

Richardson, Robert P. "Pentecostal Prophets," *Open Court*, 42 (1928): 673–80.

Seddon, A. E. "Edward Irving and Unknown Tongues," *Homiletic Review*, 57 (1909): 103–9.

Simmons, E. L. *History of the Church of God*. Cleveland, Tenn.: Church of God Publishing House, 1938.

Simpson, George Eaton. "Black Pentecostalism in the U.S.," *Phylon,* 35 (1974): 203–11.

Synan, Vinson. (ed.). *Aspects of Pentecostal-Charismatic Origins.* Plainfield, N.J.: Logos International, 1975.

Synan, Vinson. *The Holiness-Pentecostal Movement in the United States.* Grand Rapids: Eerdmans, 1971.

———. *The Old-Time Religion: A History of the Pentecostal Holiness Church.* Franklin Springs, Ga.: Advocate Press, 1973.

Tinney, James S. "Black Origins of the Pentecostal Movement," *Christianity Today,* 16 (1971): 4–6.

Williams, Jerry Douglas. "The Modern Pentecostal Movement: A Brief Sketch of Its History and Thought," *Lexington Theological Quarterly,* 9 (1974): 50–60.

Williams, Melvin D. *Community in a Black Pentecostal Church: An Anthropological Study.* Pittsburgh: Univ. of Pittsburgh Press, 1974.

Wilson, James Bright. "Religious Leaders, Institutions and Organizations among Certain Agricultural Workers in the Central Valley of California." Ph.D. diss., Univ. of Southern California, 1944.

Winehouse, Irwin. *The Assemblies of God.* New York: Vantage Press, 1959.

C. *Literature on Pentecostal Doctrine* (see also V. B., Doctrinal Literature, above)

Basham, Don. *The Miracle of Tongues.* Old Tappan, N.J.: Revell, 1973.

Bishop, A. E. *Tongues, Signs and Visions not God's Order for Today.* Chicago: Moody Bible Institute Bookstore, n.d. pamph.

Bowen, (Mrs.) T. M. *Why We Baptize in Jesus' Name.* St. Louis: Pentecostal Publishing House, n.d. pamph.

Brumback, Carl. *God in Three Persons: A Trinitarian Answer to the Oneness or "Jesus Only" Doctrine Concerning the Godhead and Water Baptism.* Cleveland, Tenn.: Pathway Press, 1959.

———. *What Meaneth This?* Springfield, Mo.: Gospel Publishing House, 1947.

Bruner, Frederick Dale. *Theology of the Holy Spirit: The Pentecostal Experience and the New Testament Witness.* Grand Rapids: Eerdmans, 1970.

Conn, Charles W. *Pillars of Pentecost.* Cleveland, Tenn.: Pathway Press, 1956.

Cross, James Adam. *Healing in the Church.* Cleveland, Tenn.: Pathway Press, 1962.

Dewar, Lindsay. *The Holy Spirit and Modern Thought.* New York: Harper & Bros., 1959.

Gee, Donald. *Concerning Spiritual Gifts.* Springfield, Mo.: Gospel Publishing House, 1947.

Hanby, S. R. *The Apostles' Doctrine.* St. Louis: Pentecostal Publishing House, n.d., pamph.

Harris, Ralph W. *Spoken by the Spirit*. Springfield, Mo.: Gospel Publishing House, 1973.

Hayes, Doremus Almy. *The Gift of Tongues*. New York: Eaton & Main, 1913.

Hoeckema, Anthony A. *Holy Spirit Baptism*. Grand Rapids: Eerdmans, 1972.

Horton, Harold. *The Gifts of the Spirit*. Bedfordshire, Eng.: Redemption Tidings Bookroom, 1946.

Horton, Wade H. (ed.). *The Glossolalia Phenomenon*. Cleveland, Tenn.: Pathway Press, 1966.

Johnson, S. C. *Twenty One Burning Subjects: Who Is This That Defies and Challenges the Whole Religious World on These Subjects?* Philadelphia: The Church of the Lord Jesus Christ of the Apostolic Faith, n.d. pamph.

Knoch, A. E. *The Exact Truth Regarding an Eternal Hell: A Reply*. Los Angeles: Concordat Publishing Concern, 1922. pamph.

Kosick, F. J. *Why Baptize in the Name of Jesus?* Winnipeg, Manitoba: n.p., n.d. pamph.

———. *Pentecostal Power and Evidence*. Winnipeg, Manitoba: n.p., n.d. pamph.

Kuyper, Abraham. *The Work of the Holy Spirit*. Grand Rapids, Mich.: Eerdmans, 1946. 1st ed., 1900.

Lemons, Frank W. *Our Pentecostal Heritage*. Cleveland, Tenn.; Pathway Press, 1963.

Mackie, Alexander. *The Gift of Tongues*. New York: George H. Doran, 1921.

Meldau, Fred J. *The Fascinating Delusion of Pentecostalism*. Denver: Christian Victory Publishing Co., n.d. pamph.

Pearlman, Myer. *Knowing the Doctrines of the Bible*. Springfield, Mo.: Gospel Publishing House, 1937.

Rice, John R. *The Power of Pentecost*. Wheaton, Ill.: Sword of the Lord Publishers, 1949.

Riggs, Ralph M. *The Spirit Himself*. Springfield, Mo.: Gospel Publishing House, 1949.

Saxby, A. E. and A. E. Knoch. *Reconciliation Tracts*. n.p., n.d. pamph. series.

Smith, (Mr. and Mrs.) P.D. *He Is Just the Same Today*. Springfield, Mo.: Gospel Publishing House, 1931.

Stagg, Frank E., et al. *Glossolalia: Tongue-Speaking in Biblical, Historical and Psychological Perspective*. Nashville: Abingdon, 1967.

Stiles, J. E. *The Gift of the Holy Spirit*. Glendale, Calif.: The Church Press, 1913.

Stolee, Haakon Jacobs. *Speaking in Tongues*. Minneapolis: Augsburg, 1963.

Thom, Robert. *The Holy Spirit and the Name*. n.p., n.d.

Unger, Merrill F. *The Baptizing Work of the Holy Spirit*. Findlay, Ohio: Dunham Publishing Co., 1962.

Van Dusen, Henry P. *Spirit, Son and Father*. New York: Charles Scribner's Sons, 1958.

Walvoord, John F. "Contemporary Issues in the Doctrine of the Holy Spirit, Part IV: Spiritual Gifts Today," *Bibliotheca Sacra,* 130 (1973): 315–28.

Westgarth, J. W. *The Holy Spirit and the Primitive Mind.* London: Victory Press, 1946.

Williams, Ernest S. *Systematic Theology.* 3 vols. Springfield, Mo.: Gospel Publishing House, 1953.

D. *The Neo-Pentecostal Movement*

Bennett, Dennis J. *Nine O'Clock in the Morning.* Plainfield, N.J.: Logos, 1970.

Bess, Donovan. "Speaking in tongues: The High Church Heresy," *Nation,* Sept. 28, 1963, pp. 173–77.

"Closely Guarded Secret," *Living Church,* July 10, 1960, pp. 5+.

duPlessis, David J. *Pentecost Outside Pentecost.* Dallas: the author, 1960.

————. *The Spirit Bade Me Go.* Dallas: the author, 1961.

Farell, F. "Outburst of Tongues: The New Penetration," *Christianity Today,* Sept. 13, 1963, pp. 3–7.

Forster, Greg S. "The Third Arm: Pentecostal Christianity," *T. S. F. Bulletin,* 63 (1972): 5–9; 64 (1972): 16–21.

Harrison, Michael I. "Sources of Recruitment to Catholic Pentecostalism," *Journal for the Scientific Study of Religion,* 13 (1974): 49–64.

Hughes, Ray H. "A Traditional Pentecostal Looks at the New Pentecostals," *Christianity Today,* 18 (1974): 1036–40.

Hutchinson, Paul F. "Open Letter to Charismatic Lutherans," *Concordia Theological Monthly,* 43 (1972): 748–51.

Jorstad, Erling. (ed.). *The Holy Spirit in Today's Church: A Handbook of the New Pentecostalism.* Nashville: Abingdon, 1973.

Kelsey, Morton T. *Tongue-Speaking: An Experiment in Spiritual Experience.* Garden City, N.Y.: Doubleday, 1964.

McCandlish, Phillips. "And There Appeared unto Them Tongues of Fire," *Saturday Evening Post,* May 16, 1964, pp. 30+.

O'Connor, Edward D. *The Pentecostal Movement in the Catholic Church.* Notre Dame, Ind.: Ave Maria Press, 1971.

Ranaghan, Kevin and Dorothy. *Catholic Pentecostals.* New York: Paulist Press, 1969.

Roberts, Oral. *The Call: Oral Roberts' Autobiography.* New York: Avon, 1971.

Sherrill, John C. *They Speak with Other Tongues.* New York: McGraw-Hill, 1964.

Williams, J. Rodman. "The Upsurge of Pentecostalism: Some Presbyterian/Reformed Comment," *The Reformed World,* 31 (1971): 339–48.

E. *Non-American Pentecostal Movement*

Calley, Malcolm J. C. *God's People: West Indian Pentecostal Sects in England.* New York: Oxford Univ. Press, 1965.

Durasoff, Steve. *The Russian Protestants.* Cranbury, N.J.: Associated Univ. Press, 1969.

Kulbeck, Gloria G. *What God Hath Wrought: A History of the Pentecostal Assemblies of Canada.* Toronto: The Pentecostal Assemblies of Canada, 1958.

Lalive d'Epiney, Christian. *Haven of the Masses: A Study of the Pentecostal Movement in Chile.* London: Lutterworth, 1969.

Parsons, Anne. "The Pentecostal Immigrants," *Journal for the Scientific Study of Religion,* 4 (1965): 183–97.

Turner, F. C. "Protestantism and Politics in Chile and Brazil," *Comparative Studies in Society and History,* 12 (1970): 213–29.

Willems, Emilio. *Followers of the New Faith: Culture Change and the Rise of Protestantism in Brazil and Chile.* Nashville: Vanderbilt Univ. Press, 1967.

Wilson, Bryan R. "The Pentecostalist Minister: Role Conflicts and Status Contradiction," *American Journal of Sociology,* 64 (1959): 494–504.

VII *Religion*

A. *General Works*

Albright, William Foxwell. *From the Stone Age to Christianity.* Garden City. N.Y.: Doubleday Anchor, 1959.

Barkun, Michael. *Disaster and the Millennium.* New Haven: Yale Univ. Press, 1974.

Cohn, Norman. *The Pursuit of the Millennium.* rev. and enl. ed. New York: Oxford Univ. Press, 1961.

Knox, Ronald A. *Enthusiasm: A Chapter in the History of Religion with Special Reference to the 17th and 18th Centuries.* New York: Oxford Univ. Press, 1961.

LaBarre, Weston. *The Ghost Dance: The Origins of Religion.* New York: Dell, 1972.

————. "Materials for a History of Studies of Crisis Cults: A Bibliographical Essay," *Current Anthropology,* 12 (1971): 3–44.

Lanternari, Vittorio. *The Religions of the Oppressed: A Study of Modern Messianic Cults.* New York: New American Library, 1963.

Lewis, I. M. *Ecstatic Religion.* Baltimore: Penguin, 1971.

Mair, L. P. "Independent Religious Movements in Three Continents," *Comparative Studies in Society and History,* 1 (1959): 113–46.

Maranda, Pierre (ed.). *Mythology.* Baltimore: Penguin, 1972.

Murray, Henry A. (ed.). *Myth and Mythmaking.* New York: George Braziller, 1960.

Otto, Rudolf. *The Idea of the Holy: An Inquiry into the Non-Rational Factor in the Idea of the Divine and Its Relation to the Rational.* New York: Oxford Univ. Press, 1965.

Sebeok, Thomas Albert (ed.). *Myth: A Symposium*. Bloomington: Indiana Univ. Press, 1965.

Thrupp, Sylvia (ed.). *Millennial Dreams in Action*. New York: Schocken, 1970.

White, Andrew D. *The History of the Warfare of Science with Theology*. New York: George Braziller, 1955.

B. *Sociology of Religion*

Douglass, H. Paul, and Edmund deS. Brunner. *The Protestant Church as a Social Institution*. New York: Harper & Bros., 1935.

Eddy, G. Norman. "Store-Front Religion," *Religion in Life*, 28 (1958–59): 68–85.

Fauset, Arthur Huff. *Black Gods of the Metroplis: Negro Religious Cults in the Urban North*. Philadelphia: Univ. of Pennsylvania Press, 1944.

Gerth, H. H., and C. Wright Mills (eds.). *From Max Weber: Essays in Sociology*. New York: Oxford University Press, 1958.

Glock, Charles Y., and Rodney Stark. *Religion and Society in Tension*. Chicago: Rand McNally, 1965.

Hine, Virginia. "Deprivation and Disorganization Theories of Social Movements." Minneapolis: Univ. of Minnesota, n.d. mimeo.

Holt, John B. "Holiness Religion: Cultural Shock and Social Reorganization," *American Sociological Review*, 5 (1940): 740–47.

Kincheloe, Samuel C. "Major Reactions of City Churches," *Religious Education*, 23 (1928): 868–74.

Moberg, David O. *The Church as a Social Institution: The Sociology of American Religion*. Englewood Cliffs, N.J.: Prentice-Hall, 1962.

Niebuhr, H. Richard. *The Social Sources of Denominationalism*. New York: Meridian, 1962.

Pope, Liston. *Millhands and Preachers: A Study of Gastonia*. New Haven: Yale Univ. Press, 1965.

Schwartz, Gary. *Sect Ideologies and Social Status*. Chicago: Univ. of Chicago Press, 1970.

Troeltsch, Ernst. *The Social Teachings of the Christian Churches*. 2 vols. New York: Harper & Bros., 1960.

Warburton, T. Rennie. "Holiness Religion: An Anomaly of Sectarian Typologies," *Journal for the Scientific Study of Religion*, 8 (1969): 130–39.

Weber, Max. *The Sociology of Religion*. Boston; Beacon Press, 1964.

Williams, Chancellor. "The Socio-Economic Significance of the Store-Front Church Movement in the United States since 1920." Ph.D. diss., American Univ., 1949.

Wilson, Bryan R. *Religious Sects*. New York: McGraw-Hill, 1970.

———. *Sects and Society: A Sociological Study of Elim Tabernacle, Christian Science and Christadelphians*. Berkeley, Calif.: Univ. Of California Press, 1961.

Yinger, J. Milton. *Religion in the Struggle for Power*. Durham, N.C.: Duke Univ. Press, 1946.

C. *Psychology of Religion*

Bourguignon, Erika (ed.). *Religion, Altered States of Consciousness and Social Change*. Columbus: Ohio State Univ. Press, 1973.

R. M. Bucke Memorial Society. *Personality Change and Religious Experience: Proceedings of the First Annual Conference*. Montreal: the author, 1965.

Davenport, Frederick Morgan. *Primitive Traits in Religious Revivals: A Study in Mental and Social Evolution*. New York: Macmillan, 1905.

James, William. *The Varieties of Religious Experience*. New York: Modern Library, n.d. 1st ed. 1902.

Kiev, Ari (ed.). *Magic, Faith and Healing*. Glencoe: Free Press, 1964.

Rose, Louis. *Faith Healing*. Baltimore: Penguin, 1973.

Sargant, William. *The Battle for the Mind: A Physiology of Conversion and Brain-Washing*. New York: Harper & Row, 1971. 1st ed. 1957.

————. *The Mind Possessed: A Physiology of Possession, Mysticism and Faith Healing*. Baltimore: Penguin, 1974.

Walker, Sheila. *Ceremonial Spirit-Possession in Africa and Afro-America*. Leiden, Neth.: E. J. Brill, 1972.

VIII   *Other Works Consulted*

Baur, John E. "Los Angeles County in the Health Rush, 1870–1900," *California Historical Society Quarterly*, 31 (1952): 13–31.

Bogue, Donal J., and Calvin L. Beale. *Economic Areas of the United States*. Glencoe: Free Press, 1961.

Bond, J. Max. "The Negro in Los Angeles." Ph.D. diss., Univ. of Southern California, 1936.

Bronfenbrenner, Uri. "Socialization and Social Class Through Time and Space," in E. E. Maccoby, et al., eds. *Readings in Social Psychology*. New York: Henry Holt, 1958.

Connelley, William E. *History of Kansas, State and People*. 5 vols. Chicago: American Historical Society, 1928.

Coser, Lewis. *The Functions of Social Conflict*. New York: Free Press, 1956.

Drake, St. Clair, and Horace R. Clayton. *Black Metropolis*. 2 vols. New York: Harper & Row, 1962.

Faulkner, Harold U. *Politics, Reform and Expansion, 1890–1900*. New York: Harper & Row, 1959.

Fogelson, Robert M. *The Fragmented Metropolis: Los Angeles, 1850–1930*. Cambridge: Harvard Univ. Press, 1967.

Gibson, Arrell M. "Lead Mining in Southwest Missouri after 1865," *Missouri Historical Review,* 53 (1959): 315–28.

Handlin, Oscar. *The Uprooted: The Epic Story of the Great Migrations That Made the American People.* New York: Grosset & Dunlap, 1951.

Hayter, Earl W. *The Troubled Farmer, 1850–1900: Rural Adjustment to Industrialism.* DeKalb, Ill.: Northern Illinois Univ. Press, 1968.

Hobsbawm, Eric J. *Primitive Rebels: Studies in Archaic Forms of Social Movements in the 19th and 20th Centuries.* New York: W. W. Norton, 1959.

Hofstadter, Richard. *Age of Reform.* New York: Vintage, 1955.

———. Anti-Intellectualism in America. New York: Vintage, 1966.

———. "Manifest Destiny and the Philippines," in Daniel Aaron (ed.), *America in Crisis.* New York: Alfred A. Knopf, 1952.

Hughes, H. Stuart. *Consciousness and Society.* New York: Vintage, 1958.

Jaher, Frederick Cople. *Doubters and Dissenters: Cataclysmic Thought in America, 1885–1918.* New York: Free Press, 1964.

Kirkland, Edward C. *A History of American Economic Life.* New York: Crofts, 1932.

Lynd, Robert S. and Helen Merrell Lynd. *Middletown.* New York: Harcourt, Brace & World, 1956.

———. *Middletown in Transition.* New York: Harcourt, Brace & World, 1937.

Osofsky, Gilbert. *Harlem: The Making of a Ghetto: Negro New York, 1890–1930.* New York: Harper & Row, 1966.

Rand, Christopher. *Los Angeles: The Ultimate City.* New York: Oxford Univ. Press, 1967.

Schlesinger, Arthur M. *The Rise of the City, 1878–1898.* New York: Macmillan, 1933.

Shannon, Fred A. *The Farmer's Last Frontier.* New York: Holt, Rinehart & Winston, 1963.

Siegel, Saul M. "The Relationship of Hostility to Authoritarianism," *Journal of Abnormal and Social Psychology,* 52 (1956): 368–72.

Thayer, George. *The Farther Shores of Politics.* New York: Simon & Schuster, 1967.

Thomas, William I., and Florian Znaniecki. *The Polish Peasant in Europe and America.* 2 vols. Chicago: Univ. of Chicago Press, 1918.

United States, Agricultural Department. *Economic and Social Problems and Conditions of the Southern Appalachians.* Washington, D.C.: U.S. Gov't. Printing Office, 1935. Johnson repr., 1970.

United States, Bureau of the Census. *Historical Statistics of the United States.* Washington, D.C.: U.S. Gov't. Printing Office, 1960.

Woodward, C. Vann. *Origins of the New South, 1877–1913.* Baton Rouge: Louisiana State Univ. Press, 1951.

Works Project Administration, Writers Project. *Kansas: A Guide to the Sunflower State.* New York: Hastings House, 1939.

Works Project Administration, Writers Project. *Texas: A Guide to the Lone Star State*. New York: Hastings House, 1940.

Zornow, William Frank. *Kansas: A History of the Jayhawk State*. Norman: Oklahoma Univ. Press, 1957.

Index

American Council of Christian Churches, 6
American Indian Pentecostals, 69, 127, 135
Apostolic Assembly of the Faith in Jesus
    Christ, 127
Apostolic Churches of Jesus Christ, 192
Apostolic Faith, The (Los Angeles), 74, 141
Apostolic Faith, The (Parham's), 50
Apostolic Faith Mission, statistics of,
    116-17, 168. *See also* Crawford, Flor-
    ence
Apostolic Faith Movement (Parham's),
    47-61, 99, 119, 128, 162, 167. *See also*
    Parham, Charles Fox
Argue, A. H., 74, 75, 100, 110, 111, 129,
    291
Arthur, Mary A., 58, 59
Assemblies of God: origins, 99, 167-8;
    Keswick influence in, 112; divisions in,
    161-5, 178-85; ecstasy in, 231; social
    character of, 119-21, 125-8, 138; racial
    attitudes of, 189-91; statistics, 116-17,
    168
Awrey, Daniel, 102, 291
Azusa mission: revival at, 66-71; spreads
    Pentecostal message, 71-4, 115, 128,
    129, 130; and Parham, 140, 190; revi-
    val declines at, 137; and sanctification,
    167, 189; and Second Coming, 79-80;
    and censuses, 125

Bailey, S. Clyde, 75, 104, 106, 208, 291
Ball, H. C., 126

Baptism in/of Holy Spirit: professional re-
    vivalists and, 37; Keswick movement
    and, 40-43; Holiness movement and,
    43, 148, 150; Pentecostal movement
    and, 4, 53-5, 83, 84, 148, 150, 174,
    232-5; Fundamentalist movement and,
    173-5; summary of doctrines of,
    289-90. *See also* ecstasy; Glossolalia;
    possession, spirit; Tongues; Xenog-
    lossy
baptism, water, 49, 59 n.46, 155, 176-88.
    See also "Oneness" Pentecostal
    movement
Barrat, Thomas Ball: childhood and youth,
    98 n.1 and n.2, 100, 102, 105, 106,
    111; and Pentecostal movement, 74,
    105, 130, 140; views on speaking in
    tongues, 16, 162, 163; biographical
    sources for, 291
Bartleman, Frank: childhood and youth,
    100, 102, 103; job record, 106-7; and
    Holiness movement, 36, 112; in Los
    Angeles revival, 64-71 *passim;* and
    Pentecostal movement, 74, 78, 141-2,
    145; and "Finished Work", 172; and
    "Oneness" movement, 178; sees de-
    cline of revival, 137, 138; social at-
    titudes of, 202, 208, 209, 212; bio-
    graphical sources for, 291
Behm, Johannes, 21, 23
Bell, Eudorus N.: childhood and youth, 102,
    104, 106, 172; and Assemblies of God,

327